The Cambridge Chaucer Companion

Cambridge Companions to Literature

The Cambridge Companion to Old English Literature
edited by Malcolm Godden and Michael Lapidge

The Cambridge Companion to Dante
edited by Rachel Jacoff

The Cambridge Chaucer Companion
edited by Piero Boitani and Jill Mann

The Cambridge Companion to English Renaissance Drama
edited by A. R. Braunmuller and Michael Hattaway

The Cambridge Companion to English Poetry, Donne to Marvell
edited by Thomas N. Corns

The Cambridge Companion to Milton
edited by Dennis Danielson

The Cambridge Companion to British Romanticism
edited by Stuart Curran

The Cambridge Companion to James Joyce
edited by Derek Attridge

The Cambridge
Chaucer Companion

Edited by
PIERO BOITANI *and* JILL MANN

CAMBRIDGE
UNIVERSITY PRESS

PUBLISHED BY THE PRESS SYNDICATE OF THE UNIVERSITY OF CAMBRIDGE
The Pitt Building, Trumpington Street, Cambridge, United Kingdom

CAMBRIDGE UNIVERSITY PRESS
The Edinburgh Building, Cambridge CB2 2RU, UK
40 West 20th Street, New York, NY 10011–4211, USA
477 Williamstown Road, Port Melbourne, VIC 3207, Australia
Ruiz de Alarcón 13, 28014 Madrid, Spain
Dock House, The Waterfront, Cape Town 8001, South Africa

http://www.cambridge.org

First published 1986
Eighth printing 2003

Printed in the United Kingdom at the University Press, Cambridge

British Library Cataloguing in Publication data
The Cambridge Chaucer companion.
1. Chaucer, Geoffrey – Criticism and interpretation
I. Boitani, Piero   II. Mann, Jill
821'.I   PR1924

Library of Congress Cataloguing in Publication data
Main entry under title:
The Cambridge Chaucer companion.
Includes Index.
1. Chaucer, Geoffrey, d. 1400 – Criticism and
interpretation. I. Boitani, Piero.   II. Mann, Jill.
PR 1924.C28   1986   821'.1   86–1293

ISBN 0 521 30422 9 hardback
ISBN 0 521 31689 8 paperback

UP

Contents

Contributors

C. DAVID BENSON, University of Connecticut
MORTON W. BLOOMFIELD, formerly Harvard University
PIERO BOITANI, University of Rome
DEREK BREWER, University of Cambridge
J. A. BURROW, University of Bristol
JOERG G. FICHTE, University of Tübingen
ROBERT WORTH FRANK JR, Pennsylvania State University
MARK LAMBERT, Bard College, New York
JILL MANN, University of Cambridge
DIETER MEHL, University of Bonn
DEREK PEARSALL, Harvard University
A. C. SPEARING, University of Virginia
PAUL STROHM, Indiana University
DAVID WALLACE, University of Minnesota
BARRY WINDEATT, University of Cambridge

Preface

This book is intended for students approaching Chaucer for the first time, at whatever stage in their lives – school, university, or beyond. Its main aim is to provide a helpful and stimulating introduction to Chaucer's text, to suggest approaches, furnish necessary explanations, provide contexts, and offer first-hand literary criticism, by means of which students may test their own responses to the works of one of the greatest English poets. The views offered in each essay are individual and to a large extent original ones; they are not intended to be résumés of the current state of Chaucer scholarship or criticism, although due account is taken of critical opinions at relevant points. We feel the student is best served by a clearly pursued line of argument, which may set off his or her own thinking, rather than an exhaustive survey of the field.

About half the essays in the collection are focussed squarely on one or more of Chaucer's major works, identifying their themes and styles, moods and tones, in such a way as to help the reader to an appreciation of Chaucer's aims and artistry in each case. Alongside these essays are others of a more general kind – focussing on literary or historical background, on style or structure – which not only present the major works in ever-different lights, but also explore their links with many of the minor poems and with other medieval literature. We hope that the combination of the two types of essay will not only give a sense of a larger context for discussion of the individual works, but will also make clear that there is no 'definitive' interpretation of, say, *Troilus and Criseyde* – rather, it can be constantly re-approached via fresh lines of enquiry.

Paul Strohm's essay sketches the general scene, both social and literary, in fourteenth-century England, and David Wallace traces the impact on Chaucer of his reading in French and Italian literature. Piero Boitani leads the reader through Chaucer's early development in the dream-poems, in which books are not just the sources but the subject of his poetry. Mark Lambert discusses the densely textured narrative style of *Troilus*, while Jill Mann focusses on its philosophical themes, on the questions of chance and destiny which Chaucer encountered in Boethius. The last section of this essay, on the *Knight's Tale*, introduces a series of contributions on the

Canterbury Tales: David Benson first discusses the tales in relation to the pilgrimage-frame, and the four succeeding essays, by J. A. Burrow, Derek Pearsall, Robert Worth Frank Jr, and A. C. Spearing, then examine selected tales grouped by mode or genre. The four final essays, by Morton W. Bloomfield, Barry Windeatt, Dieter Mehl and Derek Brewer, range widely through Chaucer's works, using comparison and contrast to illuminate larger questions of style or structure. In these essays, as in Paul Strohm's and David Wallace's, the reader will find much discussion of those of Chaucer's works which are not given separate treatment.

Because this book has an introductory function, notes have been kept to a minimum, and it has not been possible to give exhaustive documentation of the history of every critical view presented or discussed. The Guide to Chaucer Studies provided by Joerg Fichte will lead the interested student to the important works in this field whose influence has helped to shape the individual discussions in this collection, and will also clear several pathways through the dense forest of modern Chaucer criticism. The contributors to this book are the inheritors of a long and rich tradition of Chaucer scholarship, to which they feel themselves indebted. Yet in order to write freshly and freely on works which have been read and written about for six hundred years, they have inevitably had to banish from their texts and their notes many of the very works which have done most to create their own enjoyment. We hope that the final Guide to Chaucer Studies will stand as an acknowledgement of our gratitude to the labours of others. We hope also that this new volume, the joint effort of an English and an Italian editor, and the product of an international team of scholars, will help to foster in new generations of readers in all countries a love of Chaucer and an interest in Chaucer studies.

PIERO BOITANI   JILL MANN

Cambridge, July, 1985

Note on the text

The text of Chaucer used throughout for quotation and reference is *The Works of Geoffrey Chaucer*, ed. F. N. Robinson, 2nd edn (Boston/London, 1957). References are normally to individual works, with Book- and line-number; for the sake of concision, however, references to the *Canterbury Tales* are occasionally given by Fragment- and line-number (e.g. 1, 3450 = *Miller's Tale*, 3450).

Abbreviations

EETS   *Early English Text Society*
PMLA   *Proceedings of the Modern Language Association*

1   The social and literary scene in England

Social structure

MEDIEVAL social descriptions are very conscious of degree, and tend to emphasize the relatively small number of people at the top of the social hierarchy. The thirteenth-century legal commentator Bracton is representative when he divides society into those high in the ecclesiastical hierarchy (the pope, archbishops, bishops, and lesser prelates), those high in the civil hierarchy (emperors, kings, dukes, counts, barons, magnates, and knights), and those remaining (a general category of 'freepersons and bondpersons' or *liberi et villani*).[1]

Bracton's concentration on prelates and magnates is consistent with formal theory in his day, but we must remember that his category of 'freepersons and bondpersons' comprised an overwhelming majority of the fourteenth-century populace. After the cataclysmic Black Death of 1348–9, the population of England levelled off at about 3,500,000, where it remained for the rest of the century and most of the next.[2] Among these persons the 150 lords and 2,000 knights and their families upon whom Bracton concentrates would have totalled no more than 8,000–10,000, or considerably less than one-half of one per cent of the whole.[3] He is undoubtedly correct in his half-stated assumption that most of the remainder were agricultural workers, with many still bound in some fashion to the land, but other groups are apparent to the modern observer. Taken together, ecclesiastical orders probably included some 50,000 members, or just under two per cent of the whole.[4] Esquires and other lesser gentry and their families probably comprised about 30,000–40,000 additional persons. Cities were small and city-dwellers were few by standards of today. London and nearby Westminster had a population of some 40,000, and lesser cities (which we might be more inclined to call 'towns') such as Bristol, York, Norwich, Gloucester, Leicester, and Hull had populations between 10,000 and 5,000. All told, though, we might suppose that about 100,000–125,000 additional persons were 'urban' in some sense of the word.

Latent even within Bracton's commentary is another way of viewing society which encouraged more recognition of such constituent groups. His

1

division of society into the ecclesiastical hierarchy, the civil hierarchy, and the mass of other persons is based upon the traditional medieval view of the three estates (clerics, knights, and peasants).[5] Even when treated most hierarchically, the estates of society were also seen as interdependent, with each group contributing in its own way to the good of all. This notion of interdependence issued at times in an alternative view of society, as organic rather than hierarchical. This organic view – often conveyed through extended metaphors of the social estates as members of the body politic – permitted recognition of new classes of persons not clearly accommodated in the more traditional tripartite system. It is to be found less in formal statements than in sermons, statutes, ordinances, and a variety of other irregular and occasional documents.

A sermon delivered in the 1370s by Bishop Thomas Brinton of Rochester supplements the hierarchical view of society with a more organic view of the interdependence of its estates. We are all, he says, the mystical members of a single body, of which the head (or heads) are kings, princes, and prelates; the eyes are judges, wise men, and true counsellors; the ears are clergy; the tongue is good doctors. Then, within the midsection of the body, the right hand is composed of strenuous knights; the left hand is composed of merchants and craftsmen; and the heart is citizens and burgesses. Finally, peasants and workers are the feet which support the whole.[6] Similar views of society crop up in other occasional and relatively informal papers of the time. A Norwich gild ordinance of the 1380s, for example, takes note in its opening prayer of a ruling stratum composed of the king, dukes, earls, barons and bachelors; a middle stratum composed of knights, squires, citizens and burgesses, and franklins; and a broader category of tillers and craftsmen.[7]

The middle groupings in Brinton's sermon and the Norwich prayer embrace persons of different social outlook. The knights – and, in the second half of the fourteenth century, the new class of esquires – enjoyed the same *gentil* status as the great aristocrats, though clearly without enjoying the benefits conferred by the hereditary titles and accompanying revenues of the latter group. While non-*gentil*, the urban merchants (whose free status and prosperity entitled them to the titles 'citizen' or 'burgess') often enjoyed wealth considerably greater than that of most knights.[8] And even these distinctions mask variations. Many knights and esquires of the period held no land at all and had few or no military obligations, but earned their status through civil and administrative tasks which we might consider essentially 'middle class'.[9] While not *gentil*, citizens and burgesses were eligible to serve their cities and shires as 'knights' in Parliament, and some were knighted for royal or military service.[10] The ultimate standard for inclusion in these middle groupings would seem not to be rank or title, but simply civil importance and responsibility, however defined.

Chaucer's own position

Chaucer himself was a member of this middle social grouping, his place within it secured by various forms of what might be called 'civil service'. He was born in the early 1340s, in a family situation appropriate to a career of royal service.[11] His father, John Chaucer, was not only a prosperous London vintner, but had himself served Edward III in such capacities as deputy chief butler (with responsibility for certain customs collections). Chaucer's own career began in 1357 with his appointment to the household of Elizabeth, Countess of Ulster, and her husband Prince Lionel. In the service of the latter he journeyed between France and England (and was captured and ransomed during a 1359–60 military campaign in France), inaugurating a series of journeys which would take him frequently to France, twice to Italy, and elsewhere in the course of his career. Like many in his station, he married rather advantageously, to Philippa de Roet, daughter of a knight of Hainault (who had come to England in the service of the queen) and sister of Katherine Swynford (soon to be mistress and eventual third wife of John of Gaunt). In 1367, soon after his marriage, he is listed as *valettus* to King Edward III, and by 1368 he is listed among *esquiers* of the royal household. While remaining an esquire and never entering the inner circle of chamber-knights, he nevertheless continued in respected service of one sort or another until the end of his life. In 1374, he shifted from the precincts of the household to the post of controller of customs in London, assisted both by preferment from Edward III and by a timely annuity to him and to his wife from John of Gaunt. Posts and assignments continued after the accession of Richard II in 1377. The latter 1380s marked a period of comparative withdrawal from London activity, possibly tactical in nature since it roughly coincided with the years 1386–9 in which Richard II was severely challenged by an aristocratic coalition. Richard reasserted his royal prerogatives in 1389, and Chaucer soon after received his next royal appointment as clerk of the king's works. He continued in various capacities – though none of greater lustre – through the 1390s. When Henry IV supplanted Richard II in 1399, a year before Chaucer's death, he confirmed Richard's annuities and added a grant of his own.[12]

Even so spare a summary of Chaucer's civil career suggests several interesting perspectives on his life and place in society.

(1) Chaucer's position as an esquire of the royal household would have conferred *gentil* status, though he was among the more ambiguously situated members of that somewhat fluid group. Lacking the security from possession of lands and rents enjoyed by the great aristocrats and even by some of his fellow knights and esquires, Chaucer depended for his living upon his career in service. In this sense, the posts and assignments which

he held in the course of what Sylvia Thrupp has called his 'versatile' career were not just an expression of his energies or his zest for politics, but were essential to his livelihood and to the maintenance of his station in life.[13]

(2) Chaucer appears to have had a representative career, both as an esquire of the king's immediate household and as a member of the royal party beyond the immediate confines of the court.[14] He would seem to have been rather good at what he did; while not lavishly rewarded, he enjoyed frequent appointments and re-appointments while weathering the extreme and sometimes dangerous factional vicissitudes of his day. His service bridged successfully the careers of three monarchs, and he managed the extremely difficult task of being on good terms both with Richard II and with John of Gaunt and the Lancastrians, even during such points of extreme tension as Richard's clash in 1386–9 with the Appellants, an aristocratic coalition headed by the Duke of Gloucester and including Gaunt's son Henry. In a period of what Thomas Usk called 'confederacie, congregacion, & couyne',[15] Chaucer was necessarily something of a factionalist, allied like Mayor Brembre of London and Chief Justice Tresilian and others with Richard's royal party. Yet – unlike such fellow partisans as Brembre, Tresilian, and Usk, who were beheaded by the Appellants in 1388 – Chaucer seems to have understood the limits of faction, and to have tempered his activity in 1386–8 and possibly in other crucial periods as well.

(3) Patronage based on his literary accomplishments seems not to have been a major factor in Chaucer's civil career. Later we will consider several literary works which may have been written in part to console, compliment, or please his superiors, but most of the facts of·his civil career are comprehensible in terms of strictly non-literary talents and exertions. Chaucer's poetry fosters an impression of separation between his public and literary lives, as when the garrulous Eagle in the *House of Fame* chides him for his habitual withdrawal from the world of affairs to that of books and private reading:

> For when thy labour doon al ys,
> And hast mad alle thy rekenynges,
> In stede of reste and newe thynges,
> Thou goost hom to thy hous anoon;
> And, also domb as any stoon,
> Thou sittest at another book
> Tyl fully daswed ys thy look...
>
> (652–8)

The principal communities of readers

Solitary as Chaucer's own habits of reading and writing might have been, his poetry still shows a notable concern with issues of reception: with situations of telling and listening, of writing and reading, of audience reaction. This concern, in turn, encourages us to imagine the circumstances into which Chaucer actually launched his literary works – for whom he wrote them, and in what ways he expected them to be promulgated. Any attempt to answer these questions is, however, complicated by a number of situations peculiar to the society of Chaucer's day, including the coexistence of older 'oral' and newer 'literary' presuppositions; the relative infrequency of literacy in Chaucer's England; and, especially, the fragmentation of the literate populace into small and relatively self-contained communities of readers, based on considerations of language, geography, production and distribution of manuscripts, vocation, and social class.

The task of determining the boundaries of Chaucer's contemporary audience is complicated by the fact that the circumstances of oral narration in Chaucer's day could have permitted people to *hear* his work without having the occasion (or perhaps even the ability) to *read* it.[16] Chaucer himself seems occasionally unsure about whether he is primarily an *oral* or a *written* poet. We might loosely conceive of his earlier vision-poems as composed to be read aloud to an intimate audience and his *Canterbury Tales* as intended to reach a larger audience in manuscript form, with the mid-career *Troilus and Criseyde* as a watershed. Even so broad a formulation is, however, subject to uncertainties. Chaucer's tone of address to his audience is nowhere more intimate among his narrative poems than in *Troilus*, yet this poem concludes with an apostrophe ('Go, litel bok...') which certainly anticipates the circulation of his poem to an enlarged audience in manuscript form. The *Canterbury Tales* are laced with different sorts of references to hearing and reading, often within a single passage. Apologizing for his plain speech in the *Miller's Tale*, Chaucer seems to imagine his audience both as hearers and as readers of a bound manuscript:

> ...whoso list it nat yheere,
> Turne over the leef and chese another tale.   (I, 3176–7)

We might provisionally imagine Chaucer writing for an immediate, oral audience and an ultimate audience of readers, though we must add this matter of oral/written to the list of uncertainties which urge caution upon us.

If oral rendition enlarged the possible audience of fourteenth-century works, other considerations were decidedly narrowing in their effect. The already small body of literate persons in England (probably no more than five per cent of the population, even including what M. B. Parkes has called exclusively 'pragmatic' or non-literary readers[17]) was further segmented by other criteria into a number of separate 'communities of readers'. Several literary languages remained in competition throughout the second half of the fourteenth century. Though English was gradually coming to the fore, the last quarter of the century still saw Latin as the language of ecclesiastical and theological discourse, and French as the language of statecraft and civil record-keeping, as well as a literary language in some circles. Such geographically based considerations as the different dialects of English, local preference for different forms (such as alliterative as opposed to metrical verse), and physical distance were also centrifugal in their effect. Different vocational and social groupings, while anything but rigid at their outer margins, still fostered divergent tastes among such groups as the aristocracy, the gentry, and the urban middle classes. Such segmentation of the literate populace into different communities or reading publics is most dramatically illustrated by the fact that the three greatest writers of English of the later fourteenth century – Chaucer, Langland, and the *Gawain*-poet – may not have known each other's work. (Chaucer perhaps echoes the opening scene of *Sir Gawain and the Green Knight* in his *Squire's Tale*, and his Parson's dismissive allusion to poetic alliteration or 'rum, ram, ruf' may possibly embrace both writers, but neither these nor other suggestions that they knew each other's work are very persuasive.) In order better to understand how such a situation could occur, we might examine the principal literate communities of fourteenth-century England.[18]

The upper levels of the *clergy*, and especially those connected with monastic libraries and scriptoria, were naturally literate. As surviving booklists show, their continuing concern throughout the century was with theological and ecclesiastical matter written in Latin – though literature in all three languages is encountered. Some fourteenth-century manuscripts of likely ecclesiastical provenance include works in Latin, French, and Middle English, and occasionally both divine and secular works as well; Harley MS 2253, for example, not only contains a generous selection of early Middle English secular and religious lyrics, but also secular works in French and devotional works in Latin.

Members of the royal family and the fourteenth-century *aristocracy* were drawn to works in chivalry, statecraft, and occasionally theology, particularly in French. In the middle of the century, Henry, Duke of Lancaster had written a devotional treatise entitled 'Le Livre de Seyntz Medicines'. In that work, he apologizes for the quality of his native or Anglo-Norman French, on the ground that he is more familiar with English: 'Si le franceis ne soit pas bon, jeo doie estre excusee, pur seo qu jeo suit engleis et n'ai pas moelt hauntee le franceis'.[19] In style and thrust Henry's work was somewhat of the older fashion, since the mid-century provided members of the court with ample opportunity to polish their Continental French. A series of lustrous marriages brought Continent-born and -educated wives and their trains to the royal household in the course of the century, including Isabella of France (wife of Edward II and mother of Edward III), Philippa of Hainault (wife of Edward III), and Anne of Bohemia (first wife of Richard II). Additionally, the series of conflicts between England and France known as the Hundred Years War brought the two countries into inevitable association through legations, missions, and – especially – the practice of holding prisoners for ransom (after the battle of Poitiers in 1356, King John of France and a virtual court-in-exile were resident in England throughout most of an eight-year period which lasted until his death in 1364). Extant booklists throughout this period testify to a continuing interest in French literature. At the time of her death, Isabella of France bequeathed to Edward III a number of French books, including a *Brut*, deeds of Arthur, and Tristan and Isolde; she owned copies of Aimeri de Narbonne, Percival, Gawain, and other narratives as well.[20] While no bibliophile, Edward III seems to have had some interest in French romance; in one case the Issue Rolls of his reign specify 100 marks 'for a book of romance...for the King's use, which remains in the chamber of the Lord the King'.[21] Booklists of Richard II include similar romances (some possibly from his great-grandmother's bequest), and others including a 'Romance de la Rose' and a 'Romance de Perciuall & Gawyn', as well as a Bible written in French or *lingua gallica*.[22] Froissart, presenting a volume of his poems to Richard, comments that he spoke and read French very well ('moult bien parloit et lisoit le franchois'), and we have no reason to doubt his word.[23] The interest of the aristocracy was not confined to French. The Duke of Gloucester's library contained both French romances and Latin theology, and Henry IV was a reader of Latin as well.[24] Chaucer's contemporary, John Gower, claimed some encouragement from Richard II in undertaking his English *Confessio Amantis*.[25] Yet only with evidence of Henry V's preference for literature in his native tongue does English emerge clearly as the preferred literary language of the royal and aristocratic group.[26]

The situation was different among the lower echelons of the gentry – especially among those knights and esquires of the royal household and/or chancery clerks and secretaries and lawyers who comprised what might be considered the 'civil service' of the day. There, an emergent public for English literary works provided a receptive milieu for Chaucer and others as well.[27] One such writer was Thomas Usk, initially a scrivener or professional scribe who became a political factionalist and convert to the royal party. In the period 1385–7, while in temporary eclipse and awaiting the royal preferment which was to be his undoing, Usk composed a political and spiritual allegory entitled *Testament of Love*, in which he explained his still unusual choice of English as a literary language:

Trewly, the understanding of Englishmen wol not strecche to the privy termes in Frenche, what-so-ever we bosten of straunge language. Let than clerkes endyten in Latin, for they have the propertee of science, and the knowinge in that facultee; and let Frenchmen in their Frenche also endyten their queynt termes, for it is kyndely to their mouthes; and let us shewe our fantasyes in suche wordes as we lerneden of our dames tonge.[28]

Usk's probable intention in choosing English was to reach an influential audience of persons who could further his civil and factional activities. Less involved in self-promotion, but no less concerned with finding an appropriate audience for his works, was John Gower – a landed esquire with legal training, and a friend and associate of Chaucer. Gower wrote major works in French, Latin, and finally English – not, as one might suppose, from confusion, but to direct them to their appropriate audiences. His motive in composing the *Mirour de l'omme* in 1376–8 was comparatively devotional and private, and his linguistic choice was appropriately conservative. His *Vox Clamantis*, completed about 1385, was written in the voice of Old Testament prophecy, and the choice of Latin, which John Fisher calls 'the language of serious political discussion', suits his intended audience of influential clerics and, ultimately, the court. His *Confessio Amantis* (1385–93) addresses its message of political reconciliation to a still wider audience, and is thus written in English, 'for Engelondes sake'.[29]

The *citizens and burgesses* of London and other urban centres were (in Parkes' phrase) 'pragmatic readers' in the course of their business activities.[30] The question is, whither their interests turned when they engaged in more general reading. Throughout most of the fourteenth century, the answer seems to be that they turned toward service books and works of lay devotion in Latin. Study of the wills of London merchants and other gildsmen of the later fourteenth century shows them in possession of numerous service books (missals, breviaries, and graduals), works of pious devotion (psalters and legends of the saints), and occasional legal compilations.[31] Little wonder that, turning to English in the later fourteenth and fifteenth centuries, this audience sought devotional compendia (such as the *Prick of Conscience* – more popular than the *Canterbury Tales*, if we are to judge from over one hundred extant manuscripts), translations of Bonaventure, and other mystical treatises. Segments of this audience seem, as well, to have given encouragement to Chaucer's fervent contemporary, Langland.[32]

We must remind ourselves that boundaries between communities of readers tended to shift. While probably aimed at civil servants and literate gentry, Gower's *Confessio* was at least partially encouraged by the king; if *Piers Plowman* was first read by clerics, it was soon taken up by literate laypersons. An instance of how very far we are from establishing a 'sociology' of fourteenth-century taste is the case of the *Gawain*-poet, whose audience has been variously located with equal plausibility in baronial courts, among the country gentry, among Cheshire servants of Richard II, and in the monastic houses of the southwest Midlands.[33]

Chaucer's audience

Chaucer appears to have found his own community of readers among his fellow gentlepersons and civil servants, though several considerations argue against oversimplification. The embedded or fictionalized audiences within Chaucer's own poetry – such as his created audience of Canterbury pilgrims – are socially mixed, and at times his *gentils* and non-*gentils* engage in what appear to be socially based literary disagreements. We may assume at least a modest degree of social mixing within his actual audience, and several of his works do indeed appear to have been directed toward social superiors. The *Book of the Duchess* shows definite signs of intent to console John of Gaunt for the death of Duchess Blanche of Lancaster in 1368, both in the grieving knight's final return to 'a long castel' ['Lancaster'] (1318) and reference to the lost lady as 'White' ['Blanche'] by name (948). The narrator of this poem is himself somewhat more elevated socially than those of Chaucer's later efforts; unable to sleep, he bids a servant bring him a book (47), and riding forth to join a hunt he displays some hauteur in demanding of an attendant, 'Say, felowe, who shal hunte here?' (366). He is nevertheless deferential to the grieving knight, finding him neither curt nor formal and marvelling to find him 'so tretable...for al hys bale' (533–5). The relation of the narrator to the grieving knight in fact shares some characteristics of Chaucer's own probable relation to John of Gaunt: familiar in the sense that both are gentlepersons, but yet with a recognition of the rather considerable social gap between one who is simply a gentleperson and one who is at once a gentleperson and an aristocrat second in wealth and power to none in the kingdom.

Only in his short poem 'Lak of Stedfastnesse' does Chaucer appear to address Richard II directly, but Richard and Queen Anne may have been partially responsible for his ambitious but incomplete *Legend of Good Women*, with their relation to Chaucer wryly restated in his portrayal of a God and Queen of Love who set for him a trying (if not impossible) narrative task. This presumption is further fortified by the *Legend*'s points of coincidence with Gower's *Confessio Amantis* (each written in English and containing a collection of narratives of love held together by a frame which secularizes a traditional devotional form), raising the possibility that Richard and Anne were sufficiently interested in the course of English letters to give parallel charges to the two poets. If the portrayals of the God of Love and Queen Alceste are indicative, however, then certain attentions from persons in socially authoritative positions were at best to be politely endured. After all, the imperious threats of the God of Love and the inadvertent insults of Alceste ('Hym rekketh noght of what matere he take': F 365) leave Chaucer little choice but to withdraw into the defensive irony which Alfred David has seen as his characteristic strategy for dealing with socially secure members of his audience with 'limited and established literary tastes'.[34]

Chaucer's impulse to direct works beyond his immediate circle might not have been exhausted with these two efforts. Works such as his translation of Boethius and his *Tale of Melibee* may belong to the general category of 'advice to princes',[35] and the peaceable sentiments of Dame Prudence in the *Tale of Melibee* may be seen as supportive of King Richard's interest in peace with France.[36] While we have no particular evidence that Chaucer found a bourgeois readership prior to the fifteenth century, this possibility must also be entertained. Chaucer certainly had numerous associations in the London merchant classes, such as his Port of London association with Nicholas Brembre (several times mayor, and chief among the London merchant–oligarchs) or his legal surety for John Hend (prosperous draper, eventual mayor, and also member of the royal party).[37] While no documents suggest that such men were members of Chaucer's literary audience, forums and contexts existed in which they might have been. John Gower's biographer has discussed the existence in fourteenth-century England of the French-derived merchant *Pui*, an assembly of prosperous *bourgeoisie* devoted to the cultivation of balades and other *belles-lettres*.[38] Many social fraternities and gilds of the later Middle Ages provided a common meeting-place for *gentils* and merchants (for instance, the membership rolls of the Gild of St George at Norwich contain bishops and knights as well as mayors and the generality of merchants and other gildsmen and their wives).[39]

Despite such possible diversity, Chaucer's immediate circle was almost certainly composed of persons in social situations close to his own. Its members are to be sought among fellow knights and esquires of the royal household, and civil servants and lawyers of similar station in the London/Westminster area.[40] We see the outlines of such a circle in the names of those contemporaries familiarly mentioned in Chaucer's poetry: Scogan (Henry Scogan, an esquire, apparent tutor to the sons of Henry IV, and poet in his own right), Bukton (probably Peter Bukton, knight in Richard II's household and later close associate of Henry IV), Vache (Philip de la Vache, Richard's chamber-knight and eventual Knight of the Garter), Gower (lawyer, esquire, and fellow poet), and Strode (Ralph Strode, a London lawyer, who – unless we are dealing with two persons – enjoyed some standing as an Oxford philosopher–theologian earlier in his career). This circle may be filled out by our sense of other *littérateurs* in and about the court: Richard Strury (Ricardian chamber-knight and friend of the French chronicler and poet Froissart), Lewis Clifford (chamber-knight, suspected Lollard, and literary intermediary between Chaucer and the

French poet Deschamps), John Clanvowe (chamber-knight, close contemporary, and author of 'The Boke of Cupid', probably the first consciously 'Chaucerian' poem in English), and more, We may also presume the presence in this circle of educated women of similar station. Philippa of Hainault (queen of Edward III) and Anne of Bohemia (queen of Richard II) and other ladies of the court were attended by *damoiselles*, and – while court records suggest they were fewer in number than household knights and esquires – a document of 1368 lists six ladies and thirteen *damoiselles* (including Philippa Chaucer) and a document of 1369 lists forty-seven ladies, *damoiselles*, and *souz-damoiselles*.[41]

Our sense of this circle is further amplified by the familiar tone in which Chaucer often addresses members of his audience – especially in his earlier poems, and most of all in certain of his verse epistles and other occasional works. One such poem is his *Envoy to Scogan*, in which a portentous opening reference to broken statutes in heaven and a consequent deluge gives way to the jesting explanation that Scogan has upset Venus with his matter-of-factness in love. As Chaucer reminds him, Scogan has in fact gone so far as to give his lady up (instead of serving patiently like the knights of literary convention), simply because she did not respond to his overtures or 'distresse':

> Hastow not seyd, in blaspheme of the goddes,
> Thurgh pride, or thrugh thy grete rekelnesse,
> Swich thing as in the lawe of love forbode is,
> That, for thy lady sawgh nat thy distresse,
> Therfore thow yave hir up at Michelmesse? (15–19)

Associating Scogan's situation with his own (both are evidently 'rounde of shap': 31), Chaucer fears that both will suffer Cupid's revenge – consisting not of Cupid's assault, but rather his decision to leave them alone:

> He wol nat with his arwes been ywroken
> On the, ne me, ne noon of oure figure;
> We shul of him have neyther hurt ne cure. (26–8)

Chaucer concludes with reflections on his poetry (he suggests that he has recently been inactive) and friendship (he asks Scogan, kneeling 'at the stremes hed' – that is, presumably, the court – to remember him, living dully downstream). While not quite as wide-ranging, Chaucer's 'envoy' to Bukton is similarly familiar in its jocular warning of 'the sorwe and wo that is in marriage' (6). Cited as an ostensible authority on the subject of marriage is one of Chaucer's own literary creations, here as elsewhere assuming an autonomous existence outside the confines of the *Canterbury Tales*; 'The Wyf of Bathe I pray yow that ye rede / Of this matere' (29–30), Chaucer warns the prospective groom.[42]

These two poems, probable survivors of a much larger body of occasional verse now lost, confirm the existence of an 'inner circle' of Chaucer's audience which was on intimate and confidential terms both with Chaucer's store of literary devices and with Chaucer the person. Other occasional poems addressed both to men and to women – along with such moments as his address to 'every lady bright of hewe' in *Troilus* v, 1772ff – support and extend our sense of such an audience. Nimble enough to follow Chaucer's tonal shifts, acquainted enough with his verse to appreciate intertextual reference, easy enough with his company to accept and encourage jests in potentially sensitive areas – it is an audience which, in the words of Bertrand Bronson, 'must compel our admiration'.[43]

While confident in his manner of address to his immediate *hearers*, Chaucer seems less certain about the nature of his reception by those unknown persons who will be *readers* of his works in manuscript form. His ambition for such an audience has already been noted, in reference to such passages as his closing address to *Troilus* when he imagines his 'bok' entering the larger realm of 'poesye'. This imagined transition is, however, accompanied by certain anxieties, both about simple matters of transcription and also about more fundamental matters of understanding:

> ...prey I God that non myswrite the,
> Ne the mysmetre for defaute of tonge.
> And red wherso thow be, or elles songe,
> That thow be understonde, God I biseche!   (v, 1795–8)

Nice questions of interpretation aside, Chaucer need not have worried about his embrace by an enlarged fifteenth-century readership. A progressive enlargement of his readership is suggested by the evidence of manuscript dissemination: the absence or near-absence of manuscripts from Chaucer's lifetime suggests that he prepared only a limited number of copies and used them mainly as texts for oral delivery; the first extant copies of *Troilus* and the *Canterbury Tales* are relatively fine productions, evidently intended mainly for nobility in the opening decades of the fifteenth century; by 1430–40, well before Caxton's first printed edition, the rapid proliferation of less sumptuous manuscripts in paper rather than vellum suggests that his acceptance by a truly national public was complete. All told, *Troilus* exists in sixteen fifteenth-century manuscripts; the *Tales* exist in fifty-five relatively complete manuscripts (and in Caxton's two printed editions), together with eighteen segments in miscellanies and nine more fragments. Dream visions and shorter poems circulated in numerous collections of the mid-century. Moreover, these manuscripts and fragments are distributed widely, both geographically and socially. *Troilus* exists in a vellum manuscript prepared for Henry V while he was Prince of Wales and also in paper miscellanies; the *Tales* enjoyed a fifteenth-century readership so diverse as to include a future king (Richard, Duke of

Gloucester) as well as London gildsmen (as exemplified by a bequest from John Brinchele to William Holgrave, citizens and tailors of London).[44]

Chaucer as a social poet

Chaucer's poetry is complexly situated in the social context of his own time. Unlike his contemporaries Gower and Langland, he rarely if ever treats his poetry as a forum for the direct discussion of social issues of his day. The burning subject of peace with France might be addressed by Prudence's wise and pacific counsel in the *Tale of Melibee*, but only in an elliptical and proverbial way. The widespread social upheaval of 1381 known as the 'Peasant's Revolt' – in the course of which peasants and their allies from Kent and elsewhere stormed London, burned John of Gaunt's palace, and killed Archbishop Sudbury – is a subject only for glancing and bemused comment (in, for example, the *Nun's Priest's Tale*: 3394–7). Richard's near-deposition by the aristocratic Appellants and the accompanying execution of Brembre, Usk, and other of Chaucer's associates and acquaintances, is mentioned not at all. As these illustrations might suggest, Chaucer is not a very topical poet. Neither, for that matter, is he a particularly historical poet, in the sense of committing himself to faithful representation of individuals or assemblies of persons or events which he might actually have seen. While his vivid portrayal of thirty-odd pilgrims has tempted scholars to propose historical identifications, the tendency of current critical theory is to see even those characterizations most apparently drawn from life as derived largely from 'estates satire' and other literary sources.[45] Yet, granting that Chaucer is neither particularly topical nor particularly historical, in certain respects he is nevertheless profoundly social.

The pilgrims gathered at the Tabard Inn seem intended to represent neither a complete census of fourteenth-century English society nor an enumeration of its most influential ranks: the great majority of the populace who worked the land is represented only by the Ploughman; entirely missing are the great aristocrats who still controlled most of England's land and wealth. Present at least by implication, however, are all three traditional estates of medieval society: the seigneurial (represented by the Knight), the spiritual (represented by the Parson), and the agricultural (represented by the Ploughman) – together with assorted other *gentils* such as the Prioress and the Monk), and a very full review of the middle strata. While admittedly not very faithful to the numbers or proportions of fourteenth-century society, this modestly varied gathering is nevertheless presented in a way which confirms a vital premise about the relationship between social position and worldly behaviour. Jill Mann points out that the behaviour of the pilgrims on the road to Canterbury and the kinds and styles of tales they tell suggest 'a society in which work as a social experience conditions personality and the standpoint from which an individual views the world'.[46]

The pilgrimage itself is, after all, a social as well as religious event, with individuals interacting according to their social perspectives as expressed by their class (or rank) and vocation. One notices, for example, that the representatives of those traditional estates whose social responsibilities are prescribed by their place in a hierarchy mainly hold themselves aloof from the badinage of their fellow pilgrims. The Knight confines his interventions to different adjudicatory roles. The Parson chides Harry Bailly for his swearing (II, 1171) and refuses to depart from truthfulness to tell a fable (X, 31). The Ploughman does not speak. Even quasi-*gentils* like the Prioress and the Monk stand on ceremony in the end, as reflected in the Prioress' choice of a miracle for her tale and the Monk's stubborn refusal to 'pleye' (VII, 2806). In the cases of the Knight and Parson, we see evidence of the selflessness which accompanies their acceptance of the responsibilities of their social roles. Even in the case of the more self-absorbed Prioress and Monk, a certain aloof and attenuated sense of *noblesse oblige* still seems to inform their relations with their fellow pilgrims. Such restrained social conduct is at considerable variance with the bonhomie and good fellowship exhibited by their fellows. If the five gildsmen in livery are silent in the tale-telling, theirs is nevertheless the social ethic of the pilgrimage: fraternity, expressed through vital and egalitarian social interchange, is the order of the day. Certainly, quarrels based on vocational difference and other animosities constantly threaten to erupt. But the ideal of the pilgrimage is still one of amity, based on turning 'rancour and disese / T'acord' (IX, 97–8), much in the mode of those gild ordinances which seek to banish 'grucching' and 'rebellious tongues'.[47] The Merchant, in short, is not the only character attracted to 'chevyssaunce' or good deals (I, 282) – the behaviour of many of the pilgrims shows the emergence of forms of civility well-suited to the advancement of transactions in an increasingly mercantile and profit-oriented society.

Finally, social orientations of the pilgrims are reflected in the kinds of tales they tell. The Knight, the Parson, the Prioress, and the Monk all favour traditional and edifying genres – as does their apologist, the Clerk, with his unabashed endorsement of social hierarchy. Other pilgrims more clearly identified with the middle strata of society tell tales more racy in content and more situational in ethics, culminating at one extreme in the *Shipman's Tale* with its firm satiric equation of surface civility with the furtherance of 'chaffare' and the profit-motive. To be sure, Chaucer somewhat simplifies the actual state of affairs in order to suggest this socially conditioned view. While contemporary evidence *does* suggest a split in literary taste between *gentils* and others in the middle strata, that split was (as suggested earlier in this essay) probably actually grounded more on the inclination of the *gentils* toward both secular and devotional literature versus the inclination of the others toward devotional literature alone, rather than (as Chaucer seems to suggest) a clash between the *gentils'* taste for hagiographical and other elevated genres on the one hand and the taste of the non-*gentils* for fabliaux or other 'ribaudye' (VI, 324) on the other.[48] Nevertheless, Chaucer is faithful to the state of literary affairs in fourteenth-century England when he suggests that literary tastes often diverged, and that social considerations underlay the divergence.

The mingling of styles and perspectives in Chaucer's poetry has another, deeper fidelity to his social reality. The opening sections of this essay suggested that social description and social practice in Chaucer's day were moving from the static and the hierarchical to a more fluid and less hierarchical state. The penetration of new groups (such as Chaucer's own class of esquires) into the previously existing hierarchy resulted in conceptions of society as more and more internally diverse. This adjusted view in which society embraces a broadened spectrum of social groups finds a counterpart in the stylistic variety of Chaucer's own poetry – from his earlier vision poems (such as the *Parliament of Fowls*, in which the garden of love is divided into the regions of Venus and Nature, with each further subdivided into competing qualities and perspectives) to the *Canterbury Tales* itself (with its receptivity to a maximum variety of styles, genres, and their accompanying presuppositions). Again and again, Chaucer's poetry offers us an experience in which a hierarchy is postulated and then penetrated or otherwise qualified – as when the lower fowl of the *Parliament* interrupt the gentle pleas of the tercils with their 'kek's' and 'quek's' and pragmatic analysis (499) or when the drunken Miller of the *Canterbury Tales* will not abide Harry Bailly's intended order of tellers and introduces his own brand of comic 'harlotrie' (I, 3184). Chaucer's bold juxtaposition of personal and literary styles may take some liberties with the facts of personal behaviour and literary preference in his day. Even so, these stylistic juxtapositions offer an apt analogue to the complicated, varied, and dynamic social situation in which Chaucer lived and worked.[49]

Notes

1 Bracton, *On the Laws and Customs of England*, eds. and trans. G. E. Woodbine and S. E. Thorne, vol. 2 (Cambridge, Mass., 1968), p. 31.
2 The estimates given in the pioneering study of Josiah Cox Russell, *British Medieval Population* (Albuquerque, New Mexico, 1948), are now generally regarded as too low; see, among others, John Hatcher, *Plague, Population and the English Economy, 1348–1530* (London, 1977).
3 See N. Denholm-Young, *The Country Gentry in the Fourteenth Century* (Oxford, 1969), pp. 1–40.

4 Based on Russell's analysis of the 1377 poll tax, *British Medieval Population*, pp. 133, 146.

5 The rise of the theory of the three estates in eleventh–thirteenth-century France is described by Georges Duby, *The Three Orders: Feudal Society Imagined*, trans. A. Goldhammer (Chicago/London, 1980).

6 Printed in G. R. Owst, *Literature and Pulpit in Medieval England* (Cambridge, 1933), p. 587.

7 *English Gilds*, ed. L. Toulmin Smith, EETS, es 40 (London, 1870), p. 23.

8 The relative prosperity of the different estates of the realm is suggested by the different categories of the graduated poll tax of 1379; see *The Anonimalle Chronicle*, ed. V. H. Galbraith (Manchester, 1970), pp. 127–9.

9 The 1379 poll tax specifies a category of esquires who do not possess lands, rents, or chattels, but who earn their livelihood *en service* (*Anonimalle Chronicle*, p. 127).

10 M. M. Crow points out that only six of the twenty-three shire-knights in Parliament for Kent during the reign of Richard II were dubbed or formally knighted. See *Chaucer Life-Records*, eds. M. M. Crow and C. C. Olson, (Oxford, 1966), p. 364.

11 Supporting evidence for this brief summary of Chaucer's career is to be found in *Life-Records*, eds. Crow and Olson.

12 Recent examination of the evidence suggests, however, that Henry IV's response to Chaucer's needs might not have been particularly prompt. See Sumner J. Ferris, 'The Date of Chaucer's Final Annuity and of the "Complaint to His Empty Purse"', *Modern Philology*, 65 (1967–8), 45–52.

13 Sylvia Thrupp, *The Merchant Class of Medieval London, 1300–1500* (1948; repr. Ann Arbor. Mich., 1968), p. 282. On the general matter of Chaucer's social position, see Derek Brewer, 'Class Distinctions in Chaucer', *Speculum*, 43 (1968), 290–305, at p. 304.

14 As suggested by James R. Hulbert, *Chaucer's Official Life* (1912; repr. New York, 1970).

15 In 'The Appeal...', *A Book of London English, 1384–1425*, eds. R. W. Chambers and M. Daunt (Oxford, 1931), p. 29.

16 A pioneering study is Ruth Crosby, 'Chaucer and the Custom of Oral Delivery', *Speculum*, 13 (1938), 413–32.

17 M. B. Parkes, 'The Literacy of the Laity', *The Medieval World*, eds. D. Daiches and A. Thorlby, vol. 2 (London, 1973), pp. 555–78.

18 An extended – though occasionally digressive – discussion of the material of the next paragraphs is to be found in Janet Coleman, *Medieval Readers and Writers, 1350–1400* (London, 1981).

19 Ed. E. J. Arnould, Anglo-Norman Text Society (Oxford, 1940), p. 239.

20 Edith Rickert, 'King Richard II's Books', *The Library*, 4th ser., 13 (1933), 144–5.

21 *Issues of the Exchequer*, ed. R. Devon (London, 1837), p. 144.

22 Rickert, 'King Richard II's Books', pp. 144–5; *Issues*, ed. Devon, p. 213.

23 *Chroniques*, ed. J. B. M. C. Kervyn de Lettenhove, vol. 15 (Brussels, 1871), p. 167.

24 'Inventory of the Goods...Belonging to Thomas, Duke of Gloucester', *Archaeological Journal*, 54 (1897), 275–308; William Dugdale, *Monasticon Anglicanum*, vol. 1 (London, 1846), p. 41.

25 Gower, *Complete Works*, ed. G. C. Macaulay, vol. 2 (Oxford, 1901), Prol., 48*–52*.

26 Arguments may be made for Henry V and his brothers as readers of Latin, French, and English. Indications of his preference for English include the fact that Edward, second Duke of York translated Gaston de Foix's *Livre de Chasse* for him during 1399–1413 and that he possessed a copy of Chaucer's *Troilus* during the same period. See *The Master of the Game*, eds. W. A. and F. Baillie-Grohman (London, 1909).

27 See T. F. Tout, 'Literature and Learning in the English Civil Service in the Fourteenth Century', *Speculum*, 4 (1929), 365–89.

28 W. W. Skeat, *The Complete Works of Geoffrey Chaucer*, vol. 7 (Oxford, 1897), p. 2.

29 *Complete Works*, ed. Macaulay, Prol., 24. On Gower's career and literary objectives see John H. Fisher, *John Gower: Moral Philosopher and Friend of Chaucer* (New York, 1964). The deliberateness of Gower's respective choices of Latin, French, and English is underscored by the fact that, even after beginning his *Confessio* in English, he returned to Latin for his *Cronica Tripertita*, with its serious political motive of Lancastrian revisionism.

30 Thrupp, *Merchant Class*, p. 161.

31 *Calendar of Wills, Court of Hustings, London*, ed. Reginald R. Sharpe (London, 1889); discussed by Thrupp, *Merchant Class*, pp. 162–3.

32 According to John Burrow, 'We must think...of *Piers Plowman* reaching two kinds of audience – the old audience of clerks, and the new one of prosperous, literate laymen'. See 'The Audience of Piers Plowman', *Anglia*, 75 (1957), 373–84.

33 Argued, respectively, by James R. Hulbert, 'A Hypothesis Concerning the Alliterative Revival', *Modern Philology*, 28 (1930–31), 405–22; Thorlac Turville-Petre, *The Alliterative Revival* (Cambridge, 1977), pp. 40–7; Michael J. Bennett, '*Sir Gawain and the Green Knight* and the Literary Achievement of the North-West Midlands', *Journal of Medieval History*, 5 (1979), 63–88; Derek Pearsall, 'The Origins of the Alliterative Revival' in *The Alliterative Tradition in the Fourteenth Century*, eds. B. S. Levy and Paul Szarmach (Kent, Ohio, 1981), pp. 1–24.

34 Alfred David, *The Strumpet Muse: Art and Morals in Chaucer's Poetry* (Bloomington, Ind., 1976), p. 122.

35 See Richard F. Green, *Poets and Princepleasers* (Toronto, 1980), p. 166.

36 Gardiner Stillwell, 'The Political Meaning of Chaucer's *Tale of Melibee*', *Speculum*, 19 (1944), 433–44.

37 *Life-Records*, eds. Crow and Olson, pp. 281–4. Additional materials on Brembre, Hend, and other mercantile associates of Chaucer are found in Ruth Bird, *The Turbulent London of Richard II* (London, n.d.).

38 Fisher, *John Gower*, pp. 78–83.

39 *English Gilds*, ed. Toulmin Smith, pp. 443–60.

40 The argument that this group provides Chaucer's principal 'point of attachment' has been made recently by several writers; the evidence is admirably surveyed by V. J. Scattergood, 'Literary Culture at the Court of Richard II', in *English Court Culture in the Later Middle Ages* (London, 1983), pp. 29–43. Additional information on the persons mentioned in the next paragraph is available in the *Dictionary of National Biography* and in K. B. McFarlane, *Lancastrian Kings and Lollard Knights* (Oxford, 1972).

41 *Life-Records*, eds. Crow and Olson, pp. 94–9. Less persuaded that women represented a substantial portion of Chaucer's audience is Richard F. Green, 'Women in Chaucer's Audience', *Chaucer Review*, 18 (1983), 146–54.

42 More extensive discussion of these poems, in a similar vein, is offered by
    P. M. Kean, *Chaucer and the Making of English Poetry*, vol. 1 (London, 1972),
    pp. 31–8, and R. T. Lenaghan, 'Chaucer's *Envoy to Scogan*: the Uses of Literary
    Conventions', *Chaucer Review*, 10 (1975–6), 46–61.

43 Bertrand Bronson. 'Chaucer's Art in Relation to His Audience', *Five Studies in
    Literature*, University of California Publications in English 8 (Berkeley, Ca.,
    1940).

44 On manuscripts of the *Canterbury Tales* see John M. Manly and Edith Rickert,
    The Text of the Canterbury Tales, vol. 1 (Chicago, 1940), esp. pp. 606–20. On
    manuscripts of *Troilus* see Robert Kilburn Root, *The Book of Troilus and Criseyde*
    (Princeton, NJ, 1926), pp. liii–lxi.

45 Jill Mann, *Chaucer and Medieval Estates Satire* (Cambridge, 1973), esp. pp. 1–16.

46 *Chaucer and Medieval Estates Satire*, p. 202.

47 *English Gilds*, ed. Toulmin Smith, p. 97.

48 The argument that courtly audiences enjoyed fabliaux and other narratives
    in everyday settings has been advanced by Per Nykrog, *Les Fabliaux: Étude
    d'histoire littéraire et de stylistique médiévale* (Copenhagen, 1957) and has been
    restated in modified form by Jean Rychner, 'Les Fabliaux: Genre, Styles,
    Publics', *La Littérature narrative d'imagination* (Paris, 1961), pp. 41–52.

49 On Chaucer's aesthetic of juxtaposition see Charles Muscatine, *Chaucer and the
    French Tradition* (Berkeley/Los Angeles, Ca., 1957).

2 Chaucer's Continental inheritance: the early poems and *Troilus and Criseyde*

For most English people today, a first journey to the Continent comes (if it comes at all) as something of a shock. It brings us to a world that thinks, speaks and organizes itself in a language that is other than English. Our own cultural assumptions seem less secure; suddenly, we are foreigners. Such an experience of the Continent differs markedly from that of Chaucer. The London culture in which Chaucer spent most of his life was so heterogeneous, so multilingual, so much part of a greater European milieu that the passage to the Continent can hardly have struck him as a journey from familiarity to foreignness. Chaucer did not need to travel to Paris, for example, to hear French spoken, or to learn that French was the language of paramount cultural prestige as well as the *lingua franca* of international trade. Chivalry was French; romance was French; the *Roman de la Rose* – the seminal influence on vernacular poetry in the European Middle Ages – had been written by two thirteenth-century Frenchmen. English culture had been overshadowed by France and the French for three centuries.[1] In the eyes of the French poet Eustache Deschamps, Chaucer's chief merit lay in his being a 'grant translateur'; a translator, that is, from French into English.[2]

Looking back at Chaucer down the long perspective of literary history, it may seem inevitable that Chaucer should have chosen to write in English; or even that English should have chosen him. But Chaucer's choice of English, or rather of the London dialect that was to develop into what we now call English,[3] was by no means inevitable. Chaucer's friend and fellow poet, John Gower, chose to write in Latin and French as well as in English. And as Chaucer waded ever more deeply into Latin, French and Continental texts, he became ever more conscious of the comparative shallowness of his own native tradition. Social and political conditions certainly favoured Chaucer's choice of English. The fourteenth century saw English gradually superseding French as the language of royal, parliamentary and legal business;[4] and England had been at war with France, on and off, since 1338, some four or five years before Chaucer was born. But it takes more than a sympathetic political climate and good intentions to create an accomplished literary language. Our own century has seen some determined attempts to revive Scots, a literary tradition which flourished with great vigour in the later Middle Ages. Such attempts produced some brilliant early successes, such as Hugh MacDiarmid's *A Drunk Man Looks at the Thistle* (1926). But MacDiarmid, like Edwin Muir before him, was finally driven to embrace a variety of standard English by his need to explore scientific, technical and philosophical complexities. Chaucer shared such a need: his translations of Boethius' *Consolation* of *Philosophy* and the *Treatise on the Astrolabe* stimulated him to incorporate philosophical and scientific terms into his own poetic writings. The limited capacities of fourteenth-century English must occasionally have driven Chaucer close to despair – especially when he came to read the pyrotechnic brilliance of Dante's *Paradiso* and realized what fourteenth-century Italian was already capable of.

Luckily for us, Chaucer did stick with English. The tradition of English metrical romances offered some sort of foundation, albeit a shaky one, for his experiments in extended narrative. Chaucer quickly recognized, however, that his first priority as an English 'makere' was to catch up with what had been learned in France. Chaucer's Englishing of distinguished French precedents began, quietly and appropriately enough, with a diligent, literal imitation of the *Roman de la Rose*.[5] But within a remarkably short space of time – and several years before reaching his thirtieth birthday – Chaucer produced a work of original genius. The *Book of the Duchess* patently aligns itself with the *dits amoreux*, a narrative tradition that was developed out of the *Roman de la Rose* by several generations of French poets and then brought to perfection by Machaut and Froissart.[6] The alignment of the *Duchess* with the *dits* is so convincing that Froissart appears to have drawn upon Chaucer's poem for one of his own efforts in this genre.[7] But even within this larger context, the originality and distinctiveness of Chaucer's dream poem is unmistakable. Chaucer's life-long interest, for example, in communication between disparate social levels is already in evidence: the poem's centrepiece sees a narrator of middling social status and, apparently, of less than middling intelligence, attempting to make sense of the metaphorical language of a Black Knight, a figure representing John of Gaunt, the most powerful lord of the realm. The poetic texture of the *Duchess* is not of uniform excellence: the workaday diction characteristic of the English romances shows through in several patches of threadbare dialogue. But the poem's structure could hardly be improved upon. The *Book of the Duchess* is an extraordinarily assured piece of writing.

Such hard-won assurance must have been devastated by Chaucer's first full encounter with the greatest poem of the age, and perhaps of any age: the *Divina Commedia* of Dante Alighieri. Chaucer may have heard something about Dante from the many Italian merchants who passed through

London, or even from the French lyricists he had imitated and admired since his youth.[8] But in 1373 he was offered the chance of finding out for himself when he travelled to Florence on a trade mission.[9] The timing of this visit was extremely fortunate. Following a lifetime of energetic lobbying by Dante's most devoted disciple, Giovanni Boccaccio, the Florentine civic authorities finally decided (by a majority of 167 votes) to commemorate the great poet they had voted into exile some seventy years before. This commemoration was to take the form of a series of lectures, starting on 23 October 1373, to be delivered by Boccaccio himself at the Florentine church of Santo Stefano di Badia.[10] The public petition seeking these lectures was submitted in June 1373, just one month after Chaucer's return to England. Since these first *lecturae Dantis* were to appeal to a broad, mixed audience, it seems reasonable to suppose that they were a topic of current interest in literary, civic and mercantile circles during Chaucer's stay at Florence. In any event, it is quite clear that Chaucer did discover Dante at some point in the 1370s, and that this discovery was to have a profound effect on his artistic future. The poem which acts out and meditates upon this discovery is, of course, the *House of Fame*.

The *House of Fame* contains less systematic imitation of French material than the *Book of the Duchess*; Dante displaces Machaut as Chaucer's guiding light. But Machaut and the French poets are never far from Chaucer's mind at any stage of his career; their influence on the *House of Fame* is still profound.[11] Chaucer sticks with the short couplets that are the English equivalent of the *Rose*'s octosyllabics, frames his narrative within the familiar French-derived dream framework and speaks through a faintly comical narrator who, as in the *Duchess*, is led to the poem's central locale by an animal guide – in this instance by a schoolmasterly bird. But within the comfortable confines of this familiar format, Chaucer is evidently struggling with something new; something so new, in fact, that the narrator himself can barely grasp or articulate what that something might be. He tells us, repeatedly, that he is in search of 'tydinges', 'tidings' or 'news'.[12] News about what? News about love; news about fame; news about poetry. In the interests of keeping our primary focus on tracing Chaucer's evolving relations with Continental authors, we may without further discussion assume the *House of Fame* to be 'about' these newsworthy, interrelated topics of love, fame and poetry, even though no single set of assumptions about this complex poem is ever likely to unlock its enigmas and reveal a simple, essential meaning.[13] Chaucer himself seems not to have known what this poem finally amounted to: the poem ends incomplete, and the 'man of gret auctorite' (2158) who might have answered all our questions is left without a speech.

Of these three key concepts – love, fame and poetry – the most problematical within this English context of the 1370s is poetry. P. M. Kean has written that the main theme of the *House of Fame* is 'the relation of poetry to the traditions which form its material'.[14] The problem here is that there is no antecedent tradition of English poetry for Chaucer to relate to. No English 'makere' before Chaucer had dared to call himself a poet. Even in Italy, Petrarch, 'the lauriat poete...whos rethorike sweete / Enlumyned al Ytaille of poetrie' was crowned with laurel for his achievements in Latin, not in the vernacular.[15] What Chaucer first saw in Dante was the hope or dream of raising his own humble English 'makinge' to the level of poetry. Such an act might win him the fame enjoyed by the great Latin 'auctores'. Being of a modest disposition (and knowing, at this stage of his career, that he has much to be modest about) the Chaucerian dreamer ignores a request to name himself within Fame's House and denies that he has come in search of fame for himself:

> ...'Frend, what is thy name?
> Artow come hider to han fame?'
> 'Nay, for sothe, frend,' quod y;
> 'I cam noght hyder, graunt mercy,
> For no such cause, by my hed!
> Sufficeth me, as I were ded,
> That no wight have my name in honde.
> I wot myself best how y stonde;
> For what I drye, or what I thynke,
> I wil myselven al hyt drynke,
> Certeyn, for the more part,
> As fer forth as I kan myn art.'   (1871–82)

Not surprisingly, this huffy and evasive little speech only serves to exasperate Chaucer's interlocutor. So what *are* you looking for, within a House of Fame, if not fame? The dreamer struggles to explain. He resorts to his magical word 'tydinges' as if, by repeating it in an incantatory sort of way, he might suddenly be supplied with some sort of answer:

> 'But what doost thou here than?' quod he.
> Quod y, 'That wyl y tellen the,
> The cause why y stonde here:
> Somme newe tydynges for to lere,
> Somme newe thinges, y not what,
> Tydynges...'   (1883–8)

Such awkwardness and self-consciousness is not surprising in a poem which sees Chaucer trying on the poet's toga for the very first time. Dante has shown him what vernacular poetry might resemble; but Dante's Italian has forced him to realize that his own vernacular, English, is, by comparison, a blunt instrument. Chaucer, to his credit, does not shrink from such comparisons. In beginning *Paradiso*, the third and final *cantica* of his *Commedia*, Dante informs Apollo that he – Dante – upon successful

completion of his poetic task, will approach Apollo's tree and crown *himself*
with laurel. Chaucer, in beginning the third and final Book of his *House
of Fame*, informs Apollo that he – Chaucer – upon successful completion
of his poetic task, will approach Apollo's tree...and plant a big kiss on its
trunk. This pattern of retreat into self-parody recurs throughout the *House
of Fame*; Chaucer cannot yet take himself seriously as a poet. And if we
juxtapose just a portion of these last two passages we can see why. Heard
against the sonorous background of Dante's magisterial *terzine*, Chaucer's
English couplets amount to little more than a nervous squeak:[16]

> O buono Appollo, a l'ultimo lavoro
> fammi del tuo valor sí fatto vaso,
> come dimandi a dar l'amato alloro.
>   Infino a qui l'un giogo di Parnaso
> assai mi fu; ma or con amendue
> m'e uopo intrar ne l'aringo rimaso.
>   Entra nel petto mio...   (I, 13–19)

[O good Apollo, for this final labour make me such a vessel of your worthiness
as you require for granting your loved laurel.

Up to this point the one peak of Parnassus has serviced me; but now both peaks
are needed as I enter the arena that remains.

Enter my breast...]

> O God of science and of lyght,
> Appollo, thurgh thy grete myght,
> This lytel laste bok thou gye!
> Nat that I wilne, for maistrye,
> Here art poetical be shewed;
> But for the rym ys lyght and lewed,
> Yit make hyt sumwhat agreable,
> Though som vers fayle in a sillable...   (1091–8)

Chaucer makes no mention of fame here, and even the idea of 'art
poetical' makes him nervous. Following a resolute start, his invocation to
Apollo shrinks to an appeal for assistance in covering up the defects of a
lightweight and recalcitrant medium. Chaucer clearly sees that if such a
medium is to become authentically poetic – and hence capable of encompassing themes of Dantean scope and grandeur – a major overhaul is in
order. Interestingly enough, Dante himself had written a treatise on how
an illustrious vernacular (*vulgaris illustris*) might be forged from existing
Italian dialects. This Latin treatise, entitled *De Vulgari Eloquentia*, makes
diligent (but not slavish) imitation of the great Latin masters (*poetae magni*)
an urgent priority for the attainment of true vernacular eloquence.[17] So
it is that Dante hails Virgil as 'my master and my author' in the *Commedia*'s
very first canto, confides that 'long study and great love' have compelled
him 'to search your volume', and proceeds to follow in his footsteps

(literally and metaphorically) through the various landscapes of Hell and of Purgatory.[18] And in the opening Book of the *House of Fame*, Chaucer too makes a valiant attempt at 'following after' Virgil:

> I wol now singen, yif I kan,
> The armes, and also the man
> That first cam, thurgh his destinee,
> Fugityf of Troy contree...   (143–6)

This literal rendering of the *Aeneid* soon contracts to become a paraphrase (149–238), a romantic interlude (239–382), a series of exempla (388–426) and then becomes a paraphrase again (427–65) before expiring with a romancer's formula (466–7). Again, after a resolute start Chaucer's attempt at an English poetry runs rapidly downhill, offering further ironic contrasts with Dantean models and prescriptions. Another such contrast is offered in Chaucer's middle Book. In the second *cantica* of the *Commedia* Dante dreams of a golden eagle that swoops down and then carries him up into the heavens.[19] In the *House of Fame's* second Book Chaucer dreams of a golden eagle that swoops down and then carries *him* up into the heavens. But Chaucer's Eagle, having cursed and complained about Chaucer's excessive weight (Chaucer was plump), then proceeds to bore Chaucer into glassy-eyed indifference with a tedious sight-seeing commentary. So from yet another serious Dantean starting-point, Chaucer's narrative takes another turn for the comic: the would-be poet is presented as one who dangles, fat and hapless, from the claws of a big, boring bird.

But it is the very insistence and intensity of such self-parodying that most forcefully conveys Chaucer's excitement and agitation over the possibilities of the Dantean project. Within the familiar bounds of the French-derived dream poem format, Chaucer is able to measure the capabilities of his native English against the newly discovered standards of Dante's Italian. At the same time he begins exploring the complex interrelations of love, fame and poetry. This exploration is to be carried forward into *Troilus and Criseyde*, Chaucer's heroic attempt at achieving a work of Dantean stature in English. In the *Troilus*, the interrelation of our three key concepts might be formulated as follows: love inspires poetry; poetry wins fame for both poet and lovers. At first glance, the neatness of this formulation might lead us to believe that Chaucer's artistic uncertainties evaporated the moment he abandoned the *House of Fame*. But this formulation raises some awkward questions. Why labour to win fame for one lover who fears infamy and for another who is finally as indifferent to fame as he is to everything else? Why pin your best hopes for poetic fame on a secular tale of pagan love and infidelity? Such questions are not passed over in the making of the *Troilus*, but are taken up and worried over even as the poem is taking shape. The lively but limited self-assurance of the

Duchess, transformed into perplexed uncertainty in the *House of Fame*, was never to be fully recovered.

Chaucer recovered from the 'narrative débâcle'[20] of the *House of Fame* by emerging from the restrictive confines of short couplets to experiment with a longer line in various forms of verse; he even tried his hand, albeit briefly, at Dantean *terza rima*.[21] But it was a Boccaccian verse form that proved most helpful and instructive to Chaucer at this time: the evolution of Chaucerian rhyme royal, the seven-line verse form (rhyming ababbcc) of the *Parliament of Fowls* and the *Troilus*, owes much to a careful study of the Boccaccian *ottava*, an eight-line stanza of hendecasyllabic (eleven syllable) lines rhyming ababababcc. Chaucer realized the narrative potential of such a stanza in reading the *Filostrato* and *Teseida*, two Boccaccian texts which he may have brought back from Florence in 1373 or acquired a few years later. Chaucer put these two texts to very different uses. The *Filostrato* must have been put aside and mulled over in private moments for many years in preparation for the long labour of the *Troilus*. The *Teseida* was drawn upon time and again as a rich repository of narrative and iconographic motifs in a whole host of works.[22] Its story-line was ultimately to provide a source for Chaucer's *Knight's Tale*. But the *Teseida* was put to work long before this in *Anelida and Arcite*, a distant forebear of the *Knight's Tale* which has the appearance of a poetic workshop in which various stanzaic, narrative and lyric forms are put to the test.[23] The *Anelida* sees Chaucer taking his poetic role somewhat more seriously; too seriously, in fact, since the work (as Robinson so neatly puts it) is 'conspicuous among Chaucer's writings for a tendency to poetic diction'.[24] This disconcerting tendency is evident from the first in this somewhat stiff-jointed rendition of a Boccaccian invocation:[25]

> Thou ferse god of armes, Mars the rede,
> That in the frosty contre called Trace,
> Within thy grisly temple ful of drede
> Honoured art...   (1–4)

C. S. Lewis, in comparing Chaucer's diction with 'the plain style' of Gower, detects within such lines from the *Anelida* 'the germ of the whole central tradition of high poetical language in England'.[26] Such artificial diction, with its rows of tidy iambics pulling against a forced separation of subject from main verb, was much to the liking of Chaucer's fifteenth-century admirers: Lydgate, for one, commended 'the golde dewe dropes of speche and eloquence' that Chaucer 'made firste, to distille and rayne...Into our tunge'.[27] But in this, as in much else, the fifteenth-century reception of Chaucer represents a radical departure from Chaucer's own poetic agenda. The mature Chaucer strove not to gild his diction with

Latinate qualities, but rather to liberate and organize those natural rhythms and energies which were peculiar to his own native tongue. The experimental *Anelida* was left incomplete, and thereafter we see Chaucer's diction becoming ever less Latinate and ever more finely attuned to the various registers and natural nuances of an English-speaking voice. The classical world of *Troilus and Criseyde*, which is underpinned by a host of Continental and Latin texts, was to offer Chaucer endless opportunities for high-flown Latinity: but to study Chaucer at work on his sources in the *Troilus* is to see him turning down such opportunities by the dozen.[28] The *Troilus* does, of course, have its grandiloquent moments. But for the most part, the poem's first-person narrator speaks in a voice which, through painstaking art, is made to seem thoroughly natural to him. This ideal of artful naturalness in poetic diction again reflects Chaucer's diligent adherence to Dantean principles. Dante acclaims Virgil as his master, author and guide: but he never sounds like Virgil; his diction is always Italian, never Latinate. For Dante it is of fundamental importance that a poet should labour to perfect his own voice; he should not seek to borrow a voice from books or from strangers. Love of your homeland and of the language you grew up with is, after all, the most natural thing in the world. So it is that Dante's Purgatory, the most authentic homeland of poetic struggle and of artistic endeavour, is thickly peopled with poets from all over Continental Europe. At the very entrance of the Ante-Purgatory, Dante, Virgil and their companions are held spellbound by one Casella, singing one of Dante's own songs (II, 112–17). One Bolognese poet, on being acclaimed by Dante as a supreme exponent of vernacular poetry ('l'uso moderno') points to one of his poet companions as the 'miglior fabbro del parlar materno' (XXVI, 117). And this 'better craftsman of the mother tongue' is accorded the honour of speaking in his native Provençal (which Dante has troubled to learn) even within Dante's Italian masterpiece. Arnaut's greeting of Dante, his fellow poet, is respectful, friendly and fraternal:

> *Tan m'abellis vostre cortes deman...* (XXVI, 140)
>
> [Your courteous question pleases me so much...]

Chaucer must have hungered for such intelligent appreciation of his own poetic craft; he must also have recognized that there was nobody alive in England capable of offering it to him. He continued, nonetheless, to struggle towards a Dantean standard of artful naturalness in vernacular diction; and in the *Parliament of Fowls* he finally achieved it:

> The lyf so short, the craft so long to lerne,
> Th'assay so hard, so sharp the conquerynge,
> The dredful joye, alwey that slit so yerne:
> Al this mene I by Love... (1–4)

This voice, so perfectly expressive of a mind that wanders distractedly beneath the burden of a weighty, all-consuming subject, sounds quite unlike the voice which made such a stilted start to the *Anelida*. This speaker seems more vulnerable and hence more human, and less concerned with striking poetical postures. He seems, at first, to be unaware of any audience, only pulling himself together in the fourth line to tell us what his main subject is to be. From his opening lines we might have guessed his subject to be art itself: but it is love, a subject which is always intimately bound up with art in medieval writing. And although these opening lines seem so artlessly natural (even in talking around or about the subject of art) they are actually highly crafted: the opening line translates the Latin maxim *ars longa, vita brevis*; the next two lines continue the rhetorical themes of *contentio* (contrast) and *circumlocutio*; and taken together, all three lines add up to an example of *interpretatio*, saying the same thing in different ways.[29]

The opening sentences of medieval poems (and this includes the *Troilus* and the *Canterbury Tales*) are often exceptionally complex and highly wrought: it is as if the poet needs to convince us of his credentials before we commit ourselves to following his text. This holds true for the *Parliament*, too. But the *Parliament*'s opening lines, which speak with an apparently spontaneous and life-like voice that conceals painstaking elaboration of a foreign source and quiet mastery of rhetorical techniques, are also suggestively emblematic of the poem as a whole. Like the *House of Fame*, the *Parliament* offers three differing views of its declared subject, love: the first from a distant, cosmic perspective; the second from within a house of art; and the third from within a more free-wheeling, densely-peopled (or birded) milieu. Each of these three major narrative segments builds upon a major Latin or Continental, ancient or modern source.[30] As Piero Boitani indicates in the following essay, the first utilizes the fifth-century Latin of Macrobius (the 'auctour' who supplies the dream lore with which the *Roman de la Rose* opens); the second the fourteenth-century Italian of Boccaccio's *Teseida*; and the third the twelfth-century Latin of the Frenchman Alan of Lille. To complicate matters further, the transition between the second and third domains here seems to owe something to another Boccaccian text, a dream vision in *terza rima* called the *Amorosa Visione*.[31] Such a weight of source material might seem oppressive; and within the hothouse atmosphere of the temple of Venus, Chaucer himself becomes somewhat disgruntled and disaffected by the sheer weight of past writing on love. Towards the end of his temple tour he does little more than name names:

> Semyramis, Candace, and Hercules,
> Biblis, Dido, Thisbe and Piramus,
> Tristram, Isaude, Paris, and Achilles,
> Eleyne, Cleopatre, and Troylus...   (288–91)

Chaucer wanders out of this art gallery in search of 'solace' (297); and

Nature rescues him. He discovers a parliament of fowls, a gathering of birds representing every class and subclass of contemporary London society. This parliament, loosely governed by Nature herself, is initially monopolized by aristocratic voices. Such high-born birds, operating within the framework of an idealized world, would naturally sympathize with the likes of Helen of Troy, Cleopatra and Troilus. But this idealizing conception of love is soon exposed to some pungent criticisms by birds of lower degree. Duck logic may not be pleasant – it is the logic of Pandarus once Criseyde has flown – but it does ask some awkward questions about the wisdom of fidelity in a case of unrequited love:

> 'Wel bourded,' quod the doke, 'by myn hat!
> That men shulde loven alwey causeles,
> Who can a resoun fynde or wit in that?
> Daunseth he murye that is myrtheles?
> Who shulde recche of that is recheles?
> Ye quek!' yit seyde the doke, ful wel and fayre,
> 'There been mo sterres, God wot, than a payre!'   (589–95)

This movement from art-monument to a contest of impetuous, disparate voices retraces the movement from Fame's hall, where the poets stand on their metal pillars in silent rows, to the noisy, disorderly house of Rumour, a place which

> Was ful of shipmen and pilgrimes,
> With scrippes bret-ful of lesinges,
> Entremedled with tydynges,
> And eek allone be hemselve.
> O, many a thousand tymes twelve
> Saugh I eke of these pardoners...   (2122–7)

And such a movement seems prophetic of its author's entire career, as Chaucer himself was to move from the classical, noble and delimited realm of the *Troilus* to the more open territory of the *Canterbury Tales*, with its shipmen, pilgrims and pardoners. But it would be foolish to equate this with a movement from art to life, or from imitative art to art from life, or even from a derivative Englishness to a declaration of English independence. Chaucer himself warns us against forming such an equation in the latter part of his *Parliament*. Nature may look and sound like an Englishwoman but she is, Chaucer insists, of Franco-Latin origin, born out of Alan of Lille's Latin text (316–18). These English birds may sound spontaneous and unrestrained, but they still manage to keep within the bounds of a seven-line stanza rhyming ababbcc. And in concluding their parliament, these boisterous birds select a choir from within their own number, change their rhyme scheme and forget their differences in singing a roundel. Such a musical resolution to the vehement conflicts of a London parliament is, of course, a fantasy of art, not a record of life. This art is not as natural as birdsong; it is a patiently negotiated marriage between English voices and Continental forms. These birds sing in English to a tune that is borrowed not from nature but from Machaut or Deschamps:

> The note, I trowe, imaked was in Fraunce,
> The wordes were swiche as ye may heer fynde...   (677–8)

Once the *Parliament*'s roundel ends the dream dissolves and Chaucer wakes up. Offering no comment whatsoever on his dream, he returns at once to the studious pursuit of reading. These long years of study were to bear fruit in *Troilus and Criseyde*, Chaucer's magnificent attempt at achieving an English classic of extended narrative that might survive comparison with serious works of any age or language, ancient or modern. In the *House of Fame*, struggling with a vernacular which is far from illustrious, Chaucer can only eye the great 'auctores' in passing as they look down on him from their pedestals (1419–1512). Not until he has worked his way to the end of *Troilus and Criseyde* does Chaucer dare to post a claim to stand in their company. This claim, made with characteristic modesty, invites us – for the very first time – to consider the English art of an English writer as poetry, 'poesye':

> Go, litel bok, go, litel myn tragedye,
> Ther God thi makere yet, er that he dye,
> So sende myght to make in som comedye!
> But litel book, no makyng thow n'envie,
> But subgit be to alle poesye;
> And kis the steppes, where as thow seest pace
> Virgile, Ovide, Omer, Lucan, and Stace.   (v, 1786–92)

Chaucer clearly wishes us to relate his *Troilus* to those famous texts of antiquity which share his serious concern with the great themes of warfare, love and moral virtue.[32] But, at the same time, he also wishes us to associate his poem with the major texts of those medieval poets he most admired and made most use of: Boccaccio, Dante and the poets of the *Rose*. For in placing himself sixth in a poetic confraternity of six, a grouping which extends from the pagan past to the Christian present, Chaucer is deliberately upholding a precedent established by Jean de Meun and then adopted within Dante's *Commedia* and Boccaccio's *Filocolo*. Jean represents himself as following after Tibullus, Gallus, Catullus, Ovid and Guillaume de Lorris; similarly, Dante joins the company of Homer, Horace, Ovid, Lucan and Virgil as 'sixth among such intellects' ('sesto tra cotanto senno'); and Boccaccio describes himself as following in the wake of Virgil, Lucan, Statius, Ovid, and Dante.[33] The 'sixth of six' topos that is pinned to the end of Chaucer's poem functions, then, both as a badge of independent merit and as a sign that points us towards a greater, Continental context for *Troilus and Criseyde*.

This wider European context within which the *Troilus* situates itself is unified by the fundamental and pervasive influence of one key text: the *Roman de la Rose*. Chaucer remained a diligent student of the *Rose* throughout his life; Deschamps chose his words advisedly in addressing Chaucer as the 'great translator' who had 'planted the rose tree' in England.[34] And Chaucer's movements between the poetic territories of Italy and France were eased by the formative and long-lasting influence exerted by the *Rose* in both countries.[35] The Italianization of the *Rose* had got under way by 1266, several years before Jean de Meun set to work on extending the text that Guillaume de Lorris had left incomplete some forty years before. The year 1266 saw Brunetto Latini, Dante's celebrated teacher, returning to Florence after six years of political exile in France. During this period of forced idleness Brunetto had composed a poem in seven-syllable couplets known as the *Tesoretto*, which takes its inspiration from the *Rose*. This first effort at learning from the French poem was taken up by a second generation of Italian poets in a number of transitional works. One of these, the *Intelligenza*, paved the way for the Boccaccian *Amorosa Visione* and, ultimately, for the Petrarchan *Trionfi*. Another, the *Fiore* (a sequence of sonnets by a certain 'ser Durante' which imitates both parts of the *Rose*) helps clear the way for Dante's *Commedia*. It is possible that Durante and Dante are one: so Chaucer and Dante might actually have begun their poetic careers in parallel, as translators of the *Rose*. At any event, Chaucer (who had brought his own vernacular tradition through so many evolutionary stages in such a short space of time) was uniquely qualified to perceive the presence of the *Rose* within Italian texts, including Dante's *Commedia*.[36]

Chaucer thus experienced little difficulty in detecting the presence of both the *Commedia* and the *Rose* within Boccaccio's *Filocolo*, a monumentally lengthy, Italian prose version of the French romance of *Floire et Blancheflor*. It was the *Filocolo*'s fourth Book that Chaucer made most use of.[37] *Filocolo* IV appropriates landscapes from the *Commedia* and the *Rose* to explore the problematic status of a young pagan hero struggling to consummate his love affair and, at the same time, to understand that greater love which orders and governs the universe. The central Book of the *Troilus*, in taking up this exploration of the uncharted territory between pagan consummation and Christian revelation, borrows from and alludes to all three of these texts in ways that criticism has barely begun to understand.[38] Although such borrowing and allusion is at its most intense in Book III, it continues throughout the *Troilus*. Allegorical personifications from the *Rose*, such as 'Kynde', 'Daunger', and 'Feere', war within the minds of Chaucer's lovers; the conflicting views of love which separate the idealist Troilus from the pragmatist Pandarus recall the differing attitudes which separate the two authors of the *Rose*. Certain Dantean figures, often of classical origins, inspire the most complex and suggestive allusions; certain Dantean moments, such as *Inferno* v (Paolo and Francesca) or *Inferno* xxx (the juxtaposition of Troy and Thebes) cast long shadows over the entire poem. Troilus' praise of 'Benigne Love' at the height of the consummation scene (III, 1261–7) is inspired by St Bernard's prayer to the Virgin in *Paradiso* xxxIII (14–15), and the beautiful image of Criseyde's eyes as a vision of Paradise (v, 817) reminds us of Beatrice's admonition to Dante in *Paradiso* xVIII (21). Even the poem's final stanza begins with a studied imitation of lines from the *Paradiso*.[39] And the poem's tragic conclusion seems the more poignant when viewed within this Continental context, since all of its companion texts are comedies, pilgrimages to truth or love that reach their religious or erotic terminus, their designated shrine. The *Troilus* goes against the European grain; perhaps this helps to account for the narrator's acute discomfiture during the last two Books.

Within his *Filocolo*, Boccaccio purports to be following the 'true testimony' of an ancient author, one 'Ilario' (v, 97, 10). Chaucer, similarly, insists that he is bound to follow the ancient, Latin text of 'Lollius'. Both Ilario and Lollius are, of course, pious fictions, cultural ciphers expressive of a common commitment to revivifying an ancient past. They disguise the fact that both Boccaccio and Chaucer are actually reworking more modern, vernacular texts which they choose not to name. The actual source of Chaucer's *Troilus* is, of course, another Boccaccian text, the *Filostrato*. At first glance, the *Filostrato* seems a curious choice as the source of Chaucer's most serious and sustained effort at mature 'poesye'. Boccaccio was barely twenty when he wrote it; his text bears obvious signs of immaturity. Boccaccio entertains himself by striking authorish postures within the *Filostrato*; he particularly enjoys advising his youthful peers, once his love story is spent, to put a brake on their eager steps towards sexual gratification.[40] His text makes little effort to homogenize its diverse literary sources: phrases picked up, magpie-like, from writers such as Cino da Pistoia, Andreas Capellanus, and Dante (especially Dante) are stuck on to the narrative surface with great complacency and little concern for context. According to its prose Preface, Boccaccio's poem discovered its originary impulse within an assembly of courtly young lovers, the kind of assembly (real or imagined) that Chaucer was obviously at home with. But the basic narrative technique of Boccaccio's poem is actually developed out of the *cantare*, a tradition of popular narrative in *ottava rima* which has much in common with the English tradition of tail-rhyme romance.[41] The *Filostrato* did not suit Chaucer as a poetic exemplar: the English poet turns repeatedly to Dante, Machaut and the *Rose* poets when seeking more suitable models of lyric prosody or more authentic accounts of courtly sensibility.[42] But the *Filostrato* did suit Chaucer admirably as a poetic source. The *Commedia* and the *Rose*, after all, can hardly be improved upon as poetic sources. They are completed, universal texts: after hell, purgatory and heaven there is nowhere much to go. The youthful *Filostrato*, on the other hand, allowed generous room for improvement.

In choosing the *Filostrato*, Chaucer was making a deliberate, far-reaching decision about the kind of poet he wished to be and, consequently, about the kind of audience he expected to reach. He did not wish to be the kind of poet who makes things difficult for his readers and ends up by reaching only a favoured few. Petrarch anticipates that very few men will find their way into his Academy; and women are not invited. Dante is more generous: everyone is welcome at his banquet, his *Convivio*.[43] But not everyone will make it to the end of his *Commedia*; those who grow faint-hearted on entering the *Paradiso* are actively encouraged to give up reading (II, 1–9). *Troilus and Criseyde*, by contrast, is a generous, inclusive, reader-friendly text that could (and did) find a home almost anywhere: at court, at the quayside or even in the convent. It is a text which finds room for cheerful bedside banter as well as for anguished philosophical reflections. Its narrator remains on easy, familiar terms with his readership; his evolving relationship with his readers forms part of the poem's subject. These readers or listeners may, then as now, thoroughly enjoy Chaucer's poem whilst remaining blissfully ignorant of its larger cultural context and voluntarily indifferent to its learned allusions. Unlike Petrarch or Dante, Chaucer does not strive for perpetual, ingenious variety in his rhyming. He achieves moments of high drama, demanding close concentration from his readers, but he also budgets for moments when our concentration may slacken. To this end he borrows numerous tags, epithets, oaths, asseverations and other such resources from popular narrative tradition; the reader or listener may nod for a line or two. The *Troilus* employs variations of the romancer's simile 'stille as any ston' on five occasions and rhymes on 'ston' six times. Chaucer rhymes on 'two' on over twenty occasions; these include the romance tags 'eyen two' (III, 1352; IV, 750) and 'armes two' (IV, 911). And he takes full advantage of having a heroine whose name rhymes with 'seyde'.

Chaucer seems, then, to assume a double identity within *Troilus and Criseyde*. He wishes to align himself with the greatest European poets, ancient and modern. Yet he also wishes, when it suits him, to speak like an English romancer. Perhaps this is why he chooses to represent himself within the *Canterbury Tales*, first as the teller of an English stanzaic romance, and secondly as the translator (who avoids a Latin source when he can find a French one) of a 'moral tale vertuous' (VII, 940) from ancient times. Taken together, the tail-rhyme of *Sir Thopas* and the learned, pedagogical prose of the *Tale of Melibee* do amount to a recognizable caricature of their author: Chaucer as a dog who knows two tricks, romancing and translating. Perhaps we should respect Chaucer's defence of *Sir Thopas* as 'the beste rym I kan' as a candid half-truth. *Troilus and Criseyde* is, after all, Chaucer's 'beste rym'.

It is not difficult to see why Chaucer made more use of Boccaccio than of any other writer. Boccaccio shares Chaucer's ambition of establishing himself as a poet of European stature who, in company with a few Continental contemporaries, joins hands across the centuries with the great authors of antiquity. This ambition was first fired by a diligent reading of Dante. But Boccaccio also shares Chaucer's willingness to draw narrative inspiration from more popular quarters, fashioning hybrid texts which appeal to a broad range of readers. This willingness on Boccaccio's part was somewhat shortlived, however. Gradually succumbing to the influence of Petrarch and the early humanists, Boccaccio channelled most of his mature energies into Latin encyclopedism. But although he gave up vernacular verse in mid-career, Boccaccio retained a deep personal devotion to Dante. And in 1373 he was finally offered the opportunity of conducting a public celebration of Dante's great poem. But this opportunity caught Boccaccio in an awkward dilemma. He wished to honour Dante as the great poet of the Florentine vernacular. But by 1373 excessive enthusiasm for the vernacular had become unfashionable in Florence. Boccaccio struggles with this dilemma throughout the *accessus* (or introduction) to his Dante lectures. Finally he proposes that Dante actually began his *Commedia* in Latin but then switched to Italian, an inferior medium, because few noble and educated men could or would read Latin. So Latin could not make him famous; and a Latin *Commedia* 'might fall into the hands of plebeians and men of low degree'.[44] These fantastic propositions, a comprehensive betrayal of Dante's most deeply-held artistic principles, mark Boccaccio's final capitulation to the cultural pressures exerted by Petrarch and the Latin humanists.

Perhaps the very fact that Florence was finally able to rehabilitate Dante in 1373 suggests that by that time Dante's text had lost something of its revolutionary resonance. Its politics were outdated; its leading figures were long since dead, if not entirely forgotten. Its theology was outmoded; its zealous championing of vernacular poetry had passed out of fashion. And the Florentine vernacular had settled down. It had become more polished and accomplished, but could hold fewer surprises.[45] Present utterance was already conditioned and restricted by the weight of past history. English, by contrast, had little to weigh itself down with in 1373. English poetry was scarcely aware of its own existence before Chaucer's discovery of Dante. The first effects of this discovery, acted out in the *House of Fame*, were to reduce Chaucer to a state of comically ambivalent, self-conscious agitation. But as we have seen, Chaucer's self-assurance quietly grows in the course of writing the *Anelida* and the *Parliament*; and in *Troilus and Criseyde* he finally draws English into the mainstream of European poetry.

Chaucer is Dante's truest fourteenth-century continuator because it is in Chaucer's hands that Dante's text rediscovers its revolutionary potential. Chaucer came across the *Commedia* at precisely the right moment: that moment near the beginnings of a vernacular tradition when a language, although inchoate and unstable, seems (in the hands of a genius) to be marvellously malleable, infinitely adaptive, capable of almost anything. Chaucer learned many things from Dante. but the most important was, quite simply, to keep faith with his own language: a vernacular must be revolutionized from within, not patched and amended from without. The cultural prestige of French need not and (despite Petrarch's best efforts) could not be disputed: French precedents were fundamental to European literary culture. And no vernacular could hope to match the authority of Latin: for unlike Latin, no vernacular could shield itself from the effects of passing time. But it is this very inability to resist or be indifferent to changes over time that guarantees the vernacular's peculiar glory: for human experience is, after all, an experience of continual change, of growth, decay and renewal. The vernacular, not Latin, provides the most accurate mirror of the human condition. Languages change, Chaucer reminds us, 'withinne a thousand yeer';[46] and this is natural and appropriate, Dante's Adam argues, since

> ...l'uso d'i mortali è come fronda
> in ramo, che sen va e altra vene.[47]

> [...the usage of mortals is like a leaf
> on a branch, which goes away and another comes.]

Notes

1   See R. W. Southern, 'England's First Entry into Europe', in *Medieval Humanism and Other Studies* (Oxford, 1970), pp. 135–57; Elizabeth Salter, 'Chaucer and Internationalism', *Studies in the Age of Chaucer*, 2 (1980), 71–9; W. Rothwell, 'Stratford Atte Bowe and Paris', *Modern Language Review*, 80 (1985), 39–54. Donald R. Howard's forthcoming biography of Chaucer offers a fine account of Chaucer's development within this complex of domestic and European influences.

2   Deschamp's *balade* commends Chaucer, its addressee, for having served 'those who are ignorant of French': see *Chaucer: The Critical Heritage*, ed. Derek Brewer, 2 vols. (London, 1978), vol. 1, pp. 39–42; line 9, translated by Brewer, *Heritage*, vol. 1, p. 40.

3   See A. C. Baugh and Thomas Cable, *A History of the English Language*, 3rd edn (Englewood Cliffs, NJ, 1978), pp. 193–5.

4 See Baugh and Cable, *English Language*, pp. 143–54; Derek Pearsall, *Old English and Middle English Poetry* (London, 1977), pp. 189–91.

5 Chaucer refers to his translation of the *Rose* in *The Legend of Good Women*, F 327–31, G 253–7. See Ronald Sutherland, '*The Romaunt of the Rose*' and '*Le Roman de la Rose*'. *A Parallel Text Edition* (Oxford, 1967). Sutherland affirms that there is 'no reason to doubt that Fragment A of the *Romaunt*, save for a few revisions, is Chaucer's genuine work' (p. xxxiv).

6 For an excellent account of this tradition, see James I. Wimsatt, *Chaucer and the French Love Poets: The Literary Background of the Book of the Duchess* (Chapel Hill, 1968).

7 See Wimsatt, *Chaucer and the French Love Poets*, pp. 129–33.

8 See James I. Wimsatt, *Chaucer and the Poems of 'Ch'* (Cambridge, 1982), pp. 51–60, 66–8.

9 For details of Chaucer's 1373 visit to Genoa and Florence, see *Chaucer Life-Records*, eds. M. M. Crow and C. C. Olson (Oxford, 1966), pp. 32–40; D. S. Brewer, *Chaucer and his World* (London, 1978), pp. 119–31.

10 See *Esposizioni sopra la Comedia di Dante*, ed. G. Padoan, in *Tutte le opere di Giovanni Boccaccio*, ed. Vittore Branca, 12 vols., incomplete (Milan, 1964–), vol. 6; G. Padoan, 'Boccaccio, Giovanni', in *Enciclopedia Dantesca*, ed. Umberto Bosco, 6 vols. (Rome, 1970–8), vol. 1, pp. 645–50; A. Vallone, 'Lectura Dantis', *Enciclopedia Dantesca*, vol. 3, pp. 606–9.

11 See W. O. Sypherd, *Studies in Chaucer's Hous of Fame* (London, 1907), p. 13.

12 The word *tydinges* appears some twenty-two times in the *House of Fame*.

13 For a survey of recent views, see Laurence K. Shook, 'The House of Fame', in *Companion to Chaucer Studies*, ed. Beryl Rowland, 2nd edn (Oxford, 1979), pp. 414–27. See also Piero Boitani, *Chaucer and the Imaginary World of Fame* (Cambridge, 1984).

14 *Chaucer and the Making of English Poetry*, 2 vols. (London, 1972), vol. 1, p. 111.

15 See *Clerk's Prologue*, 31–3. Petrarch was crowned with the laurels of a Latin poet at Rome in 1341.

16 I follow the text of the *Commedia* established by Giorgio Petrocchi (Turin, 1975); my translation. One of the two peaks of Parnassus that Dante speaks of here was regarded as sacred to Apollo, the other to the Muses.

For a detailed consideration of Chaucer's indebtedness to specific Dantean contexts and phrasings, see Howard H. Schless, *Chaucer and Dante: A Reevaluation* (Norman, Okla., 1984).

17 See the edition (with facing Italian translation) by A. Marigo, 3rd edn, updated by P. G. Ricci (Florence, 1957), esp. II, iv, 1–3. For a convenient translation see *Literary Criticism of Dante Alighieri*, ed. and trans. Robert S. Haller (Lincoln. Nebr., 1973), pp. 3–60.

18 See *Inferno* I, 83–5. This passage is deliberately recalled by Christine de Pisan in her *Livre du chemin de long estude* (1402–3), a dream vision in which Christine 'explicitly conceives her literary career as a learned continuation of the poetic achievement of Virgil', Christine de Pisan, *The Book of the City of Ladies*, trans. E. J. Richards (New York, 1982), pp. xliii–iv.

19 See *Purgatorio* IX, 13–42.

20 Derek Brewer, *Towards a Chaucerian Poetic*, British Academy, 1974 (London, 1974), p. 8.

21 See *A Complaint to his Lady*, lines 15–22; and see *The Works of Geoffrey Chaucer*, ed. F. N. Robinson, pp. 519–20, 856.

22 See Piero Boitani, 'Style, Iconography and Narrative: the Lesson of the *Teseida*',

in *Chaucer and the Italian Trecento*, ed. Piero Boitani (Cambridge, 1983), pp. 185–99.

23 For a differing view of this poem, see John Norton-Smith, 'Chaucer's *Anelida and Arcite*', in *Medieval Studies for J. A. W. Bennett*, ed. P. L. Heyworth (Oxford, 1981), pp. 81–99.

24 *Works of Chaucer*, ed. Robinson, p. 304.

25 See *Teseida delle nozze di Emilia*, ed. A. Limentani, in *Opere di Boccaccio*, ed. Branca, vol. 2 (I, 3).

26 *The Allegory of Love* (Oxford, 1936), p. 201.

27 From *The Life of Our Lady*, c. 1410, Book II, lines 1632–4 (Brewer, *Heritage*, vol. I, p. 46).

28 See David Wallace, *Chaucer and the Early Writings of Boccaccio* (Cambridge, 1985), pp. 94–140. And see *Troilus and Criseyde: A New Edition of 'The Book of Troilus'*, ed. B. A. Windeatt, (London/New York, 1984), which juxtaposes texts of the *Filostrato* and the *Troilus*; *Chaucer's Boccaccio: Sources of Troilus and the Knight's and Franklin's Tales*, ed. and trans. N. R. Havely (Cambridge, 1980), which provides the most recent and reliable translation of the *Filostrato*.

29 See *The Parlement of Foulys*, ed. D. S. Brewer (London, 1960), pp. 48–9.

30 See B. A. Windeatt, *Chaucer's Dream Poetry: Sources and Analogues* (Cambridge, 1982).

31 See Wallace, *Early Writings*, pp. 143–6. The *Visione*, which attempts to accommodate the influence of Dante within the French-derived framework of a dream vision, has much in common with the *House of Fame*: see Wallace, *Early Writings*, pp. 5–22.

32 On this division of subject materials, see *De Vulgari Eloquentia* II, ii, 6–10 (Haller, *Literary Criticism*, pp. 34–6).

33 See *Le Roman de la Rose*, ed. F. Lecoy, 3 vols. (Paris, 1975–9), lines 10477–644; *Inferno* IV, 80–102 (102); *Filocolo*, ed. A. E. Quaglio, in *Opere di Boccaccio*, ed. Branca, vol. I, V, 97, 4–6; and see Wallace, *Early Writings*, pp. 46–53.

34 See Brewer, *Heritage*, vol. I, pp. 40–1 (Brewer's translation).

35 See David Wallace, 'Chaucer and the European *Rose*', in *Studies in the Age of Chaucer. Proceedings, No. 1, 1984: Reconstructing Chaucer*, eds. Paul Strohm and Thomas J. Heffernan (Knoxville, Tenn., 1985), pp. 61–7.

36 Both Laurent de Premierfait (who translated Boccaccio's *Decameron* into French) and Christine de Pisan (who was born in Venice and worked in various parts of France) explicitly compare the *Commedia* and the *Rose* in the early years of the fifteenth century: see John V. Fleming, *The 'Roman de la Rose'. A Study in Allegory and Iconography* (Princeton, NJ, 1969), p. 18; Maxwell Luria, *A Reader's Guide to the 'Roman de la Rose'* (Hamden, Conn., 1982), p. 201.

37 *Filocolo* IV, 31 provides a source for Chaucer's *Franklin's Tale*: see *Sources and Analogues of Chaucer's 'Canterbury Tales'*, eds. W. F. Bryan and G. Dempster (Chicago, 1941; repr. New York, 1958), pp. 377–83; for a translation, see *Chaucer's Boccaccio*, ed. Havely. The parliament of courtiers in which this source story appears is immediately preceded by a dream vision assembly of some thirty birds; the same female figure (in different symbolic disguises) governs both gatherings (IV, 12–72). The latter part of *Filocolo* IV, featuring the long-delayed consummation of a pagan love affair, influences *Troilus* III, 442–1309, that part of Chaucer's poem in which the *Filostrato* exerts virtually no influence: see Karl Young, *The Origin and Development of the Story of Troilus and Criseyde* (Chaucer society, 1908; repr. New York, 1968), pp. 139–81; *Works of Chaucer*, ed. Robinson, p. 824.

38 A brilliant start has recently been made by Winthrop Wetherbee, *Chaucer and the Poets: An Essay on Troilus and Criseyde* (Ithaca, NY, 1984). See also Young, *Development*, pp. 139–51; Wallace, *Early Writings*, pp. 133–40.

39 See Wetherbee, '*Troilus and Criseyde*', pp. 37–43, 95–6, 111–78; Wallace, *Early Writings*, pp. 133–40.

40 See *Filostrato*, ed. Branca, in *Opere di Boccaccio*, ed. Branca, vol. 2, esp. VIII, 29: 'O giovinetti...'.

41 See Wallace, *Early Writings*, pp. 73–93, 146–50.

42 See James I. Wimsatt, 'Guillaume de Machaut and Chaucer's *Troilus and Criseyde*', *Medium Aevum*, 45 (1976), 277–93.

43 The courses of Dante's *Convivio* ('banquet') are commentaries upon his own *canzoni* served to those who, through familial or civic commitments, or through being far from a university or scholarly company, have found little time or opportunity for 'speculazione': see *Il Convivio*, ed. Maria Simonelli (Bologna, 1966), I, i, 2–4. For an excellent translation (which does, however, predate more reliable editions of the Dantean text), see *Dante's Convivio*, trans. W. W. Jackson (Oxford, 1924).

44 See *Esposizioni, accessus*, 74–6.

45 See Erich Auerbach, *Literary Language and Its Public in Late Latin Antiquity and in the Middle Ages*, trans. Ralph Manheim (London, 1965), p. 318.

46 *Troilus and Criseyde* II, 23. Compare *Convivio* I, v, 9, where Dante claims that 'were those who departed this life a thousand years ago to return to their native cities, they would believe them occupied by a foreign people, so different would be the language from their own' (Haller's translation, pp. 62–3). As is pointed out by Robinson in *Works of Chaucer*, p. 818 and Windeatt in *Troilus*, p. 153, the ultimate source of *Troilus* II, 22–5 is Horace, *Ars Poetica* 69–72. The phrasing of the *Convivio* passage is, however, closer to *Troilus* II, 22–3 than any other source; and it is obviously vastly more suggestive.

47 *Paradiso* XXVI, 137–8. For a helpful guide to Dante's evolving views on the relationship of Latin to the vernacular, see J. Cremona, 'Dante's Views on Language', in *The Mind of Dante*, ed. U. Limentani (Cambridge, 1965), pp. 138–62. And for an illuminating comparison of the views of Dante and Petrarch on this relationship, see Kenelm Foster, *Petrarch. Poet and Humanist* (Edinburgh, 1984), pp. 23–48.

3   Old books brought to life in dreams:
     the *Book of the Duchess*, the *House of Fame*,
     the *Parliament of Fowls*

W HEN, in a May dream, the mighty God of Love appears to the poetic persona of Geoffrey Chaucer in the Prologue to the *Legend of Good Women*, he angrily reproaches the writer for having translated the *Roman de la Rose* ('an heresye ageyns [Love's] lawe') and composed the 'bok' of Troilus and Criseyde, which shows 'how that wemen han don mis'. In the tirade that follows, Love asks the poet whether, among all the books he owns, he could not have found 'some story of wemen that were goode and trewe' to serve as a literary model. The God is quite specific in his description of these books:

> Yis, God wot, sixty bokes olde and newe
> Hast thow thyself, alle ful of storyes grete,
> That bothe Romayns and ek Grekes trete
> Of sundry wemen, which lyf that they ladde,
> And evere an hundred goode ageyn oon badde.[1]   (G 273–7)

He cites 'Valerius', Livy, Claudian, St Jerome, Ovid, Vincent of Beauvais – indeed 'al the world of autours' both Christian and pagan could confirm to the poet that women can be true and good.

In his typically light, half-jocose, but erudite manner (he will soon mention and borrow from Dante, too), Chaucer seems to be telling us that he owns sixty books. We cannot be sure that the figure corresponds to reality – it is too round a number, and the context is not completely clear: are the sixty books exclusively 'Roman' and 'Greek', and do they deal only with 'sundry wemen'? And what does 'olde and newe' mean? Chaucer's personal library can be expanded almost *ad infinitum* by people who take every literary allusion in his works to imply knowledge of a 'book', and reduced to far less than sixty volumes by those who consider the way in which many works of literature or philosophy circulated throughout the Middle Ages as fragments in anthologies and miscellanies. A more historical approach to these problems is outlined in Paul Strohm's essay above. What interests me here is the image of himself and his library that Chaucer seems keen on presenting to his readers in this passage, the very fact that he makes Love talk to us about his books.

The God's words are extremely appropriate to the present circumstances and to this particular dreamer. For, at the very beginning of his poem (and this time in both versions), Chaucer had launched into a long hymn in praise of books and prefaced his dream of the God of Love with the portrait of himself as a fanatic bibliophile, who puts down his volume only when the overwhelming power of spring prompts him to choose the meadow and its flowers instead:

> And as for me, though that I konne but lyte,
> On bokes for to rede I me delyte,
> And to hem yive I feyth and ful credence,
> And in myn herte have hem in reverence
> So hertely, that ther is game noon
> That fro my bokes maketh me to goon.   (F 29–34)

Books are for him a delight, a faith, a passion full of reverence. The Eagle who carried him to the House of Fame had reproached Geoffrey for exactly the same reason. In his view, the poet lives a hermit's life, he ignores the real world around him and indeed his very neighbours:

> For when thy labour doon al ys,
> And hast mad alle thy rekenynges,
> In stede of reste and newe thynges,
> Thou goost hom to thy hous anoon;
> And, also domb as any stoon,
> Thou sittest at another book
> Tyl fully daswed ys thy look...   (*House of Fame*, 652–8)

Neither Richard De Bury, who wrote a *Philobiblon* to celebrate the might of books and the love we should have for them, nor his friend Petrarch, the greatest non-religious collector of books in fourteenth-century Europe, ever wrote anything like this. The comic overtone of this picture, the fact that the bibliophile is characterized as a bookworm, should not prevent us from seeing the deep seriousness which is hidden behind it and which is confirmed by the self-awareness implicit in the image. What Chaucer has the Eagle tease him for is the very source of his inspiration – not the 'tydynges of Loves folk' nor the reality of either 'fer contree' or his 'verray neyghebores', but books. The very journey to the House of Fame, begun in a temple that contains an 'Aeneid' and the purpose of which, the Eagle says, is to show the poet 'wonder thynges' and tidings of Love's folk, will become a visit to the world of books, writers and Muses, before turning into an exploration of tidings as such.

Literature is Chaucer's inspiration. A book is at the beginning and end of each of his poems until he starts composing the *Canterbury Tales*. *Troilus* is born out of a book, Boccaccio's *Filostrato*, and ends with a reference to the 'litel book', *Troilus and Criseyde* itself.[2] What takes place in the *Troilus* is but an expansion and a change into a direct source–product relationship of a phenomenon which governs Chaucer's dream poems in a more indirect fashion. After his 'labour', Geoffrey goes back home and sits at another book. In the *Book of the Duchess*, he suffers from insomnia, asks for a book 'to drive the night away' as reading is 'beter play' than 'ches or tables'. He reads his book, falls asleep, dreams, wakes up with his book beside him and decides to write a book. In the *House of Fame*, he dreams a book as a pictorial experience (the 'Aeneid' on the walls of the temple of Venus), flies, thinking of books, through the air, and encounters in the Palace of Fame the writers of books themselves. In the *Parliament of Fowls*, he reads a book, falls asleep, dreams, in his dream is promised 'mater of to wryte', visits a garden and a temple of Venus, witnesses a parliament of birds, wakes up and resorts to other books. In the Prologue to the *Legend of Good Women* he celebrates books, falls asleep, dreams about the God of Love and Alceste, wakes up, takes his books (in the F version) and starts composing his 'Legende'.

The repetition of this pattern is as significant as the variations Chaucer plays on it, and constitutes a phenomenon of great cultural relevance. For Chaucer, the book (literature) both causes the dream and exists within it. He is the first European writer to use this formula, which was to become a distinctive feature, if not a topos, of Western culture.[3] At the beginning of the fourteenth century Dante, in the episode of Paolo and Francesca, had consecrated the book as an occasion for love, sin, murder, and eternal damnation; now, in the second half of the century, Chaucer consecrates it as the key and integrating element of the dream experience – one of the fundamental activities of the human psyche – and of the creative process itself. Thus, independently of Petrarch's humanism, literature becomes one of the driving forces of European civilization. And Chaucer does indeed seem to catch and to announce, though without ostentation and as if unconsciously, the essence of all humanisms when, in the Prologue to the *Legend*, he proclaims that 'if that *olde* bokes weren aweye, / Yloren were of remembrance the keye', and when, in the *Parliament*, he explains that 'out of *olde* bokes' comes the '*newe* science'.

It is to the mechanisms, the meaning and the implications of Chaucer's dream-books and book-dreams that the following pages are devoted. And we begin with an obvious consideration. Books can be used as sources, as pure references, or as a mixture of the two. As David Wallace has shown in the preceding essay, Chaucer uses French and Italian authors as sources of several passages in his dream poems. However, he never explicitly acknowledges his verbal indebtness to, say, Machaut, Froissart or Boccaccio. He begins the *Book of the Duchess* with the quotation and summary of the episode of Ceyx and Alcyone from Ovid's *Metamorphoses*, but calls this a romance. He quotes the opening lines of Virgil's *Aeneid* when, at the beginning of his dream, he enters the temple of Venus in the *House of Fame*, Again, he does not acknowledge his source, but later, when he describes Dido's complaint in his summary of the *Aeneid* in Book I, tells his readers that if they want to know more they should resort to 'Virgile in Eneydos' and to the 'Epistle of Ovyde' (the *Heroides*). Later in the *House of Fame* he does not point out that the description of Fame is indebted to Virgil and that of the House of Rumour to Ovid. In the *Parliament*, instead, he mentions 'Tullyus of the Drem of Scipioun' just before giving us a summary of it, but carefully keeps silent on the fact that the description of the temple of Venus is translated straight out of Boccaccio's *Teseida*.

What emerges from all this is a fairly clear strategy of hide and seek. People who read or listened to Chaucer's dream poems were invited to find out where the stuff came from and were or were not, depending on the author's judgement of what was appropriate to his text and possible to his audience, given, in an exciting literary game, a clue. Would not John of Gaunt, the Black Knight who in the *Book of the Duchess* quotes 'al the remedyes of Ovyde', be able to guess that the dreamer's romance is in fact an episode of the *Metamorphoses*? Readers who were told to look up the 'Eneydos' would undoubtedly suspect that the 'table of bras' contains a translation of the most famous lines of Virgil's poem, *arma virumque cano*. They would be sent off on research of their own when they heard the poet say that he saw Homer, Statius, Virgil, Ovid, Claudian, and others stand on the pillars of the hall of Fame. On the other hand, no one probably could imagine that an as yet unknown vernacular author like Boccaccio was behind the *Parliament*'s temple of Venus.

From the beginning, then, Chaucer plays with his audience a game of intertextuality, raising expectations, stimulating cultural awareness, puzzling and overwhelming his readers with displays of erudition and at the same time relieving them with clues and a light tone. He 'translates' and popularizes, incarnating that tendency which has been seen as the culmination of the encounter between the chivalric culture of the courts and the clerical culture of the schools in fourteenth-century Europe.[4] But he often does more than that – he drops hints or explicitly refers to books which are not, strictly speaking, his sources. For instance, in the *Book of the Duchess* he says that in his dream he found himself in a chamber whose windows were 'yglased' with the story of Troy and whose walls were frescoed with 'al the Romaunce of the Rose'. In the *House of Fame* he tells his readers that if they want to know more about hell, they should turn to Virgil, Claudian, and Dante. In the *Parliament* he declares that Nature appeared to him exactly as 'Aleyn, in the Pleynt of Kynde' (Alan of Lille, in the *De Planctu Naturae*) describes her. It might be interesting to glance at a complete list of these implicit (but easily recognizable), and explicit references in the four dream poems:

Book of the Duchess: Ovid, *Metamorphoses* (Ceyx and Alcyone, 62ff); Bible, Genesis (Joseph's dream, 280–2); Macrobius, *Commentarii in Somnium Scipionis* (284–6); story of Troy (Benoit's *Roman de Troie?*, 326–31); *Roman de la Rose* (334) 'remedyes of Ovyde' (*Remedia Amoris?*, 568); Bible, Esther (987): Dares Phrygius (1070); Livy (1084); Peter Riga's 'Aurora' (*Biblia Versificata*, 1169); Ovid, *Metamorphoses* (1326–7).

House of Fame: Virgil, *Aeneid* (378); Ovid, *Heroides* (379); Virgil, Claudian, Dante (449–50); *Somnium Scipionis* (916–18); Boethius, *De Consolatione Philosophiae* (972–8); St Paul, 2 Corinthians (980–2); Martianus Capella, *De Nuptiis Mercurii et Philologiae* (985); Alan of Lille, *Anticlaudianus* (986); Virgil (1244); St John, Apocalypse (1385); Josephus Flavius (1433); Statius, *Thebaid* and *Achilleid* (1460–3); Homer, Dares Phrygius, Dictys Cretensis, Lollius (Boccaccio?), Guido delle Colonne, Geoffrey of Monmouth (1466–70); Virgil, *Aeneid* (1483); Ovid (1487); Lucan, *Pharsalia* (1499); Claudian, *De Raptu Proserpinae* (1509).

Parliament of Fowls: Cicero, *Somnium Scipionis* (*De Re Publica*, VI) (29); Macrobius, *Commentarii in Somnium Scipionis* (111); Dante, *Inferno* III (the gate, 127 and 134?); Alan of Lille, *De Planctu Naturae* (316).

Legend of Good Women, Prologue G: Chaucer, *Romance of the Rose* (255); Chaucer, *Troilus* (264–5); 'Valerius', Livy, Claudian, St Jerome (280–1); Ovid, *Heroides* (305); Vincent of Beauvais, *Speculum Historiale* (307); Dante (336); Chaucer, *House of Fame*, *Book of the Duchess*, *Parliament of Fowls*, 'Palamon and Arcite', *Boece*, Innocent III's *De Contemptu Mundi* (translation), 'Lyf of Seynt Cecile', 'Orygenes upon the Maudeleyne' (405–18); Agathon (514).

This list must be read carefully: it is fairly obvious, for instance, that Chaucer did not have a first-hand knowledge of Livy,[5] that the reference to Macrobius in the *Book of the Duchess* is probably indebted to the *Roman de la Rose* as is that to the *Somnium* in the *House of Fame*,[6] and that the mention of Agathon, the Athenian tragic poet of the Prologue to the *Legend*, is almost pure name-dropping. It is also clear that the list itself can (and will in the following pages) be supplemented by numerous references which, taken in their context, reveal knowledge of other 'books'. When the Black Knight of the *Book of the Duchess* mentions 'Genelloun', 'Rowland', and 'Olyver', he takes for granted that his interlocutor and his audience know some form of the *Chanson de Roland* or at least of the Charlemagne romances. On the other hand, the quotation from the opening lines of *Inferno* III (the threefold repetition of *Per me si va* – 'through me one goes') for the *Parliament*'s gate poses a problem. If we think that Chaucer expected his audience to recognize it even if he did not give the author's name, we must also assume knowledge of the *Commedia* to have extended beyond the circle of his acquaintances. Or was Chaucer playing a 'private' game with his intellectual friends (like Gower, who mentions Dante in the *Confessio*), whom he himself might have introduced to the great Italian poem?

Whatever we are inclined to believe on this and other issues, the list gives a fairly clear overall view of the direction towards which, within a persistently Ovidian and 'classical' horizon, Chaucer's culture moves in his dream poems. In the phase that goes from the *Book of the Duchess* to the *Parliament of Fowls* there are two general shifts – one from a culture basically founded on Ovid and the romances to an enormous widening of the *literary* spectrum in the *House of Fame* (which includes Ovid, but also relies heavily on Virgil, consecrates a number of Latin classics and medieval authors, and explicitly refers to Dante); and another from an essentially literary culture to a more philosophically inclined one, which emerges clearly in the second Book of the *House of Fame* with the mention of Boethius, Martianus Capella, and Alan (and *en passant* Aristotle and Plato, 759), and predominates in the *Parliament*, where Cicero's and Macrobius' *Somnium*, and Alan's *De Planctu Naturae* are the only two explicit references. It goes without saying that Chaucer's perusal of some Old and New Testament texts is constant. In the *Legend*, Virgil, Ovid, and Dante take over again, but the most interesting feature here is that Chaucer's own previous works are discussed in a context dominated by a meditation on the value of books 'old' and 'new'. Chaucer's dream poems begin with a book and end with a book, generally his own. His dreaming begins with Ovid's *Metamorphoses* and ends with Chaucer's own books. In this double pattern there is an extraordinary circularity and an equally staggering direct pointedness: when Chaucer dreams, a book inevitably produces another book. The 'old' book becomes 'new'. Ovid becomes Chaucer.

It is the functions of this transformation that we must now explore. In the *Book of the Duchess*, Chaucer is supposed to offer to John of Gaunt a 'consolation' for the death of his wife Blanche of Lancaster, and there are indeed several details, including the name of the Black Knight's Lady, White, to confirm this eminently 'private' occasion.[7] Yet if one reads the actual poem Chaucer has written, one hardly notices this, but rather has the impression that the images and the narrative sequence of the book raise far wider, 'public' issues such as those of love, fortune, and death. The transformation of private occasion into public concern is effected by Chaucer through a series of operations basically centred on the fictional-ization of certain motifs. The fundamental 'private' nucleus – the relation-ship between Gaunt and Blanche and her death – becomes the second, and longest, section of the dream, in which the protagonist meets a knight in black mourning his loss and complaining against Fortune, and forces him to tell the story of his love for White and finally reveal her death. But this nucleus, to which we shall soon return, is preceded by an introduction that makes the fiction much more complex. At the beginning, the poetic 'I' tells us that he suffers from insomnia, the reason of which he does not know unless it be a 'sicknesse' he has suffered for the last eight years.

Apparently, this is love. At this point, the poetic persona relates that he asked for a book, 'a romaunce', to 'drive the night away':

> And in this bok were written fables
> That clerkes had in olde tyme,
> And other poets, put in rime
> To rede, and for to be in minde,
> While men loved the lawe of kinde.
> This bok ne spak but of such thinges,
> Of quenes lives, and of kinges,
> And many other thinges smale. (52–9)

'Amonge al this' he finds a 'tale' which is the Ovidian story of Ceyx and Alcyone. In this story Ceyx loses his life at sea and his wife, Alcyone, asks Juno to put her to sleep and to show her husband's fate to her in a dream. Morpheus, summoned by Juno's messenger, takes the mortal form of Ceyx and appears to Alcyone, who dies within three days. The sleepless reader, amazed and rather sceptical, decides to offer a featherbed to Morpheus and Juno if they will put him to sleep. Hardly has he formulated his vow when he falls asleep over his book and begins to dream.

The function of the Ovidian tale is, structurally, to connect the themes of sleep and insomnia (the protagonist's problem) with the story of Gaunt and Blanche fictionalized in the second part of the poem. For in the episode from the *Metamorphoses* we have a kind of mirror-version of the Black Knight–White sequence – the story of a deep love between wife and husband, one of whom (in this case the latter) dies – and also a tale in which sleep and dreams occupy a central position. Like Alcyone, the poem's protagonist will sleep and dream, and his dream will in some way be the projection of his book and of the Gaunt–Blanche story.

The two fictionalized nuclei of the poem, preceded by the introduction, are thus thematically linked at a deep level. On the surface, they are joined to each other by an intermezzo where the logic of dreams reigns supreme. Here, as soon as he falls asleep, the dreamer finds himself, on a May morning, lying in bed naked, with birds singing all around him, in a room whose walls are covered with frescoes depicting the *Roman de la Rose* and whose windows are storiated with scenes from Trojan history and its heroes. The sun is shining and the air is 'blew, bryght, clere'. Suddenly he hears a horn, shouts, dogs, and horses. The protagonist mounts on horse, rushes out and hears that the emperor Octavian is going on a hunt. He follows the company and ends up near a tree with a small dog. Trying to catch the animal, he goes down a 'floury grene wente', a grassy path in the full bloom of spring. At its end, leaning against a great oak, stands a man dressed in black, a knight, reciting a 'compleynte' for his dead lady.

Apparently, this intermezzo has nothing to do with the first and third parts of the poem (the story of Ceyx and Alcyone and that of the Knight and his lady). In fact, it picks up at least two themes common to both. One is that of literature, represented in the first part by the romance itself, the book full of 'fables' which the protagonist reads, and in the second by the allusion to the *Roman* and the story of Troy. In the third part, this will be taken up by both Knight and dreamer. The latter invokes Socrates (717) and mentions the 'fables' of Jason and Medea, Phyllis and Demophon, Aeneas and Dido, Narcissus and Echo, Samson and Delilah (726–38). The former, in five formidable *tours de force* which establish both a common cultural ground with, and his superiority to, the protagonist (both would have been pleasing to John of Gaunt), manages to evoke the 'remedyes of Ovyde', Orpheus, Daedalus, Hippocrates, and Galen (568–72), Alcibiades, Hercules, Alexander, the great cities of the ancient world, Trojan heroes and heroines, Dares, Penelope, Lucretia, and Livy (1057–84), Achitofel, Antenor, Ganelon, Roland and Oliver (1118–23), Lamech, Pythagoras, and Peter Riga's *Aurora* (1162–9), culminating in a display of geographical–imaginary erudition which is really a jibe at the conventions of romance. Here, the Knight makes clear that Blanche was never the type of lady who sent her faithful cavaliers off to the ends of the earth, as happens in the romances (1020–33). Literature, sensibly put in its place in this passage, ties up the three parts of the poem.

The second theme common to them is that of nature. When, in the introduction, the protagonist describes his insomnia, he makes clear that this 'sickness' goes against nature:

> And wel ye woot, agaynes kynde
> Hyt were to lyven in thys wyse;
> For nature wolde nat suffyse
> To noon erthly creature
> Nat longe tyme to endure
> Withoute slep and be in sorwe.   (16–21)

Opposed to this is the book our sleepless reader picks up at night, which was written to be read and remembered 'while men loved the lawe of kinde'. The book, the *Metamorphoses*, sets the reader on the path of natural law, that sleep which has been denied him by his illness; in the same way this very book, with the dream of Alcyone it contains, also provides the Knight indirectly with an example of how to recover that harmony with nature which he has lost through his lady's death (466–9 and 511–13): because death is, precisely, the 'lawe of kinde', as the story of Ceyx and Alcyone demonstrates.[8] Nature reigns supreme in the intermezzo, in the *locus amoenus*, the 'floury grene wente' that displays its vegetable and animal plenitude, where the 'povertee' and the 'sorwes' of winter are forgotten in the quasi-celestial triumph of spring on earth:

> For hit was, on to beholde,
> As thogh the erthe envye wolde

> To be gayer than the heven,
> To have moo floures, swiche seven,
> As in the welken sterres bee.   (405–9)

Likewise, Nature later dominates the ideal portrait of the lady, a 'chef patron of beaute' according to the best poetic and social models, and 'chef ensample' of Nature's work (869–73, 908–12, 1194–8). Little wonder, then, that the story of the Knight's love for Blanche, recounted in typically courtly terms (the 'worship and the servise' the man pays to the woman), ends in marriage, supreme 'natural' bliss (1289–97). Once more, the 'private' (John of Gaunt's marriage with Blanche of Lancaster) takes on a general, 'public' significance: *amour courtois* culminates in the happy union of man and wife, who share joy and sorrow until death parts them.

Against Nature and Love fight the forces of grief, Fortune and death. In the splendid meadow where the 'sorrow' of winter is forgotten, the dreamer suddenly hears a complaint where sorrow and death dominate (475–86), and comments, with a phrase that reminds us of one used earlier for his insomnia (18–21):

> Hit was gret wonder that Nature
> Myght suffre any creature
> To have such sorwe, and be not ded.   (467–9)

The story of the Knight's love for Blanche is prefaced by his long complaint against Fortune, who played a chess game with him and who is accused of being the epitome of deception and false appearances (598–709) – Chaucer's first utterance on the theme of destiny, examined by Jill Mann later in this volume. And Blanche's beauty and the perfect union of marriage is destroyed by death, the 'natural law' which had killed Ceyx, and at the announcement of which the dream abruptly and realistically ends. When, at the end of the series of questions and answers that characterizes their exchange,[9] the Knight cries to the dreamer, 'She ys ded!', the hunt is suddenly 'doon'. The Knight walks off homewards to 'a long castel with walles white'. The bell strikes twelve, and the protagonist wakes up in his bed, with the book of Alcyone and Ceyx in his hand, ready to put his 'queynt sweven' into rhyme, to turn the book into *his* Book – the *Book of the Duchess*.

The themes of love and nature, at the centre of the three-part-plus-introduction structure of the *Book of the Duchess*, are even more overtly prominent in the three-part-plus-introduction structure of the *Parliament of Fowls*. Here, however, there seems to be no 'private' occasion behind the poem,[10] and the level of discussion is much less concrete than in the *Book of the Duchess*. We have no Knight and no lady with a story of love and death, but, instead, a dreamer–reader led by the protagonist of his dream-book, Scipio Africanus, to a garden-park of nature and love, to a temple of Venus, and to the hill where personified Nature herself presides over a parliament of birds. The central problems of the poem are examined in three successive abstract stages – the summary of a book, Cicero's *Somnium Scipionis*; the iconography of garden and temple; the animal parable of the parliament.

Throughout these phases the poet's focus is on the theme of love announced in the first two stanzas as a polyvalent and comprehensive dimension. Love is 'dredful joye, alwey that slit so yerne', 'assay...hard' and 'sharp...conquerynge'; its 'werkynge' is 'wonderful'; its phenomena are 'myrakles' and 'crewel yre'. It is an ambiguous world, in which one lives in perpetual uncertainty (6–7) and in absolute impotence ('I can na moore', 14). But Love is also a power that dominates everything: even one who, like the narrator, does not know love 'in dede', can get from books an idea of how 'he wol be lord and syre'. Love is really human life – all of it, albeit short; it is an art – the *ars amandi* – that is long and difficult to learn. And finally, as is implied by the reference to *ars longa, vita brevis*, love is the art of poetry itself, and often the object of literature:

> Yit happeth me ful ofte *in bokes reede*
> Of his myrakles and his crewel yre.   (10–11)

In other words, love is not only a feeling, but also a real culture, with its conventions and its laws.

When the narrator of the *Parliament*, who is – 'what for lust and what for lore' – an inveterate reader, picks up his book of the day, the *Somnium Scipionis*, the problem of love acquires a metatemporal and cosmic dimension.[11] We are now brought, through Scipio's dream, to the galaxy whence one can contemplate 'the lytel erthe that here is' and where the music of the spheres is heard. And we are told of life after death, of heaven, of a 'blysful place' 'there as joye is that last withouten ende'. The love that is rewarded here is love for the 'commune profyt' (46–9 and 73–7), a love which must be exercised on earth but must be detached from worldly pleasure (64–6). Clearly, this is not sensual love – it is, rather, love directed towards the *bonum commune*, love that goes beyond the individual, whose object is society and the state. The latter should be understood in the Roman sense, to which the *Somnium* obviously refers, and which was partly incorporated into the language of the English Parliament.[12] Love is the salvation and aggrandisement of the *res publica* – or, in a wider sense, of the whole of mankind.

One understands why the narrator, deprived of his book by the falling of night, and 'fulfyld of thought and busy hevynesse' as he starts getting ready for bed, declares that he has something he did not want and does not have what he wanted (90–1). It is not exactly this kind of love that he was looking for. Nor will he be any luckier in the dream which promptly begins as soon as he falls asleep after perusing his 'olde bok totorn', the *Somnium*. For here Africanus, the very protagonist of Cicero's and Macrobius' book, appears and leads him, through a Dantean gate, into a park where love reigns in a very particular fashion. As the double inscription over the gate announces, and as the visit confirms, the dreamer enters a garden which is at once a happy and a deadly place, an Eden of eternal, flourishing life and a world of total sterility; it is both a source of grace, the way to a happy end, and a 'sorweful were' where the fish die in aridity. The 'blysful place' of the *Somnium*, ultramundane and heavenly, becomes a 'blysful place' (127) in an earthly paradise, where love for the 'commune profyt' is replaced by the love with which the birds 'besyede hem here bryddes forth to brynge', that is, by procreation, and where the harmony of the spheres becomes 'ravyshyng swetnesse' of 'instruments of strenges in acord' and angelic voice of singing fowls (59–63, 190–1, 197–203). Here is the eternal joy the reader found in the vision of the *Somnium* (49 and 208), here is immortality (50–6 and 207), perennial day, constant spring, the plenitude and variety of the vegetable and animal kingdoms (172–5 and 206). Here, finally, is harmony between the world of nature and that of man, indicated subtly by the function each tree has in human life and activity – the oak to build with, the fir to sail on, the 'olyve of pees' and the 'asp for shaftes pleyne', the 'cipresse, deth to pleyne' (176–82).[13]

Yet, as the dreamer's view penetrates deeper into the garden, this Edenic universe changes. We enter the human cosmos, an artificial world where myth and courtesy – civilization as distinct from nature – are in full bloom. Here, we find Cupid and the personifications and incarnations of Eros – Beauty and Pleasure, Courtesy and Gentilesse, and many others – from the *Roman de la Rose* and Boccaccio's *Teseida*. We visit the temple of Venus, where angelic harmony is replaced by a 'swogh' of sighs hot as fire. Priapus stands 'in sovereyn place', all naked and 'with hys sceptre in honde'. The phallic image provides a prelude to the inner recesses of the temple, where the darkness thickens. There Venus, wrapped in a golden aura, with her hair unbound, her body half-covered by a film of transparent lace, reclines on her couch 'til that the hote sonne gan to weste'. Planet and goddess, courtly and sensual, Venus also represents tragic love. All around her lie the broken bows of the virgins of Diana who have sacrificed their chastity in her service, and the walls of the temple are frescoed with the stories of love and death consecrated by literature and mythology – Semiramis, Dido, Cleopatra, Helen, Tristan and Isolde, Troilus himself. Love, which is part of life – desire, which is necessary to nature – is also the negation of life, the reversal of nature. The gold that surrounds Venus is far from the flowers of white, blue, yellow and red, far from the red fins and silvery scales of the fish in the garden.

So far, love has appeared as service of the *bonum commune*, edenic plenitude, supreme moment of sensual infatuation. It has been described by means of a book, a vision, a series of images. Now, the poet introduces a lively debate between birds, an animal parable. But the implications of this are as vast as those of the preceding sections. The specific case – that of the eagle loved by three birds at once – is a courtly contest *par excellence*, but it is broadened by the introduction of Nature and the extension of the discussion to all the birds, including the less noble ones. The occasion, the annual mating of the birds on St Valentine's day, already places the *demande d'amour* within the context of natural order in general, and the problem of love itself in a perspective that is more properly philosophical. The eagle's courtly love becomes but one aspect of the general economy of nature – mating, procreation, and the perpetuation of the species. The presence of both 'lower classes' and 'nobility' (here represented by the different ranks and 'degrees' of birds) brings the problem into the sphere of the social order.

By opening the debate to the representatives of the lower classes, who have not all absorbed the courtly experience, Nature makes the *demande d'amour* apparently unsolvable. For some of the lower birds suggest solutions that contrast with the code (thus the goose maintains that the rejected suitor should choose another mate; the cuckoo recommends that all three should remain celibate; the duck scornfully rejects the whole code, 589–95), but all of them indicate, first by their noisy impatience (491–7) and then by flying away satisfied, the basic irrelevance for them of the problem itself and the socio-cultural convention it represents.

On the other hand, Nature, the 'vicaire of the almyghty Lord', follows her own logic in favouring the choice of the royal eagle, whom she herself has fashioned to her full satisfaction (636) and who is 'the gentilleste and most worthi' (635). The Nature of Alan's *De Planctu Naturae* (and of Boethius' *Consolatio*) 'keeps all things in balance and accord and... embodies their moral–natural norm'[14] – a feature that Chaucer's goddess faithfully incarnates (379–81). For her, the social order, and hence the courtly culture which it includes as an aspect of the ideal of the upper classes, is but a part of the natural order. The perfection of the universe requires plenitude and plurality – the increase and multiplication of living beings proclaimed by Genesis – as well as 'inequality'. 'It concerns the perfection of the universe', says Thomas Aquinas,[15] 'that there be not only many individuals, but that there be also different species of things, and consequently different degrees in things'. Chaucer's parliament of birds incarnates these ideas:

For this was on seynt Valentynes day,
Whan every foul cometh there to chese his make,
Of every kynde that men thynke may,   [*plurality*]
And that so huge a noyse gan they make
That erthe, and eyr, and tre, and every lake
So ful was, that unethe was there space
For me to stonde, *so ful was al the place.*   [*plenitude*]
...
That is to seyn, the foules of ravyne
Weere hyest set, and thanne the foules smale...   [*inequality*]
                                                         (309–24)

In assembling before Nature to choose a mate, the birds fulfil the supreme
law of the universe, that of 'generation', which is the one 'natural act'
to be pre-eminently directed 'to the common good'.[16] Hence, what we
witness in the third section of the *Parliament* is the preparation for
something that already took place in the second (the birds' procreation,
192), a direct consequence of the 'desire' pictured in the temple of Venus,
and an interestingly wider version of the 'commune profyt' propounded
in the first. Love is now complete.

Nature's problem, however, is still unresolved, for if reason and natural
(including social) law suggest that the eagle choose the 'royal tercel',
Nature herself 'prike[s] with plesaunce' all three of the lovers, so none of
them can claim a greater natural right than the others. The solution might
look simple to us, but is at once novel, realistic and sensible in a
fourteenth-century context:

...she
Shal han right hym on whom hire herte is set,
And he hire that his herte hath on hire knet.   (626–8)

But the lady is not ready for this, yet, and asks for a year in which to make
up her mind (647–9). Delay is a characteristic of all parliaments that
cannot decide. And the birds, singing a roundel in honour of Nature, fly
away. Their shouting awakes the dreamer, who immediately picks up
other books in the hope of some day reading something 'that [he] shal mete
som thyng for to fare / The bet'. Reading a book can be unsatisfactory.
Indeed before falling asleep the protagonist of the *Parliament* had revealed
that the *Somnium Scipionis*, which he had taken out 'a certeyn thing to
lerne', was not exactly what he wanted (90–1). The reading of the
Somnium produced the dream, the first part of which mirrors, with the
presence of Africanus, the book itself (106–8). Soon, however, this is
forgotten, and the dream develops as a visit to the park of love and the
temple of Venus. At this point, the reader's memory of another book, Alan's
De Planctu Naturae, seems to start off the second section of the dream. This,
too, is somehow unsatisfactory, in that it offers only a partial solution to

the problem it poses. Hence, more reading is required. We have here two interrelated fundamental mechanisms. One is that of the endless quest, the search for an ever-receding object that the reading of books implies. The other is the transformation of 'olde bokes' into 'newe science' – the way in which the poet, both satisfied and dissatisfied with what he has read, produces his own book by connecting his texts, relating them to each other, integrating them with his own images and ideas, by finding in them 'mater of to wryte' and supplementing it with his own 'connyng for t'endite' (167–8). For the first time in European literature, a poet lays bare before our very eyes the intellectual, cultural and creative processes by which 'tradition' is transformed by 'individual talent'.[17]

The 'newe science' consciously propounded by the discussion of Love and Nature in the three-part-plus-introduction structure of the *Parliament of Fowls* had already been at the centre of the incomplete three-part-plus-introduction structure of the *House of Fame*, where the themes of love and nature also occupy an important place. In fact, Chaucer's three early dream poems all share a series of important images. For instance, we realize that the theme of 'generation' which dominates the second and third sections of the *Parliament* is also present in the *House of Fame*, where, during the flight with the Eagle, Geoffrey beholds the 'ayerissh bestes' (clouds, mists, storms, snows, etc.) and 'th'engendrynge in hir kyndes' (965–8). Like the Scipio of the *Parliament* and of the *Somnium* (explicitly recalled in *House of Fame*, 916–18), Geoffrey also sees the galaxy, and the earth reduced to no more 'than a prikke'. The 'halles' and 'boures' of Nature in the *Parliament* are made of 'braunches'; the House of Rumour in *Fame* is made of multicoloured twigs. Yet the former are 'iwrought after [the] cast and [the] mesure' of Nature herself, whereas the latter are the product of a labyrinthine imagination. The cave of sleep described in the *Metamorphoses* story of the *Book of the Duchess* is the first image we encounter in the *House of Fame* (66–76). The garden-park is present in both *Book of the Duchess* and *Parliament of Fowls*. A temple of Venus appears in both *Parliament* and *Fame*. The *Book of the Duchess* ends with the view of a castle, the castle of Fame dominates the first part of the third book of the *House of Fame*. Frescoes on the walls feature in all three poems. We are obviously in the presence of an imagination constantly at work on the same images. Poring over his books, Chaucer is fascinated and intrigued by the 'archetypal loci' of the Western mind they present.[18]

The exploration of these in the *House of Fame* is one of the most interesting poetic enterprises of fourteenth-century Europe – a journey through tradition, myth, literature, and poetry. The self-consciousness with which Chaucer embarks on this adventure is witnessed by at least four highly significant features of his poem. First comes the discussion of the nature and causes of dreams in the long Proem to Book I. Here, in an apparently light manner, the author examines the very medium of his poetry – the dream as mode of apprehension of reality and as type of discourse, the world removed from everyday concerns yet somehow representing their sublimated or distorted projection. Then the invocations prefaced to each book attract our attention, both as conscious manifestations of a desire to enter the mainstream of 'high' tradition and as indications of a thematic programme: the god of sleep and God introduce the entire poem; Venus, the Muses, and Thought the second book; Apollo, 'god of science and of lyght', the last. Third is the fact that the protagonist is called by his real name, 'Geoffrey'. And, finally, this very poet takes here full responsibility for his sufferings, thoughts, and 'art':

> For what I drye, or what I thynke,
> I wil myselven al hyt drynke,
> Certeyn, for the more part,
> As fer forth as I kan myn art.   (1879–82)

If one adds to this the fact that Geoffrey compares his vision and flight in Book II with those of Isaiah, Scipio, Nebuchadnezzar, Pharaoh, Enoch, Elijah, Romulus, Ganymede, Alexander, and Daedalus, and evokes for his situation the names of Plato, Boethius, St Paul, Martianus Capella, and Alan of Lille, one has a full idea of how serious, in his slightly ridiculous pedantry and bookish exaggeration, Chaucer really is.

With a stroke of genius, Chaucer chooses as his central theme that of Fame, a concept which Western tradition develops throughout antiquity and the Middle Ages as omnicomprehensive.[19] A goddess from the time of Hesiod's *Works and Days*, Fame embraces the spheres of nature, death, heroism, love, chivalry, wisdom, conscience, virtue, fortune, myth, language, and poetry – the very themes Chaucer explores in his book.

A series of triads, following the tripartite structure of the *House of Fame*, will illustrate the development of these themes in the poem. The clearest sequence connects Love, Nature, and Fame.[20] The temple of Venus and the story of Dido and Aeneas in Book I are Love's domain, but, together with its pictorial and iconographic triumph, Love celebrates here its defeat. Aeneas, followed by Dido's complaint and cursed for his inconstancy, love of fame, 'delyt' and 'synguler profit' (and one thinks, by contrast, of the 'commune profyt' of the *Parliament*) leaves the queen, who kills herself. And the dreamer, going out of the temple, finds himself not in a garden, but in another *locus classicus* of the imagination – a waste land, a sterile desert where Nature is totally absent (489–90). When the golden Eagle lifts the dreamer up into the air, the flight they begin is precisely one through the world of Nature, where 'every kyndely thyng that is / Hath a kyndely stede' (730–1), where the 'ayerissh bestes' and their 'engendrynge' can be contemplated, and where the 'fetheres of Philosophye' are almost on the point of overwhelming the poet with thoughts of Boethius, St Paul, Martianus Capella, and Alan's *Anticlaudianus*. The travellers, however, do not reach the heaven of the *Somnium* nor the earthly paradise of the *Parliament*, but the House of Fame, where the goddess of renown celebrates her triumph in wealth and splendour with the Muses, the poets, and the heroes and heroines of myth. But Fame, too, is not totally positive. In her judgement of nine companies of people, she denies, grants and changes fame in a completely erratic, fickle, and unjust manner. The dreamer passes from her castle to the House of Rumour, an enormous rotating cage where crowds of anonymous, 'common' people gather to communicate and distort their news and stories to each other, and where tidings become an inextricable mixture of true and false, fly away and reach back to Fame, who gives them 'name' and 'duracioun'.

A principle of de-composition and re-composition seems to work throughout the *House of Fame*. Fame is glory, ill-repute, and rumour. Another triad to appear in the poem is that governed by Fortune, closely associated with Fame, and indeed called her 'sister' in Book III (1547), and who figures as 'destinee' in the story of Aeneas and as Chance in the House of Rumour.[21] The truth of love is polluted by deception, lack of truth (330–1), 'apparence...fals in existence' (265–6). The truth, the philosophical and scientific reality of Book II, does not withstand the action of fame, which magnifies everything (1290–2). The precise laws of nature which rule the propagation of sound are completely upset by the castle, whose foundations rest on ice. Fame herself is a mutable monster, infinitely small and infinitely great, and her Triumph is contradicted by her Judgement. In the world of Rumour, finally, 'fals' and 'soth' are 'compouned' (2108–9).

A similar process dominates in the oneiric sphere which characterizes Chaucer's journey to Fame. After discussing the nature and causes of dreams, the *House of Fame* passes through several phases that seem to find, and immediately to abandon, a correspondence with traditional types of dreams: *somnium coeleste* or *visio* as a whole, it seems to be a love-dream in Book I and to turn, at the end of the Book, into a *phantasma* ('fantome', 493). Book II, with its quotation of Scipio and Alexander, is more clearly a *visio*, but, with its reminiscences of Dante and St Paul, comes close to a beatific vision. In Book III, elements of the apocalyptic vision (1383–5) merge with those of the Triumph. Finally, with the apparition of the man of great authority, the poem breaks off with what may be seen as the overture to an *oraculum*.[22]

On one more level – that of poetry and literature – an oscillating and circular movement is a fundamental feature of the *House of Fame*. This poem begins with a poem, the 'Aeneid' painted on the walls of the temple of Venus. In Book II the Eagle gives Geoffrey an explanation of the physical nature of language – sound – and of the ambiguity that distinguishes meaning, that is, the relationship between a word and what it signifies and between a word and the speaker (1066–82). '*Fama*', say medieval etymologies, '*a fando, i.e., a loquendo*' – the word 'fame' comes from *fari*, to speak. The poets and their cycles – 'Jewerye', Troy, Aeneas, Love, Rome, Hell – figure in Book III. Finally, the tidings which the protagonist was promised by the Eagle appear in the House of Rumour as the oral molecules of narrative, covering the whole universe of nature and human activities (1960–76) already contained by the 'book', the 'Aeneid' of Book I.[23]

From the cave of sleep of the Proem to the cave of Aeolus in Book III (1583–7), the *House of Fame* is, moreover, an encyclopedia of myths both ancient and medieval and an exploration of various literary genres.[24] Aeneas' behaviour towards Dido is but the most illustrious example of that 'untrouthe' in love which recurs in endless stories of myth, from that of Demophon and Phyllis to that of Theseus and Ariadne (388–426). Daedalus, Morpheus and Aeolus dominate the imaginary world of Chaucer's poem. The entire 'chevalrie' of Africa, Europe, and Asia (1338–40) exhibits its 'armes' in Fame's hall. But myth is literature. When Chaucer recounts the 'Aeneid', he is obviously thinking of a great narrative poem such as those which, in the disguise of poetic cycles, are 'borne up' by the poets on their shoulders in Book III. But he also mentions 'olde gestes' (1515) and the popular literature of 'mynstralles' and 'gestiours', Orpheus the Ur-poet together with 'Bret Glascurion' (1197–1208). The scientific culture shown off by the Eagle agrees with the philosophical and didactic poetry of Boethius, Martianus, and Alan. When Geoffrey undergoes the mystical temptation during which, like St Paul, he knows no more whether he is there, up in the sky, 'in body or in gost' (979–82), it is hard not to remember that fourteenth-century England is full of mystical treatises. When the Eagle tells him about the 'poetrie' in which 'goddes gonne stellifye / Bridd, fissh, best, or him or here' and mentions the Raven, the Bear, Castor, Pollux, and Atalanta (1000–8), we must imagine that a courtly and cultured audience such as that for which Chaucer wrote the *Book of the Duchess* would catch the allusion to Ovid's *Metamorphoses*.

In this context, it might seem paradoxical that myth and poetry disappear in the House of Rumour, which is explicitly compared to one of the mythological, archetypal buildings *par excellence*, the 'Laboryntus', 'Domus Dedaly' (1920–1), where tidings represent the oral roots of literature. But the labyrinth is for Ovid and Virgil the place where signs are lost, unrecognizable, false like Chaucer's tidings, and the all-encompassing traditional image of life, art, the world.[25]

What Dante saw in the essence of God was, 'legato con amore in un volume, ciò che per l'universo si squaderna' (bound by love in one single volume, that which is dispersed in leaves throughout the universe).[26] Chaucer's journey to the House of Fame is a secular version of this vision – a movement from the Book at the beginning (the 'Aeneid') to the oral fragments of it at the end. These in turn go back to Fame to be ordered by her and find themselves inserted in the great cycles of poetry. Soon the shipmen, pilgrims, pardoners, and messengers who crowd the House of Rumour with their 'tydynges' will begin another journey during which they will tell each other tales to be collected in a book – the *Canterbury Tales*. Meanwhile, through the cave, temple, desert, flight in space, castle and labyrinth of the *House of Fame*, the world has become a book.[27]

Notes

1 The whole passage, G 267–312, is absent in the F redaction of the Prologue, supposedly written earlier than G.

2 And see P. Boitani, *English Medieval Narrative in the Thirteenth and Fourteenth Centuries* (Cambridge, 1982), pp. 200–1.

3 See M. W. Stearns, 'Chaucer Mentions a Book', *Modern Language Notes*, 57 (1942), 28–31.

4 G. Duby, *The Age of the Cathedrals*, trans. E. Levieux and B. Thompson (London, 1981), ch. 8.

5 Unless the mention of Livy here and elsewhere in Chaucer's works indicates that he shares the general European, and particularly Anglo-Italian passion for this author, who was being 'rediscovered' in the fourteenth century. See G. Billanovich, *La Tradizione del Testo di Livio e le Origini dell'Umanesimo* (Padua, 1981).

6 Chaucer says that 'Macrobeus' 'wrot al th'avysyoun / That he mette, *kyng* Scipioun' (and see *House of Fame*, 916–18). The *Roman de la Rose* (ed. F. Lecoy (Paris, 1968) lines 7–10) says that 'Macrobes' 'ançoit escrit l'avision qui avint au *roi* Scypion'.

7 For various correspondences, see Robinson's Introduction, pp. 266–7, and Notes, pp. 773–8.

8 See further R. O. Payne, *The Key of Remembrance* (New Haven, Conn., 1963), pp. 122–5.

9 This structures the whole of the Knight's story, as I have shown in my *English Medieval Narrative*, p. 145.

10 For speculations on this point, see Robinson's Introduction, pp. 309–10.

11 See J. A. W. Bennett, *The Parlement of Foules: An Interpretation* (Oxford, 1957), pp. 25–61.

12 See *The Parlement of Foulys*, ed. D. S. Brewer (Manchester, 1960), p. 102, n. 47.

13 See P. Boitani, 'Chaucer and Lists of Trees', *Reading Medieval Studies*, 2 (1975), 28–44.

14 P. Dronke, 'Chaucer and the Medieval Latin Poets', part A, in *Writers and Their Background: Geoffrey Chaucer*, ed. Derek Brewer (London, 1974). p. 165. The whole essay is extremely valuable in our context. In that collection, see also B. Harbert, 'Chaucer and the Latin Classics', pp. 137–53.

15 *Summa Contra Gentiles*, II, xlv, 6.
16 See *English Medieval Narrative*, p. 180.
17 'Tradition and the Individual Talent' is the title of a famous essay by T. S. Eliot published in *The Sacred Wood* (1920 and 1928).
18 I have examined the significance of these with particular reference to the *House of Fame* in my *Chaucer and the Imaginary World of Fame* (Cambridge, 1984), pp. 189–91, 193–4, 200–1.
19 For references, see *Chaucer and the Imaginary World of Fame*, Introduction and chs. 2–3.
20 See J. A. W. Bennett, *Chaucer's Book of Fame* (Oxford, 1968), chs. 1–3.
21 See *Chaucer and the Imaginary World of Fame*, p. 174.
22 *Ibid.*, pp. 180–1.
23 *Ibid.*, pp. 208–16.
24 *Ibid.*, pp. 189–208.
25 See *Chaucer and the Imaginary World of Fame*, pp. 209–10, and references therein.
26 *Paradiso* XXXIII, 86–7.
27 See G. Josipovici, *The World and the Book*, 2nd edn (London, 1979), chs. 2–3.

4   Telling the story in *Troilus and Criseyde*

Especially in its first three books, *Troilus and Criseyde* is a wonderfully textured poem: places, talk, people, are rendered with a mastery of nuance, a love of the suggestive detail, unexampled in earlier English literature. Nor is the art of the *Troilus* only an art of detail, of charming cornices and misericord carvings: *Troilus and Criseyde* has a large, clear architectural plan; it is a structure of emphatic bilateral symmetry. It is also a work which knows, and makes sure the reader knows, that it has important thematic concerns: fortune and the good things of this world; human love; fidelity. The *Troilus*, in short, has the elements of a well-made work of serious literature. But perhaps the most subtle of the things which make it not merely a worthy but a truly great poem, a poem both exhilarating and disturbing, is the way these elements are combined with and related to one another. Texture does not merely echo, enhance, unproblematically enrich, the meanings suggested by thematic statements and by structure. Almost the reverse proves to be the case; particularly as we read the second half of Chaucer's poem, our response to texture interferes with our 'proper' response to bilateral symmetry and to theme – particularly the theme of fidelity. As we move toward the conclusion of the work, *trouthe* has become both truly admirable – almost what Arveragus calls it in the *Franklin's Tale*, 'the hyeste thyng that man may kepe' (1479) – and also something we covertly dislike and are ashamed of ourselves for disliking. In the present essay I shall be discussing some of the salient features of narrative technique in the *Troilus* and also trying to show some of the ways in which texture, theme and structure are related. I shall also want to speak of the place of the poet-narrator – who, like the reader, will have trouble responding properly to the story – in the *Troilus*. Here my special concern will be the interworkings of the poet's commitment to his task and the commitment of the poem's hero and heroine to one another – their fidelity, their *trouthe*.

I begin with the poem's remarkably efficient, tightly focussed opening stanza, in which the narrator makes an implicit commitment both of and to considerable elegance:

59

> The double sorwe of Troilus to tellen,
> That was the kyng Priamus sone of Troye,
> In lovynge, how his aventures fellen
> Fro wo to wele, and after out of joie,
> My purpos is, er that I parte fro ye.
> Thesiphone, thow help me for t'endite
> Thise woful vers, that wepen as I write.   (I, 1–7)

'That wepen as I write': the audience prepares itself for a poem with a strongly dominant (for all one can yet tell, perhaps an unvaried) mood. But even earlier in the stanza there is a statement about the overarching shape of experience: 'double sorwe...Fro wo to wele, and after out of joie'. The poem which follows, one is perhaps gratified but certainly not surprised to discover, will indeed be symmetrical in structure, with various features of the rising (in medieval terms, 'comic') action of the first half recalled by features of the falling ('tragic') action of the second half.[1] One notices also, perhaps, what is *not* in this stanza: no superlatives, no suggestion of any extraordinary qualities in Troilus, Priam or Troy, to distract us from dominant mood and that idea of double sorrow. There is also, of course, no Chaucerian indirection: no frame of dreaming or reading or setting out on a pilgrimage to suggest that an attentive reader may choose to align in a number of different ways the various things the poet is telling him. No, as the old lady says in *David Copperfield*, let us have no meandering: Chaucer's initial emphases are upon the mood of the story, the shape of the story, and – thanks to the artful syntax which emphasizes 'my purpos' (the grammatical subject of the main clause of the first sentence) by holding it back for four lines – upon the poet's own commitment to something, his willing and implicitly promising the poem to follow. And this implicit promise is made, like all serious promises, to particular people for a particular time: 'er that I parte fro ye'.

The opening stanza, then, draws our attention both to the bilateral symmetry of Troilus' experience in love, and to the poet's commitment to the telling of Troilus' story. It should be noted that the two things are related: that is, self-commitment which proves successful, the kept promise, is itself a thing of bilateral symmetry: even-song and morning-song accord; what I said I would do, I have done. And like the symmetry of 'fro wo to wele, and after out of joie', the symmetry of a successful human promise is likely to entail a second half which is more difficult, oppressive than the first: it is generally easier to give our word than to keep it.

The reader who is on some level aware of these harmonics of the opening will be particularly alert to the lines which end the introduction to Book I and subtly align the heroine's fidelity with the narrator's commitment, story content with story-telling:

> For now wil I gon streght to my matere,
> In which ye may the double sorwes here
> Of Troilus in lovynge of Criseyde,
> And how that she forsook hym er she deyde.   (53–6)

The phrase 'double sorwes' brings us back to the initial stanza, and the association is made a bit stronger by the use of 'tag-ending' *ere* clauses in the two sentences: 'er that I parte fro ye'; 'er she deyde'. The story-teller's foreseen good parting from his audience, painful task faithfully completed, is put into some kind of relationship with a bad, faith-breaking parting of hero and heroine. (We should notice Chaucer's selection of 'forsook', a word which suggests betrayal as movement away.)

Thinking further about the relationship of the telling of the story and the material of the story, love which goes bad, or is not strong enough, we find a special poignancy in something Chaucer reveals shortly after his first stanza has displayed its elegance. We are made to realize that the narrator has undertaken this difficult literary task out of a generous impulse; the poem is to be a gift of love, an act of charity:

> ...if this may don gladnesse
> To any lovere, and his cause availle,
> Have he my thonk, and myn be this travaille!   (19–21)

Moreover, the poem will come into being, or the poet wishes it to come into being, not through the efforts of purposeful writer and helpful fury alone; *Troilus and Criseyde* should emerge from a context of common and loving human effort. The writer will try to 'don gladnesse' to lovers, but his chosen audience should themselves contribute to the work by praying; praying both for other lovers, and for the poet himself (22–46). As, in the early books of *Troilus and Criseyde*, the reader savours the busy-ness of Pandarus and, more generally, the atmosphere of Chaucer's Troy, the atmosphere in which the love of hero and heroine is fostered and consummated, it will be good to remember that the poem itself was to grow out of charity and a like generosity of feeling. We should also recall this general goodness of heart when, late in our reading of *Troilus*, we are disturbed to find that our responses to the story have ceased to be entirely generous.

I want now to look at the characteristics of Chaucerian Troy, that city in which the love of Troilus and Criseyde grows. It is in the presentation of this city that Chaucer shows his astonishing mastery of atmosphere and texture. This poet's Troy is the city of kindness and friendship, of an unheroic and, because not free of foibles, unintimidating loving-kindness. Minor characters are important here. Hector helps Criseyde in a socially difficult situation: he is 'pitous of nature' (1, 113), but Criseyde's beauty also has its influence upon him (115); Deiphebus loves his brother Troilus and is not only eager to help Criseyde out of a difficulty, but indignant when Pandarus speaks of her, this friend of his, as though she were a stranger (II, 1422–4); later on in the poem, when bad news comes, Trojan ladies – like all ladies, given to visiting with friends – gather at Criseyde's house to offer the solace of unexceptionable sentiments (IV, 680–730); Helen of Troy, in an astonishing transformation, becomes the very nicest lady in an affluent suburb; Troilus is the beneficiary of the human habit – still with us, the reader is glad to learn – of responding to someone's praise of a given person with still higher praise (II, 1582–9). Physically, this Chaucerian Troy is of course walled, enclosed; it is under siege, but the state of siege serves to heighten by contrast the life of peace within (cf. I, 148–50). The fighting itself is essentially off-stage, summarized rather than narrated. This city is peculiarly one of commodious, welcoming, well and discreetly staffed households: we have scenes set in the homes of Troilus, Criseyde, Pandarus, Deiphebus and, later, Sarpedon. It is a city where a kneeling hero will have a friend ready and solicitous enough to fetch him a cushion and that cushion which Pandarus brings for Troilus (III, 960–6), almost as touching as it is absurd, might be the very emblem, as Pandarus is the most extraordinary representative, of Trojanness.

This Troy is a city – or this *Troilus* is a poem – where characters, especially the hero, retreat to bed remarkably often; bed as the place of Eros is, in the *Troilus*, ambiguously related to bed as the place of infantile refuge. More generally, heroic love, the grand passion *Troilus and Criseyde* would seem to be about, is made to appear at once quite different from warm-hearted decency, and something which grows from and is nurtured by such instinctive benevolence.[2]

We are charmed, but also a bit disconcerted; which is to say we are being educated. When we began this narrative of double sorrow and weeping verses, we expected to hear about the intensity of love, and we do indeed hear about that intensity. Still, this story is not quite what we had anticipated: we have had to learn to experience intense love within the peculiar setting of the first books, heroic love in the context of niceness. Texture as rich as the texture of the *Troilus* does not simply enhance our response to theme and structure: it inevitably changes that response.

One feature of Chaucer's technique which deserves special attention both for its contribution to our sense of texture in the poem and for its intrinsic interest is his mastery of dialogue. In *Troilus and Criseyde*, talk is vitality. The association is strongly, delightfully made in the first half of the work, and variously played upon in the second half. Pandarus, the Trojan *genius loci*, is the famed and very effective speaker; when, towards the end of the poem, we learn 'a word ne kowde he seye' (V, 1729) we know that there is no hope left. The love-fostering scene at Deiphebus' house (II, 1555ff) presents diverse folk speaking diversely; in the 'falling-action' scene which is balanced against this one, the visit to Sarpedon (v, 435ff), all characters except Pandarus and Troilus are left unquoted, and thus, in contrast to the minor characters of the earlier gathering, are rather pallid, more data than persons. And there are still subtler (though, in view of the place in this work of the code of lover's secrecy, not necessarily more important) things to notice about Chaucer's dialogue than the basic speech/silence contrast. Tempo and speech-size are worked with adroitly. A sunny, comic scene may make much use of rapidly exchanged short speeches, while a sombre interview is built primarily of large blocks of speech. (Compare the Pandarus/Criseyde delivery-of-letter section (II. 1093ff) with the Pandarus/Troilus duologue at IV, 372ff.) In Chaucer's greatest presentation of talk, the first interview of Pandarus and Criseyde (II, 78ff), there is a Shavian mastery of scene rhythm, a splendid utilization of both quick interchange and long declamation.

But fully to appreciate the expressive movement of talk in *Troilus and Criseyde* (and, indeed, fully to appreciate the expressive rhythm of narration in *Troilus and Criseyde*) means to consider the particular form in which Chaucer cast his narrative: the *Troilus* is a story in verse and, more particularly, a story in stanzaic verse. The basic point is this. When an author elects to tell a tale in seven-line stanzas, one expects life in that tale (including speech) to be articulated as series of seven-line and multiple-of-seven-line units; in other words, the maker of stanzaic narrative is more conspicuously committed than is the couplet-writer (or, of course, the prose writer) to finding a certain shape in experience again and again. This is not to say that 'shape' will be a special thematic concern of any rhyme-royal narrative; but there is something right in the fact that *Troilus and Criseyde* is both stanzaic and also opens by drawing our attention to a large pattern which it is going to trace. Now *Troilus and Criseyde*, wonderfully clear in its first few lines about what it is going to do, is also the poem notorious for the trouble it finally has in coming to a stop; and whatever we make of its peculiar last pages, we will not think them quite unprepared for if we attend carefully to the way we as readers (or far better, imagined auditors) experience the longer speeches of the poem. In those longer speeches, Chaucer is having a good deal of what is in two senses liminal fun with stanza boundaries. Again and again we will have thought a given seventh line concluded a speech, only to discover a couple of seconds later that it was merely a section of that speech which so ringingly terminated. (In its technical aspects, the longwindedness of Pandarus is more amusing than the longwindedness of the Wife of Bath.) To put this another way: the opening of *Troilus and Criseyde* draws particular attention to the story's shape and anticipates the end of the matter, the parting of narrator and audience; but metrically, *Troilus* is a poem that keeps us saying to ourselves, 'ah no; there is more'. The articulation of stanzas provides, throughout the poem, reminders of the tension between the 'first-half' values of surprising abundance and the 'second-half' values of shape-holding and promise-keeping.

Now the 'more' of the *Troilus* stanzas is not a matter of quantity alone. Chaucer, in moving from speech by one character to speech by another, to narration, and perhaps back to speech again – sometimes all within seven lines – gives us effects one would have thought outside the range of stanzaic verse. Thus, the opening of that first Pandarus–Criseyde interview:

> Quod Pandarus, 'Madame, God yow see,
> With al youre fayre book and compaignie!'
> 'Ey, uncle myn, welcome iwys,' quod she;
> And up she roos, and by the hond in hye
> She took hym faste, and seyde, 'This nyght thrie,
> To goode mot it turne, of yow I mette.'
> And with that word she doun on bench hym sette.
>
> 'Ye, nece, yee shal faren wel the bet,
> If God wol, al this yeer,' quod Pandarus;
> 'But I am sory that I have yow let
> To herken of youre book ye preysen thus.
> For Goddes love, what seith it? telle it us!
> Is it of love? O, som good ye me leere!'
> 'Uncle', quod she, 'youre maistresse is nat here.'   (II, 85–98)

This would be nice enough in prose, and perhaps charming in couplets; in stanzas, it is truly exhilarating, metrical dexterity almost become a moral good. The listener receives not something in place of what was expected, but something beyond what was expected. The rhythms of easy speech do not distort the structural logic of the rhyme scheme, but unconstrainedly emerge in the stanzaic form; talk can be both talk and well-shaped rhyme royal. Thus, Chaucer's dialogues are something which equivalent exchanges in novels (which have no responsibility, no implicit contract, to be well-shaped as anything but imitations of human talk) simply cannot be: they are radically 'something more', the metrical representation of a promise being exceeded.

The first Pandarus–Criseyde interview is, I have said, Chaucer's greatest conversation scene. But this scene's mastery of stanzaic and larger rhythms is in various ways in the service of things less technical, and I do want to look here at one of those things: this is the scene where Chaucer really presents Criseyde, or presents what we might call the *other* Criseyde. Up to this time, that is, Criseyde has seemed pretty much what the original 'purpos' and indicated design required: a superlatively beautiful lady. Here one discovers that there is more to her than necessary conditions for double sorrow, more to her indeed, than her lover or anyone else in the poem can quite appreciate. She is wonderfully shrewd, agile-witted; and though we know from the beginning the one salient moral fact of her story, that she will forsake Troilus, we are endlessly interested in the nuances of her character. And we should notice also that in this interview scene and after it, our pleasure as audience involves a sort of conflict of interests, not just a combination of interests. Here Pandarus, after all, is acting to advance our hero's fortunes, and we should (unless we are trying to keep to a *very* high moral road in our reading of the poem) be on the hero's side. But we do find ourselves, for all the good we wish Troilus, taking pleasure in the fact that Criseyde is not all that easy for her uncle to manipulate, is a worthy, resourceful adversary in these verbal skirmishes. We want the scene to be a well-played match even more than we want it to be an advancing of the hero's cause. (As a good first-half scene, it will, of course, manage to be both.)

In these last pages I have been chiefly stressing the various ways in which the first half of *Troilus and Criseyde* gives its audience more than could have been expected from a poem which began by being markedly explicit about its particular concerns and insistent about its lachrymose mood: the concerns have turned out to be broader than we thought they would be, and the weeping verses proved to be not steadily weeping verses. Now a work of art is always teaching us things about ourselves while revealing things about itself, and this is certainly true of our poem: we find how easy and pleasant it is to contemplate all these unexpected, unheroic things; how responsive we are to the texture of narrative. But one might say that it is Criseyde – and, again, the Criseyde of the first interview scene – who teaches us the most flattering lesson about ourselves: if she is clever, so are we; we are clever enough to *discover* her cleverness – and thus more clever than the hero, or even her uncle, who, well into the scene, is strangely patronizing about Criseyde's intelligence (II, 267–73). We can feel more perceptive than the poet-narrator also. Chaucer is quite willing to explain, and, for comic effects, sometimes overexplain, why something is happening and what we ought to think about it. But he also knows when to leave things unexplained – sometimes because ambiguity is desirable, at other times (and this is what particularly concerns us) so that the audience may feel it understands more than the narrator, or at least does not need comments from the narrator. Exemplary in this respect is the stanza beginning at II, 141: the stanza in which Criseyde's adroitness is first discovered. Pandarus, in the part of the scene which precedes this stanza, has been arousing his niece's interest in that secret of his – Troilus' love for her – and feigning reluctance to tell the secret. There has been, thus far, no great reason to think Criseyde will be more difficult for Pandarus to manipulate than Troilus himself had been in the complementary extracting-of-the-secret scene. The first four lines of the stanza in question are, then, quite unsurprising, mere confirmation of Pandarus' ability to achieve the effects he wants:

> Tho gan she wondren moore than biforn
> A thousand fold, and down hire eyghen caste;
> For nevere, sith the tyme that she was born,
> To knowe thynge desired she so faste;

And then, in the next three lines, Criseyde comes out into the light. Rather than plead to know the secret, she becomes shrewdly acquiescent:

> And with a syk she seyde hym atte laste,
> 'Now, uncle myn, I nyl yow nought displese,
> Nor axen more that may do yow disese.'

The great line here is the one Chaucer abstained from writing: the one that would have explained why, feeling *that*, Criseyde came to say *this*: there is more pleasure for the audience in being left alone with the juxtaposition.

It is exhilarating to discover that we do not need more explanation; and it is altogether typical of Chaucer that he leaves us here feeling not that a clever author is flattering the intelligence of a fit audience, but that the writer somehow failed to notice that anything just here in his story required explanation: we are made to believe, as I have said, that only *we* are capable of fully appreciating Criseyde, of relishing her cleverness in falling back, playing the good, dutiful niece, in order to gain her end. And one should go on to stress that our discovery of this Criseyde, our clever, resourceful Criseyde, is really the type of our discovery of all the richness of texture in the poem, and particularly in the first half of the poem: we feel that there is more in the work than we could have expected to find, and also more in ourselves; that our experience keeps broadening and growing richer. And this surely is something Chaucer would have wanted the reader of any spacious narrative to feel.

The first part of the *Troilus* might be thought of as the poetry of grace: it delights by giving the reader more than was promised, more than was, perhaps, even nameable, at the poem's opening. The final part of the *Troilus* – and especially Book v – is the poetry of contract: it is itself the completing of the work explicitly described and implicitly promised by the poem's opening, and has as its subject-matter fidelity, the keeping of an agreement. The great question now is whether even-song and morning-song accord: match and symmetry are here the signs of moral health; surprises, the source of delight in the first part of the poem, are now inherently suspect or culpable. The shift here is of course in the underlying patterns of tale-telling and response rather than on the surface of the story, but it is nonetheless a very difficult shift to make, and our difficulty in making it (indeed our inability to make it completely) is part of what *Troilus* means. In his self-effacing way, Geoffrey Chaucer does have the daring of a great poet. To enrich our understanding of his matter, he will take chances, will have us feel dissatisfied: the poetry of contract is also the poetry of contraction. One may say that if the first half of *Troilus and Criseyde* is remarkable for the mastery, the ease of its narrative technique, the second half is remarkable for the riskiness, the strange moral courage of its narration. Chaucer does of course feel and want his readers to feel that on the simplest human level, what Troilus did was right and what Criseyde did was wrong. But he also wants us to feel that on that simplest human level (that is, without any consideration of larger philosophical questions) there would be something deeply impoverished in a response that was limited to this judgement and a feeling of pity for Troilus. Human experience should be richer, human response more complex, than such a judgement allows. One feels Chaucer's unease, his artistic and moral claustrophobia, given comic expression in the narrator's celebrated statement that he would excuse Criseyde if he could (v, 1097–9). That unease becomes a thing of splendour in the final leap to a Christian vision — which of course means a contract-cancelling vision. But we find that Chaucerian unease at its most disturbing in some aspects of the tale-telling.

The reader, in the first half of the poem, develops a richly specific liking for Criseyde which, being based largely on characteristics of the heroine not pertinent to the original rise-and-fall design of the work, is one of the 'extra' things of the *Troilus*. In a sort of complement to this structurally and morally excessive liking for the heroine, the reader of the second half of the poem will come to feel, and, being a good person, try to censor, repress, deny, a sense of exasperation with the decent, suffering hero of Chaucer's narrative. We do genuinely pity Troilus (if we did not, our own exasperation would not disconcert us) but we have a nagging sense of the accuracy of his self-description in Book IV: 'I, combre-world, that may of nothyng serve, / But evere dye and nevere fulli sterve' (279–80; cf. also 517–18). For 'cumber-world' (apparently a Chaucerian coinage) one should perhaps substitute 'cumber-poem' – an aesthetic encumbrance, a drag on the narrative. Chaucer's hero is faithful (always the same) but he is also, as Chaucer sees he ought to be, more than a little boring (always the same) as one follows him through two long books of despair, of hopes the reader knows to be false, of waiting for death and wishing for death. Troilus is not given, as was his model, the hero of Boccaccio's *Filostrato*, a spectacular faint on hearing the decision to exchange Criseyde for Antenor (IV, 18–20), or a serious suicide attempt when he comes to suspect that his lady has been unfaithful (VII, 33); on the other hand, Chaucer adds a long philosophical meditation by the hero, the import of which is that there is not much Troilus can do about things: 'For al that comth, comth by necessitee: / Thus to ben lorn, it is my destinee.' (IV, 958–9). At this point Pandarus is given the comic character's privilege of voicing the audience's censored exasperation (1086ff). Another Chaucerian addition to the poem is Diomede's first, wickedly brilliant courting speech (V, 106–75). The reader of that speech is disturbed to realize that he, like Criseyde, finds Diomede's speed and efficiency less appalling than he ought. If we examine our reactions closely, we see that the smile of Cassandra and the laughter of Pandarus when they recognise the dismalness of the hero's position (V, 1457; 1172) are disquieting not for what is disclosed about Troilus' sister and friend, but for what is suggested about the reader, who feels something of the same amusement – the amusement, really, of Fortune herself (IV, 6–7) at two removes. Chaucer's hero is being a true lover, faithfully going down as Fortune turns her wheel; but the reader – and indeed the narrator – are coming to feel confined and, in their exasperation, momentarily tough-minded almost to the point of feeling cruel amusement, even while they are predominantly compassionate.[3]

There is something salutary in the mere acknowledgement that one's reactions to the final, drawn-out sufferings of Troilus are decidedly mixed reactions; early in the poem we make pleasant discoveries about ourselves, and later on, some disconcerting ones. Chaucer has the great poet's ability to disturb. Our awareness of how Chaucer disturbs the reader, complicates our responses, is enhanced by a consideration of Book IV of the *Troilus* as a structural unit, a block in the composition. This penultimate book presents what may be called a ghost ending, an 'alternative', bittersweet conclusion to the story which one feels might have been the true one, but simply is rejected by an arbitrary god or fortune or author. The arbitrariness with which the Book IV conclusion is avoided – things do not happen that way just here because things do not happen that way just here – works to lessen the authenticity, the felt inevitability, of the actual, Book V conclusion. A hint of what Chaucer is up to here comes in the lines which end the 'Prohemium' to Book IV. The author calls on Mars and the Furies for assistance:

> This ilke ferthe book me helpeth fyne,
> So that the losse of lyf and love yfeere
> Of Troilus be fully shewed heere.   (26–8)

This rather suggests that the *Troilus* is to be a four-book poem, the conclusion of which we are now reaching. But what does happen in 'this ilke ferthe book'? Let me summarize in a way that will bring certain patterns out clearly. After the decision to exchange Criseyde for Antenor is made, Chaucer presents scenes with the two grieving but, in these early episodes of Book IV, separated lovers. Each of the two wishes for and is associated with death (cf. 250–2; 499ff.; 816–19; 862–3). Then comes the climax of Book IV: hero and heroine are brought together, and their individual death-wishes, death-associations, combine into a structurally and archetypically important near-death, or pseudo-death, or symbolic death. Criseyde cries, 'O Jove, I deye, and mercy I beseche! / Help, Troilus!' (1149–50) and swoons; this tragic swoon of the heroine will recall the comic swoon of the hero in the earlier consummation scene (III, 1092): there the height of the lovers' bliss was fast approaching; here, one might guess, their final woe is approaching as fast. Troilus believes Criseyde is dead and lays out her body 'As men don hem that shal ben layd on beere' (1183); he is making a fine taking-leave-of-life speech (1191–1210) and is about to kill himself when Criseyde sighs and calls out his name (1213). Realizing what has happened, she says – not, perhaps, quite realistically (cf. IV, 771–2) – that if she had found Troilus dead, she would have used his sword to end her own life. This, then, is the averted ending to the story: a Romeo and Juliet, Pyramus and Thisbe ending. And this averted ending does make the real one look somewhat arbitrary, at least where the hero is concerned: he, at least, could have died in bittersweet sorrow rather than an entirely bitter sorrow. His sufferings from this point on will seem on one level the result of what might be called *deus ex machina* continuation: if Criseyde's faint had only lasted some seconds longer...[4]

The pseudo-death, then, makes Troilus' later sufferings appear gratuitous: sufferings to be gone through not just because one cannot keep the good of this world, but because Troilus is going to lose those goods (or his one great good) in an especially painful way. This, however, does not seem to suggest much about why we should become covertly displeased with Troilus himself – though it may suggest a good deal about why we and the narrator grow impatient with the latter part of the story. To understand our exasperation with the hero himself a little better, we must look at this pseudo-death scene in a somewhat different way. Here I would invoke the axiom that in narrative a near-death usually is a ritual death, a moment of major transition. (One might think of Dante in this connection, but it is just as useful to recall *Great Expectations* or *Our Mutual Friend*: the question is one of archetypal narrative patterns, not particular influences.) Now if we do feel that this climactic incident of Book IV of *Troilus* is a ritual death, we will also feel that, in a kind of countercurrent to what is happening on the surface, Criseyde is afterwards moving back to life again.[5] We have this movement toward life in the creaturely good sense of what she says after declaring that she would have killed herself if she had found Troilus dead ('But hoo, for we han right ynough of this, / And lat us rise, and streght to bedde go, / And ther lat us speken of oure wo': 1242–4) and in the larger progress of the scene, which is from pseudo-death to Criseyde's presentation of plans to live, and to live by going from the known good place, Troy, to the frightening other place, and then returning. Her plan is, it might be said, to be not a romance heroine, but a romance hero, a Gawain or a Lancelot, undertaking a classic out-and-back adventure. (Her plans, of course, are not very good, but soundness is not the only issue here.) We should also notice that, as she begins to explain her plans, Criseyde is given one of those speeches which express the reader's censored exasperation with Troilus:

> 'Lo, herte myn, wel woot ye this,' quod she,
> 'That if a wight alwey his wo compleyne,
> And seketh nought how holpen for to be,
> It nys but folie and encrees of peyne;
> And syn that here assembled be we tweyne
> To fynde boote of wo that we ben inne,
> It were al tyme soone to bygynne.'   (1254–60)

Briefly, then, one may say that Chaucer has arranged his narrative so that the reader will on one level, the surface, always know that Criseyde forsakes the faithful Troilus, and that this is a bad thing. But on another level one senses that these two characters, Troilus and Criseyde, respond to a crisis by wishing for death, then undergo (in what is, structurally, *the* death scene of Chaucer's long, weeping love-poem) a symbolic or near-death from which one, Criseyde, emerges predominantly ready to live again and encounter new experiences, while the other seems comparatively timorous (*his* plan is for an unheroic 'stealing away') and chiefly ready to continue waiting for death even after he has, symbolically, had that death: 'But evere dye and nevere fulli sterve'. It is worth noticing also that in the early part of Book IV Chaucer even makes Criseyde seem morally superior to Troilus: she is notably more concerned with the pain he must be feeling than he is with the pain she must feel. It is especially striking that Criseyde's sympathy here transmutes the elegant double sorrow formulation of the poem's opening into something emotionally generous: 'Kan he for me so pitously compleyne? / Iwis, this sorwe doubleth al my peyne' (902–3).

The latter part of *Troilus and Criseyde* is about fidelity, but it focusses the issue of Criseyde's faithfulness in a particular way: the question of whether Criseyde will be true to Troilus, the real question, becomes for a good part of the narrative the more contractual question of whether or not Criseyde will return from the Greek camp *within ten days*. It is worth noticing that that figure of ten days starts out in what is clearly a conversational, approximating way: Criseyde says first, 'withinne a wowke or two, / I shal ben here' (IV, 1278–9) and then, 'By God, lo, right anon, / Er dayes ten' (IV, 1319–20) (Boccaccio's heroine is from the beginning more precise: cf. *Filostrato* IV, 154). Thus in the *Troilus*, a lover's wish to be reassuring produces a legalistic condition which both represents and also displaces the true issue of love. There is one interesting moment, in fact, where

Criseyde seems pushed toward despair not by her inability to remain faithful to Troilus, but by her difficulty in keeping to the ten-day agreement, and her certainty that Troilus will interpret the small failure as the great infidelity:

> And if so be that I my terme pace,
> My Troilus shal in his herte deme
> That I am fals, and so it may wel seme:
> Thus shal ich have unthonk on every side.
> That I was born, so weilaway the tide! (v, 696–700)

That part of the ten-days stipulation which is the contractualization rather than the representation of love is indirectly commented upon in Book v by the dispute Troilus and Pandarus have about the need to stay the 'contracted for' full week amid the delights of Sarpedon's house even when it is clear that the visit is doing nothing to make Troilus feel better (v, 475–97). Pandarus prevails; Troilus is, as one would have expected him to be, a man of his word, and stays the full week. It is not clear here (as it was in Boccaccio) that the host indeed would have been offended by his guests' early departure; it is not clear in Chaucer's version that this keeping to an agreed time accomplishes anything at all.

During his visit to Sarpedon, Troilus begins to impose another kind of shape on his misery: he ritualizes his grief by returning to the things associated with his time of joy. Thus he rereads the letters Criseyde sent to him in better days 'an hondred sithe atwixen noon and prime' (v, 472); he will revisit the places associated with earlier experiences (519ff.: 562ff.). Having doubled, symmetrized the happy part of his love, Troilus goes on to his more recent, unhappy experiences, and moves physically to the city gates. One remembers the pathos of Troilus on the walls, but there is also something morbid here, the movements (not suggested in *Filostrato*) of a caged animal: 'And up and down ther made he many a wente' (605); 'And up and down, by west and ek by este, / Upon the walles made he many a wente' (1193–4). In this ritualizing, this doubling of his experience, Troilus is doing something distinctly like what the poet Chaucer does when he traces on-the-way-up, on-the-way-down symmetries in Troilus' adventures in love; and the suspicion that the art of telling nicely shaped stories and the art of intensifying one's misery are closely related is made a bit stronger when one notices that it is after he has ritualized and symmetrized his experiences that Troilus realizes his life has the stuff of a narrative in it:

> ...'O blisful lord Cupide,
> Whan I the proces have in my memorie,
> How thow me hast wereyed on every syde,
> Men myght a book make of it, lik a storie.' (582–5)

In the meantime, the narrator, who has in fact undertaken to make such a book, suffers his own, smaller miseries: how painful it is for this story-teller to go through with it, to trace the pattern he proposed to trace! In the opening stanzas of Book IV, his heart bleeds and his pen quakes because of what he must now write (12–13); but perhaps, somehow, Criseyde did not quite forsake Troilus, but was only unkind – perhaps no more than that 'moot hennesforth ben matere of [his] book' (15–17); perhaps the authorities on whom this author relies have slandered the heroine (19–21). In the final book of *Troilus and Criseyde*, the narrator will move with painful, source-citing slowness through the stanzas in which he must tell of Criseyde's favours to Diomede (1030–50). These celebrated attempts to mitigate or evade the heroine's guilt are charming and humane, doing credit to the narrator's heart if not to his head. More disturbing and meaningful are the moments when he attempts to get through his self-imposed, charity-imposed obligation to deal with this final misery by emotionally disengaging himself; disengaging himself by recalling that he does, after all, know what is going to happen (e.g., v, 27–8; 766–70) or by facile moralizing (1432–5; 1748–50). Too much compassion leads to protective self-anaesthetizing; leads to it in the narrator and, even more disturbingly leads to it in ourselves, creates that undercurrent of impatience in our reaction to the hero's world-encumbering misery. It is also this sense of a nemesis of the emotions – a lack of feeling, and unresponsiveness to love, that counterbalances long fidelity and excessive feeling – which makes the late stanza on the now world-unencumbered Troilus feel terribly right; whatever we think about the particular philosophical position taken, intuitively, we know this is, indeed, the very thing that happens:

> And in hymself he lough right at the wo
> Of hem that wepten for his deth so faste;
> And dampned al oure werk that foloweth so
> The blynde lust, the which that may nat laste,
> And sholden al oure herte on heven caste.   (1821–5)

Brilliantly, our censored exasperation with and hostility toward the hero seem transformed into his hostility toward us.

With Troilus' terrible laughter we have a sort of emotional nemesis at work. With Chaucer's audacious sequence of lurching, sputtering 'concluding' stanzas (1765ff) we discover an artistic nemesis: the poem that begins by being too sure of what it is going to be, ends rather unsure of what it has, after all, been – or, more precisely, unsure of how to return from this story to the real world. Love and art require fidelity; but also room to grow and change. As a love story, *Troilus and Criseyde* overtly celebrates – and exemplifies – fidelity.; covertly, it makes us feel something of the claustrophobia which comes with fidelity rigidified, gone wrong.

Notes

1 On this symmetrical structure, see Ian Bishop's *Troilus and Criseyde: A Critical Study* (Bristol, 1981), pp. 43–4 and ff.
2 I have dealt at greater length with Chaucer's Troy and Trojans in '*Troilus*, Books I–III: a Criseydan Reading' in *Essays on Troilus and Criseyde*, ed. Mary Salu (Cambridge, 1979) pp. 105–25.
3 With the present discussion of Troilus in Books IV and V, compare Winthrop Wetherbee's *Chaucer and the Poets: An Essay on Troilus and Criseyde* (Ithaca, NY/London, 1984), pp. 205–23.
4 Compare the discussion of this 'Pyramus and Thisbe' scene, 'in a way...the climax of the poem', in E. Talbot Donaldson's *The Swan at the Well: Shakespeare Reading Chaucer* (New Haven, Conn./London, 1985), pp. 22–6.
5 See in connection with this movement back to life the provocative treatment of the poem's hero, heroine and author in Alfred David's *The Strumpet Muse: Art and Morals in Chaucer's Poetry* (Bloomington, Ind./London, 1976), pp. 27–36.

5   Chance and destiny in *Troilus and Criseyde* and the *Knight's Tale*[1]

A T a crucial moment in Book II of *Troilus and Criseyde*, Criseyde is left alone to reflect on Pandarus' astonishing revelation that Troilus is dying with love of her. And as chance would have it, at this very moment Troilus rides past her window.

> But as she sat allone and thoughte thus,
> Ascry aros at scarmuch al withoute,
> And men cride in the strete, 'Se, Troilus
> Hath right now put to flight the Grekes route!'
> With that gan al hire meyne for to shoute,
> 'A, go we se! cast up the yates wyde!
> For thorwgh this strete he moot to paleys ride;
>
> For other wey is fro the yate noon
> Of Dardanus, there opyn is the cheyne.'
> With that com he and al his folk anoon
> An esy pas rydyng, in routes tweyne,
> Right as his happy day was, sooth to seyne,
> For which, men seyn, may nought destourbed be
> That shal bityden of necessitee.   (610–23)

The vision that passes before Criseyde's eyes is a powerfully attractive one: a handsome warrior, young and strong, whose battered armour and wounded horse bear witness to his daring and bravery, and whose blushing response to the people's cheers bears witness to his humility. As she watches, Criseyde finds her emotions instinctively aroused by the sight.

> Criseyda gan al his chere aspien,
> And leet it so softe in hire herte synke,
> That to hireself she seyde, 'Who yaf me drynke?'
>
> For of hire owen thought she wex al reed,
> Remembryng hire right thus, 'Lo, this is he
> Which that myn uncle swerith he moot be deed,
> But I on hym have mercy and pitee.'   (649–55)

There is no such window-scene at the corresponding point in Chaucer's narrative source, Boccaccio's *Filostrato*.[2] There, Pandaro's departure is immediately followed by a description of Criseida's solitary reflections, in which the handsome exterior of Troiolo exercises its due influence, but which are not interrupted by his actual appearance. Only after this do we hear how Pandaro goes to Troiolo to tell him that the wooing of Criseida has been begun, and Troiolo, full of gratitude and hope, allows Pandaro to lead him to Criseida's window, where he receives a favourable glance from his lady. His gentle and amiable looks remove her remaining fears, and henceforth she fixes all her desires on this new love (*Filostrato* ii, 82–3).

On first comparing Chaucer's version with Boccaccio's, we might simply assume that Chaucer's change is made with an eye to dramatic immediacy. Instead of the imagined appearance of Troilus, Chaucer introduces the hero himself, and he places the window-scene before rather than after Criseyde's internal deliberations so as to increase its influence on her thoughts. But Chaucer does not merely move the position of the window-scene; he also doubles it. On returning to Troilus, Pandarus advises him to write Criseyde a letter, declaring his love; he suggests that Troilus should ride past Criseyde's window *as if* accidentally, while he is delivering the letter to his niece, so that he can draw her into the window to impress her with the sight of her admirer (ii, 1009–22). This plan is duly executed (ii, 1247–74), and Troilus' reward is an outward blush and inward admiration from Criseyde. This second window-scene is clearly, like the first, born of the single window-scene in Boccaccio, which indeed it resembles even more closely in being a calculated move on Pandarus' part, designed to establish contact and some kind of tacit understanding between the two young people.

Why did Chaucer go to such trouble to expand and duplicate the single brief window-scene (described in only two stanzas) in Boccaccio? Why did he fashion his narrative in such a way that the interview carefully arranged by Pandarus is preceded by an earlier encounter, dictated by nothing more than chance? The first answer, I believe, is that he wanted the comparison of the two scenes to reveal human efforts as negligible when weighed against the role of chance. The second window-scene confirms and strengthens Criseyde's attraction to Troilus (1271–4), but it is the first window-scene that has created this attraction ('Who yaf me drynke?'), and it is of key significance in the process because of its crucial positioning, occurring as it does at the moment when Criseyde is momentarily thrown off-balance by the novelty of the situation, and thus most vulnerable to impressions one way or the other. Having initiated Criseyde's internal deliberations by one chance occurrence, Chaucer follows them with two more, neither of which has any precedent in Boccaccio's narrative. Fluctuating between fear and desire, Criseyde goes to walk in her garden, and hears her niece Antigone sing a song, written by 'the goodlieste mayde / Of gret estat in al the town of Troye' (880–1), which praises love in terms that answer all Criseyde's doubts and fears (899–903).[3] She then goes to bed, with the nightingale singing beneath her window, and dreams that a white eagle tears her heart from her body, without causing her any pain, and leaves his own in its place. These experiences too have a contributory role in the 'proces' (678) by which Criseyde turns to love. We shall better understand the reasons for their introduction if we return to the initial account of Troilus riding past the window and scrutinize it more closely.

I have said that this first encounter is dictated by nothing more than chance; Chaucer makes this clear by using the adjective 'happy' ('his happy day': 621), whose root is the noun 'hap', meaning 'chance'. As Chaucer presents it, Troilus' riding past the window at that particular moment is nothing more than 'a piece of good luck'. In doubling the window-scenes, Chaucer is emphasizing chance as the crucially important determinant in the course of the love-affair. The scope of human agency is correspondingly restricted; Pandarus, fondly imagining himself the omniscient and omnipresent director of the drama, is in fact merely a contributor to, not the controller of, the dynamics of the narrative. The chance which he carefully simulates in the second window-scene has already been independently at work, making his own efforts superfluous. His skilful manipulations begin to look less like vital contributions, and more like baroque flourishes on an independently worked design.[4] Looking back to the beginning of the story, we realize that chance appropriately guides the love-affair, since it was chance that initiated it; it is 'upon cas' (I, 271) that Troilus' gaze falls on Criseyde in the temple, with such dramatic effects. Troilus himself thinks of his love as an 'aventure' (another Middle English word for chance; see I, 368), and it is consistently referred to as such by Pandarus (II, 224, 288) and also Criseyde (II, 742). Indeed, Pandarus' own intervention in the affair is dictated by the 'cas' or 'aventure' that causes him to break in on Troilus' solitary languishing (I, 568).[5]

But no sooner has Chaucer established Troilus' ride-past as due to chance, than he goes on to refer this chance to an underlying 'necessitee'.

> Right as his happy day was, sooth to seyne,
> For which, men seyn, may nought destourbed be
> Thal shal bityden of necessitee.   (II, 621–3)

And it is of 'necessitee' that Troilus complains at the other end of the narrative, in his much-discussed soliloquy on free will in Book IV. Here the sense of casualness associated with 'luck' or 'chance' has entirely disappeared; the relentless rhyming of 'necessitee' and 'destinee' that ushers in Troilus' lament (958–9) expresses his sense of being imprisoned in a tyrannical world of fate which leaves no room for the exercise of the human will or the realisation of human desires. What then is the nature of the 'necessitee' that underlies the episode in Book II, and the 'necessitee' confronting Troilus in Book IV? what is the nature of the connection between this destinal 'necessitee' and chance? and what room is left for the exercise of free will in the face of these powerful forces?

Troilus and Criseyde itself testifies to the fact that Chaucer's thinking on these questions was stimulated and directed by his reading of Boethius' *Consolation of Philosophy*, which he himself translated.[6] Boethius, confronting disgrace, imprisonment, and possible death, is brought, like Troilus, to raise questions of cosmic order – 'questions of the symplicite of the purveaunce of God, and of the ordre of destyne, and of sodeyn hap, and of the knowynge and predestinacioun devyne, and of the liberte of fre wil' (*Boece*, IV pr. 6). As he ponders the arbitrary injustice manifested in his own loss of good fortune, he observes that such injustices would better sort with a theory that the world was governed by blind chance ('fortunows hap') than with a belief in the ordering control of divine providence (IV pr. 5). Philosophy's answer to these doubts addresses itself first to the questions of providence and destiny (IV pr. 6), and then to the question of chance (V pr. 1-m. 1); finally she re-affirms the freedom of the human will (V pr. 2-pr. 6).

Crucial to Philosophy's explanation of providence and destiny is the role of time. Providence, the 'pure clennesse of the devyne intelligence', is outside of time – a separation expressed in the image of the tower, from the height of which the divine intelligence surveys all together the events which are for us arranged in temporal succession. This a-temporal providence disposes all things in an order; destiny is the manifestation of that order in time – it is a 'temporel ordenaunce'. To express this idea, Philosophy uses the analogy of a craftsman who first conceives the object he is to make, and then produces it according to his design; his conception of the object as a whole 'governs' its final form, but exists separately from its execution at all stages of the process. Using a different analogy, we could say that the relation between providence and destiny is something like the relation between a bus timetable and the actual running of the buses. The analogy is not perfect in either instance, because it is difficult to rid ourselves of the notion that the workman's design, and the bus timetable, *precede* the temporal realization that they govern – in other words, that they too belong to a temporal process. The point at which the analogies hold good is the perception that the conception and its execution exist on different planes, and that the conception embraces as a whole and immediately what can only be executed as a reality gradually and over time.

The difference between providence and destiny can thus be expressed as a difference of *perspective* – as is suggested in the text by the image of the tower, and Philosophy's repeated use of the word 'lokynge' for the divine thought (IV pr. 6). Although Philosophy talks of destiny as 'subgit' to providence, it is misleading to think of them only as two separate links in a chain of command. On the contrary, destiny and providence are merely two different names given to the same thing, which is called providence when considered as a unity out of time, and destiny when it is manifested in the linear succession of events in time. It is precisely this difference of perspective that gives rise to human doubts about providence. Bound to a temporal existence, human beings are denied a vision of the unity in which the order of providence is visible; they can glimpse only a part of the whole pattern, which inevitably appears to them as fragmentary and confused. Philosophy speaks of 'destinal ordenaunce' as 'ywoven and acomplissid' (IV pr. 6), and the image of weaving is a helpful one. In the weaving of tapestry, the design of the whole will be perceptible only when the weaving is completed; while it is in progress, the shifts in shape and colour may well seem random and confusing.

This conception of destiny helps solve the problem of necessity inasmuch as destiny is no longer perceived as the direct imposition of a divine will (whether the divinity be pagan or Christian) on helpless humanity. On Philosophy's definition, the free exercise of the human will is *part of* destiny; it is simply one of the 'moevable thynges' (IV pr. 6) whose constant interplay makes up the temporal unfolding of destiny. For us the term 'destiny' implies a pre-determining of the future, outside of the human will, whereas for Boethius, events take their place in the 'destinal cheyne' (V pr. 2) as a result of their own natural developments. The existence or non-existence of 'necessitee' is a matter of perspective; it exists only when the destinal chain is seen as a whole from the perspective of providence, since that which God sees must necessarily exist to be seen. As Philosophy puts it a little later (V pr. 6): 'thilke thing that is futur, whan it is referred to the devyne knowynge, than is it necesserie; but certis whan it is undirstonden in his owene kynde, men seen it outrely fre and absolut fro alle necessitee'. It may help us to understand this differentiation between the freedom of events within the temporal process, and their necessity within the a-temporal sphere of the divine intelligence, if we consider for a moment the status of the past, rather than the future, in relation to divine knowledge. Human beings are quite happy to think of the past as fixed and determined, merely by virtue of the fact that it has happened; it is only the future that they feel must be undetermined – that is, open to the influence of their own will. Now since divine providence 'enbraceth alle thinges to-hepe' (IV pr. 6), it makes no distinction between past, present and future. If then it is to consider the future as undetermined, the past must be considered undetermined also; conversely, the future must be perceived as determined in exactly the same way that the past is. The future is 'necessary' only in the sense that it exists (not pre-exists) in the a-temporal vision of divine providence, which beholds past, present and future in the timelessness of the eternal moment. 'Thilke God seeth in o strok of thought alle thinges that ben, or weren, or schollen comen' (v m. 2). From the human point of view, we could express the upshot of this argument by the paradoxical proposition that things are destined only when they have happened. ('The thingis thanne...that, whan men doon hem, ne han no necessitee that men doon hem, eek tho same thingis, *first er thei ben don*, thei ben to comen without necessitee': v pr. 4, my italics.) Only after they have happened are portions of the destinal pattern realized in time and made perceptible to human observers. 'Necessitee', then, does not represent the intrusion of divine control into human affairs; it is the pattern achieved by the totality of temporal events, working according to their own causes and effects.

The role of chance in this scheme of things is easily explained. Like destiny and providence, chance is a matter of perspective. 'Hap', explains Philosophy, is a name that men give to occurrences not embraced by their own intentions in initiating actions (v pr. 1). If a man ploughs a field and discovers a buried cache of gold, the discovery was intended neither by himself nor by the burier of the treasure; we call it therefore chance. Yet the event is not without causes – in this case, the hiding of the treasure and the ploughing of the field, both of which play an instrumental role. It is simply that the result of these two actions was not envisaged by either of their human performers. 'Hap' arises, therefore, from 'causes encontrynge and flowynge togidere to hemself, and nat by the entencioun of the doere' (v pr. 1). In the following metre, Philosophy illustrates this idea with the image of the two mighty rivers, Tigris and Euphrates, in whose waters a multitude of floating objects are swept together or pushed apart, as the whole mass rushes onward to the sea; in the same way, the shifts of Fortune are made one with the inexorable course of 'destinal ordinaunce'.

Turning back to our starting-point, we can see how brilliantly Chaucer has fashioned the scene in which Troilus passes Criseyde's window so that it embodies Boethius' notion of 'causes encontrynge and flowynge togidere to hemself', independent of human intention. The impression that Troilus makes on Criseyde is not only unintended by him, he is not even conscious of it; nor was it envisaged by Criseyde as she went into her closet for private thought. Even less was it foreseen or intended by Pandarus, despite his confidence that the whole world will proceed to execute his 'purpos'. Yet Pandarus is *one* cause within the larger confluence; it is his introduction of the idea of Troilus' love into Criseyde's mind that has created in her a susceptibility to a sight that would at other times have evoked no more than polite admiration. The 'flowynge togidere' of causes is thus rightly called chance ('his happy day'), since it lies outside what was envisaged by the human actors. But it can also be accurately called 'destiny', since the confluence of causes realizes a pattern. All the other occasions on which Troilus rode up this very street are not important; this one assumes significance because it connects with another contingent circumstance – Criseyde's first response to Pandarus' revelation – and thus forms part of the pattern which we are to call Troilus' destiny. The 'opyn cheyne' of the gate of Dardanus is a surrogate for the chain of destiny; open as Troilus embarks on his ride home, it closes as his passing links with Criseyde's watching. Thus the term 'necessitee' can be justified by reference of the event to its presence in the destinal pattern, out of time, in the divine thought.

The readers of Chaucer's poem are in a privileged position, since they can perceive this destinal necessity in a manner analogous to, if not identical with, that of the divine intelligence. For the pattern of destiny is, in literary terms, the pattern of the story. We feel it therefore as 'inevitable' that Pandarus' revelation should be followed by Troilus' impressive appearance, and that this in turn should be followed by Antigone's song, the nightingale, and Criseyde's dream, all insensibly steering her towards love. But we feel it as inevitable only because we know already that this is a love story, and because we are observing these individual occurrences with their known end in mind; it is because the story has, in a sense, already happened for us – we see it in 'o strok of thought' – that we can perceive its course as inevitable. The occurrences recounted are not necessary in themselves; Troilus could have ridden up some other street or returned an hour earlier; Antigone could have chosen to sing a melancholy song in which a lady lamented the loss of her lover or the torments of jealousy; it could have been a rainy night on which the nightingale uttered not a note and Criseyde fell into a dreamless sleep – the result of all this being that she woke next morning in a mood of bracing common-sense determined to hear no more romantic tales. These are not undisciplined speculations; they are justifiable precisely because this is a narrative in whose dynamics chance plays a crucial role. In order to register with full appreciation the brilliance of Chaucer's depiction of 'causes encontrynge and flowynge togidere to hemself', we must be alive to the possibility that the confluence of chance events could at every point have taken on a different form. The 'openness' of the story, our present sensation of suspense as we live through each event as it happens,[7] gives us a sense of its fluidity, its vulnerability to chance, even as our knowledge of its eventual end gives us a sense of inevitability, of its final shape as destiny. Through narrative suspense, Chaucer makes us alert to the possibility of a different story – that is, a different destiny. For *this* destiny is realized only through the confluence of contingent events; it is not fixed in advance, but in retrospect, when the pattern of 'temporel ordenaunce' (*Boece* IV pr. 6) has been worked out.[8]

Love is an area of human experience in which the retrospective nature of the realization of destiny is particularly easy to grasp, precisely because it is an experience about which it is next to impossible to use the future tense. The future-tense formulation 'I will/am about to fall in love with you' is patently absurd, while the present 'I am in love with you' implies not so much the consciousness of a present happening as of a past event – 'I have fallen in love with you' – which is achieving belated recognition. That is why Criseyde's expression of surrender to Troilus in the consummation scene of Book III – '"Ne hadde I er now, my swete herte deere, / Ben yold, ywis, I were now nought here!"' (1210–11) – is not, as some critics have held, a coy revelation that her mind had been consciously made up at some earlier date; it is rather a realization that her present situation and feelings imply – and therefore reveal – an earlier unconscious surrender, now to be made explicit.[9] Thus it is, also, that after the consummation the lovers – like all lovers – rehearse the events that have led up to this climactic end:

> Thise ilke two, of whom that I yow seye,
> Whan that hire hertes wel assured were,
> Tho gonne they to speken and to pleye,
> And ek rehercen how, and whan, and where
> Thei knewe hem first, and every wo and feere
> That passed was; but al swich hevynesse,
> I thank it God, was torned to gladnesse.   (1394–1400)

They re-interpret previous events as part of the pattern of destiny, their significance – the direction in which they were tending – now being established by the end that has been reached.[10]

The lovers have here no complaints of a destiny being forced on them; when Troilus (echoing the lover's perennial cry, 'we were meant for each other') tells Criseyde that 'God hath wrought me for I shall yow serve' (III, 1290), he is not expressing a consciousness of tyrannical control, but rather a sense of having discovered his true nature and function in life for the first time, of finding what it is that most fully expresses and engages his individual being. Their free assent, that is, is not only part of the 'confluence of causes', it is also accorded to the confluence as a whole. Free will and destiny are thus inextricably united; destiny, as I said earlier, works through the will in the subtle coalescence of outward event and inward desire.

This subtle coalescence is portrayed with extreme delicacy by Chaucer in Book II, as he traces Criseyde's response to Troilus' love. So far we have concentrated on the external occurrences – Pandarus' revelation, Troilus' riding past, Antigone's song, the dream. But equally important in the confluence of causes are the inner workings of Criseyde's mind and emotions, which are as it were the eyes into which the hooks of external incident can fall. Between Troilus' riding past and Antigone's song, Chaucer places his long account of Criseyde's deliberations (703–812). The details of what she thinks are less important than the fact that her mind appears as a seething mass of different possibilities, jostling and giving way to each other with the spontaneous movement of her emotions.[11] Within these possibilities, we can perceive the instincts towards love – and specifically, towards an ennobling love – which find an echo and a confirmation in Antigone's song. But we can also see the instincts *against* love – the fears of jealousy, emotional torment and betrayal – which could equally have found a chance echo and confirmation in the outside world; the different nature of the coalescence would have given a different turn to the story. The chances and changes that Boethius contemplates in the *Consolation* are chances and changes in the external world – loss of riches, family or friends. Chaucer adds to his representation of these instances of 'moevable destinee' the *inner* mutations which are ceaselessly at work in every human being. It is on these inner mutations that the external occurrences work; it is from the coalescence of the two that the shape of the action is born. A spherical object placed at the top of a slope will roll to the bottom because of its own sphericity as well as because of the declivity; its own nature is 'expressed' in the rolling just as much as the nature of the surrounding circumstances.[12] So Criseyde is 'expressed' in her motions towards love, even though external circumstances are needed to bring her potentialities into being.

In describing this process, I am not merely saying that Criseyde chooses to fall in love, exercising her free will in a matter presented to her for decision. This description fits Boccaccio's Criseida fairly accurately, but not Chaucer's Criseyde. For Chaucer's brilliance lies precisely in the way he makes us alive to the *involuntary* elements involved in the exercise of the will. Criseyde certainly imagines that Pandarus has presented her with a case in which she is free to choose one way or the other – she comforts herself, when he has left her, that she need not fear because

> ...man may love, of possibilite,
> A womman so, his herte may tobreste,
> And she naught love ayein, but if hire leste.   (II, 607–9)

But it is at this very point that Troilus rides past, and Criseyde finds herself unable to view the sight with the detachment she has just described; she is inevitably affected by the new knowledge she possesses.

> For of hire owen thought she wex al reed,
> Remembryng hire right thus, 'Lo, this is he
> Which that myn uncle swerith he moot be deed,
> But I on hym have mercy and pitee.'   (II, 652–5)

Tolstoy's brother Nicholas used to tell him that his wishes would come true if he first fulfilled certain conditions; the first of these conditions was to stand in a corner and *not* think of a white bear. Tolstoy commented: 'I remember how I used to get into a corner and try (but could not possibly manage) not to think of a white bear'. Criseyde's case as she thinks about *not* falling in love with Troilus seems to me of the same sort; the more she considers not doing so, the larger the position occupied in her mind by the possibility. The revelation of Troilus' love inevitably creates a new entity in her mind, a new set of emotions, of circumstances ready to form a nexus with external incidents and thus to take on the configurations of destiny.

The long and patient observation of this process in Books II and III teaches us to understand how it can be repeated, with contradictory results, in the movement towards betrayal in Book V. The changed external circumstances again exert their own pressure on Criseyde's mind, linking with her fears and her sense of emotional desolation to bring different possibilities to the fore. Again, there is no decision; the moment of betrayal is diffused through a long drawn-out process that renders it invisible. The gloomy stanza which describes the internal state of mind which is to coalesce with Diomede's external pressure in the shape of betrayal –

> Retornyng in hire soule ay up and down
> The wordes of this sodeyn Diomede,
> His grete estat, and perel of the town,
> And that she was allone and hadde nede
> Of frendes help;...

– does not conclude 'and thus she decided to stay'; it emphasizes that this is the beginning of a process whose conclusion is dispersed through a series of minute re-adjustments:

> ...and thus *bygan to brede*
> *The cause whi*, the sothe for to telle,
> That she took fully *purpos for to dwelle*.   (V, 1023–9)

We are now in the position to appreciate, not only Chaucer's debt to Boethius, but also his most original development of Boethian ideas. Boethius, as I have already suggested, sees Fortune as largely external; Chaucer on the other hand sees the processes of mutability as impregnating the inner life of man to the very depths of his being. The adjective 'slydynge', which Boethius applies to Fortune (I m. 5), Chaucer applies to

Criseyde's mind, telling us that she was 'slydynge of corage' (v, 825). Fortune, for Chaucer, is not merely apparent in the larger, more readily observable mutations in worldly affairs, it is a name we can also apply to the moment-by-moment mutations in Criseyde's mind, observable in her long soliloquy in Book II, to the opalescent shifts as one impulse or another spontaneously emerges. It is from these minute and ceaseless fluctuations that the larger movements of change are formed. In addressing Fortune with a capital F, man deceives himself into thinking that Fortune is an independent entity, existing apart from himself and from other agencies, whereas Fortune is simply the name for (what is to him) the random, the unplanned, the unforeseen, for mutability in all its manifestations, which include not only the accidents of the external world, but also the momentary oscillations within his own mind.

There is however a moment in *Troilus and Criseyde* where Fortune is associated with an external agency which apparently overrides human will – and that is the influence of the planets. At the moment when Criseyde is about to leave Pandarus' supper-party, Chaucer suddenly breaks the cheerful mood with two stanzas of gloomy foreboding.

> And after soper gonnen they to rise,
> At ese wel, with hertes fresshe and glade,
> And wel was hym that koude best devyse
> To liken hire, or that hire laughen made.
> He song; she pleyde; he tolde tale of Wade.
> But at the laste, as every thyng hath ende,
> She took hire leve, and nedes wolde wende.
>
> But O Fortune, executrice of wyrdes,
> O influences of thise hevenes hye!
> Soth is, that under God ye ben oure hierdes,
> Though to us bestes ben the causes wrie.
> This mene I now, for she gan homward hye,
> But execut was al bisyde hire leve
> The goddes wil; for which she moste bleve.
>
> The bente moone with hire hornes pale,
> Saturne and Jove, in Cancro joyned were,
> That swych a reyn from heven gan avale
> That every maner womman that was there
> Hadde of that smoky reyn a verray feere;
> At which Pandare tho lough, and seyde thenne,
> 'Now were it tyme a lady to gon henne!'   (III, 610–30)

How does this view of planetary influence sort with the views on chance and destiny that I have already outlined? And does it contradict or undermine the supposition that human will is an element in the 'causes flowynge togidere to hemself', in its assertion that 'the goddes wil' is executed regardless of Criseyde's 'leve'?

The first step in answering these questions is to identify the nature of the planetary conjunction described. Critics have, astonishingly, spent more time in trying to use this passage as a means of dating the composition of *Troilus and Criseyde* (by relating it to the real occurrence of such a conjunction) than in attempting to analyse its poetic function.[13] Poetically, the most important feature of the conjunction is that it is a malevolent one. The benevolent influence of Jupiter is outweighed by the malign effects of Saturn (described at length by the planet himself in the *Knight's Tale*), in combination with the Moon, in the unpropitious house of Cancer.[14] The conjunction therefore bodes eventual ill for the love-affair that is consummated under its auspices. But the description of the conjuction tells us more than this – it also tells us what it is that will bring about this ill. Saturn was traditionally interpreted in medieval mythic allegoresis as Time, since his Greek name, Cronos, was identified with the Greek word *chronos*.[15] The Moon is a traditional symbol of change, because of her constant waxing and waning.[16] Time and change hang threateningly over the love-affair which is shortly to be consummated; time and change bring it into being, time and change will destroy it. When understood, the planets appear not as agents of an independently exercised 'goddes wil', but as emblems (as well as representatives) of the natural forces through which the 'goddes wil' – the pattern of destiny – realizes itself. As in the Boethian scheme of things, destiny is executed by Fortune ('executrice of wyrdes'), by the individual chances that weave together the 'temporel ordenaunce' of destiny.

If this passage represents the planets as dominating human will, it is in order to show that the destinal ordinance that is being woven is one that *goes beyond* the wishes and predictions of the human contributors to it. Troilus and Criseyde are shortly to commit themselves to a consummated love as to their (beneficent) destiny, as we have seen; they assume that the pattern is now completed, it has achieved its final shape at that point. This passage reminds us that the destinal process will continue, and that the 'cas or aventure' (IV, 388) of Criseyde's exchange for Antenor will be the first in a different confluence of causes which will seal the final destiny of Troilus. The planetary conjunction images to perfection this 'double destiny'; its immediate effect is to bring the rain, cause of Criseyde's decision to stay the night, and thus, eventually, of the blissful consummation, while its ultimate effect is to subject the love-affair to the forces of time and change by which it is destroyed. Pandarus sees only the immediate effect; he rejoices in the rain that enables the execution of his will. Forgetful of the astrological calculations which he had taken care to complete before making his first approach to Criseyde (II, 74–5), he sees only that portion of the cosmological whole which is useful to his

immediate purposes. The description of Pandarus' preparations for the
supper-party shows his powers of control at their apparent zenith;
directing Troilus, coaxing Criseyde, picking a moonless night when rain
is threatening, so that the cosmos itself seems merely a tool of his grand
design. The words used of him at this point represent him as a kind of
mini-providence; his planning is referred to as 'purveiaunce', and it is
'Forncast and put in execucioun' just as divine providence is executed by
destiny (533, 521). The stanzas on the planetary conjunction reveal that
this appearance of all-embracing control is a pathetic sham. The solemn
apostrophe of Fortune introduces not only a note of foreboding but also
a sobering shift in perspective, as our vision widens with dramatic speed
from the cosy domestic interior of the dinner-party to the dizzying heights
of the cosmos, whence we glimpse humans crawling like 'bestes' on the
surface below. This dramatic effect makes clear with unforgettable impact
the limitations of human control. Pandarus' grand design is merely a feeble
fragment of a far vaster pattern, woven by mightier forces than he.

Chaucer's attempt to render the operations of chance and destiny in human
affairs was not confined to *Troilus and Criseyde*. They assume importance
in several of the *Canterbury Tales* – notably the *Man of Law's Tale*, the *Wife
of Bath's Tale*, the *Franklin's Tale*, and the *Nun's Priest's Tale*, but most of
all in the *Knight's Tale*, to which I shall devote the brief remaining space
of this essay.

As in *Troilus*, Chaucer takes pains in the *Knight's Tale* to alter his
Boccaccian source in order to emphasize the role of chance in the events
of the narrative.[17] The most striking example can be found in his altered
account of Palamon's escape from prison. In the *Teseida*, Palemone is driven
to make the attempt by discovering that Arcita has returned to Teseo's
court in disguise and is serving Emilia as her page (v, 1–8). The mechanics
of the escape are carefully and plausibly recounted, and once he is free,
Palemone goes straight to the grove outside Athens because he knows that
it is a favourite haunt of Arcita (v, 22, 33). Chaucer patiently unravels
this logically knit narrative sequence, in order to produce a narrative
dominated by chance. Knowing nothing of Arcite's presence in Athens,
Palamon simply happens (after seven years!) to escape:

> Were it by aventure or destynee –
> As, whan a thyng is shapen, it shal be   (1465–6)

The occurrence is, like Troilus' riding past the window, referred equally to
chance and destiny. Chaucer's apparent casualness in proposing the two
as alternatives is a mere narrative disguise, for here as in *Troilus* we shall
see that the one is a component of the other. He goes to the grove to hide
himself, and 'by aventure' (1506) Arcite makes for the same place. Not

only that, but 'by aventure' (1516) he wanders into the very path by whose side Palamon lies hidden, and then reveals his true identity in soliloquy. Chaucer's motive in creating this inherently improbable narrative can only have been to illustrate 'causes flowynge togidere to hemself' and creating destiny out of 'fortuit hap'. The final chance necessary to complete the pattern – in that it turns the knights' private squabble over Emily into a public contest capable of practical resolution – is the arrival of Theseus, which is duly heralded by an emphasis on destiny.

> The destinee, ministre general
> That executeth in the world over al
> The purveiaunce that God hath seyn biforn,
> So strong it is that, though the world had sworn
> The contrarie of a thyng by ye or nay,
> Yet somtyme it shal fallen on a day
> That falleth nat eft withinne a thousand yeer.   (1663–9)

The thousand-to-one chance fixes the shape of the destinal pattern for good or ill.

The rest of the narrative is equally full of chance events, most often signalled as such by the use of the key-words 'aventure', 'cas', or 'hap'. It is 'by aventure or cas' (1074) that Palamon first sees and falls in love with Emily, his fate, like Troilus', being sealed by chance – and Chaucer here alters the *Teseida*, in which the first glimpse belongs to Arcita (III, 11–12), as if to stress that it *is* simply the chance of being first-comer that will often determine a man's success in love. It is chance ('It happed', 1189; cf. 'aventure' at 1235) that brings Perotheus to Athens and thus effects Arcite's release. We are made conscious also of the alternative stories that chance could dictate, as Palamon and Arcite each speculate on various ways in which Fortune might produce events to favour the other's suit (1240–3, 1285–90). Finally, the tournament which Theseus decrees shall determine who is to marry Emily is a vast amphitheatre for chance ('fallyng nys nat but an aventure', 2722). Acknowledging, with true wisdom, the limitations of human control, Theseus eschews making the choice himself; not denying or combatting the role of chance, he merely provides a civilized context within which it can operate. The final chance of Arcite's death after victory is thus a blow, but not a crushing one, since Theseus' role throughout the narrative constitutes an acknowledgement of the powers of chance and an illustration of readiness to adapt to it.

However in the *Knight's Tale* as in *Troilus*, at an important moment in the poem we might be tempted to think that the course of events is *not* dictated merely by chance, but by the will of higher powers. For the *Knight's Tale*, like *Troilus*, represents human affairs as subject to planetary influence.[18] Just before the tournament, Palamon and Arcite pray to Venus

and Mars respectively to grant their wishes, and Chaucer temporarily
abandons the human plane of his narrative to show us the heated debate
that then breaks out between the conflicting celestial powers. For Palamon
and Arcite, Venus, Mars, Saturn, and the rest are 'gods'; when we look
closer, however, we can see that it is not as deities but as planets that they
exert power. Saturn's speech makes this plain:

> 'My cours, that hath so wyde for to turne,
> Hath moore power than woot any man.
> ...
> I do vengeance and pleyn correccioun,
> Whil I dwelle in the signe of the leoun.'   (2454–5, 2461–2)

It is because Saturn's sphere is the outermost in the planetary order (his
course thus being widest of all) that his influence dominates the planets
beneath him.[19] His overruling influence means that the lesser influences
exerted by Mars and Venus will resolve themselves into a malevolent
pattern; his sending of a 'furie infernal' to startle Arcite's horse is an
anthropomorphic representation of a cosmological phenomenon. It is
because Mars and Venus are planets, and not independent pagan deities,
that Palamon and Arcite win their favour; both knights take care to make
their pleas at the astrologically correct hour, when the planet's power is
at its height,[20] and response to human prayers follows according to a
quasi-physical law of cause and effect. The importance of this is that we
perceive that the planets act according to their nature, not according to
their whims. Their representation in human shape means we can 'read'
their behaviour in two ways – first, as the result of their own independent
wishes, and second, as the result of inevitable natural processes. As we
shift between these two views – from free agents to naturally impelled
forces – we are instructed in the illusions of control; we see that the
apparently independent movers are themselves moved by other powers.

The shift from the human to the cosmological plane has a similarly
instructive effect. Like the dramatic widening of vision in the passage
concerning the planets in Book III of *Troilus*, it expands way beyond the
possible reach of any sort of human control the kinds of causes which we
conceive as flowing together to make up the pattern of human destiny. We
are allowed, by poetic licence as it were, a fleeting glimpse of the hidden
causes behind what appears to the human onlookers as the chance
('aventure', 2703) of Arcite's fall (as if, in Boethius' example, we were
privileged to see the man burying the gold and thus to know the 'cause'
of its being found). But in being vouchsafed this glimpse, we are only being
shown one more cause, not the final cause that lies behind all of them.
We have a shift in perspective, not the complete vision which belongs only
to providence, seeing 'alle thinges to-hepe'. We have left the human

plane; we have not left the cosmos, or the realm of time. It is in Theseus' final speech that we perceive this most fully. His opening reference to the 'Firste Moevere' reminds us that there is a power beyond the planets, by which they are moved. They do not operate of their own volition; their power is only a secondary one. *A fortiori*, the same holds good for human beings. Only from the perspective of the First Mover, which is forever inaccessible to mortals, could the final causes of events be understood, and the shape which would give them final meaning be perceived. Theseus emphasizes our perception of 'temporel ordenaunce' as a series of individual destinies, whose end is determined by the natural processes of change and decay – the tree falls, the river runs dry, man dies. The larger shape, the whole of which these individual experiences are part, remains hidden; human beings can perceive only what Boethius calls the 'entrechaungeable mutacioun' (IV pr. 6) by which the processes of decay and renewal work themselves out. The planets too are part of this 'entrechaungeable mutacioun'; they are not the agents by which it is set in motion.

Since man is bound to time and change, he must embrace these conditions of his existence, for good or ill. But time and change do not always bring disaster. Theseus' humble acknowledgement of the inevitability of change and death concludes with an attempt to realize the beneficent possibilities created by the shifting kaleidoscope of chance. Arcite's death is irreversible, but it provides the chance to create a new configuration with the marriage of Palamon and Emily. Whereas at the end of *Troilus* chance works to close off possibilities, here there survives the opportunity, gladly perceived and realized by Theseus, to move forwards, to allow the process of mutability to carry one on to happiness. Caught in the realization of his tragic destiny, Troilus perceives 'necessitee' as a cruel trap; in the more optimistic configurations of the *Knight's Tale*, we can see that it is possible to 'maken vertu of necessitee' (3042) – not merely to 'grin and bear it', but to transform necessity *into* 'vertu', to respond to the pattern as it forms with a recognition of its passing chances for good, as well as the faith that its final shape will be revealed as concordant with the 'cheyne of love'.

Chaucer's thinking on the question of whether the world is governed by 'fortunous hap' or by a benign ordering power, is fundamental to his most serious poetry. In reading that poetry, we must in consequence give due attention to his presentation of *event*, rather than focussing on the 'characters' of Criseyde and Troilus, or Palamon and Arcite, as sole determinants of the narrative development. We must be alive to his use of words like 'cas', 'aventure' or 'destinee' (and to others, such as 'entencioun', 'purveiaunce', 'ordinaunce', 'governaunce', which also belong to his exploration of Boethian problems)[21] as signalling his reflections on the nature of the forces which work on human beings, and the extent of their own possibilities for action. Chaucer is outdone by none in his ability to reproduce the idiosyncratic details of human speech and action, but his deepest interest in investigating human psychology is to uncover the subtlest manifestations of time and change at work in human emotions, shaping the course of our lives.

Notes

1 The issues dealt with in this essay have been discussed by numerous other writers, and it is not possible to indicate in detail points where my own treatment corresponds to or diverges from theirs. The reader is referred to some particularly important contributions: Howard R. Patch, 'Troilus on Determinism', *Speculum*, 6 (1931), 225–43; Morton W. Bloomfield, 'Distance and Predestination in *Troilus and Criseyde*', PMLA, 72 (1957), 14–26; Walter Clyde Curry, 'Destiny in *Troilus and Criseyde*', in *Chaucer and the Mediaeval Sciences*, rev. edn (New York, 1960), pp. 241–98. All three articles are reprinted in *Chaucer Criticism*, eds. Richard J. Schoeck and Jerome Taylor, 2 vols. (Notre Dame, Ind., 1961), vol. 2; Bloomfield's article is also reprinted in *Chaucer's Troilus: Essays in Criticism*, ed. Stephen A. Barney (London, 1980.)
2 Comparison of the two texts is easiest in the edition of *Troilus and Criseyde* by B. A. Windeatt (London/New York, 1984), which places the Italian text alongside corresponding passages in Chaucer; here no parallel is given, but the source of the scene in *Filostrato* II, 82 is noted.
3 For a more detailed demonstration of this, see Jill Mann, 'Troilus' Swoon', *Chaucer Review*, 14 (1980), 319–35, at pp. 320–1.
4 This is even more true of his efforts in the bedroom scene of Book III; see Mann, 'Troilus' Swoon', pp. 325–6.
5 For the numerous other examples of these and connected words which play a part in the development of this theme in *Troilus*, see *A Concordance to the Complete Works of Geoffrey Chaucer*, eds. John S. P. Tatlock and Arthur G. Kennedy (Gloucester, Mass., 1963).
6 The most comprehensive study of Chaucer's debt to Boethius is Bernard L. Jefferson, *Chaucer and the Consolation of Philosophy of Boethius* (Princeton, NJ, 1917).
7 The most obvious example of suspense is the ending of Book II ('O myghty God, what shal he seye?': 1757), but the whole Horaste story, for example, increases narrative tension and our sense of precariousness up to the consummation scene.
8 In the preceding essay, Mark Lambert shows how Chaucer deliberately fashioned the parting scene in Book IV as an 'alternative ending' to the story; had Criseyde not revived from her swoon in the nick of time, we should have had a Romeo-and-Juliet-type ending, which would have made this a story of fidelity unto death, rather than a story of classic betrayal.
9 See further Mann, 'Troilus' Swoon', p. 330.
10 I owe this point to Dr Philip Davis of the University of Liverpool.
11 For a subtle, sensitive and full analysis of Criseyde's internal monologue and its relations to the surrounding narrative, which coincides very closely with the next section of my discussion, see Donald R. Howard, 'Experience,

Language and Consciousness: "Troilus and Criseyde", II, 596–931' in *Medieval Literature and Folklore Studies: Essays in Honor of Francis Lee Utley*, eds. Jerome Mandel and Bruce A. Rosenburg (New Brunswick, 1970), pp. 173–92; repr. in *Chaucer's Troilus*, ed. Barney.

12 This analogy is based on those devised by the Stoics to express their theory of necessity and free will (see A. A. Long, *Problems in Stoicism* (London, 1971), p. 180); there is of course no question of Chaucer having direct knowledge of these theories, but he seems independently to have arrived at similar ideas.

13 See the articles listed by F. N. Robinson in the Introduction to his Explanatory Notes on the poem, p. 811, and more recently, J. D. North, 'Kalenderes Enlumyned Ben They: Some Astronomical Themes in Chaucer', *Review of English Studies*, ns 20 (1969), 129–54, 257–83, 418–44, at pp. 142–4. John J. O'Connor ('The Astronomical Dating of Chaucer's *Troilus*', *Journal of English and Germanic Philology*, 55 (1956), 556–62) insists on the storial significance of the conjunction, but relates it to the fall of Troy and the heavy rain, rather than to the ultimate outcome of the love-affair. Chauncey Wood (*Chaucer and the Country of the Stars* (Princeton, 1970), pp. 47–8) also focuses on the rain, which he sees as a bathetically deflatory result of so awe-inspiring a conjunction.

14 Cancer was the mansion of the Moon (North, 'Kalenderes', p. 136), and would thus strengthen her influence. Jupiter at first seems the 'odd man out' in this predominantly malevolent grouping. I suggest that here, as in the *Knight's Tale*, he has a double role: first, as one of the seven planets (in which role he brings the short-term happiness experienced by the lovers), and second, as a mythic representative of the power of the Christian God, the providence which lies behind the whole conjunction and subjects it to its own ultimate plan.

15 Isidore of Seville, *Etymologiae* VIII. xi. 31: *Vnde et eum Graeci Cronos nomen habere dicunt, id est tempus, quod filios suos fertur devorasse, hoc est annos, quos tempus produxerit, in se revolvit...*

16 See *Romaunt of the Rose*, 5331–50; *House of Fame*, 2114–16; *Complaint of Mars*, 235, for the moon as an image of change.

17 Excerpts from Boccaccio's *Teseida*, including those which form a source for the *Knight's Tale*, are to be found in *Chaucer's Boccaccio: Sources of Troilus and the Knight's and Franklin's Tales*, ed. and trans. N. R. Havely (Cambridge, 1980).

18 For an astrologically based interpretation of the whole poem, see Douglas Brooks and Alastair Fowler, 'The Meaning of Chaucer's *Knight's Tale*', *Medium Aevum*, 39 (1970), 123–46.

19 In the medieval cosmological scheme, the planets were thought to move in concentric spheres, arranged in the order: Moon, Mercury, Venus, Sun, Mars, Jupiter, Saturn. Then came the sphere of the fixed stars, and finally the Primum Mobile or First Moving Sphere, which moves all those beneath it. God is the First Mover of the whole cosmos. For a brief account, see Edward Grant, *Physical Science in the Middle Ages* (Cambridge, 1971), chapter V, 'Earth, Heavens and Beyond'.

20 See John Livingston Lowes, *Geoffrey Chaucer* (London, 1934), pp. 10–13.

21 For a discussion of Chaucer's use of the last three words to develop Boethian themes, see Jill Mann 'Parents and Children in the "Canterbury Tales"' in *Literature in Fourteenth-Century England*, eds. Piero Boitani and Anna Torti (Tübingen/Cambridge, 1983), pp. 165–83.

6   The *Canterbury Tales*: Personal drama or experiments in poetic variety?

READERS sometimes neglect what is most extraordinary about the *Canterbury Tales*: its dazzling variety of stories and styles. Although story-collections were a recognized literary form long before Chaucer (and were especially popular in the late Middle Ages, as shown by Boccaccio's *Decameron* and the *Confessio Amantis* of Chaucer's friend John Gower), no other example of the genre contains the radical literary individuality of the *Canterbury Tales* nor creates such complex relationships among its different parts. Chaucer himself had earlier experimented with the form in the unfinished *Legend of Good Women*, but the *Legend* is a disappointment to most Chaucerians, largely because its stories of suffering women are so similar in approach and content. Monotony also mars a story-collection within the *Canterbury Tales*: the apparently endless tragedies of the *Monk's Tale* are finally halted by the Knight because he finds them too pessimistic, though some readers welcome the intervention because the stories have become boring. Yet boring is the last word one would use to describe the *Canterbury Tales* as a whole. The collection is energized by unexpected juxtapositions of styles and subject matter, so that, for example, a long romance of ancient heroism comes before a short, witty tale of local lust and an account of alchemical swindlers follows a story about ancient martyrdom.

For many, the clearest signals of the variety of the *Canterbury Tales* are the sharply differentiated tellers and their intricate relationships before, after, and sometimes during the tales. No other story-collection has a frame that is so lively and dynamic. In contrast to the uniformly aristocratic company of the *Decameron* or the two speakers in Gower's *Confessio* (the Lover and Genius), Chaucer's pilgrim-tellers come from a wide range of late medieval clerical and lay estates: a delicate squire rides next to scurrilous churls and worldly businessmen next to a poor but saintly parson. Like the rural retreat from the plague that occasions the *Decameron*, the Canterbury pilgrimage is presented as a real event, but unlike the Italian work, whose careful symmetry demands that each of the ten characters tell a tale on an assigned topic on each of ten days, the English narrative permits violent interruptions and unexpected changes in direction.

The plan of tale-telling in order of social rank which is apparently intended by the Host is quickly subverted beyond repair when the drunken Miller insists that he, and not the Monk, will tell the second Canterbury tale and 'quite' the Knight's noble sentiments (I, 3120–7). But before the Miller can begin, the Reeve angrily speaks up and vows to answer in kind the slanders he anticipates. As the journey proceeds, more surprises occur: two tales are abruptly cut off, while two others remain unfinished, probably deliberately so. A quarrel breaks out between the Friar and Summoner during the Wife of Bath's performance (which also contains an interruption by the Pardoner), and they continue it before and within their own tales. Later, two strangers ride up to join the company, and, soon after, the Cook is called upon for a story (though an incomplete tale had already been assigned him in the first fragment), but he proves too drunk and falls from his horse. Although Chaucer includes himself as a member of this boisterous company and even tells two tales (to no great approval), he adopts the role of benign incompetence familiar from his earlier works and insists that he is only a reporter with no power over the words and actions of others (I, 725–38). As a result of such narrative diffidence, the *Canterbury Tales* contains no logical order of events or explicit hierarchy of values, but all remains in flux and on the road. That the work is unfinished undoubtedly makes it seem all the more life-like.

The originality of the frame narrative has encouraged many to see the relationship between the pilgrims and their tales as the central achievement of the *Canterbury Tales*. Although such an approach had been developing for over two hundred years, the most influential modern exponent of the so-called 'dramatic theory' is undoubtedly George Lyman Kittredge. In *Chaucer and His Poetry*, Kittredge argued that the individual tales are not told in Chaucer's own voice, but that each is a dramatic expression of the personality of its particular teller: 'the Pilgrims do not exist for the sake of the story, but *vice versa*. Structurally regarded, the stories are merely long speeches expressing, directly or indirectly, the characters of the several persons. They are more or less comparable, in this regard, to the soliloquies of Hamlet or Iago or Macbeth.'[1] Kittredge's view has been adapted and made less extreme by later dramatic critics, but his central assumption – that the Canterbury pilgrims have complex, believable personalities that intimately inform their individual tales – is still widely, if unsystematically, accepted today, with few feeling the need to justify its validity. The dramatic interpretation has surely contributed much to our understanding of the *Canterbury Tales*, especially by calling attention to its diversity, but the crippling limitation of the approach is that it leads readers to concentrate on what is less interesting and less knowable in the work: the characters of the tellers instead of the poetry itself. The special genius of the *Canterbury Tales* is not so much its frame narrative, fascinating as that can be, as it is Chaucer's radical literary experiments. We must look beyond the supposed personalities of the pilgrims to the poetic individuality of the tales themselves.

Those who see the *Canterbury Tales* as a drama of personality naturally make much of the magnificent descriptions of the pilgrims in the *General Prologue*; indeed, many readers in past centuries seem to have read no farther. Yet Chaucer's opening portraits are most extraordinary not because they give a full and realistic picture of late medieval English life (though they have much to tell us), still less because they contain psychologically believable individuals, but because of their literary skill and wit. The usual medieval character portrait is static and distant, as Chaucer himself demonstrates when he suddenly, and surely ironically, mimics it briefly to describe Criseyde, Troilus, and Diomede in Book v of *Troilus and Criseyde* (799–840). At its most elaborate, medieval characterization is often nothing more than an interminable list of the subject's physical parts, as in the following very brief excerpt from Paris' first sight of Helen, taken from the standard medieval history of Troy and itself adapted as a model of portraiture in an influential medieval rhetorical manual: 'He also admired how her even shoulder-blades, by a gentle descent to her flat back, with a depression between them, joined each side gracefully and pleasantly. He admired her arms, which were of proper length to induce the sweetest embraces, while her hands were plump and a little rounded, and the slender tips of her fingers, which were proportionally long, revealed ivory nails.'[2]

In contrast to such dull, trivial inventories, the portraits in the *General Prologue*, while equally detailed, are dynamic and vivid. The variety that distinguishes the *Canterbury Tales* as a whole is fully present from the very beginning. Chaucer's pilgrims are arranged in no clear order or hierarchy, as his disingenuous apology ('My wit is short, ye may wel understonde': I, 746) makes clear, and their descriptions vary in length, point of view, and tone. The longest (the Friar's) is sixty-one lines, the shortest (the Cook's) only nine; some emphasize what the pilgrim wears, some what he does, some what he thinks. Although the Knight is described quite formally from the outside, we go inside the mind of the Monk to share his private, rebellious thoughts. Chaucer does not restrict himself to a single consistent narrative voice in the *General Prologue*, as is sometimes claimed, but is variously naive and shrewd, devout and worldly – bluffly endorsing the murderous Shipman one moment, while slyly questioning the Physician's religious faith and business practices the next. The standards of judgement continually shift: the pretensions of the Merchant or the

Man of Law produce social satire, while the Pardoner is condemned and the Parson praised in strictly Christian terms. The portraits are built on memorable details and telling insights, such as the Prioress' careful table manners and unsophisticated French or the simple pleasures of municipal office enjoyed by the wives of the Guildsmen. Few readers can forget the Cook's 'mormal', the Miller's wart, and the Franklin's hospitality ('It snewed in his hous of mete and drynke': I, 345), or the terrifying countenance of the Summoner and the ambiguous sexuality of the Pardoner.

Given such diverse and energetic portraits, it is all too easy to imagine the Canterbury pilgrims as fully developed and psychologically complex characters, like those we know from the realistic novel or popular film. Scholars have even argued that Chaucer must have had real-life models and suggested specific names, but the latest studies confirm what some earlier readers understood – the *General Prologue* describes types rather than specific individuals. In the eighteenth century, Dryden and Blake argued that the Canterbury pilgrims illustrate universal categories of human nature, and in her recent *Chaucer and Medieval Estates Satire*, Jill Mann has shown that the portraits are largely based on material from the traditional descriptions of different occupational 'estates'.[3] As the labels Knight, Miller, Prioress, and even Wife suggest, the *General Prologue* describes professions rather than believable personalities, and many of its pilgrims are composite portraits of an estate. No single warrior could have fought in all the battles attributed to the Knight, just as the Monk and Friar exemplify the full range (and not just some) of the vices associated with their respective callings.

Even when the *General Prologue* far transcends standard medieval portraiture and seems most complex, the result is not the rounded, believable characters required for dramatic interpretations so much as intriguing, incomplete puzzles. Chaucer often creates the illusion of life-like individuality through brief insinuations, as in the famous couplet about the Man of Law ('Nowher so bisy a man as he ther nas, / And yet he semed bisier than he was': I, 321–2) or the observation that 'ther wiste no wight' that the Merchant 'was in dette' (I, 280). But such lines suggest more than they actually state. They are so framed that the reader may guess, but cannot certainly know, how busy the Lawyer actually is, or whether no one recognizes the Merchant to be in debt because he is not or because he has hidden it so well. Chaucer's most subtle portraits stubbornly avoid final judgement and thus allow a range of interpretation. The courteous and 'pitous' Prioress, for instance, has been seen as everything from a corrupter of holy office to an attractive, if sentimental, woman of style. Such diversity of opinion is a tribute to Chaucer's skill, but the reader who chooses any single view, and interprets the tale in its light, runs the risk of serious distortion because of a subjective reaction to a brief and deliberately ambiguous portrait. The *General Prologue* rarely provides characterization that is specific or clear enough for the reader to have any confidence that it will be more than generally useful in understanding the tale that follows.

The pilgrims are not developed much further in their later appearances on the road to Canterbury. When he so desires, Chaucer can create characters as complex and convincing as any in medieval literature, as we see most memorably in *Troilus and Criseyde*, but the frame of the *Canterbury Tales* suggests that the poet did not concern himself overmuch with the psychological depth or consistency of his pilgrim-narrators, though we must not forget that the work is unfinished. Many of the pilgrims – such as the Squire, Physician, Second Nun, and Shipman – make only the briefest appearance, or none, outside the *General Prologue*. More revealing are the frequent inconsistencies between what we are told about a pilgrim in his portrait and what we discover later. Consider the contrast between the stiff, secretive Merchant in his portrait and the reckless husband who freely exposes his marital troubles in the prologue to his tale. The pleasure-loving Monk of the *General Prologue* also seems to have little in common with the cleric of the same name who ignores the Host's suggestive repartee in order to tell his solemn tragedies; similarly, the old age of the Reeve, which is so important in his prologue, is not mentioned in his portrait. Of course, clever readers will be able to construct a consistent character even out of the most random and contradictory materials, but in so doing they must supplement what the poet has written with their own inventions, and thus they rarely agree with one another.

If most of the Canterbury pilgrims are relatively undeveloped and appear only briefly after the *General Prologue*, there are some striking exceptions. Three pilgrims especially, who are often at the centre of dramatic interpretations of the *Canterbury Tales* – the Canon's Yeoman, the Wife of Bath, and the Pardoner – come forward in the body of the work to give detailed accounts of their lives. Yet even though all three possess extraordinary narrative energy, and contribute much to the total effect of the *Canterbury Tales*, none has great depth of character because each is more of a dramatic voice than a believable personality. We see a performance rather than the psychological causes behind it. Like Chaucer's other pilgrims, the three are essentially occupational types and what they tell us about themselves has only a general relationship to their stories.

The *Canon's Yeoman's Tale* shows the flexibility of the Canterbury frame and its potential for narrative surprise. The pilgrims are travelling through 'Boghtoun under Blee' when they are suddenly overtaken by a hard-riding canon and his yeoman to whom the narrator responds strongly (for example, 'it was joye for to seen hym swete!': VIII, 579). The Host's initial questioning of the Yeoman prompts extravagant praise of the Canon and his achievements, including the claim that he can pave the road 'al of silver and of gold' (VIII, 626). When Harry wonders why such a distinguished man is dressed in filthy rags, the Yeoman laments that his master will never prosper, and then begins to divulge the failures that alchemy has brought. The Canon attempts to stop these revelations, but when he fails he flees the company in 'sorwe and shame' (VIII, 702), leaving the Yeoman to tell all: 'Syn that my lord is goon, I wol nat spare; / Swich thyng as that I knowe, I wol declare' (VIII, 718–19).

The exciting drama in the *Canon's Yeoman's Prologue* is one of the best-developed scenes in the frame narrative, and perhaps shows Chaucer exploring the possibilities of the form at a late stage of the *Canterbury Tales*. But we should not confuse any of this with genuine psychological realism. Why does the Yeoman change so quickly from excessive praise of his master to bitter condemnation? Why does he decide now, within minutes of joining the pilgrims, to confess everything to Harry Bailly? One could imagine circumstances and motives that would make his actions plausible – and many dramatic critics have – but Chaucer does not even bother to try. He is more interested in the result of the Yeoman's decision to confess than in establishing the psychology that brought it about. As often, the primary purpose of this prologue is to introduce the subsequent tale.

The *Canon's Yeoman's Tale* itself has interested dramatic critics because its first half, which is less a story than a hodgepodge of alchemical lore, is drawn from the teller's own experiences. Critics often read Chaucer's tales as though they were as personally revealing as Browning's dramatic monologues, but, in fact, the *prima pars* of the *Canon's Yeoman's Tale* is the only explicitly autobiographical tale (as opposed to prologue) in the entire *Canterbury Tales*:

> With this Chanoun I dwelt have seven yeer,
> And of his science am I never the neer.
> Al that I hadde I have lost therby,
> And, God woot, so hath many mo than I.   (720–3)

As the last line of the quotation suggests, however, the *prima pars*, though autobiographical, is only superficially personal. The Yeoman and his experiences are offered as a demonstration of the errors of many; he is not an individual, but an exemplum: 'Lat every man be war by me for evere!' (737).

The first half of the tale is less about the Canon's Yeoman than about his profession. It tells us almost nothing special about the teller because its subject from first to last is the 'cursed craft' (830) and 'elvysshe nyce loore' (842) of alchemy. Indeed, the word 'craft' occurs more often here than in any other tale. Thus dramatic narration need not mean personal disclosure: as early as the *House of Fame*, Chaucer understood how effectively a vivacious speaking voice could present technical information, especially scientific lore. Although the Eagle who lectures 'Geffrey' so authoritatively on the way to the House of Fame makes the journey delightful for the reader, he has no more than a cartoon personality. Similarly, the colloquial, breathless, occasionally confused voice in the *Canon's Yeoman's Tale* defines no individual psychology (the Yeoman has been judged at various times both stupid and shrewd), but instead illustrates the mixture of chaos and enthusiasm among all alchemists. The most memorable detail we learn about the Canon's Yeoman is purely external and generic to his task (his leaden complexion from too much blowing on the fire). The voice accomplishes its task – it is flexible, aware of the audience, and lively. It has kept us interested while demonstrating the delusions of alchemy, but we have learned nothing idiosyncratic or personal about the Yeoman. The dramatic voice is nothing more, and nothing less, than a brilliant narrative device.

The second part of the *Canon's Yeoman's Tale*, about another canon who tricks a greedy priest into believing he knows how to turn base metal into silver, is told in the same animated voice, with even more moral outrage: 'This false chanoun – the foule feend hym fecche!' (1159). Despite the teller's explicit denial, dramatic critics often assume that the Yeoman is actually speaking about his master; but the narrative logic is surely wrong (why would the confessing Yeoman suddenly turn coy?), and there is no reason to believe that the Canon and his Yeoman are crooks – everything we are told suggests they are victims of a sincere belief in the science. The delight some readers find in developing such faint hints of personal drama is misplaced and distorts the purpose of the tale. Chaucer wants us to understand the folly of alchemy, not the folly of one or two individual pilgrims. The *Canon's Yeoman's Tale* is an extended occupational portrait. The first part of the tale demonstrates one of the vices of alchemy (deluding oneself), while the second part demonstrates another (deluding others); the connection between the two is thematic rather than personal. The dramatic consistency of the tale is further undermined by its conclusion (1388–1481), in which a more learned and thoughtful voice than we have heard before assesses the pros and cons of alchemy before advising that men should wait for God to reveal its secrets. The different tone will bother only those who imagine that the tale has been told by a complex and believable personality throughout. In fact, the most interesting relationships are literary rather than dramatic; not between the Canon's Yeoman and his tale, but, for instance, between the sterile work and hellish fire of the *Canon's Yeoman's Tale* and the fruitful work and divine fire of the preceding *Second Nun's Tale*.

The Wife of Bath is undoubtedly the most fully and consistently developed of the Canterbury pilgrims. Her prologue is the longest in the *Tales* and offers a clever defence of marriage as well as detailed and roughly chronological accounts of her five husbands. Alison was apparently a great favourite with readers from the start. Chaucer himself cites her twice, in his *Envoy to Bukton* and within the *Merchant's Tale*, and it has been persuasively argued that her role grew over the years, perhaps in response to public demand.[4] If so, her evolution is something like that of Shakespeare's Falstaff, whom she resembles in so many other ways. Like him, she derives from an allegorical source, possesses great verbal powers, and represents an exaggeration of one aspect of human nature more than a convincing human being. Like Falstaff also, the Wife has moments of real pathos – the regret for her lost youth or her troubles with her fifth husband, Jankyn, for instance – but the reader never knows quite how to take these scenes because everything important we think we know about her comes from her own mouth.

Like the Canon's Yeoman, the Wife of Bath has a distinct speaking voice, though it is heard only in her prologue. In the first part, before the interruption of the Pardoner, the Wife produces a travesty of traditional Christian teachings about marriage with her brilliant misuse of medieval logic and Biblical quotation. Question: Should one marry more than once? Answer: Christ's views on this are difficult to understand, but certainly God's 'gentil text' to 'wexe and multiplye' is clear enough – and look at all Solomon's wives (9–44). Question: Is virginity commanded? Answer: If so, where would new virgins come from? and does not a household need wooden vessels as well as gold? and why then were humans given 'membres of generacion' (62–134)? The wife's eclectic arguments never seriously threaten orthodox thought, but their cleverness is wonderfully entertaining. Later, we see more evidence of her terrifying fluency when she repeats a speech used on her old husbands that masterfully combines false reasoning ('And sith a man is moore resonable / Than womman is, ye moste been suffrable'), stunning vulgarity ('Is it for ye wolde have my queynte allone?'), and magnanimous generosity ('Wy, taak it al! lo, have it every deel!': 441–5). Despite her opening claim to follow 'experience' rather than 'auctoritee', the Wife of Bath is an intellectual *manqué*, a would-be clerk, who, like Falstaff, is fully powerful only in language.

The other long autobiographical prologue in the *Canterbury Tales* is that of the equally verbal Pardoner. When he interrupts the Wife, the Pardoner calls her a 'noble prechour' (III, 165), a subject on which he is an expert. Now in his own prologue, he explains his use of the pulpit to impress the 'lewed peple' (437) and make them give him money. The Pardoner is a master of the techniques of pious deceit, and his descendants can still be found today in revival tents and on television broadcasts. Like the expert huckster he is, the Pardoner knows all the tricks of the trade. He puts on a multi-media show that includes papal bulls and fake relics, but his most effective skill is his use of words. His verbal devices include 'olde stories' (436), 'false japes' (394), and indirect attacks on his personal enemies (412–22); his showy Latin quotations (344–6) are balanced by a sniggering reference to a wife sleeping with two or three priests (369–71). The Pardoner is justly proud of his command of language. With his 'hauteyn speche' he makes his words ring out 'as round as gooth a belle' (330–1), and the effect is spectacular: 'Myne handes and my tonge goon so yerne / That it is joye to se my bisynesse' (398–9).

Like the Canon's Yeoman, the Wife of Bath and the Pardoner are primarily dramatic voices. Their prologues contain magnificent performances, but they do not reveal individual personality. Instead of believable human beings, the Pardoner and the Wife are verbal artists, skilled users of words. However much the reader enjoys their linguistic virtuosity, nothing that either says can be trusted. Most of what we know about them is what they themselves choose to tell us in their prologues, and a persistent theme of both is their ability to manipulate others with false speech. Because we have no way of verifying the truth of what either says, the reader who desires to define the 'real' Pardoner or Wife behind the performances can do so only subjectively. We may suspect that the Wife's final relationship with Jankyn was not as harmonious as she asserts, or wonder about the jolly wenches the Pardoner boasts of having in every town, but we can be no more certain about these claims than about anything else either says. As a result, critics have some justification for arguing that the Pardoner is everything from damned to comic to Christ-like, and that the Wife of Bath is either a lusty lover of life or a pitiful example of the wages of sin.

The mistake is to imagine that Chaucer has given a full and consistent human personality to either. Despite the many lines devoted to them, both the Pardoner and the Wife, like the other Canterbury pilgrims, are essentially occupational types. Although the Wife's prologue may seem intimate because it concerns domestic life, all that she ever talks about is her profession — marriage. We hear nothing about weaving (her first vocation) and no details of the extra-marital sexual encounters she hints at; other parts of her life, like her gossips or pilgrimages, are mentioned only when directly relevant to her husbands. The Pardoner is equally professional. For all his seeming revelations, his skill in the pulpit is really all that we know about him and the only subject of his apparently personal prologue. Although Chaucer has developed them far beyond their original models in the *Roman de la Rose*, the Wife and Pardoner retain an allegorical core: she is the standard nightmare of medieval antifeminism and he the corrupt preacher he boasts himself to be. This is not to say that either is dull or simple. As dynamic allegorical characters such as Gluttony or Lady Meed in Langland's *Piers Plowman* demonstrate, literary vitality and excitement are not the same as psychological realism. In fiction, it is often the purity of a characterization that makes it memorable.

Although the Pardoner and Wife of Bath are highly developed in their prologues, the relationship between these pilgrims and their tales is not especially revealing. The *Wife of Bath's Tale* is much shorter than the preceding prologue. The story of the old hag who wins back both youth and a vigorous husband can be read as the Wife's wish-fulfilment, if one so desires, but the voice of the teller has changed completely. The style of the tale is more reserved and objective than that of the prologue (only an early dig at friars reminds us of the earlier tone), and the delicate speeches in the tale on gentility, poverty, and age sound nothing like the Wife's aggressive materialism and impudent self-confidence. The *Pardoner's Tale* is more closely connected to its teller (it purports to be his standard homily), but for all its use of preaching techniques, its resemblance to an actual sermon is probably not great. Moreover, while the melodramatic denunciation of the three tavern sins is clearly appropriate to a corrupt preacher, the profundity and quiet austerity of the exemplum of the 'riotoures' seem far beyond his understanding. There is no reason to believe that either part reveals anything about the Pardoner as a man. As with the Canon's Yeoman, the most fruitful relationships are literary rather than personal. Rather than pursuing the elusive psyches of even these highly developed pilgrims, the reader would do better to look closely at how the *Wife of Bath's Tale* differs from other experiments with romance narrative in the *Canterbury Tales*. Similarly, one might compare the *Pardoner's Tale* with Chaucer's other forms of Christian instruction in the collection, or examine its inner conflict between two kinds of religious poetry – the flamboyant denunciation in contrast to the haunting exemplum. We know very little that is certain about the personal lives of the Wife and Pardoner, but the poetry of their tales is fully available to all for literary analysis and comparison.

Although few, if any, of the tales reveal the psychology of their pilgrims in any significant way, Chaucer has so designed the *Canterbury Tales* that there is usually some kind of correspondence between teller and tale. The poet himself calls attention to this in a warning to fastidious readers before the *Miller's Tale*:

> The Millere is a cherl, ye knowe wel this;
> So was the Reeve eek and othere mo,
> And harlotrie they tolden bothe two.   (I, 3182–4)

Note, however, that the relationship Chaucer claims here is extremely broad and the general result of class rather than individual personality – a low-born pilgrim will naturally tell a low story.

The natural appropriateness of tale to teller is clearly demonstrated in the first fragment of the *Canterbury Tales*, the most finished part of the work and the best indication of what the whole would have been like had Chaucer lived to complete it. After the *General Prologue*, the noble Knight's philosophical story of chivalry, love, and 'gentilesse' is followed, as Chaucer warns, by three ribald fabliaux told by churls. Elsewhere in the *Canterbury Tales*, a similar congruity between estate and kind of story is common. The two nuns tell religious tales, the Squire and Franklin tell romances, and the Pardoner and Parson explore the effects of sin. Sometimes the relationship may be even more specific. The voice of the pompous Man of Law has been detected in his highly rhetorical tale of the trials of Custance and that of the plain, clever Clerk in his story of Griselda.

But despite such general agreement, the intense, personal association between teller and tale automatically assumed by followers of the dramatic theory is rare in the *Canterbury Tales*. The classical learning of the *Knight's Tale*, the polished art of the *Miller's Tale*, the moral delicacy of the *Friar's Tale*, the cleverness and learning of the *Summoner's Tale*, and the dogged didacticism of the *Monk's Tale* – none of these qualities, but rather their reverse, is suggested by what we know of the pilgrims outside the tales. Perhaps the most extreme disjunction of teller and tale is the contrast between the rough, murderous Shipman of the *General Prologue* and the cool, sophisticated art of the *Shipman's Tale*.

Given such loose connections between teller and tale, dramatic readings of the *Canterbury Tales* are frequently either banal (the *Knight's Tale* fits the Knight because it is about chivalry) or highly imaginative (the *Prioress's Tale* has been said to reveal its teller to be everything from a frustrated mother to a vicious anti-Semite). Even worse, the approach sometimes leads critics to assume that the supposed limitations of a pilgrim mean that the tale assigned to him or her is severely flawed or even deliberately bad. Tales so regarded are often moral or religious works, such as the *Tale of Melibee* or the *Prioress's*, *Second Nun's*, *Man of Law's*, *Physician's*, and *Clerk's Tales*, but others, including the *Squire's Tale* and *Franklin's Tale*, have been similarly dismissed. It is possible that Chaucer wanted most or all of these tales to be read ironically, but it is more probable that the dramatic approach is being used to support modern prejudices about what makes a good story.

Dramatic interpretations sometimes manage to trivialize Chaucer's greatest achievements by associating them too closely with their assigned tellers. A flagrant example is the attempt to read the Merchant into the extraordinary tale of the marriage of old January to 'fresshe' May. Neither the secretive Merchant of the *General Prologue* nor the recklessly confessional husband of the *Merchant's Prologue* has much in common with the protagonist of the *Merchant's Tale*, despite the circular reasoning by which dramatic critics derive the biography of the Merchant almost entirely from the story of January, after which teller and tale are, not unsurprisingly, found to be in remarkable agreement. The relationship between the *Merchant's Prologue*, in which the Merchant briefly and bitterly condemns his wife of two months, and the tale that follows is introductory rather than psychological. The Merchant's complaints are a conventional piece of medieval antifeminism, not a significant revelation of individual personality. They serve nicely to prepare the reader for a tale about married woe, but they do not begin to define the specific shape of that tale – the Merchant's problems with his wife are different from and more familiar than January's. It is reductive in the extreme to derive all the complexity and dark brilliance of the *Merchant's Tale* from the simple disappointments of a new husband. January is one of Chaucer's greatest achievements in moral characterization, but the pilgrim Merchant is little more than a stock figure. The *Merchant's Tale* warns us to trust the tale and not the teller.

I am not, of course, arguing that the dramatic frame has no purpose in the *Canterbury Tales*, only that it, along with the portraits in the *General Prologue*, has been given too much of the wrong kind of attention by some readers. Chaucer often uses a pilgrim's voice to make complex information more lively, as we have seen with the antifeminism of the *Wife of Bath's Prologue* or the alchemical lore of the *Canon's Yeoman's Tale*. The frame narrative offers the reader a more ordinary, frequently comic world between the powerful fiction of the tales themselves. The dramatic introductions often do little more than generally prepare us for what is to come, and the episodes between pilgrims that conclude some tales are rarely their thematic or artistic culmination, though they are often so regarded. The coarse foolery at the end of the *Pardoner's Tale*, for example, during which the Host angrily insults the Pardoner, has often dominated critical discussions at the expense of the infinitely greater tale of the three revellers. Like the Host himself, who is so active in this realm, the frame often provides indirect and deliberately misleading comment on the tales, perhaps something like the grotesques in the margins of medieval manuscripts. For all its value and originality, the pilgrimage narrative should not become more important than the tales it encloses.

Perhaps the greatest contribution of the frame is that its personal conflicts point to the more important literary conflicts of the *Canterbury Tales*. When the drunken Miller interrupts to 'quite' the *Knight's Tale*, the human drama is only a brief and general moment of class antagonism (the two pilgrims never actually address one another), but the artistic drama that results from the juxtaposition of their two different tales begins the extraordinary variety of the *Canterbury Tales*. Imagine how different the *Tales* would be if, as originally planned, the long and philosophical *Knight's Tale* were then followed by the interminable tragedies of the Monk. How many would want to read further? Instead, Chaucer uses the Miller's rudeness to establish the principle of literary diversity that distinguishes the entire collection.

As I have suggested throughout this essay, the Canterbury tales are a series of literary experiments rather than a drama of personalities. The undeniable variety of the collection comes from the conflicting artistries of the tales themselves. Stylistically, not one of the Canterbury tales is much like any other. Each is a unique work with its own distinct poetic, a poetic that ranges from large literary elements, such as narrator and dialogue, down to the specifics of imagery, allusion, and vocabulary. Even more remarkable, the special artistry of an individual tale remains consistent throughout, almost as if Chaucer had created a different poet for each. I know of no other literary work so constructed, for the various tales are not a group of parodies or only generally unlike; instead, each is a fully worked out expression of a special kind of poetry. This radical stylistic variety, and not the relations between tale and teller, is the central achievement of the *Canterbury Tales*.

The *General Prologue* first prepares us for the coming drama of style with its many different kinds of pilgrim portraits, and Chaucer further shows us how to read the *Canterbury Tales* in the two works he assigns to himself – the clever parody *Sir Thopas* and the dull if worthy *Melibee*. Although much critical ingenuity has been spent trying to define the vague and contradictory figure of 'Chaucer the Pilgrim', the significant drama in this episode is the literary opposition of the two tales themselves. *Thopas* and *Melibee* reveal no clear pilgrim personality, but they do suggest the outer boundaries of Christian literature. Though a delightful exercise in aesthetic burlesque, *Thopas* is so self-indulgent and insubstantial, so empty of theme and *sentence*, that it risks confirming the worst fears of medieval moralists about the frivolity and falsity of poetry. In contrast, the admirable but plodding *Melibee* threatens to undermine its didactic mission by putting its audience to sleep. Through the deliberate artistic opposition of his own two tales, Chaucer reveals the intricate dialectic of styles in the *Canterbury Tales*, while suggesting that effective Christian poetry will need to combine the moral meaning of *Melibee* with the literary skill of *Sir Thopas*.

Chaucer's art of literary contrast and experiment is found throughout the *Canterbury Tales*. It begins with the juxtaposition of the *Knight's* and *Miller's Tales*, whose differences go far beyond the change from romance to fabliaux, and near the end we find an equally complex relationship between the paired tales of the Second Nun and Canon's Yeoman, which are opposite in form and theme, but share similar kinds of imagery. Chaucer even creates poetic variety within a single tale. The first part of the *Pardoner's Tale* (the sermon on the tavern sins) is as corrupt as it is skilful – a dazzling, manipulative, and superficial harangue designed to sell pardons, but one that offers no real understanding of sin or help against it. Yet the second part of the tale (the exemplum of the three rioters searching for Death) is completely different in tone and effect: the melodramatic rhetoric of the sermon instantly gives way at line 661 to a powerfully understated and symbolically charged narrative that succeeds as both an exciting story and a vehicle for serious Christian instruction. The two different kinds of preaching in the *Pardoner's Tale* suggest both the dangers and the opportunities of moral fiction.

The literary variety of the *Canterbury Tales* occurs even among tales that ought to be most alike. Although rarely discussed by dramatic critics, and then only generally, the radical stylistic differences among stories of the same genre are the clearest proof of the unique poetic sensibilities created for each of the Canterbury tales. The several romances in the collection, for example, are significantly different from one another. A similar literary variety occurs in the religious tales. The *Prioress's Tale* and the *Second Nun's Tale* both tell of an innocent martyr whose death is a triumph of Christian faith, yet the first is a lyrical exercise in affective piety, while the second is an austere and intellectual work that makes complex use of dialogue and imagery. Perhaps the most surprising example of literary experimentation within a single genre occurs in the fabliaux. The *Miller's Tale, Reeve's Tale, Shipman's Tale,* and *Merchant's Tale* all contain the same basic situation (a husband is cuckolded by a younger man whom he himself has introduced into the household), yet no two share anything like the same artistry, since each contains its own unique poetic voice, only a little of which can be attributed to the different tellers.

The stylistic individuality of Chaucer's fabliaux is found in everything from their different narrators and wooing scenes to their special use of imagery and vocabulary. For instance, each of the fabliaux has its preferred kind of speech: quick and witty exchanges in the *Miller's Tale*; flat and frequently inarticulate expression in the *Reeve's Tale*; sophisticated, manipulative dialogue in the *Shipman's Tale*; and long, often interior monologues of great psychological and moral depth in the *Merchant's Tale*. Or consider a more precise example: literary and learned allusions are virtually non-existent in the Reeve's and Shipman's tales, but extremely important, though completely different, in the Miller's and Merchant's tales. The allusions in the *Miller's Tale* are drawn largely from popular sources like contemporary songs or the mystery play, while those in the *Merchant's*

Tale are more frequent, more various, and more complex: stories from the Bible and the classics, especially, introduce new standards of judgement to the world of the fabliau that expose the corruption of January and May while offering images of hope.

The *Reeve's Tale* has sometimes been slighted by critics in favour of the more flamboyant *Miller's Tale*. But when the two are read together and compared as experiments in the possibilities of a genre, the special virtues of the *Reeve's Tale* become apparent, such as its glorious glossary and profound understanding of the physical and social constraints of the real world. Perhaps the clearest proof of the unique and accomplished artistry of the *Reeve's Tale* is the Northern dialect spoken by the two Cambridge students. For this one tale and its particular poet, Chaucer creates an unprecedented and sophisticated literary device he never uses again. Some critics have also dismissed the *Shipman's Tale*, mistaking its individual, understated artistry for inferiority. The work lacks some of the successful literary elements of Chaucer's other fabliaux only because its special accomplishments lie elsewhere, especially in the long dialogue of seduction between wife and monk whose subtlety is unmatched elsewhere in the *Canterbury Tales*.

Because it recognizes only relationships sanctioned by the frame narrative, the dramatic approach has hindered the detailed and wide-ranging literary comparisons between individual tales and among groups of tales sketched above. Such comparisons are essential to genuine understanding of the *Canterbury Tales*, for they alone permit us to begin to appreciate the intricate drama of style that Chaucer has created. The *Canterbury Tales* is a collection of absolutely different kinds of poetry; each contributes a special artistic vision, and thus a special view of the world, to the collection as a whole. Even the most comic tales are charged with the literary and thematic individuality that makes the *Canterbury Tales* so exciting and challenging. Too often the dramatic theory has concealed or trivialized the extent of that poetic range by asking us to concentrate on the lesser thing (the pilgrims) rather than the greater (the tales themselves). Although the *Canterbury Tales* has been enjoyed for almost six hundred years, the full achievement of Chaucer's experiments in poetic variety remains to be explored.

Notes

1 George Lyman Kittredge, *Chaucer and His Poetry* (Cambridge, Mass., 1915), p. 155.
2 Guido delle Colonne, *Historia Destructionis Troiae*, trans. Mary E. Meek (Bloomington, Ind., 1974), p. 71.
3 Jill Mann, *Chaucer and Medieval Estates Satire* (Cambridge, 1973). The comments of Dryden and Blake are most conveniently found in *Geoffrey Chaucer:*

The Critical Heritage, ed. D. S. Brewer, 2 vols. (London, 1978), vol. I, pp. 166–7 and 249–60.

4 R. A. Pratt, 'The Development of the Wife of Bath', *Studies in Medieval Literature in Honor of Professor Albert Croll Baugh*, ed. MacEdward Leach (Philadelphia, 1961), pp. 45–79.

7   The *Canterbury Tales* 1: Romance

T H E term 'romance' is not an exact one. Applied to medieval writings it denotes a large area whose outer limits are by no means easy to define. Yet most readers of English literature have some notion of what a typical romance is like, a notion derived mainly from the tales of Arthur and the Round Table. The hero of such a romance will be a knight who engages in perilous adventures, riding out and frequently fighting, sometimes to win or defend a lady, sometimes to defeat enemies of the realm, and sometimes for no evident reason at all. It should be said straightaway that the reader who turns to Chaucer's great story-collection in search of such a typical romance will be disappointed; for the five Canterbury 'romances' to be discussed in this chapter are all, in one way or another, divergent from that stereotype. It is as if Chaucer, who seems so much at home in the fabliau, the miracle of the Virgin, and the saint's life, felt less easy with the very genre which we regard as most characteristic of his period, the knightly romance.

The only poem of Chaucer which has an Arthurian setting – indeed, the only poem in which he so much as mentions Arthur, apart from a passing reference in the *Romaunt of the Rose* – is the *Wife of Bath's Tale*. The opening line of this tale, 'In th'olde dayes of the Kyng Arthour', holds out the promise that here for once Chaucer is going to try his hand at the most traditional kind of knightly romance. Yet by the end of the poem's first paragraph this expectation is already shaken:

> In th'olde dayes of the Kyng Arthour,
> Of which that Britons speken greet honour,
> Al was this land fulfild of fayerye.
> The elf-queene, with hir joly compaignye,
> Daunced ful ofte in many a grene mede.
> This was the olde opinion, as I rede;
> I speke of manye hundred yeres ago.
> But now kan no man se none elves mo,
> For now the grete charitee and prayeres
> Of lymytours and othere hooly freres,
> That serchen every lond and every streem,
> As thikke as motes in the sonne-beem,

Blessynge halles, chambres, kichenes, boures,
Citees, burghes, castels, hye toures,
Thropes, bernes, shipnes, dayeryes —
This maketh that ther ben no fayeryes.
For ther as wont to walken was an elf,
Ther walketh now the lymytour hymself
In undermeles and in morwenynges,
And seyth his matyns and his hooly thynges
As he gooth in his lymytacioun.
Wommen may go now saufly up and doun.
In every bussh or under every tree
Ther is noon oother incubus but he,
And he ne wol doon hem but dishonour.   (857–81)

The ostensible purpose of these scintillating lines is the same as that of the opening of *Sir Gawain and the Green Knight*: to set the ensuing story in Britain's great age of wonders, the reign of King Arthur. Yet, whereas the *Gawain*-poet's introduction is serious and single-minded, Chaucer's is comic and distracted. It may appear that the Wife of Bath (for the voice is distinctly hers) here turns a traditional comparison upside-down. Arthurian romancers commonly compare modern times unfavourably with the grand old days of Arthur; but the Wife at first speaks as if, for women at least, things are better nowadays. In Arthurian times women lived in continual fear of being raped by the 'elves' or fairy creatures with which the land was then filled; but now these incubi have been driven out by the pious activity of the friars: 'Wommen may go now saufly up and doun'. This flattery of friars may remind us that the Wife of Bath belongs to that class of 'worthy wommen of the toun' with whom the Friar on the pilgrimage was especially 'wel biloved and famulier', according to the *General Prologue*. Such women were, in fact, notorious for their susceptibility to sweet-talking friars. Yet the Wife is a tough character, who can look after herself. Perhaps the Friar's laughing compliment at the end of her prologue irritated her ('This is a long preamble of a tale!'). At any rate, one may detect a note of sarcasm in her response to the Host's call for a tale:

'Al redy, sire,' quod she, 'right as yow lest,
If I have licence of this worthy Frere'.   (III, 854–5)

The mock submissiveness of these words prepares the way for the deceptive sweetness of the tale's opening. For the Wife does not in reality treat modern friars as an improvement on their elvish predecessors. Her description of friars blessing everything in sight 'as thikke as motes in the sonne-beem' is not merely ridiculous; it also has something of that horror of the swarm so vividly evoked later by the Summoner's dreadful account of thousands of friars swarming out of the devil's arse like bees from a hive

(III, 1692–6). Nor are women, she suggests, actually safe with friars from sexual attack. Their only comfort is that the friar has not inherited the elf's power of infallibly causing conception: 'he ne wol doon hem but dishonour'. Nothing but dishonour! By comparison, the olden days of King Arthur emerge as something like a golden age for women. We may notice, looking back, that the Wife first describes Arthurian fairies, not as lustful male incubi, but as a happy band of dancing ladies:

> The elf-queene, with hir joly compaignye,
> Daunced ful ofte in many a grene mede.   (860–1)

This brief but memorable glimpse of the queen of the fairies and her company of ladies does much to establish the character of the Arthurian world as the Wife is to portray it in her tale. It is essentially a feminine world, dominated by women both human and fairy. The fairy element is not obvious, for the old hag who turns into the beautiful young wife is never explained as an elf-woman. But neither does she turn out to be, as in the three other surviving English versions of the story, a human girl bewitched by a wicked stepmother.[1] Indeed, she is not explained at all. Yet the circumstances in which the knight first encounters her clearly associate her with the 'joly compaignye' of the queen of the fairies. Under the forest eaves he comes upon a company of four and twenty ladies dancing; and it is after they have mysteriously vanished that he first sees the old hag sitting on the green. This is enough, in a land 'fulfild of fayerye', to establish her true identity.

The dominance of women in the fairy world evoked by the Wife of Bath is striking. The hero of the tale is a man, a 'lusty bacheler' of Arthur's court; but he is not named, like Florent in Gower's version of the story or Sir Gawain in the other two versions. Nor is he, like Gower's Florent, a 'knyght aventurous'. The masculine activities of adventure and feats of arms play no part in his story. Riding back from a day's hawking he commits, it is true, the ultimate act of male domination, when he rapes a passing girl; but, unlike an incubus or a friar, he does not go unpunished. His act of 'oppressioun' delivers him, in fact, into the hands of the women – Arthur's queen and her ladies, and also the elf-woman. His life is made to depend on his ability to determine what women most desire; and the answer to that question, when he discovers it, proves to affirm their claim to supremacy:

> 'Wommen desiren to have sovereynetee
> As wel over hir housbond as hir love,
> And for to been in maistrie hym above'.   (1038–40)

Chaucer's only 'Arthurian romance', then, turns out to be a fairy tale, told by a woman and dominated by women. Perhaps this is how Chaucer thought of Arthurian stories – strange as that may seem to a reader of Malory. In his tale the Squire speaks of 'Fairye' as the country out of which Gawain might come again (96); and the Nun's Priest skittishly associates an Arthurian book with women readers:

> This storie is also trewe, I undertake,
> As is the book of Launcelot de Lake,
> That wommen holde in ful greet reverence.   (VII, 3211–13)

Chaucer probably had in mind here the French *Lancelot*, which formed part of the great thirteenth-century Vulgate Cycle of Arthurian stories. This is the very book which, in a memorable episode in Dante's *Inferno*, the two young lovers Paolo and Francesca were reading together when they first kissed. Dante himself had certainly read the *Lancelot*, for he recalls a tiny episode from the book, to brilliant effect, in the *Paradiso* (XVI, 14–15); but it may be surmised that he, like Chaucer, regarded knightly romance as a form of agreeable light reading to which no serious fourteenth-century poet should devote more than passing attention.

If this was indeed Chaucer's attitude, it may seem strange that he should have assigned to himself, of all the Canterbury pilgrims, the tale which comes closer than any other of his works to being a story of knightly adventure; but his *Tale of Sir Thopas*, as nearly all readers have noticed, is an outright burlesque. Adventure, as it figured so largely in the romance of chivalry, seems never to have attracted Chaucer's interest. His account of how Jason and Hercules 'soughten the aventures of Colcos' occurs in a context that directs attention not to male heroism but to female suffering (as part of the legend of Hypsipyle and Medea in the *Legend of Good Women*); and the only other Chaucerian hero who sets off in search of adventure is Sir Thopas himself. Having fallen in love with an 'elf-queene', Thopas rides out into the 'contree of Fairye'. There he encounters her monstrous guardian, a three-headed giant called Sir Olifaunt ('Elephant'), whereupon he hurries home again to fetch his armour. There follows an elaborately circumstantial arming scene, very much in the romance manner, after which the knight sets out again to meet the giant. Chaucer is careful to explain that Thopas conducts himself on this second sortie exactly as a 'knyght auntrous' or adventurous knight should – sleeping in the open with his helm as a pillow, and drinking nothing but spring water:

> Hymself drank water of the well,
> As dide the knyght sire Percyvell
>   So worly² under wede,
> Til on a day –   (915–18)

At this point, however, the Host can stand no more, and he tells Chaucer to stop: 'Thou doost noght elles but despendest tyme'. Perhaps Harry

Bailly here voices his creator's thought about those shapeless and inter-minable adventures which occupy so many medieval romances. Yet it may be noticed that even in this ridiculous context, just as in the *Wife of Bath's Tale*, the thought of the elf-queen inspires Chaucer (himself described as 'elvyssh' in the *Prologue to Sir Thopas*) to an imaginative response:

> 'Heere is the queene of Fayerye,
> With harpe and pipe and symphonye,
>   Dwellynge in this place'.   (814–16)

The strange potency of Chaucer's fairy queen, with her entourage of instrumental music and dancing ladies, impressed her on the mind of the next great English poet; for Spenser's Faerie Queene is her descendant. The episode where Spenser's Arthur falls in love with the 'elf-queene' seen in a vision as he sleeps in a forest glade (*Faerie Queene* I, ix, 8–15) is directly modelled upon the episode in *Sir Thopas* where the hero falls in love in just the same fashion:

> 'Me dremed al this nyght, pardee,
> An elf-queene shal my lemman be
>   And slepe under my goore'.   (787–9)

Spenser, the devoted subject of Queen Elizabeth I, evidently found much that was congenial in the fairylands of the *Wife of Bath's Tale* and *Sir Thopas*, where knights and even three-headed giants submit themselves to mysterious female powers.

Yet Chaucer's *Sir Thopas*, whether or not Spenser realized the fact, is first and foremost a literary *jeu d'esprit* – a pointed burlesque, not of romance in general, but of the English romances of his day. Modern readers acquainted only with *Sir Gawain and the Green Knight* will miss the immediate point of the joke, for Chaucer's target was a quite different kind of fourteenth-century poem, not much read today but popular in its time: older rhymes such as the romances of Bevis of Hampton and Guy of Warwick (both mentioned in *Sir Thopas*, 899), and newer works such as the two Arthurian pieces composed by Chaucer's contemporary Thomas Chester, *Lybeaus Desconus* and *Sir Launfal*.[3] Chaucer signals his intention plainly enough in the first stanza:

> Listeth, lordes, in good entent.
> And I wol telle verrayment
>   Of myrthe and of solas;
> Al of a knyght was fair and gent
> In bataille and in tourneyment,
>   His name was sire Thopas.   (712–17)

No contemporary reader, and few modern ones, could mistake this for
Chaucer's own poetic voice. He nowhere else uses the tail-rhyme stanza
which was such a favourite with hack poets of his day: there was evidently
something ludicrous, to his more fastidious ear, in the effect of the two
short 'tail' lines linked by a thumping rhyme. The appeal for attention to
a listening audience, vulgarly addressed as 'lordes', strikes a popular note;
and the epithets 'fair and gent' seem to owe their connection with battle
and tournament helplessly to the exigences of rhyme. There are also other
wrong notes in the stanza more difficult for a modern ear to detect.
'Entent', here coupled with the rhyme-tag 'verrayment' (which Chaucer
does not use elsewhere), always has a final -e in Chaucer's serious writings:
'entente'. 'Thopas' is obviously a ridiculously fanciful name for the tale's
Flemish hero; but it can also be shown, more surprisingly, that to preface
a knight's name with the title 'Sir' was regarded by Chaucer, as by his
French contemporaries, as a vulgarism. He employs the form only in *Sir
Thopas*, where it is scattered so promiscuously that even a giant can be
dubbed 'Sir Olifaunt'.

The next two romances to be considered, those of the Squire and the
Franklin, were intended by Chaucer to stand side by side in the completed
Canterbury collection. Taken together they may be distinguished from the
Wife of Bath's Tale and *Sir Thopas* in their treatment of that essential
ingredient in romance, the marvellous. Arthurian Britain, according to the
Wife of Bath, is a land full of fairy, and the Flanders of Sir Thopas, though
comically mundane in itself, abuts upon the 'contree of Fairye'. Both tales
accept the fairy as a potent source of marvels which require no further
investigation or excuse. Things are different in the Tartary of the *Squire's
Tale* and the Brittany of the *Franklin's Tale*. Here wonders have, or may
have, natural causes. In the *Squire's Tale* an emissary from the King of
Araby and Ind brings four gifts to the Tartar king Cambyuskan and his
daughter Canacee, each possessing marvellous powers: a brass horse, an
unsheathed sword, a mirror, and a ring. The people of Tartary, so far from
accepting these wonders as the commonplaces of romance, look for
explanations and precedents. The long passage describing their various
speculations (189–262) shows Chaucer at his best. How can a brass horse
fly? Some think it may be 'of Fairye'; others recall the flying horse Pegasus
and the wooden horse of Troy; and one sceptic suggests that it may be
nothing but 'an apparence ymaad by som magyk, / As jogelours pleyen
at thise feestes grete':

> Of sondry doutes thus they jangle and trete,
> As lewed peple demeth comunly
> Of thynges that been maad moore subtilly
> Than they kan in hir lewednesse comprehende;
> They demen gladly to the badder ende.   (220–4)

Since the *Squire's Tale* is unfinished, the truth of the matter is never revealed; but we may notice that the most sceptical of the explanations canvassed by the Tartars serves in the *Franklin's Tale* to account for the great marvel of the disappearing rocks. Set the task of removing all the rocks from the coast of Brittany – apparently an 'inpossible', as he complains – the lovesick squire Aurelius first prays to Apollo for a miracle, but without result; and it is only when he consults a scholar of Orleans who has learned from his books of natural magic the science of producing 'apparences' that Aurelius is able to produce the desired effect: 'It semed that alle the rokkes were aweye'. But only 'semed'. In this tale the marvellous is an illusion, like the tricks played by conjurors at feasts (1139–51).

Although the tales of the Squire and the Franklin are coupled together and share a playful interest in the rationalization of marvels, they are otherwise very different. The *Squire's Tale* presents problems because it is unfinished. It has been suggested that the 'wordes of the Frankeleyn to the Squier', which follow the fragmentary tale in the manuscripts, are to be read as an interruption of the Squire's performance, similar to, though much more polite than, the Host's interruption of *Sir Thopas*. Certainly the fragment as we have it does reveal some Chaucerian characteristics. Of the elaborate plot projected in lines 661–9, which was to involve separate or intertwined exploits of Cambyuskan and each of his three children, we are given only the sentimental episode of Canacee and the lovesick falconess. The promise 'of aventures and of batailles' remains tantalizingly unfulfilled, just as in *Sir Thopas*. Yet the Franklin's flattering comments do not sound like an interruption ('In feith, Squier, thow hast thee wel yquit'), and it may be questioned whether Chaucer could have trusted either his readers or the scribes who copied the *Tales* to understand them as such. His two undoubted interruptions, when Harry Bailly stops Chaucer and when the Knight stops the Monk, are both clearly signalled by the phrase 'Namoore of this!' (VII 919, 2767). It seems preferable, all things considered, to suppose either, with Edmund Spenser, that the rest of the *Squire's Tale* has been lost (*Faerie Queene* IV, ii, 33), or else, with John Milton, that the tale was simply 'left half-told' (*Il Penseroso*, 109). In any case, the admiration expressed by both Spenser and Milton for this 'work of noblest wit' makes one hesitate to accept the opinion of some modern critics that the *Squire's Tale*, like *Sir Thopas*, is unworthy of its author.

The tale contains, in fact, some of the richest passages of poetic narrative to be found in Chaucer. The description of the arrival of the Arabian emissary at the Tartar feast is as vivid as the *Gawain*-poet's description of the Green Knight's arrival at Camelot, with which it is often compared. Even better is the account of how the great feast ends in the small hours, not long before daybreak:

> The norice of digestioun, the sleep,
> Gan on hem wynke and bad hem taken keep
> That muchel drynke and labour wolde han reste;
> And with a galpyng mouth hem alle he keste,
> And seyde that it was tyme to lye adoun,
> For blood was in his domynacioun.
> 'Cherisseth blood, natures freend,' quod he.
> They thanken hym galpynge, by two, by thre,
> And every wight gan drawe hym to his reste,
> As sleep hem bad; they tooke it for the beste.   (347–56)

Later poets' personifications of Sleep use language more poetical ('O soft embalmer of the still midnight'), but none is more powerful than this. The goodnight kiss so strangely bestowed with a yawning mouth by Sleep is received by the revellers with an answering yawn. The repetition of 'galpyng', supported by the haunting repetition of 'blood' in the intervening lines, creates a powerful narcotic effect, anticipating the more famous infectious yawn which brings Pope's *Dunciad* to an end. Equally vivid is the ensuing account of how young Canacee (who has prudently gone to bed early) gets up at dawn the next day to walk in the park. It is just after six in the morning,

> And in a trench forth in the park gooth she.
> The vapour which that fro the erthe glood
> Made the sonne to seme rody and brood;
> But nathelees it was so fair a sighte
> That it made alle hire hertes for to lighte.   (392–6)

The sun, discoloured and magnified by low-lying morning mists, casts a peculiar light over the ensuing scene, in which Canacee encounters the grieving falcon, perched in a tree 'for drye as whit as chalk'.

It seems that the *Squire's Tale* was planned as one of those complex, multi-track stories which inspired Dante (again no doubt recalling the French *Lancelot*) to speak of the 'exquisite intricacies of Arthur' – but with oriental rather than Arthurian materials. Yet the fragmentary condition of the poem leaves its precise character in doubt. The Franklin, by contrast, clearly announces his tale as belonging to that species of romance known as the Breton lay:

> Thise olde gentil Britouns in hir dayes
> Of diverse aventures maden layes,
> Rymeyed in hir firste Briton tonge;
> Whiche layes with hir instrumentz they songe,
> Or elles redden hem for hir plesaunce,
> And oon of hem have I in remembraunce,
> Which I shal seyn with good wyl as I kan.   (709–15)

The Breton lay had its origin in the twelfth century, when minstrels from Brittany performed their 'lays' or songs in the households of France and England. Their lays were essentially musical performances, sung to the harp in the Celtic 'Briton tonge'; but since the emotions they expressed were commonly attributed to characters in stories (Tristan's Lament, as it might be), the performers made a point of explaining the narrative context of their songs in French. It was from these accompanying narratives that the French poetess, Marie de France, claimed to derive the matter for her collection of twelve romantic verse-narratives, written in England in the time of Henry II (1154–89). The 'diverse aventures' rhymed by Marie and her imitators are conveniently characterized in the English Breton lay *Sir Orfeo*,[4] which Chaucer probably knew:

> Sum bethe of wer and sum of wo,
> And sum of joie and mirthe also,
> And sum of trecherie and of gile,
> Of old aventours that fel while,
> And sum of bourdes and ribaudy,
> And mani ther beth of fairy;
> Of al thinges that men seth
> Mest o love forsothe thay beth.   (5–12)

Among these varied subjects the English poet here gives pride of place to the fairy and especially to love – the two themes which together may be taken to characterize the Breton lay tradition which Marie established. In her poems, as in such English lays as *Sir Orfeo* and *Sir Launfal*, it is not adventure or feats of arms that interest the poet, but the world of fairy and the joys and sorrows of love.

Chaucer may not have read Marie de France;[5] but it seems that the feminine type of romance which she played a part in establishing appealed to Chaucer more than the tales of derring-do which so delighted Sir Thomas Malory. In the *Franklin's Tale*, Arveragus is presented as an adventurous knight who wins Dorigen by 'many a labour, many a greet emprise'; but these exploits are no more than mentioned, and when after a year of marriage Arveragus sets off, as knights were supposed to do, to escape from uxorious idleness and keep honour bright by the exercise of arms, the narrative does not follow him. We are merely told that he

> Shoop hym to goon and dwelle a yeer or tweyne
> In Engelond, that cleped was eek Briteyne,
> To seke in armes worshipe and honour;
> For al his lust he sette in swich labour.   (809–12)

It is startling to hear the chief business of so many romances – seeking honour in arms – thus dismissed in a single couplet. 'Swich labour'! The heart of the *Franklin's Tale* lies elsewhere. Although the Franklin does not share with the Wife and Marie their interest in the fairy, in his tale as in theirs woman plays the dominant role. The chief concern of the tale is with Dorigen and her feelings, and its most characteristic moments are when she piteously laments her absent husband (852–94) and her present dilemma (1352–1458). In these passages especially the poem comes very close to being another Legend of Good Women. Not for nothing did the Scots poet Gavin Douglas say of his master Chaucer that 'he was evir, God wait, all womanis frend'.

Like the Breton lays described in *Sir Orfeo*, the *Franklin's Tale* deals above all with love: the married love between Dorigen and Arveragus, and the passion of Aurelius for Dorigen. In one of Marie de France's poems a lady expresses the opinion that no gentleman would seek to win love by virtue of his lordly power ('par seignurie') because love can be worthy and honourable only between equals: 'Amur n'est pruz se n'est egals' (*Equitan*, 137). The same essentially courtly thought is expressed by the Franklin:

> Love wol nat been constreyned by maistrye.
> Whan maistrie comth, the God of Love anon
> Beteth his wynges, and farewel, he is gon!
> Love is a thyng as any spirit free.   (764–7)

Already in the twelfth century writers saw that this doctrine created difficulties, on the one hand because the courtly lover was supposed to be his mistress' servant, and on the other because the husband was supposed to be his wife's master. Chrétien de Troyes solved this problem by affirming that, in an ideal romantic marriage, the man is at one and the same time superior (lord), equal (friend), and inferior (servant); and it is this mysterious paradox that the Franklin invokes in his account of the relationship between Dorigen and Arveragus (791–8). Dorigen is at once lady (superior), wife (inferior), and love (equal) to Arveragus.[6] Such is the Franklin's solution to the problem of sovereignty in marriage. But his tale is not, as discussions of the so-called Marriage Group suggest,[7] concerned solely with love in marriage. The same noble principle, that 'love wol nat been constreyned by maistrye', triumphs also in the case of the squire Aurelius. By engineering the disappearance of the rocks and holding Dorigen to her rash promise, Aurelius does indeed attempt to 'constrain' her love; but in the event he cannot bring himself to 'doon so heigh a cherlyssh wrecchednesse / Agayns franchise and alle gentillesse' as to force her against her will. He releases her from her promise.

The behaviour of Aurelius places the refusal of mastery in love in its relation to more general doctrines of 'gentillesse'. Commonly in medieval romance one character finds himself or herself subjected to the will of another by virtue of a vow or promise, and stands to suffer in consequence. Since nobility of soul obliges any romance hero to keep his pledged word, the story will seem all set for a painful conclusion; but this is averted by an answering nobility in the adversary, who waives his rights and releases the hero from his obligations. This pattern of reciprocal nobility or 'gentillesse' – submission on the one hand, release on the other – can be traced in the happy endings of many romances, most obviously in the scene at the Green Chapel in *Sir Gawain and the Green Knight*. In the *Wife of Bath's Tale*, the old hag's attempt to 'constrain love by mastery' seems to be leading to an unhappy conclusion when she demands, not only that the young knight should honour his promise to marry her, as he is prepared to do, but also that he should accept her as his love: '"My love?" quod he, "nay, my dampnacioun!"' The impasse is comically prolonged by the hag's ensuing lecture on 'gentillesse' and the virtues of poverty and old age, as if the happy ending were to depend on the knight's readiness to abandon his prejudices against ugly old working-class women. And so, up to a point, it does; for in response the chastened hero goes so far as to employ a triple form of address which implies exactly the romantic married relationship described by the Franklin:

> 'My lady and my love, and wyf so deere,
> I put me in youre wise governance'.   (1230–1)

This improved act of submission finally triggers the moment of release. Not only does the old hag turn into a beautiful young woman, but she also appears to have waived her claim to one-sided 'maistrye':

> A thousand tyme a-rewe he gan hire kisse,
> And she obeyed hym in every thyng
> That myghte doon hym plesance or likyng.   (1254–6)

In the case of the *Franklin's Tale*, the happy ending depends upon two such moments of 'release' (the word is used at lines 1533 and 1613), both of which manifest 'franchise and gentillesse' in the characters involved. Impressed by the resolve of both Dorigen and her husband that she should honour her promise, and moved to pity by the woman's distress, Aurelius releases her from her obligation; and he himself is released from his debt to the scholar of Orleans by a further act of 'gentillesse' on the part of his creditor:

> 'But God forbede, for his blisful myght,
> But if a clerk koude doon a gentil dede
> As wel as any of yow, it is no drede!
> Sire, I releesse thee thy thousand pound'.   (1610–13)

Thus the tale can end, like its closest analogue in Boccaccio's *Filocolo*, with a question: 'Whiche was the mooste fre, as thynketh yow?' It has been suggested that the Franklin's insistence on the fact that generosity of spirit can manifest itself in clerks and squires as well as in knights betrays some uneasiness about his own claim to be accepted as a gentlemen; but this is borne out neither by the historical evidence about franklins nor by the character of the tale itself. Franklins had every justification for regarding themselves as gentlemen, albeit of the country sort; and this franklin's tale, so far from appearing the work of a social climber, may claim to express more fully than any other Middle English poem that generous and humane spirit which marks the best medieval courtly writing, from the time of Marie de France and Chrétien de Troyes onwards.

Of all the tales under discussion here the *Knight's Tale* least resembles other medieval romances, French or English. Its source is an Italian poem, the *Teseida* of Giovanni Boccaccio; and the *Teseida* claims to be not a romance but an epic. It is indeed one of the first attempts in a European vernacular to match the twelve-book epics of antiquity. Its title declares this ambition: 'Teseida' from 'Teseo' (Theseus), as 'Aeneid' from 'Aeneas'. In reality, Boccaccio's poem is something of a hybrid, for the story of the two young Thebans Palemone and Arcita and their rivalry for the hand of the beautiful Emilia might well have figured, stripped of its neo-classical trappings, in one of the popular Italian romances of the time; but the poem's epic form marks it out as an altogether more ambitious, not to say pretentious, literary production. Chaucer, of course, could not incorporate a twelve-book epic in his Canterbury anthology; yet even his version, much abbreviated and with most of the epic machinery removed, is itself a complex and many-sided work, which cannot without discomfort be described simply as a romance.

Literary historians sometimes associate the rise of romance in the twelfth century with the increased interest manifested at that time in individual experience. Certainly the heroes and heroines of Marie and Chrétien are activated chiefly by personal considerations, especially the desire for honour and for happiness in love. In this respect, Palamon and Arcite may be accounted typical romance heroes. Although the *Knight's Tale* is not, like so many of Chaucer's works, dominated by a female character, it is the two young knights' love for Emily which exclusively preoccupies their minds, once they have glimpsed her from their prison window. From that moment on, they are lovers and nothing else, in the best romantic tradition. Their love turns them instantly from sworn brothers into sworn rivals; and it is for love that they fight each other, first in the grove and then at the great tournament. Some readers have seen differences in character between them, but it is doubtful whether Chaucer intended any. The prison scene in which Arcite argues that, although Palamon in fact saw Emily first, he himself was the first to love her 'paramours' since Palamon mistook her for a goddess, does not prove Arcite to be a less romantic type than his companion. The argument is obviously a desperate sophistry. Arcite loves Emily quite as much as Palamon does, and in exactly the same fashion.

When he later prays to Mars for victory in the tournament, he has Emily just as steadily in mind as does Palamon when he prays for Emily herself to Venus. The only significance of Arcite's choice is that it lays him open, most unhappily, to the equivocating judgement of the planet-god Saturn, who neatly resolves the problem at his expense by granting him what he asked for, not what he wanted.

If there were no more to the *Knight's Tale* than this, it might rank as a piece of sentimental courtly casuistry, to set beside the episode in the *Parliament of Fowls* where three eagles each swear undying devotion to the same female bird – the problem in both cases being to decide how such a situation can be resolved, given that 'gentils' cannot be expected to seek consolation elsewhere when disappointed in love. But the young people in the *Knight's Tale* do not pursue their private ends in isolation: they belong to a larger world with other concerns, best represented by Theseus, Duke of Athens. The full title of Boccaccio's poem was *Teseida delle Nozze d'Emilia*, or 'The Theseid, Concerning the Nuptials of Emily'. Whilst indicating the poem's romantic subject, this title gives pride of place to Duke Theseus, whose campaigns against Amazons and Thebans occupy the first two of Boccaccio's twelve books. Boccaccio's ambition to be the first Italian poet to sing of feats of arms in a manner worthy to be compared with that of Virgil or Statius (*Teseida* XII, 84) evidently failed to inspire a similar ambition in Chaucer, who shows his customary impatience with such subjects by cutting most of the fighting out. Yet Theseus remains a dominating figure in the English poem. The Knight begins his tale with Theseus, introducing him as 'lord and governour' of Athens and conqueror of many nations. It is in these capacities that he exerts his influence over the lives of Palamon and Arcite. First, after his conquest of Thebes, he imprisons the two young Theban princes for ever and without hope of ransom – evidently treating them as war criminals along with their dead leader, Creon, who had put himself beyond the pale of humanity by refusing burial to the bodies of the dead. Later, when he comes upon the two young men fighting in the grove, it is Theseus who decrees and organizes the tournament which is to settle their fate. And finally it is Theseus who, after Arcite's death, proposes the marriage between Palamon and Emily, so securing a bond between Athens and Thebes. By these and other actions, Theseus manifests his concern for matters of foreign relations and public order which have no place in romances such as the *Wife of Bath's Tale*. Unlike Alice's Arthurian Britain, the Knight's ancient Greece has a political dimension. Its great ceremonial occasions – the tournament, the obsequies of Arcite, the parliament at which Theseus proposes the marriage – are not mere scenes in a romantic pageant. They represent man's attempts to accommodate and civilize the anarchic and inescapable facts of aggression, death, and love, as social life requires.

The attitude of Theseus to Palamon and Arcite changes in the course of the story: they are first enemies beyond the pale, then threats to public order at home, and at last friends. Insofar as they are romantic lovers, his attitude to them is best represented in the speech which he makes when he comes upon them fighting in the grove. This oration, beginning 'The god of love, a, *benedicite*!', opens in a spirit of outright mockery. The Duke remarks pithily on the folly of lovers who can so put their lives at risk for the sake of a woman who does not even know that they love her:

> 'She woot namoore of al this hoote fare,
> By God, than woot a cokkow or an hare!'   (1809–10)

But the speech then modulates into a tone of sympathy and forgiveness, as Theseus recalls that he himself, though now a sober married man, has in his time been made a fool of by the overpowering force of love:

> 'But all moot ben assayed, hoot and coold;
> A man moot ben a fool, or yong or oold, –
> I woot it by myself ful yore agon,
> For in my tyme a servant was I oon.'   (1811–14)

Theseus speaks here as a mature man who has passed through and beyond the stage of life represented by Palamon and Arcite. Like Shakespeare's *A Midsummer Night's Dream*, which owes much to Chaucer's poem, the *Knight's Tale* displays the preoccupations of young love in a large human context, exhibiting both their utter naturalness and also their funny side. As Shakespeare's Theseus observes:

> Lovers and madmen have such seething brains,
> Such shaping fantasies, that apprehend
> More than cool reason ever comprehends.

There is also a still larger context within which Chaucer sets his romantic adventure – no less than the universe itself, represented in the *Knight's Tale* by the classical gods. In the pre-Christian Brittany of the *Franklin's Tale* Apollo can evidently do nothing for his votary, but in pagan Athens the gods wield real power. It is only when the issue between Palamon and Arcite is taken up by Venus and Mars that it achieves a kind of solution. Yet that solution, engineered by 'the pale Saturnus the colde', raises profound questions about the order of things – questions similar to those raised by Dorigen in her complaint to God about the black rocks which, she says, 'semen rather a foul confusion / Of werk than any fair creacion'. These two poems have a philosophical dimension lacking in the other Canterbury romances. What chiefly interests Chaucer, however, is not so much the philosophical ideas themselves as the way human beings select and adopt them according to mood or occasion. If Dorigen is prompted by the Breton rocks to reflect on problems of evil and pain in the universe

(865–93), it is perhaps only because they threaten her beloved husband. Once he is safely home, one hears no more of that particular difficulty, just as in the third book of *Troilus and Criseyde* Criseyde stops thinking about 'fals felicitee' (III, 814) once she discovers that Troilus is not in fact, as Pandarus has maintained, angry with her. Similarly in the *Knight's Tale*, imprisonment prompts Palamon and Arcite to some deep Boethian reflections on the vanity of human wishes (1251–67) and the miseries of life (1303–27); but once the young men regain their freedom, such considerations are soon forgotten. Some readers have found in the more settled pessimism of Theseus' father Egeus the true voice of the tale: 'This world nys but a thurghfare ful of wo'. But one might equally well see that speech as a typical old man's utterance, or as a customary half-consolatory response to the fact of death. It is rather Theseus who, from his commanding position as a mature man and a 'governour', makes the most impressive philosophical utterance in the poem, when he addresses the Athenian parliament: 'The Firste Moevere of the cause above...'. This oration (the opening of which Chaucer derived not from Boccaccio but from Boethius) expounds a universal order in which partial and transitory things have their origin in a first cause which is itself eternal and unchanging. Since death is inevitable in the sublunary world, Theseus argues, it would be folly for Palamon and Emily to go on grieving for Arcite – especially since the circumstances of his death were so honourable:

> 'Why grucchen we, why have we hevynesse,
> That goode Arcite, of chivalrie the flour,
> Departed is with duetee and honour
> Out of this foule prisoun of this lyf?'   (3058–61)

Yet even these grand truths are being used – and in this case for a very practical purpose, to introduce the proposal that the Theban prince should marry Emily. Theseus speaks not as a philosopher but as a governor, whose business it is to make the best of an awkward human situation, and who is also (we may infer from lines 2973–4) interested in linking the royal houses of Athens and Thebes by marriage. He is so little a philosopher that, in flat contradiction of his earlier argument, he can go on to offer Emily and Palamon the prospect of 'o parfit joye, lastynge everemo' in their marriage.

The *Knight's Tale* does indeed end in the 'parfit joye' of mutual love in marriage:

> For now is Palamon in alle wele,
> Lyvynge in blisse, in richesse, and in heele,
> And Emelye hym loveth so tendrely,
> And he hire serveth al so gentilly,

> That nevere was ther no word hem bitwene
> Of jalousie or any oother teene.
> Thus endeth Palamon and Emelye;
> And God save al this faire compaignye!   (3101–8)

This is the customary happy ending of romance. Each of the two other Canterbury romances completed by Chaucer leaves its hero and heroine united in the same fairy-tale felicity: 'parfit joye' in the *Wife of Bath's Tale* (1258), 'sovereyn blisse' in the *Franklin's Tale* (1552). Yet it is a measure of the greater seriousness of the *Knight's Tale* that the happy ending here seems a fragile and questionable thing, shadowed by thoughts of suffering and death and especially by the memory of Arcite's dying words (2777–9):

> 'What is this world? what asketh men to have?
> Now with his love, now in his colde grave,
> Allone, withouten any compaignye'.

Notes

1 The three English analogues are all printed in *Sources and Analogues of Chaucer's Canterbury Tales*, ed. W. F. Bryan and G. Dempster (Chicago, 1941; repr. New York, 1958). See Gower's Tale of Florent, *Confessio Amantis* I, 1841–6; *The Marriage of Sir Gawaine*, part 2, stanzas 16–17; *The Weddynge of Sir Gawen and Dame Ragnell*, lines 691–3.

2 For the 'worly' in line 917, see J. A. Burrow, 'Worly under Wede', in *Essays on Medieval Literature* (Oxford, 1984), pp. 74–8.

3 Chester was possibly an acquaintance. A Thomas de Chestre appears together with Galfridus Chaucer among those to whose ransoms the King contributed in 1360. Both men had been captured by the French during the campaign of 1359–60. See *Chaucer Life-Records*, ed. M. M. Crow and C. C. Olson (Oxford, 1966), pp. 23–4. For all his lack of interest in fighting as a poetic subject, Chaucer was not without military experience.

4 *Sir Orfeo*, ed. A. J. Bliss, 2nd edn (Oxford, 1966), pp. 2–3.

5 But see Jill Mann, 'Chaucerian Themes and Style in the *Franklin's Tale*' in *The New Pelican Guide to English Literature*, ed. Boris Ford, vol. I, part I (Harmondsworth, 1982), pp. 133–53.

6 Compare the end of Chrétien's *Cligès*, where the heroine Fénice, after Cligès wins her in marriage, is said to continue to be his *amie* and his *dame* as well as his *fame*. These terms correspond to the Franklin's *love*, *lady*, and *wyf* (v, 796–7). What Chaucer calls the 'lawe of love' is the same in both poets.

7 The suggestion that the tales told by the Wife of Bath, Clerk, Merchant and Franklin were intended by Chaucer to form a debate on the subject of marriage was originally made by George Lyman Kittredge, 'Chaucer's Discussion of Marriage', *Modern Philology*, 9 (1911–12), 435–67; repr. in *Chaucer: Modern Essays in Criticism*, ed. Edward Wagenknecht (Oxford, 1959).

8   The *Canterbury Tales* II: Comedy

COMEDY of one kind or another is present in a large number of the *Canterbury Tales*, and pervasive in the links between tales, but we are concerned here with those tales where the narrative structure and expectations are those of comedy as a specific genre. There are six such tales, those of the Miller, Reeve, Shipman, Merchant, Friar and Summoner, and a seventh, that of the Cook, which is left unfinished but which was certainly going to belong to the genre. The fact that we know this, from only fifty-eight lines, is an indication of the general firmness of the initial structure of expectation of Chaucerian comedy, the codifiability of the preliminary ground-rules, whatever strain or defiance those rules may be subjected to in Chaucer's subsequent development of the story. Anticipatory indications of the nature of a particular tale are often given by what we know or suspect of the character of the pilgrim who tells it, and the comic or satirically abusive prologues to five of these tales are important in creating expectation; but even without such clues we should know, from elements built into the narrative structure, the rules of the narrative game we were being invited to play.

The time is the present, and the story is introduced as an up-to-date report on a contemporary 'slice-of-life'. There is nothing of what 'olde stories tellen us' (*Knight's Tale*, 859). The place is the homely known world of town or village, usually in England. The Miller's and Reeve's tales are slily set in or near the two university towns of Oxford and Cambridge (Trumpington is 'nat fer fro Cantebrigge': I, 3921), as if to give a broad and impartial view of the principal preoccupations and activities of university students, and the *Cook's Tale* is set in London, 'oure citee' (4365). The *Friar's Tale* speaks of 'my contree' (1301), again communicating that sense of the known and familiar, while the *Summoner's Tale* is set in Holderness, in Yorkshire. The French setting of the *Shipman's Tale* in 'Seint Denys', with Paris and Bruges figuring in the action, would have seemed homely enough, and quite different from another French setting, that of the *Franklin's Tale*, near Penmarch, in Brittany, with all its romantic associations. The *Merchant's Tale* is set in Pavia, in Lombardy, which may have had a reputation in English eyes as a 'city of sin': whatever the connotations, in this as in other respects the *Merchant's Tale* proclaims itself 'different'. Apart from these matters of setting, in time and place, there is also a distinctive tone about Chaucer's comic tales which helps to mark them off as a genre, a reductive tone, resembling a clinical analysis of the inhabitants of a zoo. Only in this type of tale would we be told of a merchant 'That riche was, for which men helde hym wys' (*Shipman's Tale*, 2) or of the desire of an old man for a wife, 'Were it for hoolynesse or for dotage' (*Merchant's Tale*, 1253) or be given an unoutraged description of a wife 'that heeld for contenance / A shoppe, and swyved for hir sustenance' (*Cook's Tale*, 4421–2).

More important than any of these features, however, in contributing to the distinctiveness of the sense of genre in Chaucer's comic tales are the assumptions we are asked to share in reading them. In romance, to take a contrasting type of tale, we are asked to accept for the purposes of the story that there are noble ideals of behaviour, fidelity to which is the means through which human existence is validated, through which life is shown to be meaningful. So Arveragus speaks of 'trouthe' (*Franklin's Tale*, 1479), and Arcite, in dying, of 'trouthe, honour, knyghthede' and the other values he admires (*Knight's Tale*, 2789). In religious tales and saints' legends, an equally self-transcending system of values operates, in this case proving the significance of life through the demonstration of its ultimate insignificance in relation to life eternal. Comedy sets all this aside, and asserts that there are no values, secular or religious, more important than survival and the satisfaction of appetite. Characters who may be temporarily under the illusion that things are otherwise, such as Absolon or January, are given short shrift. The injunction is not 'be noble', or 'be good', but 'be smart'. Our extreme satisfaction in seeing Nicholas, in the *Miller's Tale*, receive his come-uppance is not based on a perception of moral justice being done – the idea that he is 'scalded in the towte' (3853) because he has committed adultery is too trite for words – but on the comic justice of 'the biter bit'. Nicholas makes himself vulnerable because he ceases to be smart, and tries to play the same trick on Absolon that Alison has already played: this is not the behaviour of a cunning animal, which is what the comic hero is expected to be.

It will be seen that Chaucerian comedy, on this definition of it, differs markedly from comedy as classically defined, that is, as a socially normative literary form, working to correct our behaviour through making us laugh at the ridiculousness of vice and folly. This is the comedy of dramatists like Jonson or Molière, or of theorists like Bergson or Meredith.[1] In Chaucer, though, the social norms are not clearly displayed and moral norms are often openly subverted, as when the narrator of the *Miller's Tale*, after licking his lips over the description of Alison, comments in conclusion:

She was a prymerole, a piggesnye,
For any lord to leggen in his bedde,
Or yet for any good yeman to wedde.   (3268–70)

For the reader to reassert the moral norm by attributing the neglect or
subversion of moral value to the narrator's inadequacy is a trick that has
often been tried, but mostly by people who think laughter unimportant or
who have misunderstood the rules of this particular game. This is not to
say, of course, that satire, done from well-established normative positions,
is not present in these comic tales: the complacency and gullibility of John
the carpenter, the ludicrous philandering of Absolon, are classics of
satirical comedy. But the tales as a whole are not satirical comedies: one
would have to ask, satirical of *what?* and Chaucer will not return any
simple answer, or any complicated one for that matter. The case may
seem different with the Friar's and Summoner's tales, but even there the
satire is made part of a mutual exchange of abuse and thereby pushed
away from any authoritative moral centre. The wickedness of summoners
and friars remains the theme of the two tales, respectively, but not their
point.

At the same time that one rejects moralistic interpretations of Chaucerian
comedy, one should not allow one's enthusiasm for immorality to go
so far as to encourage an alternative kind of assertiveness – that the comic
tales are a 'celebration of life', a universal subversion of established values,
a kick up the behind for all orthodoxies. The popularization of the views
of Bakhtin in the West has led to a good deal of insistence on the presence
of this kind of 'festive comedy' in Chaucer, as in Shakespeare.[2] In a certain
basic way, of course, laughter always offers a kind of psychic release which
is assertive of life, especially when we laugh at the blaspheming of what
is revered, the breaking of taboos, the open practice of verbal obscenity,
the explicit depiction of excretory and sexual functions. There is also
release of another kind in the denouements of these comic tales, where in
every case the climax, after much build-up of tension and expectation,
involves the final acting-out of some trick, accompanied by delightful
surprise and reversal. The moments when we realize that Nicholas's call
for water – '"Help! water! water! help, for Goddes herte!"' (3815) – is
going to be construed by the carpenter in his tub as the announcement
of the predicted deluge, or that Aleyn, thinking he has got into bed with
his fellow student, has snuggled up to the miller, are moments of almost
cathartic physical release. Laughter here is a renewal of vitality: it does
not, however, mean anything beyond itself, in relation to life (as distinct
from art), or constitute a 'celebration of life', that is, of life in its physical
functions (as if those functions were more 'real' than intellectual,
emotional or spiritual functions). Chaucer's comic tales exist no more to

celebrate life than to criticize immorality: 'realism' is not in question, and the narrative assumptions we are asked to make are no more realistic than those we are asked to make in romance.

It is important at this stage to introduce a distinction between the Friar's and Summoner's tales and the other four (or four-and-a-bit) tales, and to appropriate the technical term fabliau to apply to the latter group. The term is often used broadly for all comic tales of low life involving trickery, but there is much advantage in restricting it, in discussing Chaucer, to the tales involving marriage and sex, and setting aside the Friar's and Summoner's tales for later discussion. The four tales remaining are capable of quite strict definition as fabliaux, as tales, that is, in which a bourgeois husband is duped or tricked into conniving at the free award of his wife's sexual favours to a clever young man. Such tales are widespread in European tradition, and well known from being included in such numbers in Boccaccio's *Decameron* or in French collections such as the *Cent Nouvelles Nouvelles* ('A Hundred New Stories'). There are very few examples in English: indeed, Chaucer's are almost the only examples of the genre as more strictly defined. It was long believed, because of a convenient assumption about social class and social morality, that the fabliaux could only have been enjoyed by the lower classes, or the bourgeoisie at best, but this belief has been shown to be unfounded,[1] and indeed it seems on the face of it unlikely, given that the pillars of petit-bourgeois society are constantly the objects of ridicule, and that the humour of the stories often relies on quite a subtle understanding of the courtly behaviour that is travestied.

In practice, Chaucer blurs this distinctive sense of audience, this sense of a sophisticated courtly group laughing at the animal antics of their inferiors, perhaps because his idea of his potential audience in the *Canterbury Tales* is much more generous and comprehensive. He allocates the telling of the tales, by a shrewd dramatic stroke, to the kind of people that they are about, suggesting half-playfully a kind of merging of pilgrimage-reality and tale-reality (the appearance in the *Miller's Tale* of a servant who, like the Miller himself (3129), is called Robyn and has a special way with doors (3466; cf. *General Prologue* 550) is the most whimsically audacious example of this), and subsuming the real audience (us) in the fictional one (the pilgrims). He also apologizes in advance, in the *General Prologue*, for telling such coarse tales, explaining that, as an honest reporter, he must report exactly what was said, however 'rudeliche and large' (734) he has to speak, and he returns to these tongue-in-cheek excuses in introducing the *Miller's Tale*. It is hard to believe that Chaucer was genuinely embarrassed by what he was doing: it is all part of the fun, and all part of the system of dramatic subterfuges that Chaucer has worked out in the *Canterbury Tales* to give himself the freedom he needs to do what he wants to do as a writer. The freedom, however won, was worth winning, for the four fabliaux are, without exception, amongst the supreme achievements of his artistry.

The association of fabliau with romance needs a word more said about it, since the two literary forms seem to exist in a complementary relationship. Romance asserts the possibility that men may behave in a noble and self-transcending manner; fabliau declares the certainty that they will always behave like animals. The one portrays men as superhuman, the other portrays them as subhuman. Neither is 'true' or realistic, though we might say that our understanding of what *is* true gains depth from having different slanting lights thrown upon reality, so that beneficial shock, enrichment, invigoration is given to our perception of the world. Romance and fabliau complement one another, and Chaucer encourages us to look at them thus by setting the *Knight's Tale* and the *Miller's Tale* side by side. Each type of story makes a selection of human experience in accord with its own narrative conventions or rules. Out of the interlocking of these and other different types of story, in the general medieval hierarchy of genres, or in the *Canterbury Tales* as a whole, grows the social relevance of literary forms, the fabliau amongst them.

The narrative structure of Chaucer's four fabliaux has already been briefly described. Before going on to deal in detail with the manner in which he works variations on this structure in individual tales, it may be worth pausing to refine the model a little. The basic ingredients are three, a husband, a wife, and an intruder, though the functions of the last two may be duplicated in more complex plots. The intruder is always a man: it is possible to imagine a modern fabliau in which it was a woman, but not a medieval one. The husband belongs to the petit-bourgeoisie, or, if that term means nothing in the Middle Ages, to the world of successful tradesmen; the *Merchant's Tale* is, as often, exceptional, in that the husband is a 'knyght'. The wife is younger than her husband, or, if not younger, still with some unsatisfied sexual potential. This is briefly and devastatingly indicated, for instance, in an aside in the *Reeve's Tale*, when John leaps on the good wife: 'So myrie a fit ne hadde she nat ful yoore' (4230). The wife of the fabliaux is not, it must be stressed, promiscuous, and there is no suggestion that the affair in which she is engaged is a matter of regular occupation. This is not because Chaucer is mealy-mouthed where Boccaccio is (quite often) frank, but because he can thereby increase the amount and quality of the intrigue. The 'intruder' is usually younger than the husband, or at least, as in the *Shipman's Tale*, explicitly more sexually active. More importantly, he belongs to a different class, being usually a student or other kind of cleric or religious, and therefore more clever, flexible and mobile than those with whom he is temporarily (as lodger or guest) accommodated. He is a member of a classless intellectual elite who, in being shown as a predator upon the conventional marital and materialistic values of the bourgeois, can be brought into an implicit alliance with the aristocracy. The *Merchant's Tale* is once more the exception, and there is no doubt that the nastiness of the tale is much increased by the fact that the intruder is a squire of January's own household, and furthermore one who plays a subordinate part in the intrigue to the wife.

It is not difficult to speak of Chaucer's fabliaux in this way, with the plot-elements and characters abstracted as functions, and it is not a distortion of the nature of the fabliaux to draw attention to the narrative rules upon which they operate. But the success of Chaucer's poetry is in the manner in which he works variations on these set patterns, defies expectation, tests the tolerance of the form and the habitual perceptions of the reader, and creates four poems which are as enjoyable for the ways in which each is unique as for the ways in which they fit a pattern.

The *Miller's Tale* is Chaucer's greatest achievement in the genre, and in many ways the most perfectly accomplished of all the *Canterbury Tales*. It seems to overflow with high spirits, and to convey, despite the nasty and painful events it describes, a sort of genial gusto. It is full of music and amorous serenading, whether Nicholas practising on his 'gay sautrie' (3213) and singing *Angelus ad Virginem* (thinking, perhaps, of himself as the angel Gabriel and Alison as the prospective 'virgin') or Absolon setting about his midnight 'gyternynge' (3363) at the famous 'shot-wyndowe'. The allusions to music often have a strong sexual suggestion, as when Nicholas turns his attention to his instrument after his exciting interview with Alison:

> Whan Nicholas had doon thus everideel,
> And thakked hire aboute the lendes weel,
> He kiste hire sweete and taketh his sawtrie,
> And pleyeth faste, and maketh melodie.   (3303–6)

The most notable of these allusions, and the one that seems to capture the spirit of the tale, is the brief description of the love-making of Nicholas and Alison after they have tiptoed down from their tubs into the vacant marital bed: 'Ther was the revel and the melodye' (3652). The little touch of lyricism here is not dissipated by the further musical allusion that follows, when we are told that they went on enjoying themselves 'Til that the belle of laudes gan to rynge, / And freres in the chauncel gonne synge.' (3655–6). A contrast between the two kinds of 'music' is implied, but with no more than genial perfunctoriness. The notion that some critics have that the religious reference acts as a reminder of Nicholas and Alison's wickedness is heavy-handed in the extreme. Nicholas and Alison have their 'bisynesse', and the friars have theirs: there is no competition. References to the church and the religious life of the community are frequent in the tale, but essentially as part of the unnoticed furniture of everyday urban life and part of the tale's incomparable substantiality. That Alison should go, after being well 'thakked aboute the lendes' by Nicholas, to the parish church, 'Cristes owene werkes for to wirche' (3308), is charmingly inapposite, but to call it 'ironical' would be to load the tale with a moral freight it has no purpose to bear.

The quality of lyricism in the tale is further enhanced by its exuberant travesty of courtly language and behaviour. It is a very 'literary' fabliau. The elaborate description of Alison, for instance, comes at just the point where the heroine would be described in a romance, and it is a beautifully observed parody of the conventional top-to-toe inventory. In itself, too, it is a subtle mixture of the vulgar and the artfully seductive: bedizened in black and white silk, in the latest out-of-date provincial fashion, and with a brooch planted in her cleavage 'As brood as is the boos of a bokeler' (3266), she is yet as lithe as a weasel, 'wynsynge' like a young colt, and her breath smells, unforgettably, one would think, of apples 'leyd in hey or heeth'. To try to 'contain' such a picture within a moral or satirical frame of reference would be to deny the irresistible impression of animal vitality, indeed of innocence. So too when she acts out her little scene with Nicholas: he is the impassioned lover, ready to 'spille' if his desires are not satisfied (3278), and she is the coy mistress, threatening to cry out (but not too loud) if he does not remove his hand from her 'queynte'. She does not thoroughly understand why she should be, even temporarily, under this nice restraint (any more than a colt 'in the trave': 3282), but she obliges with a decent if brief show of reluctance.

Absolon, of course, is a more obvious satirical target, and his efforts to play the courtly lover are genuinely ludicrous. He has had some success with the flighty local barmaids, but he is a deal too circumspect for your true courtly lover, who would not expect to have to take a nap in order to prepare for his night's doings (3685) nor to chew 'greyn and lycorys' (3690) to make his breath sweet. When he arrives at the 'shot-wyndowe' to devastate Alison with his guitar, he gets everything wrong: the echoes of the Song of Songs (3698–3707) are in a good courtly tradition, but not the emphasis on his 'sweating' for love nor on his desire for her as that of the 'lamb after the tete'. He also calls her, twice, his 'lemman', which is a coarse form of address, and hilariously inappropriate to his pretensions as a lover.[4]

In addition to the lyricism and gaiety that these allusions give to the tale, there is also an unexpected generosity, as well as a great fertility of comic invention, in Chaucer's portrayal of his characters. John the carpenter is the most notable example: set up at the start as that traditionally licensed victim of satire, the old man who marries a young wife, he is portrayed as richly complacent and gullible. The congratulations he offers himself on his simple honest Christian faith, and the way it has helped him avoid getting into the state Nicholas is in, are unforgettable:

> 'I thoghte ay wel how that it sholde be!
> Men sholde nat knowe of Goddes pryvetee.
> Ye, blessed be alwey a lewed man
> That noght but oonly his bileve kan!'   (3453–6)

His readiness to accept Nicholas's fantastic story of the coming flood shows another kind of simple faith, and perhaps no great reluctance to be cast in the role of a second Noah. Yet his concern for Nicholas, who has been missing all weekend, is quite good-natured and unselfish, and his first reaction to the news of the flood is to think of his wife: '"Allas, my wyf! / And shal she drenche? allas, myn Alisoun!"' (3522–3). There is enough here to give us a twinge of sympathy, but no more. Chaucer's control of our emotional responses of engagement and sympathy, responses such as are totally alien in the tradition of fabliau, is consummate. He allows us the delightful apprehension of a momentary intrusion of feeling, and then resumes his splendid fooling.

The high spirits of the tale are of course best exemplified in Nicholas, who has all the attributes of 'our hero', the master of plotting and connoisseur of intrigue. Notice what lengths he goes to in order to secure Alison's company on *Monday* night when the carpenter has been away in Oseney all the previous weekend. To have sneaked into bed with Alison then would have been, one feels, no challenge. When he is describing the escape from the flood, one senses that he has almost got carried away in the delighted contemplation of his own imaginative creation:

> 'Thanne shaltou swymme as myrie, I undertake,
> As dooth the white doke after hire drake.
> Thanne wol I clepe, "How, Alison! how, John!
> Be myrie, for the flood wol passe anon."
> And thou wolt seyn, "Hayl, maister Nicholay!
> Good morwe, I se thee wel, for it is day."'   (3575–80)

Nicholas's wit and vitality carry all before them, but his downfall comes when he tries to repeat the trick Alison played on Absolon: this is a lapse from the high standard of cunning and inventiveness we expect of him, and he is duly punished. Absolon deserves his moment of triumph. Alison, by contrast, escapes scot-free, and quite properly so, according to the laws of the comic fabliau, not because she has done nothing wrong but because she has done nothing that betrays her nature. Throughout she behaves like the healthy animal she is, quick, alert, high-spirited, where Absolon has fantasies of the various animals he might be – a lamb seeking its mother's teat, or a cat playing with Alison-mouse (3347). The ending of the tale, with its catalogue of punishments (3850–3), has the air of justice meted out, but it is not a moral justice.

Fertility and richness of invention characterize the tale. but also a high degree of technical accomplishment. The dropping of hints is unobtrusively neat: the mention of Nicholas's skill in astrology and his ability to predict 'droghte or elles shoures' (3196) and of Absolon's unfortunate squeamishness of farting (3338) are delightful anticipations of significances still to be fulfilled. Absolon's certainty that the itching of his mouth is a sign of kissing 'at the leeste wey' (3680) is one of many prophetic puns that detonate by delayed action. The careful specification of the height above street-level of the 'shot-wyndowe' – 'Unto his brest it raughte, it was so lowe' (3696) – is of course vital to the ensuing action. Most cunningly devised is the long dormancy of the flood-plot, and the reader's sudden realization that Nicholas' cry for water will reactivate it. This is a sublime moment of almost pure aesthetic pleasure. Add to this what Muscatine has called the 'overpowering substantiality' of the tale,[5] and one sees the loving care Chaucer has lavished upon it. The density of detail, the sense of town life extending into deep perspective behind the foreground action, is extraordinary.[6] It is present in the architecture of John's house, down to the gable that looks out upon the garden, over the stable (3572); in the ramblingly uninformative account of John's whereabouts given by the anonymous 'cloisterer' (3661); in the nocturnal activities of Gerveys the blacksmith (3761), who had to work at night, of course, because the things he was mending were needed by day; and perhaps above all in the series of references to the mystery plays. The bustle and business of the street-plays comes vividly alive in the allusions to the Miller himself speaking 'in Pilates voys' (3124) and to Absolon playing Herod 'upon a scaffold hye' (3384) – perhaps in a slightly 'camp', effeminate way? And Chaucer hints mischievously at the effect mystery plays might have on the average citizen in describing John's spectacular ignorance of the whole point of the Noah story.

The *Reeve's Tale* has much of this same substantiality, in its account of the Cambridge college background, the activity of flour-milling, the weary chase through the fens after the runaway horse, and above all in the evocation of the darkened bedroom of the night's encounters. It is remarkable, though, how a tale so similar in structure and technique can create such a totally different impression. Gusto and geniality give way to a spirit of meanness and vindictiveness; the only music to be heard is the cacophony of the family snoring (4165) and the only 'courtly' allusions are in the contemptuous reference to the miller's wife's absurd pretensions to be a lady (3942–3). Both the *Miller's Tale* and the *Reeve's Tale* make a stronger impact individually because of the effect of contrast, a measure of Chaucer's skill in juxtaposition in his mature work on the *Canterbury Tales*.

The tale seems to be concentrated on its destructive purpose, and everything serves the Reeve's revenge upon the Miller. Where the *Miller's*

Tale began with a seductive description of Alison, the Reeve begins by presenting the miller of his tale as a target to be attacked and destroyed. His violence, his thievery and his pride in his lineage are singled out for attention, and then systematically rebuked and punished in the most painful and humiliating way. He himself is beaten up not only by the students but by his own wife, his ill-gotten flour is restored to the students by his own daughter, and that daughter herself, of whom he had such hopes, is now thoroughly shop-soiled:

> 'Who dorste be so boold to disparage
> My doghter, that is come of swich lynage?'   (4271-2)

Even his hospitality in allowing the students to lodge with him is given no chance to register sympathetically because of his sneering remarks about the students' book-learning (4122-6). His wife is portrayed with open contempt, and there is no hint of affection in the picture of his daughter and her coarsely nubile charms:

> This wenche thikke and wel ygrowen was,
> With kamus nose, and eyen greye as glas,
> With buttokes brode, and brestes rounde and hye;
> But right fair was hire heer, I wol nat lye.   (3973-6)

The students themselves have nothing of Nicholas about them and are not attractive in their own right. They are oafish fellows, and Chaucer takes some care to present them as northerners and to have them speak in a passable imitation of fourteenth-century northern dialect: that the miller can be shown to be outwitted and put down by such bumpkins makes him even more to be derided.

A particular edge is given to the tale's nastiness by the manner in which sexual activity is portrayed. Chaucer has removed from the original story, as told in a French fabliau,[7] the element of sexual attraction that first draws the one student to the daughter and then the other to the wife. Aleyn and John act simply out of revenge and because the family snoring is keeping them awake. There are no musical allusions or lyrical overtones: they jump on the women like animals: 'He priketh harde and depe as he were mad' (4231) and the fact that the women find they like it impugns only the miller's pride and virility. The little parody of the *aube*-scene (the lovers must part because of the approach of day) has Aleyn taking his leave of the daughter, Malyne, more because he is exhausted, it appears, than anything:

> Aleyn wax wery in the dawenynge,
> For he had swonken al the longe nyght.   (4234-5)

His vows of undying fidelity are perfunctorily echoed by Malyne, who has the grace 'almoost' to weep (4248), but who is chiefly concerned to hand over her father's hard-won cake of flour.

Systematically, it appears, those touches of lyricism and generosity that graced the *Miller's Tale* have been stripped away, and the fabliau used as a machine for the Reeve's vindictive purposes. Something of the tale's special tone might be related to the character of the Reeve, who seems bent on revenge even before he has heard the supposed attack on himself (also a carpenter) in the *Miller's Tale*. He is the kind of man who makes a profession of taking offence, and who makes a slimy pretence of self-righteousness to cover his envious and suspicious nature. His own prologue is a remarkably disgusting piece of self-ingratiating self-abasement. In pressing the narrator upon our attention in this way, Chaucer is bound to make us conscious of him, at least at one level, as we read his tale: certainly the sense of vindictive purpose is strong, and there are pointed allusions to the quasi-legal sanctions that justify getting one's own back (4181, 4321). But it would be wrong to make this 'the meaning' of the tale: the rumpus in the bedroom at the end is in the best manner of high-spirited fabliau, and the most we might say is that Chaucer has given our laughter an edge of uneasiness by having us share it with the Reeve. From a larger point of view, one might see the *Reeve's Tale* as the inseparable companion of the *Miller's Tale*. They are the Jekyll and Hyde of fabliau; the one necessarily belongs to and comments upon the other.

The *Shipman's Tale* has no dramatic context in the pilgrimage, and its brevity has often encouraged people to think of it as 'basic' fabliau. It is in fact a subtle and highly contrived variation on the form which has its own individual character. At first, by comparison with the Miller's and Reeve's tales, it seem easiest to characterize by negatives. It has no violence and no very explicit depictions of sexual activity, no courtly allusions, no lyrical fantasies, and no-one seems very much upset by what happens. The narrator seems quite happy with the world he inhabits, and there is very little satirical comment, except such as is implicit in reporting such a world without comment.

It is in terms of such blandness that the tale is most acutely characterized. Throughout no-one speaks openly or directly or honestly to anyone else, neither in rage, scorn nor desire. Everyone is politely diplomatic, careful not to offend and not to reveal any real purpose or feeling. The scene between the wife and the monk in the garden is a beautifully decorous comedy of manners, with each delicate advance towards mutual understanding carefully planned and signalled. The monk's playful insinuation of her husband's inadequacy in bed (at which he has the grace himself to blush) encourages the wife to speak of her other dissatisfactions; they exchange vows of secrecy; the monk discovers that he has always been waiting for this moment of intimacy; the wife's need of money seals the bond. It is like making love over the counter, and in some strange way the exchange of money seems to legitimize rather than corrupt the encounter. Nothing of this comes out in the open, of course. The wife sees what she does as a perfectly reasonable business transaction, and the monk, though there may be an element of calculation in his carefully regulated tipping of the members of the merchant's household (46), and certainly an accomplished skill in his technique of asking for a loan (269–80), is not portrayed as a scrounger or a predator.

The merchant, however, is the most unexpected beneficiary of the general complacency. He too is treated soberly, even generously. His avarice is not stressed, except by his wife, and he has a careful tedious explanation to his wife of why he has to spend so much time on his accounts:

> 'Wyf,' quod this man, 'litel kanstow devyne
> The curious bisynesse that we have'...   (224–5)

He speaks as if this is not the first time he has had to do this kind of explaining. The same quality of carefully fostered good nature comes over in his response to the monk's request for a loan. It is a generous response, of course, and the hundred francs are immediately promised. The promise, however, is followed by the careful qualification:

> But o thyng is, ye knowe it well ynogh,
> Of chapmen, that hir moneie is hir plogh.   (287–8)

He wants to remind the monk that ready money is not easily come by in the finance business, that it is not a little thing for him to do, that it *is* a loan, at the same time that he wants to appear generous. One recognizes the desire to be thought well of, or to think well of oneself, and it comes out again in the merchant's later rebuke to his wife for not having told him of the return of the loan. He is annoyed because he feels he might have been thought by the monk to have arranged to meet him in Paris in order to ask the monk for his money back. We are specifically told that this was not his intention (338), and the merchant cannot bear the thought of a generous intention wasted.

The wife has her own problem when she hears of what the monk has in fact done – that is, borrow the money from her husband to give to her (in exchange for a night in bed with her) so that she can pay her debts. She now owes the money to her husband too. But sex comes to the rescue again, and she pays her husband in the same coin as she paid the monk. So the hundred francs has gone the rounds, and so has the wife, and no-one seems much the worse for the experience. In fact, there is hardly a ripple on the surface of surburban life. There is a good deal of insight in this tale into the power of money, into the nature of sex as a commodity, and into the subterfuges of self-deception. The tale is coldly exhilarating in its total disregard of familiar moral decencies.

The *Merchant's Tale* is quite different, and certainly Chaucer's most ambitious exercise in the fabliau form, so ambitious in fact that it threatens to explode the form into something like a modern 'black comedy'. It is a more powerful poem than the *Miller's Tale*, and expands on the technique of that tale with extensive lyrical interpolations (the marriage ceremony 1709–41; January's love song, 2138–48), rhetorical digressions (e.g. 1783–94, 2057–68), a long mock-encomium on marriage at the beginning, and a mythological episode of Pluto and Proserpina at the end. There are, as in the *Miller's Tale*, many subtle verbal anticipations and echoings: January's comparison of his sexuality to the evergreen laurel (1466) is echoed in the laurel in the garden where he is cuckolded (2037); the wax to which he compares the pliability of the desired wife (1430) is echoed in the wax that the wife uses to make a copy of the key to the garden (2117). The fabliau nucleus is still there, in the episode of the pear-tree, but is almost an afterthought to a rich and strange performance.

One was aware of a sneering malevolence in the *Reeve's Tale*. Here that tone is continuous and raised to a high pitch of stridency. The opening account of January's desire to get married drips with contempt for such old fools, and the mock-encomium of marriage is openly sarcastic at times rather than mockingly ironical. The description of the marriage ceremony is cynically reductive: the priest comes forth,

> And seyde his orisons, as is usage,
> And croucheth hem, and bad God sholde hem blesse,
> And made al siker ynogh with hoolynesse.   (1706–8)

Not merely this travesty of marriage, but marriage as such, seems to be sneered at, and the same Thersitean voice is heard in the comments on January's energetic imitation of the Song of Songs: 'Swiche olde lewed wordes used he' (2149). The voice throughout is that of the clerical misogynist, and is expressive of that cynicism about sexuality generally which is the legacy of religious celibacy. It is the rhetoric of a disordered and mutilated consciousness, and Chaucer gives to it an extraordinary Swiftian power.

January himself is something more than the traditional *senex amans*. To the disgust traditionally associated with that figure Chaucer adds a lurid physical reality:

> And Januarie hath faste in armes take
> His fresshe May, his paradys, his make.
> He lulleth hire, he kisseth hire ful ofte;
> With thikke brustles of his berd unsofte,
> Lyk to the skyn of houndfyssh, sharp as brere.   (1821–5)

The images of sexual possession as eating (1419), the fantasies of prolonged rape (1757–61), the haste, the barrelfuls of aphrodisiacs (1807), give a partly comic effect, but always with an undertone of disgust and repulsion. It is as if someone were telling a dirty story and insisting on going into detail, materializing every innuendo. The effect is shocking and disorientating, for there seems no centre of consciousness that we can draw to except the one that is disgusted and fascinated by sexuality. What is more, January is granted a kind of deformed moral consciousness, so that he is constantly preoccupied with whether what he is doing is right or lawful. Hence his long debates with his advisers, and with himself, and his pathetically confident explanation to May that what he is about to do to her, previously wrong, is now, by virtue of 'trewe wedlok', right: 'For we han leve to pleye us by the lawe' (1841). There is no need to be reminded how alien to fabliau is the stimulus to feeling and moral reflection, however perverted, that we are given in the *Merchant's Tale*.

A further strange twist to the tale is given by the portrayal of May and Damian. They would conventionally in a fabliau have the advantage and merit of youth, and some quality of gaiety and vigour would hang about their liaison. But they lack even January's vitality. God knows, says the narrator, what May thought of January's wedding-night performance, suggesting, in his prurient way, the unspeakable horrors of maidenly innocence violated – but then he tells us, with equally characteristic bluntness: 'She preyseth nat his pleyyng worth a bene' (1854). The coldness of the appraisal is as shocking as any of January's excesses, and the narrator's subsequent sneering remarks about her 'pitee' (1986, 1995), his gratuitous bit of information about the fate of Damian's love-letter (1954), suggest not a healthy animal vitality but a perverted cold sexuality. Damian is no more than a poodle to this lady dog-trainer and it is indeed to a fawning dog that he is compared when he returns to court and smothers January with his obsequious attentions (2014). January's own overheated sexual fantasies come to seem almost natural by comparison. His blindness, too, creates a grudging sympathy in us, and in him a kind of insight, as when he speaks to May of his 'unlikly elde' (2180) and his awareness of how he may appear to her. The corrupted understanding seems more and more to be that of the narrator.

The ending restores the lighter and more spirited mood of fabliau, and May's trick is a good one. If the ending suggests that January will do well to cherish the illusion she has put him under, and that happiness is truly the perpetual possession of being well deceived, then that is no more than we expect of fabliau. The sense of trespass, however, in the tale as a whole, remains. Chaucer, in suggesting to us all sorts of themes of moral and emotional significance, has violated all the expectations of the genre without creating any alternative order for the understanding of the tale.

There is a character called Justinus, whose name suggests that he should represent some point of vantage in the story, some resting-place for the reader's bewildered moral consciousness; but he turns out to be wise only in the cynicism of embittered experience. There is no escape from the horror of sexuality. The attribution of the tale to the Merchant solves no problems, since there is no way in which the tale can be 'contained' within what we can legitimately assume about his character. The most we can say about the prologue, and its account of the plight of the unhappily married Merchant, is that it may be part of some process of revision in which this disturbing tale was accommodated to a more conventional complaint against marriage.

The Friar's and Summoner's tales lack something of the immediacy of appeal of the fabliaux, since they deal with specialized kinds of medieval corrupt practice, and not with sex and marriage, but they are both masterpieces of satirical anecdote. Though not strictly speaking fabliaux, they operate according to the same basic comic rules, namely, that the criterion by which human beings are judged successful is the extent to which they find means fully to satisfy their appetites and manipulate the world, by their smartness, to their will. What Chaucer has done is to absorb satire of the professional activities of summoners and friars into the dramatic comedy of the exchange of abuse between the Friar and Summoner. Moral outrage at what they describe each other as doing is a proper preliminary response, but it is swallowed up in laughter, since what the narrators try to do is to prove not that their victims are knaves but that they are fools. They know perfectly well that to demonstrate their opponent's success in villainy will cause no wound, since there is nothing to be ashamed of in following one's rapacious nature. To demolish one's victim effectively, he must be shown to be stupid, and both the Friar and the Summoner do this in the same way, by portraying their victims as pathetically gullible. Both the summoner of the *Friar's Tale* and the friar of the *Summoner's Tale* misunderstand things that would be obvious to the meanest intelligence, mistake the surface for reality, the letter for the spirit, and end up destroying themselves through their own stupidity.

The *Friar's Tale* is quite brief. It begins with the expected attack on the fictional summoner, but soon the story takes over, and we gradually forget the pilgrim-Friar and pilgrim-Summoner, engrossed as we are in the summoner's meeting with the mysterious yeoman. The revelation of his identity is gradual, with all sorts of hints and ironies to follow up; the summoner's embarrassment about his own profession, meanwhile, makes him more pathetically contemptible than being accused of robbing a hundred widows:

> He dorste nat, for verray filthe and shame
> Seye that he was a somonour, for the name.   (1393-4)

The hilarity of the tale begins when the devil-yeoman reveals his identity. We naturally expect that the summoner will show some sign of apprehension, or at least some sign that he realizes something significant is happening. But no: he seems impenetrable to all understanding, and preoccupied with the devil's skill in shape-changing. He behaves like a con-man who has met a fellow trickster, and is so persistent in his trivial enquiries that the devil begins to show a certain exasperation, as if irritated that he has been sent on a special mission to capture a soul of such banality. Through all the subsequent incidents of the carter who curses his horse and does not mean what he says and the old widow who curses the summoner and does, the summoner remains impervious to any perception but of the grossly literal. Twice invited to think again or to repent (1522, 1629), he seems not even to understand what he stands to lose. The joke against the summoner is not that he is snatched off to hell but that he will not even realize where he is when he gets there.

The Summoner's response is violent, and his immediate riposte, concerning the dwelling-place of friars in the nether regions, is appropriately anal. This anality is wittily prolonged into the tale, with puns on 'ferthyng' (1967), 'fundement' (2103), and 'ars-metrike' (2222), and of course the denouement is a great fart. All this may seem very suitable to a man whose diet was all 'garleek, oynons, and eek lekes' (1, 634). However, the story he tells is not vile and reeking of the sewer, but cool, witty, and precisely judged. The portrait of the friar at his characteristic activities of hypocritical wheedling, and 'glosynge' ('Glosynge is a glorious thyng, certeyn': 1793) takes up the great bulk of the tale, and it is done with superb skill and panache. One notices the accustomed smoothness with which he shoos the cat off the most comfortable seat and takes its place (1775), the amorous suggestiveness of his address to Thomas' wife and the little variation he introduces into the fraternal kiss ('and chirketh as a sparwe / With his lyppes': 1804–5), the air of ascetic self-denial and true Franciscan charity ('But that I nolde no beest for me were deed': 1842) with which he orders his gourmet dinner. There is even something quite engaging about his quickness of wit in getting out of difficult situations. Suddenly realizing that the household of which he is such a close friend has suffered a bereavement of which he should have apprised himself, he lays on immediately an imaginary funeral service in which he galvanizes the whole brotherhood into activity,

> 'With many a teere trillying on my cheke,
> Withouten noyse or claterynge of belles'.   (1864–5)

The last detail is a shrewd bit of quick thinking: the bells, if they had sounded, would have been heard. So too when Thomas complains that all his gifts to the different friars have done him no good:

The frere answerde, 'O Thomas, dostow so?
What nedeth yow diverse freres seche?
What nedeth hym that hath a parfit leche
To sechen othere leches in the toun?
Your inconstance is youre confusioun...
A! yif that covent half a quarter otes!
A! yif that covent foure and twenty grotes!
A! yif that frere a peny, and lat hym go!
Nay, nay, Thomas, it may no thyng be so!
What is a ferthyng worth parted in twelve?'   (1954–8, 1963–7)

He is a true ancestor of Falstaff, and we are obliged to pay laughing respect, in the very teeth of morality, to such vitality.

Towards the end of the tale, however, the friar seems to 'go into automatic'. His sermon on Ire is queasily irrelevant, and his demands on Thomas become more peremptory and blatant. He falls over-eagerly for Thomas's trick, and then, ridiculously, seems more put out by the absurdly impossible problem in 'ars-metrike' he has been set than by the grossness of his humiliation. All our memory of the quarrel between the Friar and the Summoner, all possibility of morally based satire on the friar, seem swallowed up in the conclusion of the story, in the posing of the puzzle of the divided fart and its fantastically imaginative solution. Humour gets the better of satire, and Chaucer, as often, seems to prefer complicity with the world of his creatures to moral criticism.

Notes

1 The essays of Henri Bergson ('Laughter') and George Meredith ('An Essay in Comedy') are conveniently available in *Comedy*, ed. Wylie Sypher (New York, 1956).

2 Mikhail Bakhtin, *Rabelais and his World*, trans. Helene Iswolsky (Cambridge, Mass., 1965). For skilful use of Bakhtin in relation to the *Miller's Tale*, see Alfred David, *The Strumpet Muse: Art and Morals in Chaucer's Poetry* (Bloomington, Ind./London, 1976), pp. 94, 104–5.

3 The traditional view is that of Joseph Bédier (*Les Fabliaux*, 1893) and is opposed by Per Nykrog, *Les Fabliaux: Étude d'histoire littéraire et de stylistique médiévale* (Copenhagen, 1957). For a convenient summary of opinions, see D. S. Brewer, 'The Fabliaux' in *Companion to Chaucer Studies*, ed. Beryl Rowland (Toronto/New York/London, 1968), pp. 247–67. There are important qualifications to Nykrog's view, suggestive of a looser and more heterogeneous audience for fabliau, in Charles Muscatine, 'The Social Background of the Old French Fabliaux', *Genre*, 9 (1976), 1–19.

4 See E. Talbot Donaldson, 'Idiom of Popular Poetry in the Miller's Tale', in *English Institute Essays 1950*, ed. A. S. Downer (New York, 1951), pp. 116–40; repr. in the author's *Speaking of Chaucer* (London, 1970), pp. 13–29.

5 Charles Muscatine, *Chaucer and the French Tradition: A Study in Style and Meaning* (Berkeley/Los Angeles, Ca./London, 1957), p. 226.

6 J. A. W. Bennett, *Chaucer at Oxford and at Cambridge* (Oxford, 1974), provides ample historical documentation to confirm this critical impression of the *Miller's Tale* and the *Reeve's Tale*.

7 For analogues to Chaucer's fabliaux, see Larry D. Benson and Theodore M. Andersson, *The Literary Contexts of Chaucer's Fabliaux; Texts and Translations* (Indianapolis, Ind./New York, 1971).

9   The *Canterbury Tales* III: Pathos

T HE narratives we may call 'tales of pathos' – the tales of the Man of Law, Clerk, Physician, Prioress and Monk – make greater demands on a modern reader's historical sense and imaginative sympathies than probably any other grouping in the *Canterbury Tales*. An understanding reading can be rewarding, however, in several ways. They introduce us to modes of thinking and feeling central to fourteenth-century experience, illuminating aspects of Chaucer's world he otherwise left unexplored. They also testify to his passionate interest in the many forms of story flooding the late medieval world. Not of least importance, several of his greatest achievements are found here.

'Tales of pathos', however, are not a genre. No two narratives are the same: they include a saint's life, a miracle of the Virgin, a series of *de casibus* stories, a religious romance, an expanded exemplum, and a tale. These tales vary, too, in the degree of pathos aimed for and achieved. The *Second Nun's Tale* and the *Monk's Tale* – with one striking exception – are only marginally pathetic, whereas the *Clerk's Tale*, the *Prioress's* and the *Man of Law's* are intensely so. Nevertheless, they may be properly considered together. They share a narrative mode and a method of treatment, they possess several features in common, and they make essentially the same demand on a modern reader and are best understood and appreciated by reference to certain characteristics of fourteenth-century experience and mentality.

Unlike so many of Chaucer's narratives, they are in no way comic. Chaucerian irony is also absent. There is little or no complexity. Characters are generally one- or two-dimensional, motivated by a single virtue: constancy, patience, simple piety. The treatment of scene tends to be abstract. The action is played on a bare stage, so to speak. The narratives concentrate on crucial incident, moments of extreme threat, pain, distress, anguish. Or, if there is a happy ending, tearful bliss.

Chaucer's principal artistic concern (with the *Monk's Tale*, again, possibly an exception) is to produce a strong emotional effect. The situations – death of a child, separation of loved ones, being set adrift at sea, martyrdom – in themselves arouse feeling. Special attention is given to the emotional reaction of the central character, and, often, of witnesses,

143

and of the narrator as well. Additional devices to heighten feeling and involvement may be used: apostrophes, *exclamatio*, allusions charged with religious significance and emotional associations. Such non-narrative, rhetorical passages often alternate with dramatic scenes. The aim is to involve the audience and persuade them to an empathetic posture.

This, of course, is the essential nature of the pathetic. It is a mode of artistic representation that seeks to evoke pity and compassion in the beholder and to elicit tears of sympathy. Pathos, however, is out of fashion today. Except, perhaps, for the literature of brutality and violence, and for pornography, our age resents having its feelings worked upon, particularly its sense of pity. Appeals for food for starving children and funds for victims of disaster may make some use of pathos, but art may not. Receptivity to pathos is very much a matter of the taste of an age. Nineteenth-century British readers, Leigh Hunt, Wordsworth, Matthew Arnold, among others, responded with special enthusiasm to the tales considered here.

We will accept the tragic in art, but not the pathetic. The distinction between the two is helpful for a sharper understanding of this mode. The difference lies primarily in the nature of the central characters and of their relation to the action. In pathos, they must be victims, that is, they must be passive, not active agents who struggle in some fashion, however futile, against opposing forces and even contribute to their own destruction, as in tragedy. In pathos the central character is a suffering figure, and this suffering arouses our sympathy. If the suffering is totally undeserved, even stronger feeling is evoked, and so innocence is a characteristic of the pathetic victim. So also is weakness, an inability to struggle. The power-lessness of the victim is yet more dramatic if the hostile force acting on him or her is by contrast strong, brutal, evil, and immune to the claims of weakness and innocence.

Pathos, we have said, is dependent on the taste of the times, and Chaucer's age was unusually receptive to it, especially though not exclusively in the area of religion. In fourteenth- and fifteenth-century literature and art, religious pathos was powerful and pervasive. Three of our tales are religious in genre and subject, and there are references to 'icons' of religious pathos in two others. The account of Ugolino in the *Monk's Tale* is without overt religious allusion, but its language and imagery are rich in religious and biblical resonances.[1]

This deep vein of religious pathos has several sources. In a variety of ways religion in this period fed and aroused strong feelings of pity, joy, terror, hope. The church did not depend on the teaching of formal doctrine alone. It also reached layfolk by appeals to feeling. The horrors of hell were graphically drawn in sermons and confessional manuals, in illuminations in Books of Hours, and in paintings on interior church walls. Sermons, lyrics, the mystery cycles, and art vividly recreated the sufferings of Christ and the anguish of the Virgin in the several stages of the Passion, the tender joy of the Nativity, the fearful flight into Egypt.

Behind much of this lay a phenomenon known as the humanization of Christ, well established by Chaucer's time. The human nature of Christ had become as significant for worshippers as the divine. Representations of the Crucifixion in the ninth and tenth centuries show a remote, austere God commanding awe and reverence. The thirteenth and fourteenth centuries present a suffering, dying man petitioning the beholder's compassion and tears, as do the swooning Virgin and the weeping Magdalene. Pictorial representations of this suffering, mortal God, loved and mourned by a mother and dear companions, call for a human, empathetic response. Lyrics report the Passion in lurid detail or express the sorrow of one meditating on the scene: in some, Christ speaks directly from the cross to the reader, bidding him see how He suffers. Many portray Mary's grief, often uttered directly by her.

A powerful agent in this humanization of Christ was the religious form called the meditation. Originally a monastic exercise, it was later adopted by lay persons. The meditant concentrated his or her thoughts on scenes or subjects that would bring home forcefully the crises of the human condition: death, the pains of hell, the bliss of heaven, one's sinfulness, God's goodness, the urgency of repentance. Scenes from the life of Christ, and of the Virgin, proved especially effective. Written meditations served as guides. None was more popular than a thirteenth-century work by an anonymous Italian Franciscan, the *Meditations on the Life of Christ*. More than two hundred manuscripts survive, and the Latin version was translated into many vernaculars, including Middle English.

Two facts about the *Meditations* are relevant here. First, it added freely to the Gospel accounts of Christ's life, drawing on apocryphal writings, the *Golden Legend*, and the author's fertile imagination. A complete 'domestic' history was created, in which the bond between the Virgin and Christ was stressed insistently. We learn how the infant cried in pain at the circumcision and how Mary wept to hear him cry. We are told that during the years in Egypt the Virgin sewed and spun to earn money, and the five-year-old child Jesus went about in search of work for his mother. The Gospel's silence on the years between Christ's twelfth and thirtieth years is filled by an account of his life with his family, sometimes helping his foster-father Joseph, sometimes assisting his mother by setting the table, making the beds, and doing other household chores. A Christ is created with whom all can identify.

Secondly, the reader of the *Meditations* (and of other meditations) is constantly urged to participate in the action and to respond empathetically to the scene presented. The language is now vivid and detailed, now charged and emotive, and from time to time the reader is told to step into the scene. At the Nativity, the meditant should kiss the infant's feet: 'beg His mother to offer to let you hold Him a while. Pick Him up and hold Him in your arms. Gaze on His face with devotion and reverently kiss Him and delight in Him'. After visiting the Holy Family in Egypt, on leaving the meditant should 'kneel before them and take leave of them with tears and deep sympathy, for they were exiled and driven away from their country for no reason'. On the road to Gethsemane, the meditant is urged to 'Look at Him well, then, as He goes along bowed down by the cross and gasping aloud. Feel as much compassion for Him as you can, placed in such anguish, in renewed derision.'[2]

The influence of the *Meditations* was enormous. So also was the cult of the Virgin. She won adoring partisans as the most merciful resource in the pantheon. She became not just the mother of God, but of all mankind. She could be turned to in desperation as one willing to intercede for a poor sinner when all else had failed. Her humility and her obedience made her a model for all; her compassion also invited imitation. As a human mother she shared the basic experience of womankind; as a mother who had witnessed her son's death at the hands of remorseless men she knew the bitterest agony of a parent. In her miracles she is seen to be especially responsive to the helpless and the innocent, and especially alert to the tragedies of commonplace domestic life. She became an icon of pathos and a model of compassion.

The spirit of Franciscan piety also infuses this vein of late medieval spirituality. St Francis' devotion to the wounds and suffering of Christ and to the Virgin, his tears at the thought of their pain, his encompassing humanity and compassion, embracing the humblest and most despised – indeed, his love and tears for all created things, whether a leper, a cricket, or a stone – make him the patron saint of pathos. In reading these narratives, his influence in these centuries should not be forgotten. He might well have been Chaucer's ideal audience.

Finally, what can we deduce concerning Chaucer's own religious attitude? His primary image as a comic artist and an ironist may be difficult to reconcile with his role as an artist of the pathetic. (Charles Dickens, however, is not too remote a parallel.) But there is no reason to doubt that he shared the religious faith of his time. Such evidence as we have suggests that he was directly, devoutly religious, with a special love for the Virgin Mary. The faith and the fondness are demonstrated by his translation, probably early in his career, from the French, of 'An A B C to the Virgin'. The 'Retractation' attached to the conclusion of the *Canterbury Tales*, near the end of his life, is an explicit statement of faith and repentance. His fondness for the Virgin seems confirmed when the Prioress praises her reverently in her *Prologue* and then recounts one of her miracles. His translation of the life of St Cecilia, which eventually became the *Second Nun's Tale*, with its fervent, carefully fashioned Invocation to the Virgin, suggests no wavering in his middle years. Let us turn to it first.

We know from the *Prologue* to the *Legend of Good Women* (F 426) that the translation of St Cecilia's life preceded the Canterbury project by several years. We should see it, therefore, as an act of personal devotion. Saints' lives were a popular form all through the medieval period, and the numerous translations into Old English and Middle English served an increasingly literate lay public for whom Latin was a closed book. In the second half of the thirteenth century Jacobus de Voragine had made an encyclopedic collection of saints' lives, the *Golden Legend* (*Legenda Aurea*), organized around the church calendar. This in some form was Chaucer's source for roughly the first two-thirds of his narrative, after which he switched to a longer version of the legend, the *Passio S. Caeciliae*.

Whatever his personal reasons, it was a good choice as a narrative. It is unified in theme: from beginning to end, St Cecilia is devoted to the work of conversion. It is climactic in its action, moving from the personal scene of her wedding night, when her vow of chastity leads to her husband's acceptance of her faith, through an ever widening circle of conversions and accompanying martyrdoms, to the dramatic confrontation with the Roman prefect Almachius and St Cecilia's martyrdom by fire and sword (beheading).

Chaucer had great respect for his original and claimed to be following it faithfully (VIII, 24–6). He did so, up to about line 354. But changing his source there, he began to cut skilfully, eliminating speeches that delayed the action and moving quickly to the climactic scenes. It is, then, 'something more complex than an ordinary translation', it is 'in some sense a new work'.[3]

His greatest gift here is, nonetheless, his beautiful translation, a remarkable example of the translator's art, faithful to its original but with no evidence of strain or awkwardness. The language moves with the naturalness and ease of an original creation. This is especially evident in the handling of the verse form, the rhyme-royal stanza of his middle period (seven decasyllabic lines rhyming ababbcc). It is the stanza of the *Parliament of Fowls* and *Troilus and Criseyde*. He used it also for three other narratives in the present grouping, the tales of the Man of Law, Prioress, and Clerk. These are also translations essentially, though treated more freely. Whatever other reason Chaucer may have had for employing the stanza, it served him well as a translator.

Though St Cecilia's story ends in martyrdom, it qualifies only marginally as a tale of pathos. True, she is innocent, and she is helpless against Roman power and is, finally, a victim. Nevertheless, she is too strong a figure to evoke our pity in any insistent fashion. Valerian's affection for his brother is touching, as are Tiburce's simple, direct acceptance of his new faith and St Cecilia's chaste kiss of welcome on his breast. These human moments soften the tone. People weep at dramatic scenes. But St Cecilia's vigorous, contemptuous challenging of the Roman Almachius has a touch of the heroic. (Some readers think it unduly arrogant, but this is the standard posture of martyrs before their pagan accusers.) Her heroic stance continues through her martyrdom to the end. There may be some pathos in her isolation, but it is not stressed. The challenge to the reader of this tale is to search out and respond to the spirit of reverence which pervades the narrative and its language.

Like all saints' lives, its message is the special grace of God revealed in the saint's power of conversion, unshakeable faith, and the willing, even joyful, acceptance of the torments of martyrdom in witness of that faith's truth and power. The narrative pits simple faith against literal-mindedness and disbelief, and demonstrates the penetrating power of faith's vision as against the blindness of false or inadequate belief. This is done first engagingly, and in a low key, through St Cecilia's husband, Valerian, and his brother, Tiburce, and then, more dramatically, through the menacing, frustrated Roman prefect, Almachius. The simplicity of Valerian and Tiburce, both before and after conversion, is charming. They penetrate the illusion of the literal and see truth. Almachius never does. His power against St Cecilia can be exercised only with divine permission. She triumphs over him in her life and in her death.

Lucifer, Adam, Samson, Hercules, Nebuchadnezzar, Belshazzar, Zenobia; the 'Modern Instances': Pedro of Spain, Peter of Cyprus, Bernabò, Ugolino; Nero, Holofernes, Antiochus, Alexander, Caesar, Croesus.

The seventeen brief narratives that constitute the *Monk's Tale* are *de casibus* tragedies, telling of 'falls' (*casus*) from greatness. Boccaccio had compiled a great number of such narratives in his *De Casibus Virorum Illustrium* (1363). Chaucer borrowed some of his information for the *Monk's Tale* from this work, and it may have inspired his much less extensive collection. Or perhaps it was the *Roman de la Rose* of the preceding century, which also had a brief *de casibus* passage. In the next generation after Chaucer John Lydgate produced the lengthy *Fall of Princes*, working from a French translation of Boccaccio's work. The form continued to be popular into the sixteenth century, where the collection known as *A Mirror for Magistrates* went through many editions.

Chaucer collected his material from a variety of sources – the Bible, Boethius, Dante, the *Roman de la Rose*, as well as Boccaccio. For three of the four 'modern instances' he probably drew on the knowledge of contemporaries. It was a diligent and responsible selection, not a casual gathering. The individual narratives are, for the most part, interesting as stories. (They are best read one at a time, not all in one sitting.) Their greater appeal was as history in a popular, accessible form at a time when books were hard to come by. And they are presented here as history (VII, 1973–4), to which the *de casibus* genre gave a pattern.

More important, it presented history in the form most acceptable, as a moral guide. History's chief value was exemplary, to give men and women examples from the past by which they might be warned and advised. The moral taught is to beware of Fortune. The narratives tell of persons who stood in 'heigh degree' but fell from their position of power, wealth, or fame and lost all, including, finally, their lives. They are often responsible for their own destruction by their folly or their pride, but the active agent in their fall is Fortune.

Fortune and her wheel, on which kings and heroes rose and fell, were a medieval cliché, but a powerful image nonetheless. Life was terrifyingly uncertain in the fourteenth century. More to the point, Fortune had support in philosophy and had a role in the divine plan, spelled out for all to see in Boethius' *Consolation of Philosophy*. This was one of the most influential books of the Middle Ages and one Chaucer had translated and knew well; its importance to *Troilus* and the *Knight's Tale* has already been discussed in this volume by Jill Mann. Boethius defined the nature and role of Fortune. Ever changeable, Fortune rules over the mutable, impermanent, secondary 'goods' of this world, such as fame, riches, and power, as opposed to the immutable, eternal, primary good, the love and pursuit of goodness itself. No man can be secure until he has, in fact, been forsaken by Fortune (II pr. 1). But who can avoid giving some hostages to Fortune?

The leading figure in these narratives is neither helpless nor innocent and so hardly qualifies as an ideal subject for pathos. It is possible, however, that the 'fall' in itself produced a more emotional reaction then than it does today. In a culture so hierarchical, the spectacle of loss of power or fame or riches may have been radically threatening and distressing. Some of the illustrations in a manuscript of the French translation of Boccaccio's *De Casibus* verge on the pathetic and the sentimental. The Monk begins by saying, 'I wol biwaille...'. And the Knight stops the Monk, not because the stories are dull – Chaucer did not work in order to bore his audience – but because he found their 'hevynesse', that is, their sadness, disturbing. (The interruption is an ingenious way to bring a collection of brief stories to a dramatic conclusion.) The stories may then have been received with some intensity of feeling, even a sense of pathos.

This possiblity is reinforced by the inclusion, without apology, of one of the most pathetic tales Chaucer ever told. He took it from a scene in the ninth circle of Dante's *Inferno*, and dropping the gruesome context, heightened the inherent pathos. It tells of the imprisonment and death by starvation of Count Ugolino of Pisa and his three children, the oldest only five. The youngest (aged three) voices his hunger (the last speech in Dante), cries from day to day, and dies. Seeing their father gnaw at his arms in his grief, the other two children misunderstand it as hunger and offer him their flesh. Chaucer, correctly, makes this the last speech we hear: 'And after that, withinne a day or two, / They leyde hem in his lappe adoun and deyde' (2453–4). Though the father's grief is not ignored, the focus is on the innocent children: 'Allas, Fortune! it was greet crueltee / Swiche briddes for to putte in swich a cage!' (2413–14). It is a beautifully carved cameo of the pathetic art. All the elements are there in perfect balance: extremity of situation, helplessness, innocence, powerful familial and emotional ties, sensitive language, and restraint.

The narrative assigned to the Man of Law had a long and complex history but came to Chaucer from a source close at hand, the Anglo-Norman *Chronicle* of Nicholas Trivet (c. 1335). There are many versions in many languages. It recounts the adventures of a beautiful woman falsely accused, who in consequence suffers many trials but is ultimately exonerated and restored to happiness. Chaucer's fellow poet, John Gower, also using Trivet, told the story in his *Confessio Amantis* (II, 587–1598). In the next generation, Thomas Hoccleve told a variant version. *Emaré* and *Le Bone Florence of Rome* are two Middle English romances using the theme. The story obviously had strong contemporary appeal.

Trivet, including it in his *Chronicle*, presented it as an incident in the history of early England. The story is a romance; Trivet gave it a strong hagiographical colouring, making of it a kind of secular saint's life. Chaucer disengaged the story from its chronicle setting but preserved and even intensified the religious elements.

The story is set in a distant time, before Christianity had come to England; and in exotic places – early Rome, pagan Syria, pagan Northumbria. The heroine, Custance, an emperor's daughter, is twice set adrift alone in the open sea. There are treacherous plots, providential rescues, separations of child from parent (Custance from her father), husband from wife and child (King Alla from Custance and his infant son), and tearful reunions.

The extraordinary adventures and reunions of romance do not require divine intervention, but they can be easily accommodated to it. The same situations can be found in a number of saints' lives, some of which have been labelled 'hagiographical romances'. The legend of St Eustace, for example, recounts the separation, first, of wife from her husband and two sons, then of the sons from their father and from each other, with all parties finally united by a series of coincidences. There are dramatic adventures and rescues. In the life of Mary Magdalene, a king is forced to abandon his wife (believed dead) and newborn child on an alien shore; returning two years later, he finds both alive. The saints' lives merely emphasize the hand of God in these wondrous experiences. The marvellous becomes the miraculous.

The extreme situations of romance lead naturally to moments of pathos, heightened by the religious elements. There was also a scattered rhetoric of pathos, which Chaucer drew on, especially in this narrative.[4] To give added dignity and import to his heroine's misadventures, he supplies allusions to classical figures and events (190–203, 288–94, 400–3). The astounding survivals are placed in a dignifying pattern of divine protection by allusions to similar miraculous events in sacred history and hagiography (470–504, 639, 932–45). Rhetorical apostrophes further heighten emotional tension (at least fifteen; for example, 267–71, 295–315, 358–64, 631–7).

All these devices focus ultimately on Custance and her trials. She is a classically pathetic heroine, beautiful, saintly, innocent, helpless, victimized. Epithets applied to her – fair, innocent, humble, meek, wretched, weak, woeful (see 682, 719, 918, 932, 978) – constantly remind us of her virtues and her pathetic circumstances. Chaucer gives her four dramatic scenes: her departure from Rome for Syria, her being set adrift there, the accusation of murder, and being set adrift again. Of these, the first and fourth are most fully developed. The first, building on a single sentence in Trivet, is elaborately worked up, especially by the use of rhetorical devices. It is a nicely calculated addition. It establishes her at once as a pathetic figure, giving her an emotional aura which never fades. The last, her departure from Northumbria, is her climactic scene. The method here is primarily dramatic. The compassion of the Virgin at the Crucifixion is invoked to equate, obliquely, with Custance's overwhelming fear for the safety of her infant son. There are pathetic tableaux: Custance lulling the weeping child and spreading her headscarf over its little eyes ('little' is a key adjective in Chaucer's vocabulary of pathos); her final walk across the sand quieting her child; her last words – 'Farewel, housbonde routhelees!' – not a speech of defiance but a final cry of pain that crystallizes the pathos of her plight. The scene is mounted with consummate skill, arousing and condensing feelings of pity and pain. The spectators' tears confirm the pathetic moment and they are also, in fact, a kind of stage direction to the reader.

The image of Custance that emerges is powerfully evocative, and its greatest power is inherent in the essence of her situation which Chaucer has perceived. His imagination was seized by the fact of her *aloneness*. In each scene we see how alone, how isolated, she is. The rhetoric and epithets merely reinforce a moving truth. 'Allas! Custance, thou hast no champioun!' (631) the narrator is made to exclaim when she is falsely accused of murder, and Chaucer goes on to write one of his starkest, most moving passages:

> Have ye nat seyn somtyme a pale face,
> Among a prees, of hym that hath be lad
> Toward his deeth, wher as hym gat no grace,
> And swich a colour in his face hath had,
> Men myghte knowe his face that was bistad,
> Amonges alle the faces in that route?
> So stant Custance, and looketh hire aboute.   (645–51)

Even after her return to Rome she lives unknown to her parents for twelve years until King Alla's coming releases her from her spiritual isolation.

Custance embodies Chaucer's perception of the isolation of women in his day – or of upper-class women, at least – and his sense of its poignancy. Saying farewell to her parents as she departs for her marriage of conversion as well as convenience, she exclaims, 'Wommen are born to thraldom and penance, / And to been under mannes governance' (286–87). Used as counters in the games of power politics and economic manoeuvre, separated, possibly forever, from friends and family to marry, often, men they had never seen in countries totally alien, queens, duchesses, and ladies, whom the narrator appeals to for understanding of Custance's isolation, very probably would have understood all too well. And Chaucer here, and in the *Clerk's Tale*, seems to have understood too. It may even explain the rather awkward stanza about Custance's wedding night. The imaginative embodiment of isolation in the character of Custance is the narrative's real achievement.

Chaucer used a different technique of rhetorical elaboration to give weight to the *Physician's Tale*, an incident from Livy's *History of Rome*. He probably first found it in the *Roman de la Rose*, where it is used as an exemplum. He attempts to turn it into a self-sufficient narrative; knowing it comes from Livy, he tells it as a true story (155–57). But in Livy, the father's desperate action, beheading his daughter to save her from a tyrant's lust, dramatized the desperation of a political situation. As a purely human drama, however, it raises questions at a human level: is the father's action justified? is it responsible or merely cruel? The setting in pagan Rome rules out any appeal to Christian doctrine.

In consequence, the issue becomes abstract: the responsibilities of parental power and governance in relation to the priceless quality of youthful beauty and goodness, innocence and chastity. A long introductory passage poses the issue, using the rhetorical *descriptio* of so much courtly poetry, with its twofold division: here the *effictio*, describing the young daughter Virginia's beauty, though laudatory, is abstract (rose and white complexion, golden tresses); the *notatio* or moral description is more elaborate, endowing Virginia with manifold virtues: chastity, humility, abstinence, temperance, patience, eloquence, modesty, industry. Just as her name cannot help but suggest the Virgin, so also her virtues (and her beauty) are those invariably ascribed to Mary, making Virginia infinitely precious.

A long *digressio* establishes the theme of parental responsibility by addressing governesses, fosterers, and finally parents. It urges these last not to slacken in teaching virtue, warning them that the worst treason is the betrayal of innocence. Setting a bad example or being negligent in chastising them may cause their children's destruction.

The narrative proper then begins and proceeds briskly. Chaucer summarizes the enthralment of the governor Apius by Virginia's beauty and his plot to possess her by the trumped-up charge that she is a stolen slave. Two 'courtroom' scenes follow. In one, Apius, sitting in his consistory, pronounces his false judgement (his 'sentence': 177, 190). In the other, Virginius, sitting in his 'halle' (207), pronounces *his* 'sentence' (224). The parallel scenes contrast false, corrupt judgement with responsible though unbearably painful true judgement.

This scene is the moment of pathos: parent and child, an impending cruel separation, expressions of strong feeling (218, 221, 223, 231, 235–36), Virginius' face pale as ashes, his aching heart (209, 211), Virginia's tears and swoons, and her final, touching plea to her father that 'with his swerd he sholde smyte softe' (252). There are no bystanders to heighten feeling. Father and daughter are alone. There is one biblical reference, to the parallel dilemma of Jephthah and his daughter. The Abraham–Isaac story would probably also have come to his audience's mind.

Chaucer's purpose seems to have been to tell a striking story in the pathetic mode. The long introduction is unwieldy, however, and the reader totally unsympathetic to pathos will find little to please. But Boccaccio told the same story in *De claris mulieribus* and Gower in the *Confessio Amantis* (VII, 5131–306). The very extremism that troubles a modern reader was no doubt part of its appeal and provides a further insight into the taste of the age.

The Prioress tells a miracle of the Virgin, a popular devotional form that often revealed a striking predilection for the weak and innocent and for the virtue of simplicity. In one miracle Mary saves from dismissal a priest who knows only one mass. In another, a simple-minded girl who can recite only *Ave Maria gratia plena Dominus tecum* receives a sign of special grace. The Virgin also protects those who show her special devotion: sinful monks, for instance, who forget their vows of chastity but not her worship. Her miracles also frequently deal with pathetic situations: a young wife, pregnant, who kills herself in a fit of mistaken jealousy, is revived; a mother's only son who dies is restored to her.

The miracle Chaucer selects combines the simplicity so greatly revered with the devotion to the Virgin so amply rewarded. The simplicity and devotion are demonstrated by a seven-year-old boy, who kneels before every statue of the Virgin he passes and recites the *Ave Maria*. They are revealed further in his determination to learn the *Alma redemptoris*, though he does not know what the Latin words mean. It is enough for him that it is an anthem in praise of the Virgin, and he sings it every day going to and from school through the Asian ghetto.

The simplicity and innocence, and the helplessness, are those of childhood, a fact we are never allowed to forget. The words 'litel', 'smal', 'yong', 'child', 'children', 'boy', 'innocent' are used again and again. (Perhaps here is the voice of the Prioress.) They solicit the reader's tender sympathy for the child and his devotion, horror and pity at his manner of death.

Pathos is likewise elicited for the mother, a widow, alone and poor, in her anxious night of waiting and her journeys through the streets, as, half out of her mind, she searches for her child. It is a mirror image of the Virgin's tearful search for the twelve-year-old Jesus when separated from him at the Temple. The many references to Mary as mother suggest an equation of the widow's suffering and the Virgin's compassion at the Crucifixion.

Feeling is further enhanced by the ruthless power and evil of the child's destroyers. The murder scene is swiftly rendered, the ruthlessness embodied in the rapid succession of verbs: 'hente', 'heeld', 'kitte', 'caste' (570–1). The repellent anti-Semitism is offensive to us, and some critics see it as a bitter comment on the Prioress. But it is an unhappy fact that anti-Semitism was endemic in the late Middle Ages. And the Virgin was the arch-enemy of heretics, and of Jews. They are targets in a number of her miracles, which often ended with massacres or enforced conversions. It is more reasonable to conclude, however reluctantly, that Chaucer did not see beyond the prejudice of his age and took the story simply because it served his purpose.

That purpose was to demonstrate the Virgin's power and her surpassing tenderness and mercy. The narrative does that, and so does the language. Constant references celebrate her name, her blessedness above all other mortals, her mercy (510, 532, 538, 543, 550, 566, 618–19, 654, 656, 664, 678, 690). And so does the pathos. For the tender feelings generated are transferred to the Virgin herself. Tears of sorrow and joy are a fitting and welcome tribute. In fourteenth- and fifteenth-century art she often floats in an aura of tenderness and tears. She does so here.

The Clerk tells an immensely popular narrative, originally a folktale. Boccaccio introduced it to the literary world as the last story in his *Decameron* (1353). Petrarch recast it into Latin (1373-4), and in the next twenty years there appeared another Italian version, two French translations, one of which was given even wider circulation by its inclusion in a Parisian merchant's book of guidance for his young wife (*Le Ménagier de Paris*, c. 1393), and a French dramatization (1395). Chaucer used Petrarch's Latin and one of the translations. Clearly a nerve was touched by this story of a peasant's daughter who promised complete obedience to the marquis who married her and kept that vow without a murmur though he tested her obedience inhumanly.

Its appeal six hundred years ago can best be understood, first, by reference to the high value that religious teaching placed on humility, obedience, and patience, the virtues Griselda displays so abundantly. Pride is, of course, the deadliest of the seven deadly sins, and the remedy against pride is humility (cf. the Parson, x, 387, 475). The archetypal examples of humility, and its attendant virtue, obedience, were Christ and the Virgin. Christ is 'the Master of humility'. God's descending into human form and Christ's submitting to the indignities and torments of the Passion were the ultimate acts of patience and obedience. The Virgin was cited even more insistently as a practitioner of these virtues. In her years at the Temple, one of her seven requests was for 'humility, patience, benignity, and meekness'. Her humility, said one commentator, was the celestial ladder by which God descended to earth. Her obedience and humility at the Annunciation are a constant theme.

The Parisian merchant who copied the story for his wife did so in recommending wifely obedience, though he hastened to add he would never make such extreme demands on her. Griselda's story takes place, of course, within the context of a marriage, and in one sense it is about marriage. This fact alone makes her conduct unbearable to a modern reader. But the tale is neither foremost nor finally a demonstration lecture for husbands and wives. Its larger import, deriving from Petrarch's version, is the major reason it gripped so many. Her story dramatized for them the teaching that God tests his people. The tragedies of life are evidence enough for that. And it dramatized the humility required of the truly devout before God and the absolute obedience demanded in the face of that testing, a humility and obedience that frail mortality found difficult and, often, impossible. This is one source of the tale's poignancy. The racking demands on Griselda are extreme reflections of less drastic though surely painful testings of the faithful and devout. Her triumph chides them and reminds them how far short they have fallen.

Chaucer heightens this religious dimension. He adds the allusion to Job (932–8). More subtle are the touches by which he casts over the figure of Griselda the shadow of the Virgin. Her absolute humility is Mary's virtue. Her beauty and her early maturity (211–12, 218–20) are also reminiscent of Mary. Treatments of the Virgin stressed her beauty, and her maturity and wisdom even as a young girl in the Temple. Like the Virgin, Griselda is poor and never idle; the detail of her spinning while watching the sheep (223–4) is a pointed reference. There is an oblique allusion to the Nativity (206–7); the marquis' announcement that he wishes to take her as his wife on condition she obey him absolutely and her unquestioning acceptance arouse echoes of the Annunciation (see especially 292–4). To make this connection may seem blasphemous, but it is not. The scene is different in all but one or two details, and the echo is of the faintest, but the echo is there.

The association of Griselda with the Virgin draws to her much of the tender feeling surrounding Mary. It also makes more acceptable Griselda's patience and suffering by invoking the experience of that other rare mortal. The pathos depends on our believing in Griselda's agony. Her language and reactions with Walter conceal and deny any pain – do so outrageously when he demands she give up her second child (617–72). But this is the obedience God demands. We penetrate to her real feelings in various ways: her farewell to her daughter (547–72) and to her son (679–83), her gentle admonitions to Walter when she leaves his house (813–89) and when she meets his new bride (1032–43).

Griselda's self-contained dignity is what finally exalts her. She is another of Chaucer's isolated women, isolated by her poverty, her low birth, her vows of obedience to her husband, her separations, her firmness, her suffering. She moves alone, in marriage, in childbirth, in bereavement, a powerful image of the isolation of the human soul. The narrative's method is accumulative pathos. She never weeps, nor are we urged to weep, until the climax. Then there is a storm of feeling, expressed most tellingly in the iron grasp on her two children, when Griselda at last is not alone with her love and her pain. And then she recovers her dignity, rising, abashed at her trance. And for the first time we have a sense of Walter and Griselda together (1113).

For some, Walter is an even greater problem than Griselda. Today we would call him obsessed. The narrator protests at his cruelty (460–2, 621–3), and this, together with Chaucer's humanization of the tale, his greater 'realism', it is claimed, make Walter's monstrous actions and Griselda's improbable obedience all the more implausible. But her alliance with the image of the Virgin roots her conduct in a laudable mode of action, and the realism makes her suffering a human suffering that we can respond to. As for Walter, critics forget that life at times can be monstrous.

We must remember, finally, that obedience was demanded not only by religion but by many social relationships in the fourteenth and fifteenth centuries: wife to husband, fief to feudal lord, subject to superior. Humility and subservience on one side, arrogance and outrageous demand on the other were often the order of the day in a society so hierarchical. The strain on psyche and ego may be imagined. And these were the centuries in which that hierarchy was beginning to show signs of stress and change. In religion many hungered after a more personal relationship with divinity. The increased circulation of money, the growth of trade, a slightly accelerated social mobility must have called into question in many instances the absolute rigidity of former relations of inferiority. This may be the real nerve the story touched. Though the narrative holds up absolute obedience as the ideal, it also acknowledges the terrible demands that can be made in its name and their irrationality, and above all it gives imaginative and sympathetic recognition to the price of obedience, the suffering it can entail. Griselda captures the imagination not only for her 'patience', her obedience. She does so even more because of her great pain. We can identify with that. Chaucer's restraint and his sensitivity make it possible. Griselda is his greatest triumph in the pathetic mode.

In *Anatomy of Criticism* Northrop Frye places pathos in the category of the low mimetic, of domestic tragedy. Most of us will live our lives in the low mimetic mode. We shall not dwell or end in epic or heroic tragedy. Pathos, then, is rooted in a level of experience common to most humankind. Behind the melodramatic and extreme situations which it employs and which we hope we shall never know are experiences that are commonplace and familiar: the loss of a parent, the death of a child, a separation of husband and wife. The emotions dramatized in pathos are emotions we shall know: terror, grief, overwhelming joy. We shall probably never know the agony of the loss of a kingdom, but we shall all know, at some time, the grief caused by the loss of someone we love.

Pathos may seem alien because it works with extremes. It willingly tramples over probability if need be to portray these extremes – of goodness, of evil, of suffering, of faith, of innocence. From this pushing to extremes arises its abstract character. Qualifications and complexities do not interest it. Pure innocence, pure evil, pure goodness are what it wants, and it cuts away everything extraneous to get them. It needs them in order to get the strong emotional effect it aims for. This employment of extremes and this pursuit of emotional impact are precisely what the modern reader objects to as forced and dishonest. But the truth is that at moments of strong feeling we do simplify and exaggerate. When we weep for a dead friend we forget all faults and he or she becomes for the moment pure generosity, or pure goodness. When we explode with anger the object of our wrath becomes villainy personified. Pathos is more honest about, and less afraid of, raw feeling than is irony.

The simplicities of the tales of pathos are what is most difficult for a modern reader to accept. Yet simplicity is their essence, and they demand a corresponding simplicity in the reader if they are to receive a proper response – T. S. Eliot's 'condition of complete simplicity / (Costing not less than everything)'. The tears that flow in such abundance in these narratives and the tears so ardently sought from the reader are valued as cleansing, redeeming, and above all revelatory. The mask dissolves and the shared humanity and weakness are declared. When the hero weeps, he becomes one with the least of his followers.

And if the art of the pathetic is not the highest art, it is not necessarily a cheap or easy art. True, the effect of pathos may be achieved easily, or cheaply. But what a particular culture will accept as legitimate devices for achieving pathos – what it is truly strongly moved by – must be allowed the artist as legitimate resources. And there can be a skilful and an honest art of the pathetic, where situation, language, and mode of treatment justify the emotional effect sought for. That skilful and honest art may be found in Chaucer's tales of pathos.

Notes

1 See Jill Mann, 'Parents and Children in the "Canterbury Tales"' in *Literature in Fourteenth-Century England*, eds. Piero Boitani and Anna Torti (Tübingen/ Cambridge, 1983), pp. 165–83.
2 *Meditations on the Life of Christ: An Illustrated Manuscript of the Fourteenth Century*, trans. Isa Ragusa, eds. Isa Ragusa and Rosalie E. Green (Princeton, N.J., 1961), pp. 38, 76, 331.
3 Sherry L. Reames, 'The Sources of Chaucer's "Second Nun's Tale"', *Modern Philology*, 76 (1978), 128–9.
4 Thomas H. Bestul, 'The *Man of Law's Tale* and the Rhetorical Foundations of Chaucerian Pathos', *Chaucer Review*, 9 (1975), 216–26.

10   The *Canterbury Tales* IV: Exemplum and fable

In medieval culture a widely accepted hierarchy of discourses set moral teaching above narrative yet established strong expectations that the two would be connected. Stories were necessary to illustrate general truths and make them memorable, while, in an age suspicious of the dangers of fiction, the claim to teach was necessary as justification for story-telling. The two most obvious forms the link could take are named in this essay's title. The exemplum has been defined as 'a short narrative used to illustrate or confirm a general statement'.[1] Exempla or 'ensamples' often purport to be true stories or stories that could be true and thus, in their literal sense, they offer evidence to support doctrine. Fables are *un*true stories – invented fictions or pagan myths – and were often seen as allegories, requiring interpretation to uncover a truth hidden beneath the surface. Boccaccio defines 'fabula' as 'a form of discourse, which, under guise of invention, illustrates or proves an idea; and, as its superficial aspect is removed, the meaning of the author is clear'.[2] From early times, classical mythology had been interpreted thus: Jupiter was taken to represent some aspect of the Christian God, or, as Boccaccio explains, Mercury's visit to rebuke Aeneas means that Aeneas was roused by 'remorse, or the reproof of some outspoken friend'.[3] A common type of invented fiction is the beast-fable: stories of the cock and fox or the lion and mice, manifestly untrue but devised to teach truths amusingly, especially to schoolchildren. Beast-fables, by a translation back into human terms of the human behaviour attributed to animals, might illustrate prudential morality ('beware of flattery'); they might also be interpreted as allegories, so that, as Henryson explains of the last of his *Moral Fables*, the mouse symbolizes the human soul, the toad to which she attaches herself to cross a river, and from which she then cannot escape, symbolizes the body, the river the world, and the kite that destroys both creatures is death. But Chaucer shows little interest in allegorical interpretation or hidden meanings. He is a literalist, and for him the beast-fable tends to become a fictional exemplum, while classical myths are 'fables' in the sense of being the mistaken truths of 'olde tyme... / While men loved the lawe of kinde' (*Book of the Duchess*, 52–6). For Chaucer 'fable' usually means simply fiction, as opposed to 'storyal soth' (*Legend of Good Women*, 702).

159

The idea that doctrines can best be conveyed by stories has a long history in Christian thought. Gregory wrote that 'there are many who are drawn to love of the Heavenly Kingdom more by exempla than through direct preaching',[4] and exempla were increasingly used by preachers from the thirteenth century on. Chaucer's Pardoner grasps Gregory's point and evidently owes to it much of his success as a preacher: first he shows his listeners his forged documents, next his spurious relics, and

> Thanne telle I hem ensamples many oon
> Of olde stories longe tyme agoon.
> For lewed peple loven tales olde;
> Swiche thynges kan they wel reporte and holde.   (VI, 435–8)

Repeatedly in his tales Chaucer or his characters, whether or not their purpose is homiletic, follow the same practice. 'Ensamples many oon' can also provide the basis for complete literary works. Mannyng's *Handlyng Synne* is a lengthy penitential handbook in which schemes such as the commandments and sins are expounded through exemplary narratives, all allegedly true. Gower's *Confessio Amantis* uses the penitential framework, adapted to the 'religion of love', for an immense collection of narratives exemplifying sins against Cupid. And Chaucer himself made exemplification the basis for two story-collections: the *Legend of Good Women*, where, despite his claim that elsewhere he wrote of unfaithful women only to discourage infidelity 'By swich ensample' (*Prologue* F 474), Cupid imposes on him the penance of collecting stories of faithful women; and the *Monk's Tale*, a collection of 'ensamples trewe and olde' (VII, 1998) relentlessly demonstrating Fortune's unreliability.

Similarly, Chaucer frequently exploits the idea that stories can be justified if they exemplify doctrines. Several of the least obviously edifying *Canterbury Tales* end by claiming to have demonstrated some instructive truth. The *Reeve's Tale* allegedly endorses the proverbs that 'Hym thar nat wene wel that yvele dooth' and 'A gylour shal hymself bigyled be' (4320–1); the *Merchant's Tale* purports to show that 'He that mysconceyveth, he mysdemeth' (2410); and from the *Canon's Yeoman's Tale* we learn that God's enemies never prosper (1476–9). It does not take such questionable cases, though, to suggest that the link between story and doctrine is likely to be tense. Sufficient ingenuity in the teller can make almost any story illustrate some doctrine or other; yet stories have an energy of their own which resists subordination to doctrinal purposes. The very details in the narrative that make it vivid and memorable may well diverge from the doctrine supposedly served and even make us question it. Conversely, while the teller's ingenuity in adapting his story to an exemplary purpose may well help to make it stick in our minds, the more aware we are of that ingenuity the more likely we are to suspect his motives and thus to resist his design upon us.

It must be admitted, though, that modern readers are apt to be biassed against the very possibility of exemplary narrative by scepticism about the validity of general truths. Primitive societies live on proverbs, pithy generalizations which transmit the structure of their communal consciousness, and cannot therefore be repeated too often. In our culture, the concept of general truth last flourished in the Augustan age, and it is nearly two centuries since Blake angrily opposed that concept with his assertion that 'to Generalize is to be an Idiot. To Particularize is the Alone Distinction of Merit'.[5] Even though much literary interpretation still, and perhaps inevitably, involves the substitution of general truths for narrative particulars, we are likely to doubt whether stories can effectively teach doctrines, and to agree with D. H. Lawrence, Blake's twentieth-century heir, that true morality in literature does not take the form of explicit teaching but 'the trembling instability of the balance'.[6] So perhaps we should not assume too readily that Chaucer shared these marked prejudices. Nevertheless, in his clearest instances of exemplum or fable he does acknowledge the tension of the relationships between stories and doctrinal truths. Whatever Chaucer consciously intended, the four tales considered here (the *Friar's Tale*, the *Pardoner's Tale*, the *Nun's Priest's Tale*, and the *Manciple's Tale*) seem to offer a series of demonstrations of ways in which stories do something other than convey the meanings to which they are explicitly yoked. I examine the four in the accepted manuscript order simply to avoid imposing on them a sequence of my own. What emerges may be a growing scepticism on Chaucer's part about the link his age expected between narrative and moral wisdom; but the *Canterbury Tales* is too rich and various a collection to serve as an exemplum or fable illustrating the 'truths' of late-twentieth-century thought about literature.

The *Friar's Tale*, often described as a fabliau, is best considered as an exemplum. Its story, of a grasping official who enters into partnership with a devil in human disguise and is eventually carried to hell as his prey, was used as an exemplum by medieval preachers. One Latin sermon describes it as a *narratio jocosa* (merry tale) which nevertheless teaches man to avoid certain vices;[7] and there as in Chaucer the victim's anonymity adds to the tale's exemplary air. The *Friar's Tale* conspicuously lacks the boisterous sexual and excretory humour of fabliaux, relying instead on ironic wit and quiet inevitability. The devil in it distinguishes between 'sleyghte' and 'violence' as means of earning his keep (1431); the whole tale is one of 'sleyghte', in which 'violence' is unnecessary because of the victim's eagerness to rush towards damnation.

The moral the Friar draws is explicit: we should pray God to help us resist diabolic temptation, for

> 'The leoun sit in his awayt alway
> To sle the innocent, if that he may.'   (1657–8)

This composite quotation from Psalm 10. 8–9 – 'He sitteth in ambush...in private places, that he may kill the innocent...he lieth in wait in secret like a lion in his den' – serves adequately as a general moral, but when we attempt to relate it closely to the story it begins to seem odd, for the summoner who is the devil's victim is plainly *not* innocent. Influenced by antagonism towards the pilgrim-Summoner, the Friar depicts a summoner who is unquestionably guilty, and whose guilt accords with the reputation and probably the reality of the medieval archidiaconal court he serves. A recent study of records of such courts speaks of their 'singleminded concentration on profit from sexual offences'.[8] The archdeacon's court tried people for moral and other ecclesiastical offences – 'But certes, lecchours dide he grettest wo' (1310). For those convicted, corporal punishment was normal – 'They sholde syngen if that they were hent' (1311) – but might be avoided by paying a fine. The summoner's task was to find sinners and bring them to court or collect the fines; the Friar's summoner surreptitiously keeps half for himself. He is, in the Friar's coolly insulting catalogue, 'A theef, and eek a somnour, and a baude' (1354) – a bawd in procuring immorality in order to uncover it. No 'innocent', then; and to catch him the devil need only be a patient lion. Medieval devils are generally boisterous figures, much given to oaths and fireworks, but the one in the tale is not 'the devel blak and rough of hewe' (1622) the widow mentions, but one disguised as a smart yeoman, wearing huntsman's green, with only the black fringes on his hat to hint at his true nature. He answers the summoner's questions 'in softe speche' (1412) and even prefaces the announcement of his damnation with a polite 'be nat wrooth' (1634). Yet the devil in his true shape and 'The peynes of thilke cursed hous of helle' (1652) are only just offstage, and the story derives piquancy from our knowledge of the horrors concealed by its restrained and elegant surface.

It is that surface, polished with irony, that makes the tale such an effective exemplum. Irony demands differing levels of understanding, and in the *Friar's Tale* there are several. Unusually, Chaucer does not take us into his confidence, and at first we are no more aware than the summoner that the 'gay yeman' (1380) he meets is a devil. There are the black fringes, to be sure, huntsman's garb suits the devil, and the liminal area where they meet, 'under a forest syde' (1380), is likely to be perilous; but at first we are simply amused at the summoner's calling himself a bailiff because he is so ashamed of his true occupation. Even when his fellow bailiff explains

that he dwells 'fer in the north contree' (1413) (the devil's supposed home)
and that he expects to see the summoner there eventually, the penny may
not drop, until he announces, smiling slightly, 'I am a feend; my dwellyng
is in helle' (1448). The parallels the summoner has delightedly noted
between his way of life and his new companion's now take on extra force,
and we see how appropriate it is that a devil should inspire him to such
ready disclosure of his lack of conscience or desire to be shriven.

A gap in understanding remains. The summoner preys ruthlessly on
others, and he has been described in images that link him with predatory
animals – hawks, hunting-dogs, shrikes. The devil too is a huntsman, and
one who readily admits his quest for prey: 'ryde wolde I now / Unto the
worldes ende for a preye', he says (1454–5), and to the summoner's
question whether devils have fixed shapes he answers that they assume
such appearances 'As moost able is oure preyes for to take' (1472). The
summoner cannot emulate such shape-shifting, yet it never strikes him
that the prey his new companion now seeks could be himself. He curiously
questions him – why do devils work so hard? do they create new bodies
for their human appearances? – and even when the devil impatiently
warns him that

> Thou shalt herafterward, my brother deere,
> Come there thee nedeth nat of me to leere,   (1515–16)

he still sticks to his agreement to share takings. Next, when they encounter
a carter whose cart is temporarily stuck and who is consigning 'hors and
cart and hey' (1547) to the devil, the summoner foolishly urges the devil
to take them. Last, as culmination of his stupid complacency, he proposes
to demonstrate to the devil how to extract twelve pence from the old widow.
'Taak heer ensample of me' (1580), he patronizingly urges, not grasping
that *he* is to be the subject of an exemplum constructed (under divine
providence) by the devil. And when she consigns him most sincerely to the
devil, unless he repents, and he answers with equal sincerity that he will
never do that, the devil takes him, and there is still no sign that he grasps
what has happened.

The devil has explained that 'somtyme we been Goddes instrumentz'
(1483), and we seem to recognize providence working through the story
and bringing the summoner his just reward. The neatness of the plot
suggests this; so does the way in which he unconsciously conspires in the
irony against himself by making remarks with double meanings. The devil
assures him that '"I wole holde compaignye with thee / Til it be so that
thou forsake me." / "Nay," quod this somnour, "that shal nat bityde!"'
(1521–3). And when, trying to persuade the widow to part with her
shilling, the summoner remarks, 'My maister hath the profit, and nat I'
(1601), he is thinking of the archdeacon, while really his master is already

the 'hard... and daungerous' lord of hell (1427). Finally, he rashly swears that if he excuses her, 'the foule feend me fecche!' (1610).

The emotional coolness and formal elegance of the *Friar's Tale* are matched by a more marked intellectual content than its sermon analogues possess. The summoner's curiosity about hell, though idle, receives learned answers, distinguishing the purposes the devils serve, their degrees of power over men's bodies and souls, and the means by which they adopt human forms. Such learning is vain because ultimately unnecessary for one who will soon be able to see for himself: so the devil warns,

> ...thou shalt, by thyn owene experience,
> Konne in a chayer rede of this sentence,
> Bet than Virgile, while he was on lyve,
> Or Dant also.   (1517–20)

But the warning is itself learned, with its academic setting and references to pagan and Christian authorities on hell. The tale focusses on 'entente', a concept crucial to penitential theology. Friars specialized in preaching and confession, and the *General Prologue* stresses the Friar's claim to possess 'power of confessioun' (218) greater than a parish-priest and his profitable use of this power. This interest is reflected in his tale. The source of sin is not deed but 'entente'; this is what any confessor must scrutinize to assess the penance necessary before absolution can be granted. The tale is full of casual references to 'entente' in the general sense of 'purpose', but it eventually isolates the word's penitential sense. The devil, more scrupulous than the summoner, declines to accept what the carter offers because 'It is nat his entente, trust me weel' (1556); and when the cart is freed and the carter blesses his horses instead, the devil explains that 'The carl spak oo thing, but he thoghte another' (1568). For intention to be complete, thought must correspond to words; this fundamental principle of the trade of both is understood only by the devil. The widow, infuriated by the summoner's claim to her new pan 'For dette which thow owest me of old' (1615), consigns him and the pan to the devil; the devil, kneeling, asks her, 'Is this youre wyl in ernest that ye seye?' (1627); she confirms that it is, the summoner confirms that it is not his 'entente' (1630) to repent, and, all necessary conditions being satisfied, the devil carries off the widow's donations. We are left to imagine what the pan's use will be in hell – perhaps to boil the summoner.

Q.E.D. seems the appropriate conclusion to this neat demonstration of sin and punishment; but the tale has another layer of meaning which complicates its exemplary function. The Friar's antagonism towards the pilgrim-Summoner has been manifest since they threatened tales against each other's professions in the *Wife of Bath's Prologue*. The Friar's provocation is not, as satirists and preachers like to claim, 'The strong

Antipathy of Good to Bad', for he is as scandalously guilty as the Summoner of perverting the church's penitential apparatus; it is rather the contempt of a smooth-talking extortioner for a bullying one. The Summoner threatens that his tale will grieve the Friar's heart; the Friar promises that his will arouse laughter. He aims to show his social and intellectual superiority and destroy the Summoner with derision. The antagonism is as much professional as personal: 'we' friars, he proudly claims, are exempt from summoners' jurisdiction, and the Summoner angrily responds that prostitutes too are 'out of *oure* cure' (1333). In the tale, the Friar's professional *parti pris* betrays itself in the studied insolence with which he treats his fictional summoner, not only disclosing his insatiable greed but also emphasizing his stupidity in failing, right to the last, to grasp his role as chosen victim. But gradually something more disturbing emerges: the Friar's contempt for the summoner shades into admiration for the devil who so coolly tricks him. The self-control, the weary tolerance of the victim's fatuous questions, the theological learning – all these surely belong to the Friar himself, and by the end he has identified himself completely with the triumphant devil. After his general warning against the lion's ambush, he impudently begs us to pray that summoners repent before the devil seizes them. Yet, all unknowingly, he has revealed the truth of what the pilgrim-Summoner says later: small marvel that the Friar knows about hell, for 'Freres and feendes been but lyte asonder' (1674).

In one way the *Pardoner's Tale* is a simpler case than the *Friar's Tale*. A pardoner was licensed by the church to supply absolution to sinners whose penitence showed itself in their willingness to make financial contributions. This system, in theory a means by which sinners could gain access to the church's 'treasury of grace', was in practice open to gross corruption; and Chaucer's Pardoner is among the most disreputable pilgrims. He preaches to stir up appetite for his wares; asked to tell a tale, but urged by the respectable pilgrims to make it 'som moral thyng' (VI, 325), he pauses to drink, and then offers them a sample of the way he usually preaches. His prologue describes his preaching technique, and his tale is a specimen sermon. He calls it a 'moral tale' (460); it is in fact an exemplum which has subsumed its sermon, so that moral exhortation is merely an interlude in the narrative. The general truth it illustrates is defined in the text on which he always preaches: *Radix malorum est cupiditas* (the desire of money is the root of all evils) (1 Timothy 6.10). His purpose in preaching is to gain money; yet, just as his normal audience of 'lewed people' are taken in by the rags and bones that he calls relics, so they are moved by his exemplum against *cupiditas* – and with good reason.

The tale is a perfect instance of exemplary narrative. Its characters are anonymous: three revellers who, on learning that a companion has been slain by 'a privee theef men clepeth Deeth' (675), set off drunkenly to find and kill Death, are directed by an old man down a 'croked wey' (761) to a heap of coins under a tree, and end by killing each other to possess them. As in the *Friar's Tale*, their story is shaped with extreme neatness. The revellers do 'find death' under the tree, and the self-destruction of sinners seems to disclose the working of divine providence to punish *cupiditas*. Like the Friar's summoner, they are blind to the ironies they enact: one says that if he could possess all the treasure himself,

> Ther is no man that lyveth under the trone
> Of God that sholde lyve so murye as I!   (842–3)

without recognizing that he is even then before God's judgement-seat. It is 'the feend, oure enemy' (844) who suggests that he should poison his fellows; but, except that the tavern where it begins is 'that develes temple' (470), that is the tale's only reference to the devil. Diabolic intervention is unnecessary when men are so set on damning themselves. Their story is driven by a feverish energy quite different from the restraint of the *Friar's Tale*. Their life is crammed with 'riot, hasard, stywes, and tavernes' (465); learning of their companion's fate, they leap up 'al dronken in this rage' (705) to seek Death; they run to the tree the old man points out; one agrees to 'renne to the town' (796) to fetch refreshments, and, having purchased 'strong and violent' poison (867), he then runs to borrow bottles for it; the others 'ryve hym thurgh the sydes tweye' (828) and then drink the poison. Only in recounting the triple death does the Pardoner speak with restraint (and then only to break out in violent exclamations against the sins that caused it); otherwise his narrative style enacts a life restlessly driven by appetite.

In certain ways the tale's imaginative power exceeds its exemplary function. Thus the old man is an enigma of a kind rarely found in a poet more given to complexity than to mystery. Asked why he lives so long, he answers that it is because no man will exchange youth for his age, and goes on to describe in chilling and suggestive detail the misery of a life spent searching for death;

> ...on the ground, which is my moodres gate,
> I knokke with my staf, bothe erly and late,
> And seye, 'Leeve mooder, leet me in!'   (729–31)

The old man, 'al forwrapped save [his] face' (718), is like a swaddled baby trying to re-enter the womb. There are hints about him of the Wandering Jew, of the Pauline 'old man', of Death himself; but the impossibility of fitting him completely into any pre-existing category leaves us baffled and disturbed as by a dream rather than instructed as by an exemplum.

Again, though the tale claims to illustrate the specific danger of *cupiditas*, it does not separate this sin from others, but mingles sins together, creating a sense of the metamorphic energy of a sinfulness that eludes categorization. The Pardoner's homiletic 'interlude' passes through drunkenness, lechery, gluttony, gambling, blasphemy – sins originating in the tavern and intricately interconnected. Blasphemy receives particular emphasis, especially in the form of swearing by the parts of Christ's body. Of the three revellers we are quickly informed that

> Oure blissed Lordes body they totere, –
> Hem thoughte that Jewes rente hym noght ynough,   (474–5)

and the tale echoes with such oaths, illustrated by the Pardoner –

> 'By Goddes precious herte,' and 'By his nayles,'
> And 'By the blood of Crist that is in Hayles,
> Sevene is my chaunce, and thyn is cynk and treye!'
> 'By Goddes armes, if thou falsly pleye,
> This daggere shal thurghout thyn herte go!'   (651–5)

– and demonstrated by the revellers. The idea that oaths repeat the mutilation of Christ's body makes them blasphemous indeed, but at the price of a materialism comparable to the supposition that death is a person. The tale discloses a world dominated by such materialism: like a Bosch painting, it is full of dismembered bodily parts possessing a hideous life of their own. In the prologue the Pardoner's neck, hands, and tongue seem to operate autonomously as he preaches; and the tale gives independent life to belly, throat, mouth, gullet, tongue, nose, face, 'flessh, and blood, and skyn' (732), bones, sides, neck, and finally 'fundement' and 'coillons'. The Pardoner's false relics are similarly multilated parts of animals – 'pigges bones' (I, 700) and 'a sholder-boon...of an hooly Jewes sheep' (VI, 350–1) – but even if genuine they would still be bits of bodies. The Pardoner's world is not only one of sinful materialism, where marrow is knocked out of bones to 'go thurgh the golet softe and swoote' (543); it is one where the church itself presents holiness in the form of bodily fragments.

The *Pardoner's Tale* is about blasphemy; it also enacts blasphemy. The revellers' aim that 'Deeth shal be deed' (710) is an attempt to usurp Christ's role, as prefigured in Hosea 13.14: 'O death, I will be thy death'. The three of them form an evil Trinity, and when 'the worste of hem' (776) embarks on his plan to kill the youngest he sends him to fetch 'breed and wyn' (797), the elements which by transubstantiation become Christ's body and blood. When the two murder the third, they 'ryve hym thurgh the sydes tweye' (827), as Christ's body was riven on the cross and as oaths tear it once more. We know from *Piers Plowman*[9] that a current blasphemy was that the Crucifixion was not a willing sacrifice but a conspiracy by two members of the Trinity against the third; the *Pardoner's Tale* offers an enactment of this blasphemy, followed by a sacramental meal that kills its participants.

All this enriches without contradicting the tale's exemplary function: it remains, for the Pardoner's normal 'lewed' audience, a vision of the power and self-destructiveness of sin that would surely be effective in arousing fear and repentance. But, as in the *Friar's Tale*, the exemplary narrative is framed by a narratorial 'entente' that complicates matters. The Friar betrayed his 'entente' inadvertently; the Pardoner's is openly proclaimed in advance. Preaching against *cupiditas*, yet, he says, 'I preche of no thyng but for coveityse' (424), and his prologue is a detailed exposition of his motives and methods. It derives from a non-realistic literary convention of confession, to which Chaucer has given a more inward significance. The Pardoner's 'confession' may flatter the pilgrims by revealing to them the tricks he practises on the 'lewed peple', but, beyond that, he is characterized in the *General Prologue* and his own prologue as a man who shamelessly flaunts his abnormal appearance and sexuality. His power over his audiences derives ultimately from a persistent self-exposure, in which calculated histrionicism cannot be distinguished from psychopathological compulsion.

We may be amused by his account of his pulpit techniques, but his callousness about the spiritual consequences is horrifying: what does he care if the souls of his listeners 'goon a-blakeberyed' (406) when they die? What is most frightening, though, is that his techniques work. The demonstration-sermon becomes a real sermon; we cannot remain comfortably separated, along with the pilgrims, from the 'lewed' audience; we too are gripped by the exemplum of the three revellers, and when the Pardoner concludes we are all too ready to be deceived by his promise not to deceive us, a promise in which truth itself is forced to serve his ends of profit and power:

> And lo, sires, thus I preche.
> And Jhesu Crist, that is oure soules leche,
> So graunte yow his pardoun to receyve,
> For that is best; I wol yow nat deceyve.   (915–18)

His whole way of life is a blasphemy, of which the enacted blasphemy of his tale is but a further display; but suppose it leads us not a-blackberrying but to Christ's pardon? suppose the damned preacher can really bring us to salvation? Which side is this double agent really on? In a sense, then, the persuasive force of the *Pardoner's Tale* may be strengthened by our knowledge of the teller's vicious purpose; but only at the cost of a fundamental disturbance in the relation between narrative and moral teaching. The power of narrative becomes merely aesthetic; poetry is reduced to the culinary art in terms of which the Pardoner contemptuously describes his preaching:

> ...in Latyn I speke a wordes fewe,
> To saffron with my predicacioun,
> And for to stire hem to devocioun. (344–6)

The separation of fiction from moral 'entente' leaves even exemplary narrative exposed as mere lies – an insight which will be taken up by the Parson as the tales close.

The *Pardoner's Tale* itself, however, ends with a characteristically Chaucerian swerve away from the darkness it has opened up. The Pardoner overreaches himself in inviting the Host to be the first to kiss his relics. Harry angrily rejects them for the fakes they are –

> Thou woldest make me kisse thyn olde breech,
> And swere it were a relyk of a seint,
> Though it were with thy fundement depeint! (948–50)

– yet in doing so he comes dangerously near to calling in question the pilgrimage's goal, for the breeches of St Thomas were one of the most precious relics at Canterbury.[10] As often in this tale, we seem on the verge of a Protestant conclusion; but instead the Host turns on the Pardoner himself, with his dubious sexuality, and proposes that his testicles should be severed as a relic and 'shryned in an hogges toord' (955). This last and most violent image of dismemberment goes too far for the Knight, who insists that they should make peace. 'Anon they kiste, and ryden forth hir weye' (968) – leaving behind a fearsome apprehension.

The *Nun's Priest's Tale*, Chaucer's only beast-fable, tells how the cock, Chauntecleer, is frightened by a nightmare in which he is seized by a doglike yellowish-red beast with black tips to its ears and tail. His wife, Pertelote, argues that dreams have merely physiological causes; thus he has no reason to fear, and should simply take 'digestyves / Of wormes' and 'laxatyves' (2961–2). But Chauntecleer has learned from his extensive reading that dreams are prophetic, and he devotes 167 lines to 'ensamples olde' (3106) demonstrating this. His first two exempla are of considerable length and have many properties of the exemplary tales we have discussed: unnamed characters, stories full of authenticating detail and building skilfully towards a climax that seems predetermined and perhaps divinely ordained. The first is especially absorbing, a horror story in miniature of a pilgrim to whom his separately lodged travelling companion appeared thrice in dreams, the first time to say that he was going to be murdered and the last time, 'With a ful pitous face, pale of hewe' (3023), to say that he had been murdered and his body was in a dung-cart. So it proved to be. This perfect exemplum is also a perfect proof of the tense relationship between narrative and doctrine. Chauntecleer himself, moved by his own story, declares what it teaches:

> O blisful God, that art so just and trewe,
> Lo, how that thou biwreyest mordre alway!
> Mordre wol out, that se we day by day.   (3050–2)

We may well agree, for the more completely the story engages us, the more likely we are to forget its intended moral – not 'Mordre wol out' but, as Chauntecleer then hastily recalls, 'Heere may men seen that dremes been to drede' (3063). This pattern of forgetfulness is repeated by Chauntecleer in respect of his whole collection of exempla. Its 'conclusioun' for him is that 'I shal han of this avisioun / Adversitee' (3151–3); so we might expect him to be depressed and wary. In fact he is so pleased with himself for having defeated his wife by his masculine display of learning that he is greatly cheered, and, having patronizingly disposed of her with a mistranslated Latin quotation, he summons his obedient hens, copulates 'twenty tyme' (3177) with Pertelote, and struts about, a marvellous parody of complacent male stupidity: 'Hym deigned nat to sette his foot to grounde' (3181). For Chauntecleer, then, a collection of exempla has led to a conclusion quite contrary to his original purpose in telling them. (Similarly in the *Franklin's Tale* Dorigen's twenty-two exempla of ladies who preferred death to dishonour, intended to nerve her to commit suicide, actually fill in the time till her husband returns, so that he can settle her problem differently.)

Exempla collections, as we have seen, can also form complete works; and the tale preceding the Nun's Priest's is such a collection. The Monk proposes to recount a series of 'tragedies'. They tell of falls from high estate to misery, and he repeatedly urges us to 'Be war by thise ensamples trewe and olde' (1998) of the unreliability of Fortune. Whatever Chaucer's intentions when he began the collection, its effect as it proceeds becomes one of both monotony and incoherence. The exempla all illustrate the same truth, yet the exemplary purpose obscures the point of each individual story, failing even to distinguish between deserved and undeserved falls. We are relieved when, after the seventeenth tragedy, the Knight interrupts, saying that such stories are depressing (and boring, adds the Host), and the Nun's Priest is named as the next teller. The Monk's final exemplum rounds off the collection by repeating the definition of tragedy with which he began. Moreover, this last exemplum is that of Croesus, which is also one of Chauntecleer's list of exempla, so we may assume that the interruption and the juxtaposition of the two tales are not random.

The *Nun's Priest's Tale* is designed as a parody of exemplary tragedy. The tragedy of Croesus tells how he had a dream which was correctly interpreted by his daughter as foretelling his death; in the tale of Chauntecleer, the hero has a dream which is misinterpreted by his wife as not foreboding any harm. In the latter tale, the tragic outcome, having been extensively lamented in advance, is then narrowly averted, but the moral remains the same:

> Lo, how Fortune turneth sodeynly
> The hope and pryde eek of hir enemy!   (3403–4)

The Monk's exempla are 'trewe and olde'; the story of Chauntecleer is as true as that of Lancelot, 'That wommen holde in ful greet reverence' (3213). A tragedy compared to the destruction of Troy, Carthage, and Rome, and, in a witty parody of Geoffrey de Vinsauf's rhetorical textbook, to the death of Richard Lionheart, but which has animals as its characters and then does not occur after all, is hardly to be taken seriously. The full apparatus of rhetorical high style is applied to Chauntecleer's story. It is related to history, scientific lore, elevated philosophical debate, and the language in which this is done is not intrinsically debased; yet a powerful contextual irony operates as we are recurrently reminded that 'My tale is of a cok, as ye may heere' (3252). Men are perhaps as ridiculous as Chauntecleer in their self-important supposition that moral generalizations of significance or utility can be drawn from their lives; only for a dim rhetorician does it remain a 'sovereyn notabilitee' that 'worldly joye is soone ago' (3209, 3206).

'Taketh the moralite, goode men', the Nun's Priest urges those who think his tale 'a folye, / As of a fox, or of a cok and hen' (3438–40). Some have seen this injunction as implying hidden allegorical significance. The cock, it has been suggested, is the priest, the widow who owns him the church, and the fox is the devil. (Perhaps indeed its black tips may remind us of the black fringes on the devil's hat in the *Friar's Tale*.) Or perhaps the fox is a heretic or a friar rather than the devil – perhaps all three. Or it may be that the tale is an allegory of the fall of man, with the cock as an Adam misled by his wife, but this time avoiding expulsion from the garden at the last minute. Many such suggestions have been made; but their multiplicity and contradictoriness tell against them, and it is difficult to find evidence to suggest that Chaucer seriously intended any of them (or indeed that any medieval narratives in English have systematic but concealed allegorical significances). We are left to be amused by the occasional hints of hidden meaning and their utter incongruity with a farmyard world in which the only morality is instinctive and prudential – eating, copulating, avoiding death.

The story in the form the Nun's Priest tells it was probably known to Chaucer as a sermon exemplum.[11] It is thus an appropriate tale for a priest; nor does it lack non-allegorical moral applications. There are those concerning Fortune and 'worldly joye' quoted above. There are conflicting generalizations about dreams: Pertelote's 'Ne do no fors of dremes' (2941) and Chauntecleer's

> By swiche ensamples olde maistow leere
> That no man sholde been to recchelees
> Of dremes...   (3106–8)

There is a cluster of antifeminist morals: *Mulier est hominis confusio* (3164: woman is man's confusion), which Chauntecleer mistranslates as 'Womman is mannes joye and al his blis' (3166); and the Nun's Priest's generalization that 'Wommennes conseils been ful ofte colde' (3256), which he then hastily blames on Chauntecleer. There is advice about flatterers, addressed specifically – 'Beth war, ye lordes, of hir trecherye' (3330) – and then stated more generally at the conclusion. There is a further pair of divergent morals drawn from the story by the chief participants: Chauntecleer's

> For he that wynketh, whan he sholde see,
> Al wilfully, God lat hym nevere thee!

and then the fox's

> God yeve hym meschaunce,
> That is so undiscreet of governaunce
> That jangleth whan he sholde holde his pees.   (3431–5)

The Nun's Priest advises, 'Taketh the fruyt and lat the chaf be stille' (3443), but his tale offers such a selection of fruits that we are at a loss to know which to select as '*the* moralite'. The beast-fable has here become a mock-exemplum as much as a mock-tragedy, making fun of that determination to project meaning and pattern on to his life which betrays man's vanity, and the absurdity of which is manifest when it is attributed to animals.

Though the shortest completed *Canterbury Tale*, the *Manciple's Tale* is one of the most baffling; and though it seems the clearest instance of an exemplum, with a sixty-four-line moral beginning, 'Lordynges, by this ensample I yow preye, / Beth war...' (309–10), its exemplary function is strangely distorted. A sense of cross-purpose begins with its prologue. The Host points out that the Cook has fallen drunkenly asleep and says that his penance must be to tell a tale, but the Manciple intervenes with an offer to take his place, followed by a violently sarcastic verbal assault. The Cook is angered, but helplessly drunk; the Host, however, warns the Manciple that if he tells a tale against the Cook, the latter may take revenge later by revealing the Manciple's dubious accounting practices. Instantly the Manciple agrees that this would be undesirable, claims that he was only joking, degrades the Cook by offering him yet more drink, and proceeds with a tale of a different kind. Chaucer has appeared to be preparing for another pair of tales motivated by professional antagonism, but the Manciple prefers jeering discretion to valour. The power of drink, often associated with conviviality and uninhibited self-expression, is now seen as debasing and as leading to silence. If this is a foretaste of the celebration dinner when the pilgrims return, one would prefer to remain uninvited, and Chaucer's own comment –

> O thou Bacus, yblessed be thy name,
> That so kanst turnen ernest into game!
> Worshipe and thank be to thy deitee!   (99–101)

– can only be read as savagely ironic.

Like Bacchus in the prologue, the 'Phebus' who is the tale's 'hero' is no real deity, and classical fable becomes little different from exemplary narrative. Living on earth as a 'lusty bachiler' (107), he had a white crow which could speak and sing beautifully, and a wife whom he guarded jealously but who, in his absence, was unfaithful with her worthless lover. The crow saw this happening and told Apollo; he angrily slew his wife with his bow, but then regretted his act, broke his bow and musical instruments, and punished the crow by turning it black and depriving it of speech and song. The moral, learned, the Manciple says, from his mother, is 'Kepe wel thy tonge, and thenk upon the crowe' (362).

This simple story is amplified in a way apparently designed to enrich its moral force but actually serving to confuse interpretation. Apollo is praised for his singing, playing, shooting, 'his manhede and his governaunce' (158), but his role is utterly undignified, as a jealous husband who is cuckolded and then foolishly punishes the truth-teller. Denouncing the crow, he apostrophizes his dead wife:

> O deere wyf! o gemme of lustiheed!
> That were to me so sad and eek so trewe,
> Now listow deed, with face pale of hewe,
> Ful giltelees...   (274–7)

Yet the crow had offered 'sadde tokenes' (258) of the wife's infidelity, and her guilt is a narrative datum. The operatic pathos of Apollo's speech works only if we forget that his view of his wife is self-deceptive fantasy. Should we then sympathize with the wife, as victim of his jealousy? Far from it: the tale is rancid with antifeminism. The truth that it is impossible to govern natural impulses is demonstrated by the Manciple's insertion of three exempla into his exemplum: a caged bird always tries to escape, however luxuriously kept; a cat will reject dainty food, 'Swich appetit hath he to ete a mous' (180); a she-wolf on heat will accept any mate, even the 'leest of reputacioun' (185). The Manciple adds,

> Alle thise ensamples speke I by thise men
> That ben untrewe, and nothyng by wommen,   (187–8)

but this is plainly another expedient withdrawal. Why otherwise should his last 'ensample' concern a *she*-wolf, and why should he go on to describe the wife's lover, like the she-wolf's mate, as 'of litel reputacioun' (199)? His real opinion, plainly, is that 'Wommen and bestes been but lyte asonder'. Yet the nameless rival, mentioned only with contempt, can clearly expect no more approval than the wife; and thus the crow remains as the sole possible recipient of our sympathy. He at least, evidently an exception to the Manciple's generalization about caged birds, does his duty to his master and suffers for it, but his way of revealing the truth is comically tactless: 'This crowe sang, "Cokkow! cokkow! cokkow!"' (243). Even he appears infected by the malice of the prologue, and it is hardly surprising that Apollo denounces his 'tonge of scorpioun' (271), that the story-teller consigns him to the devil (307), or that the moral concerns guarding one's tongue.

A story may perhaps be an effective exemplum although its characters are all foolish or contemptible, but even the moral of the *Manciple's Tale* is self-cancelling. Its argument for keeping quiet, though scarcely heroic, would naturally appeal to a man with as much to hide as the Manciple evidently has. But a sixty-four-line speech in favour of silence is absurd, and still more so, in this antifeminist context, when its garrulity is attributed to a woman. The mother monotonously repeats 'My sone'; she finds innumerable long-winded ways of saying 'Don't talk'; and this praise of silence, like its source in the Epistle of St James[12], leaves the impression of a gigantic tongue babbling uncontrollably.

To determine Chaucer's purpose in the *Manciple's Tale* is difficult. Lacking the neatness and inevitability appropriate to exempla, it may be read as parody of 'the romanticized moral fable'[13]; but I am not confident that it can be read consistently in these terms. Parody in Chaucer is almost always contextual rather than stylistic, and in this case there is no firm context such as that provided for the *Nun's Priest's Tale* by the *Monk's Tale* and its interruption. Various speeches pull in opposing directions; the tale seems to offer not a stable, even if inverted, hierarchy of story and meaning, but a cluster of divergent discourses in unstable equilibrium. Something similar might be said of the *Canterbury Tales* as a whole, but there the overall effect is of plenitude – 'God's plenty', in Dryden's famous phrase – while in the *Manciple's Tale* it is of exhaustion, sour verbalism from which the only exit is silence.

The end of the collection is near, and those critics may be right who see self-reference in this penultimate tale. Like the Manciple, Chaucer held positions in which success must have depended on guarding his tongue, and the Manciple, whose words express not truth but only the speaker's interest, may be an unflattering self-portrait. Apollo is the god of poetic inspiration: shot down in mid-flight by the Franklin's interruption of the *Squire's Tale*, he is now an earthly, demythologized figure, who ends by destroying his divine attributes. Apollo's crow, which could 'countrefete the speche of every man...whan he sholde telle a tale' (134–5), sounds like the poet of the *Canterbury Tales*, while as the voyeur who tells of an illicit love-affair, he recalls the narrator of the *Troilus*. Self-reference is suggested, too, by the long speech about language which the Manciple inserts after describing Apollo's cuckolder as his wife's 'lemman' (205). Begging forgiveness for such 'knavyssh speche' (205), he first quotes a saying employed in the *General Prologue* as a defence of artistic freedom – 'The word moot nede accorde with the dede' (208: cf. I, 742) – and then argues that, though an unfaithful wife of noble rank is conventionally called her lover's 'lady' and one of low rank 'his wenche or his lemman' (220), the acts they perform are identical. (The tale's characteristic antifeminist bias reappears as 'lemman' becomes female, not male.) The effect of the speech is now to destroy artistic freedom, by reducing stylistic variety to social prejudice and the matter of courtly poetry to mere coarseness. If this is all the poet can say, silence may be the best outcome; yet even the argument for silence is cancelled by uncontrollable garrulity. What follows is the *Parson's Prologue*, in which the Parson, about to tell the final tale, denounces 'fables and swich wrecchednesse' (34), offers instead 'Moralitee and vertuous mateere' (38), and proceeds to tell, in prose, the only tale with no narrative element. The attempt, embodied in exemplum and fable, to make narrative serve general truth is finally abandoned; and it is tempting to see the self-destructive cynicism of the *Manciple's Tale* as a springboard designed to project the collection towards the Parson's puritanism and its own end.[14]

Notes

1 J. A. Mosher, *The Exemplum in the Early Religious and Didactic Literature of England* (New York, 1911), p. 1.

2 *Boccaccio on Poetry*, trans. C. G. Osgood (Princeton, NJ, 1930), p. 48.

3 *Ibid.*, p. 69.

4 *Dialogues* 1, Prol. 9, cited by Charles Runacres, 'Art and Ethics in the *Exempla* of *Confessio Amantis*', in *Gower's Confessio Amantis: Responses and Reassessments*, ed. A. J. Minnis (Cambridge, 1983), p. 107, n. 2.

5 Marginalia to Reynolds' *Discourses*, from *Poetry and Prose of William Blake*, ed. Geoffrey Keynes (London, 1939), p. 777, also cited by Runacres, p. 112, n. 17. For fuller discussion of exemplification and the reaction against it, see

J. A. Burrow, *Ricardian Poetry* (London, 1971), pp. 82–92, and *Medieval Writers and Their Work* (Oxford, 1982), pp. 107–18.

6   'Morality and the Novel', from *D. H. Lawrence: Selected Literary Criticism*, ed. Anthony Beal (London, 1956), p. 110.

7   G. R. Owst, *Literature and Pulpit in Medieval England* (Cambridge, 1933), pp. 162–3.

8   Thomas Hahn and Richard W. Kaeuper, 'Text and Context: Chaucer's *Friar's Tale*', *Studies in the Age of Chaucer*, 5 (1983), 67–101, at p. 74.

9   C x, 35–9, ed. Derek Pearsall (London, 1978).

10 Daniel Knapp, 'The Relyk of a Seint: A Gloss on Chaucer's Pilgrimage', *ELH*, 39 (1972), 1–26.

11 A. Paul Shallers, 'The *Nun's Priest's Tale*: an Ironic Exemplum', *ELH*, 42 (1975), 319–37.

12 Sheila Delany, 'Doer of the Word: the Epistle of St. James as a Source for Chaucer's *Manciple's Tale*', *Chaucer Review*, 17 (1983–4), 250–4.

13 Richard Hazelton, 'The *Manciple's Tale*: Parody and Critique', *Journal of English and Germanic Philology*, 62 (1963), 3.

14 Among the studies by which I have been influenced in writing this chapter but which are not mentioned in the preceding notes, I should like to record the following:

Peter Dronke, *Fabula* (Leiden, 1974).

Douglas Gray, *Robert Henryson* (Leiden, 1979), ch. 2.

Stephan A. Khinoy, 'Inside Chaucer's Pardoner?', *Chaucer Review*, 6 (1971–2), 255–67.

R. T. Lenaghan, 'The Irony of the *Friar's Tale*', *Chaucer Review*, 7 (1972–3), 282–94.

Jill Mann, 'The *Speculum Stultorum* and the *Nun's Priest's Tale*', *Chaucer Review*, 9 (1974–5), 262–82.

Stephen Manning, 'The Nun's Priest's Morality and the Medieval Attitude toward Fables', *Journal of English and Germanic Philology*, 59 (1960), 403–16.

Anne Middleton, 'The *Physician's Tale* and Love's Martyrs: "Ensamples mo than Ten" as a Method in the *Canterbury Tales*', *Chaucer Review*, 8 (1973–4), 9–32.

Gerald Morgan, 'The Self-Revealing Tendencies of Chaucer's Pardoner', *Modern Language Review*, 71 (1976), 242–55.

Przemysław Mroczkowski, 'The *Friar's Tale* and its Pulpit Background', *English Studies Today*, 2nd ser., ed. G. A. Bonnard (Berne, 1961), 107–20.

Lee W. Patterson, 'Chaucerian Confession: Penitential Literature and the Pardoner', *Mediaevalia et Humanistica*, n. s. 7 (1976), 153–73.

Derek Pearsall, 'Chaucer, the *Nun's Priest's Tale*, and the Modern Reader', *Dutch Quarterly Review*, 10 (1980), 164–74.

Derek Pearsall, 'Chaucer's Pardoner: the Death of a Salesman', *Chaucer Review*, 17 (1982–3), 358–65.

Malcolm Pittock, 'Chaucer's Pardoner and the Quest for Death', *Essays in Criticism*, 24 (1974), 107–23.

James F. Rhodes, 'Motivation in Chaucer's *Pardoner's Tale*: Winner Take Nothing', *Chaucer Review*, 17 (1982–3), 40–61.

V. J. Scattergood, 'The Manciple's Manner of Speaking', *Essays in Criticism*, 24 (1974), 124–46.

Martin Stevens and Kathleen Falvey, 'Substance, Accident and Transformations: A Reading of the *Pardoner's Tale*', *Chaucer Review*, 17 (1982–3), 142–58.

J.-Th. Welter, *L'Exemplum dans la littérature religieuse et didactique du moyen âge* (Paris, 1927).

11 Chaucerian realism[1]

Realism is a complex word with many meanings. As applied to literature, it is mainly used to refer to a work which reproduces (more or less) the details of the external reality of the subject, and (to a lesser extent) an objective, unbiassed presentation of the inner reality of the human characters who people the story. Fidelity to actuality, to a true representation of the world, both outer and inner, is the key meaning of the term. 'Mimesis' (noun) and 'mimetic' (adjective) are words (taken from Aristotle's *Poetics*) which are also frequently used with the same functions as 'realism' and 'realistic', although often in a broader sense. Both words refer to the attempt to reproduce in literary and other arts the world as it appears to our mind.

In all probability, no subject in literary theory has been more quarrelled over, argued about, and commented on than that of realism. Yet in spite of certain recurrent themes and a good amount of repetition, new aspects of this eternally fascinating subject do appear at times and a more precise understanding of the nature of art becomes possible. Charles Muscatine's *Chaucer and the French Tradition* enabled us to look at Chaucerian and medieval realism in a new, or perhaps I should say old, way. He made us see that it is a style and not merely a reproduction of life. Realism, in other words, has a strong conventional element in it, going back in large measure to French models. A medieval writer writes realistically not merely by observing and selecting materials from life around him but also by imitating the features of the realistic style. Realism in Chaucer, and in other medieval writers, is not merely an imitation of life but also of the characteristics of certain kinds of literature. As Muscatine writes, 'The literature of the [medieval] bourgeois tradition is "realistic" or "naturalistic" but it neither attempts nor achieves the reportorial detail of the modern fiction describable by these labels. It is based, even more clearly than the realism of the novel, on a circumscribedly conventional style. It is full of exaggeration, of caricature and grotesque imagination.'[2]

The great Chaucerian critics of the first half of the century were unconsciously under the influence of the contemporary climate which saw realism as a vivid 'slice-of-life' and as the highest expression of literary art. They tended, therefore, to see the dramatic and circumstantial element in Chaucerian narrative to the exclusion of the conventional and stylistic element – the details themselves rather than how they were used. More recent criticism, doubtless also under the influence of the contemporary climate, in which Kafka has replaced Zola in esteem, has focussed rather on the symbolic aspects of experience, which seem to offer clues to a deeper 'truth to life'. But most people, even today, prefer literature to be 'true to life' and interpret that principle in a mimetic way. Symbolic, fantastic and illusionary writing are looked upon by many readers as untrue, and hence a waste of time. In order to identify and define Chaucer's realism, or perhaps more exactly realisms, we must look at the matter in a broader way than our nineteenth- and early twentieth-century forebears. It is certainly assumed by most readers that Chaucer is a realistic writer, especially if their knowledge of his writings is confined to the *Canterbury Tales*, but inasmuch as the word has many meanings, in order to discuss it properly we must try to understand what we mean by the term and how it applies to Chaucer. As Nelson Goodman writes, 'realism, like reality, is multiple and evanescent, and no one account of it will do.'[3]

There is good reason why realism in general is such a popular subject in literary theory and criticism, for in one way or another one might say that it is central to any discussion of literature or even art. As the ancient theory of imitation or mimesis testifies, art must claim to be real in some sense if it is to be taken at all seriously. The whole problem lies, of course, in what sense or senses art is real. In an immediately obvious sense, it is patently not real. Art objects are not natural, and all art objects are human creations of some sort. They are made up. Yet in another sense, they must be real if they are worthy of engaging the attention of human beings. And art has engaged and continues to engage the attention and endeavours of men in various capacities. Art is in some way both real and unreal at the same time. The sharpness of the real–unreal dichotomy comes out very clearly in Gilbert Murray's comment on the *Iliad:* 'If you take up the Iliad as a record of history, you will soon put it down, exclaiming, "Why, this is fiction!" But if you read it as fiction, you will at every page be pulled up by the feeling that it is not free fiction.'[4]

Two hundred years ago, David Hume wrote more vigorously: 'Poets...though liars by profession, always endeavour to give an air of truth to their fictions; and where that is totally neglected, their performances, however ingenious, will never be able to afford much pleasure.'[5] The irony of this statement turns ultimately against Hume, for poets are liars only in order to be true to life in its deepest sense. That life is more than sense experience, more than the 'fact', is a principle all great writers have subscribed to. They have understood, as Hume did not, that one must lie in order to get at the truth.

Yet Hume raises a very fundamental issue here. Why in order to deny mere sense experience must writers pretend that what they are writing is true? Why this 'air of truth'? In attempting to answer this question, we must discriminate among realisms,[6] as we have been taught to discriminate among romanticisms. In order to make use of such a protean word as 'realism' at all, we must give it, as we must to all general words in the humanities, many meanings if appearances are to be saved. My main purpose is to look into one of the meanings of this word as it may be applied to narrative, especially Chaucerian narrative.

A basic realism in narrative is concerned with the establishment of an air of truth or plausibility to a tale. Narratives use such strategies to avoid the accusation of lying. This type of realism may be called 'authenticating realism' and is to be found in one way or another in almost all narratives. It is fundamentally concerned with the truth-claim of the narrative and although related to it, is very different from ordinary realism. This realism of truth may be achieved in various ways, not all incompatible with each other. Frames of various sorts are popular for this purpose. Benjamin Constant's *Adolphe* opens with a fake publisher's foreword in which the publisher explains how the hero's story fell into his hands when he met him in Calabria. Stendhal tells us, in an address to the reader at the beginning of *The Charterhouse of Parma*, how the story which he is about to tell was told him in Parma toward the end of 1830 by the nephew of a friend of his, a canon of Parma. *Gulliver's Travels* opens with a letter from Captain Gulliver to his cousin Sympson the publisher, followed by Sympson's address to the reader. We also find more elaborate framing devices used in whole or in part to authenticate a narrative or narratives as in the *Decameron*, the *Arabian Nights* and the *Canterbury Tales*, the last of which is our main concern here.

More frequently, however, we merely find an 'I' in the story, the presumed narrator who may or may not bear the author's name. In medieval narrative, the 'I' is usually the literary equivalent of the author. Sometimes the 'I' may participate in the action of the story which he is presumably narrating, and sometimes he is merely an observer. If there is a frame, he may appear in it – as in the *Canterbury Tales*. This authorial 'I' is a creation of the author and serves, among other things, to give 'an air of truth' to the tale.

There are also other methods of authentication used by writers. Sometimes authentication may be obtained by the tone of the authorial voice alone. This method too is not inconsistent with the others we have discussed but is, on the contrary, always an accompaniment of every narrative. In some narratives there is neither a frame nor an 'I' but merely a voice. In such cases, the tone of the narrator's voice serves as a kind of control and a guarantee of authenticity or on some occasions deliberate inauthenticity. We read a narrative not only for the story but for the authenticating voice. In one way or another a narrative must not only present a story but an authentication of that story. In other words, a story must also present a solution to its epistemological problem. How are we to know that the story is true or presumably true? The suspension of disbelief is a fundamental process in narrative art. Part of the privilege of reading a narrative is to know in some measure the teller or assumed teller and the claims of his authority.

In much modern literature, tricks are played with the authenticating level. As Stephen Spender writes, 'the mode of perceiving itself [in modern fiction] becomes an object of perception, and is included as part of the thing perceived'.[7] We find figures such as the author himself in his own name talking about writing the book he is actually giving us or the 'unreliable narrator' used in Henry James' novels and those of others.[8] However, tricks on the authenticating level are not unknown in earlier times. Cervantes, for instance, used a mythical Arab historian in *Don Quixote*. The 'I' is used in an extremely confusing fashion by Vincente Espinel in his *Relaciones de la Vida del Escudero Marcos de Obregón*, a seventeenth-century novel.[9] Or the obvious parodic realistic authentication of Dickens' *Pickwick Papers* provides another example. However, the deliberate manipulation of the authenticating level to raise problems of perception and truth is largely a modern characteristic. In some cases, we even find the absolute destruction or abolition of a narrator or even 'tone of voice'. As we shall see later, however, all authenticating devices not only authenticate, they also call attention to the need for authentication and hence to the *in*authenticity of the work of art.

When an artist plays tricks with his authenticating level, he is not normally giving up the truth-claim of his story but is putting it on to another level – the level of the real world as seen in his title or chapter headings or preface or what you will. This particular type of authentication raises many difficult problems which need further investigation.

Finally, details of background in the tale itself or in the outside of the inner tale – in the world of the frame or the world of the 'I' – may be used to gain authenticity. Localities, names, dates, and so forth may give an air of truth. These naturalistic and realistic details are very characteristic of the nineteenth- and twentieth-century realistic novel, but they may be found at all times in narrative art. Certain periods seem to favour this type of authentication over others, but although it has been most widely and consistently used in the past two hundred years, it is an old device and by no means the invention of modern times.

The authenticating level joins, in a way, the reader to the reporter in a shared intimacy. The reader or hearer is asked to accept the truth of something which is being told to him, and he is left free to accept the tale

if he wants and to interpret it as he sees fit. The choice is up to him to
accept or reject the plausibility of the tale. When the authenticating level
is presented in the form of a presumed experience which has happened to
the narrator or the voice telling the tale, as is very common, the narrator
is taking the reader into his confidence and allowing him to judge the tale
as the narrator judges it. The reader and the narrator are sharing an
experience together. This makes for the kind of closeness which comes
from allowing someone to speak to you. One is prepared to believe and to
suspend disbelief. Since the rise of writing and printing, the greater need
to create authenticating intimacy has led to more complicated authenticating devices. The ironies are deep here, for the teller and the reader both
know that the story is not true, or at least not entirely true, in the sense
of its having really happened, but that if the tale is to be told in a satisfying
manner, they must both pretend together.[10]

When we look at Chaucer's authenticating devices, we see that from the
very beginning of his literary career he put a great deal of care into them.
His favourite device, as with most medieval writers, was the dream. It is
perhaps hard today to think of the dream framework as an authenticating
device, but as even a superficial study of dream theory shows, dreams,
especially 'in the morning', that is, late, after the food has been digested,
are bearers of revelation and true. The dream frame has been much
misunderstood. For much of the past, it served to suspend disbelief and to
obtain credence. The dream may be fantastic, but it really happened. The
dreamer is also an 'I' so that the basic credibility may be maintained. A
man telling his own dream usually tells the truth. The dream framework
gives us then two authenticating devices *per se*, the dream itself and an
'I'. The dream frame has other functions as well, for the tone established
and the facts set forth tend to heighten the meaning of the dream itself,
ironically or directly, but its chief function is in a very basic sense to
establish the presumed reality and truth of the story. In the *Book of the
Duchess* the voice speaking the poem tells us of his insomnia and
unhappiness (probably from love) and how he read a book 'this other
night' to 'drive the night away' (1–49). He is presumably telling us about
some of his constant problems. The first forty-three lines are in the present
tense. Then at line 44 we move into the past. He is telling us of a particular
experience – the reading of the story of Ceyx and Alcyone – which is to lead
into his narrative. The past tense signals this shift to a particular
experience. The story of Ceyx and Alcyone, which deals with faithful love
beyond death, tells us how love can overcome death and prepares us
to accept the mourning knight in the story. But it also has the detail and
circumstantiality of truth. The tone is intimate – yet with the distance
objectivity, irony, and self-awareness can give. The 'I' falls asleep as he

finishes the tale, and in his dream we are given the story of the grieving knight set in a partially ideal landscape such as we often find in dreams. After he has unburdened himself and the dreamer has asked his famous question and received his answer, the knight rides away.

The dreamer then awakes and tells us that he must 'put this sweven in ryme / As I kan best, and that anoon' (1332–3). The poem ends with the line 'This was my sweven; now hit ys doon' (1334). I have completed my task; this was my real dream. These words echo the line just before the dream is introduced 'Loo, thus hyt was, thys was my sweven' (290). The last sentence drives us back to the beginning of the dream and the beginning of the poem. The circle comes full close. A circle is a most appropriate organization of a frame for a story about death for the thought of the unceasing round of death for all men is one of the traditional consolations for bereaved humans. All men die, it happens again and again.

The frame is then detailed and quasi-personal. It provides its own rationale as well as authenticating the content of the dream and presenting a counterpointing tale to that of the grieving knight within the story. There are three unhappy lovers in the *Book of the Duchess*: the dreamer, Alcyone, and the knight. But the dreamer is speaking to us and telling us of the other two, and his rather indefinite sorrow, as well as the general circumstances of his dream, authenticates the sorrow and story of the others.

The inner story is full of dialogue and circumstantial detail, but it is set in an ideal and somewhat unreal landscape. The ideality of the *Book of the Duchess* lies almost exclusively in this setting. Every other level is presented in as life-like a fashion as possible, but the inner background with its aroma of timelessness and unreality makes all the difference. The boundary between the frame and the inner story is firm. There is a 'real' world and a 'dream' world, and each is kept completely separate as a unit from the other, unlike the procedure in *Piers Plowman* where the reader is often haled back into the 'real' world. The third world, the real world revealed by the title is, as always, real and direct although only briefly given. The world of the title is real, the world of the frame is presented as real, the world of the inner story is presented as made up by, to use a modern term, the unconscious of the dreamer and contains real and ideal details.

If we turn to *Troilus and Criseyde*, we find a different frame – a frame which distances us from and authenticates the inner story by history and the historical consciousness. Here it is not a dream which separates the frame from the story as in the *Book of the Duchess*, but the past and time of which we are made constantly aware. The 'I' of *Troilus and Criseyde* is constantly bringing us into the present, authenticating the story by the pose of the historian. The narrator is bound by history. The contrast between past and present in *Troilus and Criseyde* gives us a feeling of timelessness, of the spatialization of time,[11] while within the world of the story itself we get a lively sense of the passage of time which is a strong realistic device. Time is of the essence of narrative, which is, as Lessing long ago pointed out, sequential, but narrative writers all more or less try to transcend this limitation without at the same time destroying completely the temporality of narrative. Samuel Johnson speaks of diversifying narrative by 'retrospection and anticipation'.[12] Chaucer knew this secret as all his narratives show.

The setting of the inner story is Troy but re-created with much vividness.[13] Both the frame and the story are equally alive and presented with great psychological acuity. There is no ideal level in *Troilus and Criseyde*, although Troilus himself and perhaps even Criseyde are idealistic characters. But the setting of the world of the frame against the world of the story takes us out of time[14] and gives an ideality of immobility to the work. As a result, the naturalism in the inner story set in this contrast gives us a stronger sense of reality than we get from the *Book of the Duchess*. However, both frames are realistic in the ordinary sense of the word, but they present us an individualistic not a social world. Both 'I's' are directly responsible for the inner story – one as dreamer, one as historian.

With the *Canterbury Tales*, however, to which we now turn, it is a social as well as personal world which authenticates the inner stories. Chaucer has moved from dream and past history[15] to a report on the contemporary world and present history, producing thereby yet another variation on the numerous ways of giving a realistic effect. The *Canterbury Tales* has always been considered Chaucer's greatest realistic masterpiece, but I think we should look a little more closely at the way in which Chaucer gains this realistic effect and also ask ourselves whether it is as realistic as is generally assumed. Like the *Book of the Duchess* or the *Romance of the Rose*, it is set in the present, but in the frame we are given a social world, not an individual's problem or attitudes. Part of the sense of vitality and plenitude which comes from a reading of the *Canterbury Tales* is due to the variety and extension of the frame. The stories, as we shall see, vivid as many of them are, do not give us this same sense of fullness. Unlike the *Book of the Duchess* but like *Troilus and Criseyde*, the two worlds of frame and story interpenetrate. Between stories we move back into the firm setting of the frame. And occasionally the frame interposes itself into a story, as when the Friar accuses the Summoner of lying after he begins his tale or when a character in the *Merchant's Tale* alludes to the Wife of Bath.

The frame of the *Canterbury Tales* is in the form of a pilgrimage to the shrine of St Thomas in Canterbury. The pilgrim's tale of his voyage is a well-known literary genre, although until the later Middle Ages it was normally in Latin. It is a religious genre which catered to human curiosity about other lands and strange places and which stimulated religious piety.

The pilgrimage is also a key metaphor for life from the religious sphere. We are all pilgrims on the way to the heavenly city, and every journey, but especially a religious one, reflects the basic pattern of existence. We are all homeless, exiled from paradise, looking for a return to our true home which is heaven, of which the earthly paradise was the foreshadowing. No doubt Chaucer had this religious dimension in mind when he chose a pilgrimage as a frame. The introduction to the last tale, that of the Parson, makes this quite clear. But a report of a pilgrimage is also a true report of an experience, and it is customary to report it in the first person. The authentication of a real pilgrimage lies in the personal participation of the pilgrim. In the *Canterbury Tales* the reporting pilgrim is the Chaucer figure, and it is on his authority that we must accept the truth of his story about events and tales. As we have already said, the vividness and circumstantiality of the *Canterbury Tales* seem to come largely from both the choice and treatment of this frame, so much so that some scholars have tended to reduce the individual tales of the work to mere appendages of the frame and its characters, as David Benson's essay in this collection has shown. The reason behind Kittredge's opinion that 'the pilgrims do not exist for the sake of the stories, but *vice versa*,' and that 'the stories are merely long speeches expressing, directly or indirectly, the characters of the several persons',[16] is that it is in the authenticating device of the work, in the frame, that Chaucer's circumstantial and dramatic verisimilitude most strongly appears. In an age which admired realism in narrative art, Kittredge's judgement would be especially welcome.

Let us look at the individual stories. Individually, they too have their authenticating devices, but since things are complicated enough we shall not discuss them here but get to the content of the tales themselves. The *Knight's Tale* is not realistic in any direct sense: the characters are very stylized, as disputes over whether Palamon or Arcite is the more worthy show, and Emily is little more than a bone over which the dogs fight. We are told about her beauty; we do not see it. The story is laid in the past, and the action has a pageant–tapestry-like quality, with much description and decorative detail. The Miller's and Reeve's tales, on the other hand, are full of circumstantial detail, and they are laid in contemporary England. Yet as stories, both are so improbable as to be grotesque. The whole scheme of Nicholas in the *Miller's Tale* is so fantastic that in terms of everyday realism it is absolutely unbelievable. It depends on a remarkable credulity on the part of the carpenter, on a series of incredible coincidences, and above all on an unreal world in spite of all the detail with which it is recorded. Then too the plan, even if it went as Nicholas had hoped, could only work once. For a pleasant run of adultery, it was the worst possible scheme. Many of these points can also be made concerning the *Reeve's Tale*, although it is more credible in some ways.

The *Man of Law's Tale* lacks circumstantial realism and is laid in a vague past and for the most part in strange countries. The *Wife of Bath's Tale* is set in Arthurian England among characters who never could have existed. Here, as in most of Chaucer's tales, we get a most lively dialogue. But the tale is fundamentally a fable. The *Friar's Tale* is a story of the supernatural, while the *Summoner's Tale*, in spite of its great circumstantial detail, has many of the characteristics of the fabliau as we have presented them in our brief comments on the *Miller's Tale*, and displays a most grotesque wit.

The *Clerk's Tale* has strong symbolic overtones, is laid in Italy and has a most incredible plot. The climax of the *Merchant's Tale* is extremely unrealistic, and it is peopled by figures with names like January and May, Placebo and Justinus. Yet it too has much circumstantial detail. The *Squire's Tale* is set in Asia and is frankly a tale of the supernatural.

The *Franklin's Tale* is by no means fundamentally realistic. It is set in pagan Brittany and depends on magic for the success of its story. The locale of the *Physician's Tale* is ancient Rome, and the rather summary story cannot be called realistic in the ordinary sense of the word. The *Pardoner's Tale* is an exemplum with little characterization and with a supernatural atmosphere. The *Shipman's Tale* is another fabliau with much circumstantial detail and a fantastic plot. The *Prioress's Tale* is a miracle of the Virgin, set in Asia. *Sir Thopas* is a parody of the romances which gains its effect by exaggerating their already incredible events and descriptions. The *Tale of Melibee* is more or less a string of proverbs and moral apophthegms. The *Monk's Tale* does have some historical realism, but here history is being used for moralizing purposes, not for its own sake.

The *Nun's Priest's Tale* is a charming beast fable. The *Second Nun's Tale* is a saint's life. The *Canon's Yeoman's Tale* is perhaps the most realistic of all the *Canterbury Tales* in the sense that we have been using the term 'realism'. Yet it is also one of Chaucer's least interesting tales. The *Manciple's Tale* is a mythological story from Ovid; and finally the *Parson's Tale* is not a tale at all, but a moral tractate.

As we look over this list, we see that actually none of these tales, with the possible exception of one, can compare in realism, in the sense of reproduction of the details and events of ordinary life and their credibility, with the frame of the *Canterbury Tales*. It is the authenticating part of the work, the frame, that gives us that strong sense of real life that the poem affords. Now it is true that Chaucer's dialogue and characterization in many of the tales do reflect such a sense, but practically none of the tales can stand up in full measure as realistic, as true to perceived life. If some are realistic in one regard, they are apt to be unrealistic in another. At times, they are not even as realistic as Langland's *Piers Plowman*. The feeling of the action in the tale is real, as it is in almost all narrative, but the plot is often improbable either because of its deficient or accidental causality or because of its dependence upon the supernatural. The frame has a strong temporal quality which always makes for realism, but the stories themselves tend to move out of time or to do incredible tricks with it.

The *Canterbury Tales* is, however, realistic in a way that *Piers Plowman* is not because it has an authenticating frame which gives us a strong sense and feel of contemporary English life. It is the frame which creates the fundamental realism of the work. Of the two worlds of the *Canterbury Tales*, that of the frame conveys a strong sense of the workaday universe, that of the stories, in spite of many realistic aspects, really an ideal world which is stylized and patterned. And it is to the frame that Chaucer returns again and again.

Of course, by all this I do not mean to imply that, in a more profound sense, in the sense that all great art is real, the tales, or most of them, are not real too, but in the narrower sense, most of the tales are not as satisfyingly naturalistic as many critics seem to assume. When they are realistic their realism is very much a stylistic matter with skilful use of naturalistic elements in dialogue, diction or subject matter (bourgeois life).

Where did Chaucer get this notion of a realistic authenticating frame? It is hard to find before Chaucer's time consistent circumstantial realism used to any degree in English literature, with the exception of religious literature. Chaucer's realism of detail in the authenticating frame seems to be largely original with him.[17] He no doubt took some suggestions from earlier works, and possibly from the dream-vision prologue as Cunningham has suggested,[18] but I suspect that the realistic climate of the later Middle Ages in art and literature and about which Huizinga has written so eloquently led him to his original notion of using elaborate circumstantial social detail without relying on the dream convention as in the *Book of the Duchess* or the historical approach as in *Troilus and Criseyde* to give him what every narrative writer needs – his authenticating realism. In other words, Chaucer's originality from this point of view consists in combining the truth claim of his major authenticating device with a circumstantial realism.

Let us look at the *Canterbury Tales* from another point of view. I wish to stress that background in narrative is much more complex than is commonly realized and that in a way the naturalistic realism of narrative art often lies more in the background properly defined than in the foreground. A narrative must reproduce or indicate the real world at two points – in its extreme foreground of action and in its extreme background, the world of titles, summaries and epigraphs. In between, the levels may or may not be realistic. When we speak of realistic fiction in the normal sense of the term, we mean fiction which is realistic in some of these in-between regions, for the other two levels must be realistic.

What I call the extreme foreground of every piece of fiction is the inner action. I choose action as the extreme foreground because with Aristotle I assume that action is fundamental to both narrative and drama. It may be defined as the movement and contacts of the characters in deeds and words. In any narrative the description of this action must be realistic. The parts may not fit in a probable way or the deeds and dialogue may be untrue so that the plot itself may not be credible, but the *action* itself must be described as if it actually happened. When a personified knight attacks a dragon, both unreal creatures, we must have a description of a real fight, not necessarily with full detail, but the fight must give the impression of a real combat between two beings of some sort. When Don Quixote attacks a windmill, however deluded or unlikely the action may be in its context in real life, it is described in a realistic way as if a man were really attacking a windmill. When K. is taken into custody in Kafka's *The Trial*, the description and dialogue indicate a real arrest. It is in this sense that I believe the extreme foreground of all fiction must be realistic.

However, the sequence of the action – the plot – may not be likely, probable or 'true to life'. It may be controlled by some tight intellectual scheme rather than by verisimilitude. But what is done is done realistically. The characters too who participate in the action may or may not be like real people or animals. They may have various degrees of reality. They may be real internally, that is psychologically or symbolically, but unreal externally, that is naturalistically, or *vice versa*. Or they may be unreal in both regards. The locale or setting of the inner story may or may not be portrayed realistically. Some stories are set in the past or the future, both imaginary, some are set in an ideal landscape, some merely suggest a background and some are set in a very natural setting of nature and artifacts or society, or in various degrees of the three. It is the fullness of this natural setting which gives the nineteenth-century novel much of its realistic quality. It is not an invention of the nineteenth-century; the kind of detail with its social and class dimension which evokes a special atmosphere was, however, something new which helps to create the feeling of a 'slice-of-life'.

When we move out of the inner story on the authenticating level, whether it be a frame, an 'I' or merely a voice, one of its main purposes is to give the reader a feeling that the story is true. We have tried to argue that the special quality of the realism of the *Canterbury Tales* lies in the circumstantial realism of its authenticating level. This level often does have circumstantial detail, but it is by no means universal. A tone of voice, for instance, may merely convey authority, not circumstantial surface reality. But the authenticating level of a narrative is concerned with realism in a fundamental way, for it must make possible the suspension of disbelief and is basically though not exclusively concerned with an epistemological question. It must try to validate the story which is being told. However, it may also reinforce the inner story or ironically counterpoint it or be used to shift perspective. Ironically, however, the authenticating level also in a way makes us more aware of the fact that the inner story is a creation which needs authenticating.

Finally, we move out of the story to the level of the author speaking directly to the audience without *persona* or any mask, to which we have already briefly alluded. In most narrative this level is only made known to us by the title of the tale, or by the table of contents, or summaries or chapter headings or divisions if some are given. Here is a man telling us directly or occasionally ironically what he is doing as he sees it. He usually writes in the present tense about his subject, how he is dividing it, and occasionally what he thinks about it. When he is being ironical, he is being ironical to us directly. We are out of the world of the story, listening to the author being as objective as he can be about his intentions.

Chaucer in the *Canterbury Tales* complex makes more use of this level than most readers are aware of.[19] At the beginning of the work he tells us 'Here bygynneth the Book of the Tales of Canterbury', even before he breaks into that famous description of the showers of April. Before every tale and every section and subsection, mostly in English, but occasionally in Latin, he tells us directly what he is doing or sometimes what he has done, as, for instance, 'Here endeth the Wyf of Bathe hir Prologe'. Occasionally these comments are more than merely neutral, as, for instance, 'Bihoold the murie wordes of the Hoost to the Shipman and to the lady Prioresse'. Note, incidentally, the immediacy of the imperative 'behold'. Finally at the very end of the work, we have Chaucer's retraction in which, in two or three paragraphs, he, following a long tradition, asks God to remember those works of his which lead to virtue and to forgive those 'of worldly vanitees' and his 'leccherous' lays. Here is the voice of the Christian man, Chaucer, speaking in deadly seriousness.

In each case, Chaucer takes his readers out of the work of art back into the real world where he is speaking to them quietly and directly, in the present time. He uses no *persona* here beyond the natural *personae* of all human beings when speaking publicly, and continually reminds us in these titles and comments that the poem is his creation and his world and that he is master of both. Sometimes he tells us how to divide one of his stories into parts; sometimes he directs our attention to some point. The creator of these titles and comments is not the pilgrim who is reporting the Canterbury pilgrimage, although he is related to him very closely. He is speaking to us from another part of his being.

I have up to this point been stressing for the most part how Chaucer gave his *Canterbury Tales* a sense of reality. Now it is necessary to backtrack a bit and argue that he is also showing us its unreality and untruth. For

Chaucer in the *Canterbury Tales* by means of various devices which we have discussed brings us into a real world and then transcends it by his art and his presence. His art and his presence distance his readers or audience from their own world so that they can see its meaning as he interpreted it. Yet because his subject was set in the contemporary world on the authenticating level, he is in a profound sense satirical. The first step, the precondition of all satire, is objectivity. But in order to create an objectivity in his readers toward his story, he must also establish the unreality of the real world. The dialectic between real and unreal is handled in a masterly fashion and creates one of the fascinations of the *Canterbury Tales*.

Professor Wolfgang Clemen in speaking of Chaucer's early poetry has said that he created there a 'new realism of the unreal'.[20] This, at least as it applies to the *Book of the Duchess*, is perhaps overstating the case, but it contains much truth. I would urge that in the *Canterbury Tales* Chaucer's problem was just the opposite. He had to create a new unreality of the real so that the real could be brought into art in a manner proper to the illusion of art. This task he accomplished in various ways – by his individual stories, by his selection of the facts, by his comments on his poem. But it is also achieved by the elaborate structure he made of the different levels of the work so that the reality of the world of Chaucer and of the authenticating level is balanced by an unreality in the tales and by the unreality of constantly shifting us back into various levels because this movement makes us aware of the manipulating role of the artist.

The tales themselves have subtle meaning, and often have strong realistic elements, but in practically every case they have a strong ideal base of some sort. They are meaningful in themselves in various ways and in their relation to the frame. The authenticating frame, however, except for its suggestion of life itself and for its authenticating power, has little narrative meaning by itself. It exists for the characterization of the tellers and for the tales they tell. This is generally true of authenticating devices. They do not exist for themselves. Although we may delight in the authenticating level, as we certainly do in the frame of the *Canterbury Tales*, from the point of view of narrative we read it for the inner story or stories and for the relation between the frame and the story. We cannot reduce the tales to the characters of the frame as Kittredge suggested without killing the work as narrative art. The experience of reading the *General Prologue* is not for its narrative itself but for what is to come. If we read it for itself, it is for the portraits, the humour or the expressive power. Yet ironically as I hope I have shown, it is the frame which gives a strong sense of ordinary circumscribed reality to the whole work as narrative.

The *Canterbury Tales*, unfinished as it is, is a complex work of art, and by looking at its variety of realisms and unrealisms we gain a deeper sense of its profundities. We demand illusion and reality, but illusion which seems real and, of course, which reflects reality. All of Chaucer's work is realistic in the sense that it shows us a truth about life; at the same time all his tales, even the fabliaux, are illusory, but we must be constantly alert to the nature and sources of both realism and illusion in Chaucer. The overall tone of action and events in both *Troilus and Criseyde* and the *Canterbury Tales* is not realistic in the usual sense of that word, although individual characterization, descriptions and a number of episodes are. Chaucer is a realist in his portrayal of human nature, in his descriptions and voice, but not of all actions and not of the story line. The tension created by the interplay of real and unreal in the *Canterbury Tales* provides one of the great pleasures of the work, and is an essential part of its genius.

Notes

1 The present essay is based on an article of mine published about twenty-two years ago. Parts of the original are reprinted by permission of the publisher from 'Authenticating Realism and the Realism of Chaucer', by Morton W. Bloomfield, in *Thought*, 39 (1964), pp. 335–58 (New York: Fordham University Press), copyright © 1964, Fordham University Press.

2 *Chaucer and the French Tradition* (Berkeley/Los Angeles, Ca., 1957), p. 58. Although there is a realistic French style, mainly in the fabliaux, it is no longer clear that it is actually a bourgeois creation. Per Nykrog argues cogently that the fabliaux arise in the same social circles as the courtly romances and were written basically to mock the bourgeois. See his *Les Fabliaux: Étude historique littéraire et de stylistique médiéval* (Copenhagen, 1957).

3 See his 'Three Types of Realism', *Partisan Review*, 51 (1984), 285–8, wherein he makes some interesting distinctions within artistic realism.

4 *The Rise of the Greek Epic* (Oxford, 1907), p. 158.

5 *Treatise of Human Nature*, I, iii, 10, ed. L. A. Selby-Bigge (Oxford, 1928 edn), p. 121.

6 See Wayne C. Booth, *The Rhetoric of Fiction* (Chicago, 1961), pp. 53ff *et passim*.

7 'A Short History of the Pers. Pron. 1st Sing. Nom.', *The Struggle of the Modern* (London, 1963), pp. 133–4.

8 See Wayne Booth, *The Rhetoric of Fiction*, pp. 339–74. I doubt whether we can find an absolutely unreliable narrator much before the nineteenth century, although the narrator may be ironical about himself as in the *Canterbury Tales*, as one might be in real life.

9 See George Haley, *Vincente Espinel and Marcos de Obregón, A Life and Its Literary Representation*, Brown University Studies xxv (Providence, R.I., 1959), pp. 65ff.

10 A good example of how unawareness of the authenticating level in narrative may lead to misinterpretations may be seen in Ernest Hoepffner, *Aux Origines de la nouvelle française*. The Taylorian Lecture (Oxford, 1939), pp. 11ff, where Hoepffner argues that Marie de France believed in the magic and supernatural in which her *lais* abound because she says these unnatural experiences really happened.

11 On spatialization of time, see Joseph Frank, 'Spatial Form in Modern Literature', reprinted in revised form from *The Sewanee Review* 1945 in *Criticism, The Foundations of Modern Literary Judgment*, eds. Mark Schorer, Josephine Miles and Gordon McKenzie (New York, 1948), pp. 379–92.

12 *Lives of the English Poets*, ed. George Birkbeck Hill (Oxford, 1905), vol. I, p. 170 (Life of Milton).

13 See John McCall, 'The Trojan Scene in Chaucer's *Troilus*', *ELH*, 29 (1962), 263–75.

14 At the very end, Chaucer achieves a complete victory over time by moving Troilus to a pagan heaven and the 'I' to the contemplation of the Trinity.

15 Although, as Ralph Baldwin points out, Chaucer does juxtapose present and past in the General Prologue when, although presumably at the Inn before the journey, he describes the pilgrims as he could have known them only after the journey started. This technique is similar in part to that used more frequently in *Troilus and Criseyde*. See Baldwin's *The Unity of the Canterbury Tales* (Copenhagen, 1955), pp. 54–7. James V. Cunningham, 'The Literary Form of the Prologue to the *Canterbury Tales*', *Modern Philology*, 49 (1951–2), 172–81, argues with great persuasiveness for the similarity of the *General Prologue* to the dream-vision prologue, especially that of the *Romance of the Rose*.

16 *Chaucer and His Poetry* (Cambridge, 1915), p. 155.

17 The frame of the *Decameron* actually works in the opposite way from that of the *Canterbury Tales*. Except for the plague, the frame creates a kind of ideal world. The stories on the other hand are for the most part more 'realistic' than the Canterbury tales.

18 See note 15 above.

19 These titles may be the work of scribes. It is impossible to prove that they are Chaucer's, but I am making this assumption here.

20 In his address to the Fifth Triennial Convention of the International Association of the University Professors of English in Edinburgh in August, 1962.

12   Literary structures in Chaucer

'TH'ENDE is every tales strengthe...' as Pandarus tells Criseyde, and the *Canterbury Tales* as a whole and in many of its parts – as well as some of Chaucer's other works – suggest both the significance and also the challenge and strain that Chaucer found in inventing an appropriate close to the structures that he had created in his poems.[1] This essay outlines Chaucer's characteristic uses of such literary structures, and the particular place of an ending as the 'strengthe' in the distinctive forms of artistic wholeness that Chaucer's poetic structures represent. It is not only in Chaucer's many poems that are not brought to a close – the *House of Fame*, the *Anelida*, the *Legend of Good Women*, the *Cook's Tale*, the *Squire's Tale* – but also in those works where Chaucer does provide a conclusion, such as the ending of the *Troilus*[2] or the ending of the whole *Canterbury Tales* with the *Parson's Tale*, that the poet's sense of the ending as a difficult and special part of the 'strengthe' of a literary structure is felt.[3]

While *Troilus and Criseyde* is Chaucer's greatest single completed work and his most fully achieved and accomplished literary structure, the nature and extent of completedness in the *Canterbury Tales* is uncertain, and poses special problems in analysis. It is a work which is completed in different ways at different levels. The individual tales are highly finished within themselves, but the interlinking structure that frames them – of which enough has been written to establish the course of the whole – still bears signs of work in progress. Chaucer's last literary will and testament in the *Retractions*[4] at the end of the *Canterbury Tales* does however suggest that at some point, perhaps perforce, the poet saw himself as having finished with the tales, presumably much in the state reflected in the Ellesmere manuscript, where the structure and order of the series of 'Fragments' which form the *Canterbury Tales* most probably represent the state of composition that Chaucer had reached and then rounded off.[5]

But if, by comparison with the more characteristically 'Gothic' structures of many of his other works, the *Troilus* is Chaucer's most symmetrically constructed poem, reflecting in its five-book symmetry the lessons of classical models,[6] the range of Chaucer's literary structures only confirms the underlying patterns in his structural techniques. In most of his poems, as in the *Troilus*, Chaucer builds the old story into a new structure marked by his distinctive disposition of prologues, interpolated passages and framing structures, which contain the narrative within a commentary that has transformed meaning by the time the poem reaches its resolution in the structure Chaucer has devised ('That thow be understonde, God I bieseche!' *Troilus* v, 1798).

To begin with beginnings is to notice Chaucer's recurrent introduction of prologues into the structures of his poems, and also of various kinds of prefatory section more broadly defined. In this, it has been suggested, Chaucer is working within the structural principles of much Gothic art, with its disposition towards effects achieved by juxtaposition, and such comparisons with the procedures of medieval artists and builders seem true to the daring and subtlety of Chaucer's own approach to structure.[7] The construction of the dream poems strikes the modern reader as Chaucer's most 'Gothic' structural technique, where phases and episodes of the dreamer's observing experience are juxtaposed with others in the manner of the 'panels', 'masses' and 'blocks' juxtaposed in the plastic arts. In poems of this sort, as in pictures, to juxtapose materials is to suggest some thematic relation, and it is precisely in this creation of a new structure, by conjoining and coordinating elements drawn from a range of his reading, that Chaucer's dream poems are original.[8] The dream poems make distinctive use of a prefatory or prologue phase, which establishes a theme against which subsequent reading experience in the poem is registered and played off. The dreamer's bed-time reading in the *Book of the Duchess* of the story of how a loving wife, Alcyone, comes to acknowledge the death at sea of her husband Ceyx, forms a poignant prologue and mirroring precedent for the dreamer's subsequent conversation in his dream with the Man in Black, who is grieving for a dead wife. In the *Parliament of Fowls* the dreamer's initial reading of the *Dream of Scipio* forms a comparably appropriate prologue to the thematic structure of the poem, just as in the *House of Fame* the poet's vision in dream in Book I of a kind of mural of the Dido legend establishes awareness of problems of literary truth-telling as an important thematic first movement to the poem, which is drawn upon during the rest of the poem's structure.[9]

Indeed, when we are talking of the poet of the *General Prologue*, it is scarcely necessary to stress how much literary potential Chaucer clearly saw in the play between some decisively established body of initial information and the work that follows. The whole conception of the *Canterbury Tales* as a collection of stories within the framework of the tale-telling on the pilgrimage to Canterbury is the most ambitious instance of Chaucer's inclination throughout his artistic career to re-interpret received materials by setting them within 'frames' of various forms, 'frames' which through Chaucer's structural devising enable the received story to be read within a context constructed to extend and give super-added meaning to the borrowed story-shape. As the Fragments of the *Canterbury Tales* now stand, it is only the Physician's and Shipman's tales at the openings of Fragments VI and VII which baldly open without an introduction of some kind, and the interplay between such prologues and what follows will often suggest ironic discontinuities which are one of Chaucer's characteristic ways of exploiting his prologues and prefaces.

Apart from Chaucer's distinctive use of prologues in the framework to the *Tales*, he also develops comparable structural techniques within the construction of some of the tales themselves, as with the tales of the Physician, Merchant, and Pardoner. Part of the creative process in structuring such tales involves Chaucer's conjoining of his narration of some pre-existing story with an ample and thematically important first phase or preface, so that the received story can be re-interpreted within a new context. In the *Physician's Tale* the story – of how the Roman father kills his beloved young daughter rather than allow her to be dishonoured by a corrupt judge – is provided in Chaucer's new structural disposition with an opening discourse on the balance between nature and nurture and on the upbringing of children (9–104). In a short tale this preface takes up some first third of the whole structure and, by thus establishing a context, gives more substance to what is only a brief brutal incident in Livy and a passing exemplum in the *Roman de la Rose*. Whatever ironic incongruities may be seen between this 'education prologue', the character of the Physician, and the logic of the borrowed story, such added possibility for layers of meaning has been created by Chaucer's interpolation of this prefatory phase before the narrative itself. Similarly in the *Canon's Yeoman's Tale*, the lengthy first 'Part' is a hectic account of the processes of alchemy, followed in the second 'Part' by the narrative of the tale itself, which stands in pointed juxtaposition with this technical first 'movement' of the Yeoman's utterance as a whole.

Even more striking as a comparable structural disposition is the way Chaucer develops the opening phase of the *Merchant's Tale*. Before the narrative begins to fulfil its fabliau pattern, Chaucer has introduced the lengthy prefatory discourse of well over a hundred lines ('To take a wyf it is a glorious thyng...': 1268ff), enumerating the joys and by implication the sorrows of marriage. This substantial 'panel' of generalization is interpolated between January's initial inclination to marry, in the first lines of the tale, and the teller's eventual pursuit of the narrative line suspended during this theoretical quasi-preface ('For which this Januarie, of whom I tolde...': 1393). Indeed, the prejudiced debate on matrimony which January now conducts (1399ff) – which opens up a range of reference and comparison unlikely to slip from the reader's awareness during the rest of the tale – also fits with a wider pattern in Chaucer's structural techniques, which involves the early introduction of some substantial passage to give a new context to the unfolding of the ensuing story-shape. In the *Nun's Priest's Tale*, Chaucer's version of the fable of the cock and fox, the cockerel's prescient dream of his fate prompts a discourse and dispute on the truth of dreams which is almost a third of the length of the whole tale, so that the narrative of the tricking of the cock does not get under way until sometime past the mid-point of the tale (3187ff). This virtuoso 'preface' of prejudiced argument and anecdotage so establishes the question of predestination that the unfolding story-pattern of the familiar fable cannot but be seen in relation to what has gone before, just as in the *Summoner's Tale* — by the interpolation of the friar's preaching against anger into the spare narrative of fabliau – a distinctive 'block' of discourse is held in ironic juxtaposition with the narrative inside the newly constructed whole and so extends the meaning of the fabliau.

It is through his use of the structural possibilities of prologue and frame for a borrowed story-line that Chaucer achieves such decisive effects in the *Pardoner's Tale*. The very old tale of the fools who set off to seek and kill Death is provided with two consecutive 'prefaces': not only the Pardoner's confession of his preaching practices in his Prologue, but then the full and exclamatory exposition of the relevant sins, on which the Pardoner embarks between briefly introducing the characters of his tale and then returning to them, hundreds of lines later, to set the narrative going (483–660). The juxtaposition between this prefatory phase and the ensuing story has a dreadful aptness, and lends a moral momentum to the exemplary tale which the Pardoner knows how to bring to a rhetorical climax (895–903), although the framing structure of the tale then leads through a series of different experiences of ending, frames within frames, boxes within boxes: the first, accomplished ending with the Pardoner's 'sample' exemplum; the second, jagged ending with his attempt to transfer the closing effects of the exemplum to the pilgrims, and the angry débâcle with the Host; the third and imposed ending in reconciliation and continuity, at once sublime and ludicrous ('Anon they kiste, and ryden forth hir weye'). It is through the structure of such a frame that Chaucer releases the fullest force in the traditional tale which serves as his 'source'.

When Chaucer's structural technique in using his sources and analogues is examined, it becomes clear that there is no paradox in the fact that Chaucer invents so few stories yet is so inventive a story-teller. Chaucer's inventiveness will often consist in an 'art of context', of creating a structure which enables an interaction between materials which Chaucer has had the perceptiveness to bring together. In this sense Chaucer's most innovative wielding of structure lies in his technique of 'contextualizing' received materials.

While it is evidently a simplification of the creative process, it is perhaps helpful to think of the story-shape, the narrative pattern of his 'original', as an outline structure held within Chaucer's imagination as he invents his own version through such techniques as constructing a frame, emphasizing or suppressing certain parts, interpolating substantial passages both narrative and non-narrative, within the overall shape of the original or traditional story. While Chaucer also creates his own interpretation of received matter through closer stylistic effects, some of his most characteristic re-interpretation of sources is achieved through structural techniques, as in such diverse tales as the Man of Law's and the Manciple's. In the *Man of Law's Tale* Chaucer is at work interpolating added passages into the received story-line in a way that punctuates but respects the structure of the original narrative. In the *Manciple's Tale* the teller's interpolations into the original story-line are so lengthy and substantial that it is the 'framework' of intervention into the narrative which now provides the main continuity and holds the story-shape within its structure.

As Chaucer in the *Man of Law's Tale* composes into his own stanzas from the uninterrupted prose of his source in Trivet's Anglo-Norman chronicle, he also punctuates thematically by inserting a succession of interpolations at key points, such as the exclamations on the lessons of the stars (197–203, 295–315), on Satan (358–71), on God's miraculous powers to preserve His servants (470–504), on Custance's predicaments (645–58), on drunkenness (771–7), on lechery (925–31). Through such formal non-narrative interpolations, and the elaborate added prayers (449ff, 841ff), the tale of Custance is taken over substantially unchanged – and even highlighted – as a story-shape, but re-structured from within by an added pattern of commentary.

If in the *Man of Law's Tale* story is interpolated by commentary, in the *Manciple's Tale* commentary is interpolated by the received story from *Metamorphoses*. First, the narrative scene is set: that Phoebus has a caged crow and that he jealously loves his wife, hoping to keep her faithful. But now intervenes a lengthy discourse on the impossibility of thwarting natural instincts (160–95). The narrative resumes long enough to relate that the wife indeed had a lover, but before anything can happen another passage of commentary discusses the appropriate use of words for things, including lovers (207–34). Eventually the narrative is resumed and the crow punished for its pains by the ungrateful god. The last third of the tale's whole structure is now occupied by the Manciple's prudent moralization of his fable (309–62), a passage which expresses the cautiousness and limitedness of his character.

As a narrative of metamorphosis set within a framework of moralization the *Manciple's Tale* ends, at the level of both story and interpretation, with a resolution that puts it at one extreme of the wide range of relatively open and closed forms of ending in Chaucer's works. The genres where narrative arrives at perhaps the most resolved conclusions are fabliau and hagiography, while some of Chaucer's other poems are variously open-ended, both by design as in the *Book of the Duchess*[10] and the *Parliament of Fowls*,[11] and by default, as in the poems which Chaucer left uncompleted,

In some of these unfinished works the natural point of ending seems so close to the point at which Chaucer's writing breaks off that the absence of that ending is all the more intriguing. The *Legend of Good Women* is evidently incomplete as a series, but the last legend of *Hypermnestra* breaks off unfinished even though the source material has been used up in what exists and the narrative seems effectively at an end. Perhaps that was the problem: the source in *Heroides*, couched as a letter from the heroine, by definition could not narrate the writer's own end, and that Chaucer evidently stalled at the task of providing an appropriate conclusion suggests his sense of the need and the difficulty of an ending. More famously unfinished and difficult, the *House of Fame* breaks off just as it teasingly anticipates the arrival of some authoritative figure who may have resolved the impasse the poem has reached, and the anticipation of a conclusion beyond the confines of the existing poem resembles the ending of the *Parliament of Fowls*, whether or not the lack of a formal close reflects Chaucer's difficulty in providing a resolution of the issues raised in the *House of Fame*.

Whether the much more fragmentary state of *Anelida and Arcite* or the *Squire's Tale* reflects Chaucer's unwillingness or inability to complete them, they also resemble each other precisely in an open-ended structural pattern by starting with the promise of action but moving into the essential immobility of a set-piece 'complaint', itself a closing device in some of Chaucer's short poems (like the *Complaint of Mars*), where a brief narrative prefaces and provides the context for an elaborate concluding 'complaint', in a transition in pace and focus which achieves a closural effect.

If these fragmentary structures of poetic openings suggest difficulties in closing poems that Chaucer turned away from, in few narrative poems could closure be more fittingly and climactically achieved than in such fabliaux as the Miller's, Reeve's or Shipman's tales, where a vigorous plot of 'tricks' is worked through to its resolution.[12] With Nicholas's cry of 'Water!' (I, 3815) or the *double entendre* of 'taille' (VII, 416), the plot 'clicks' satisfyingly shut and completes the reader's expectations of the tale, just as the *Friar's Tale* comparably 'turns' upon the fulfilment of the literally meant force of an oath, which is prepared for and anticipated in the earlier agreement between summoner and devil. With such tales the falling out of sheer plot bulks larger in the reader's pleasure than in most other types of story in the *Canterbury Tales*, and the closure of the *Summoner's Tale* shows both Chaucer's relish for fabliau and the special role he accords the ending of a story as the solving of a problem, the answering of a question. Through the incongruously elaborate and pseudo-scientifically precise arrangements for dividing the donation of the fart, the tale finds its resolution in an image in the mind's eye of the cartwheel, here focussed and defined with the dignity of an invention, almost a piece of machinery, the mechanism of a 'process', which resolves the problem set in the tale and brings it to an achieved close beyond which the fabliau could not be continued. Such use of the image left in the mind's eye by the pear tree at the ending of the *Merchant's Tale* comparably brings that tale to a close upon a 'memorial' image of the action[13] to which the dispute between Pluto and Proserpina affords a framing reinforcement of meaning. Indeed, the closing of the *Franklin's Tale* as it paces itself towards its final *demaunde* 'Which was the mooste fre...?' suggests that endings are sometimes to be savoured in the posed deliberateness of their patterns, not rushed or pre-empted until their shape is complete: 'Herkneth the tale er ye upon hire crie... / And whan that ye han herd the tale, demeth' (v, 1496–8).

Working on looser plots, some of Chaucer's other tales – like the lives of the saintlike – rest more on patterns of enduring than intervening in events. But the differences in Chaucer's art of closure between the *Prioress's Tale* and the *Second Nun's Tale* on the one hand, and the *Man of Law's Tale* and the *Clerk's Tale* on the other, underline the important role of the ending in resolving such tales. As the central figures of the Prioress's and Nun's tales are candidates for sainthood, both story-patterns complete themselves with a sense of triumphant deliberateness: the miraculous discovery of the body of the little 'clergeon' and its ceremonious enshrinement bring the tale to a conclusion in ritual confirmation of the new saint, while in the Nun's tale, as in many saints' legends, the violent scene of Cecilia's martyrdom – with its iconography of the three wounds – concludes the tale with a powerful image. By comparison, in the *Man of Law's Tale*, the story of the saintly wife Custance with its patterns of endurance and survival generates no such climactic concluding action but has a succession of 'discoveries' and endings – reunion of husband and wife, reunion of daughter and father, death of husband and return to father, death of father, death of heroine – as the tale quietly follows the cycles of human life to exhaustion. A comparable pattern in Griselda's endurance in the *Clerk's Tale*, because of Chaucer's alteration of the internal balance of the tale, demands a more complex form of closure, drawing on the structural techniques of some of Chaucer's most distinctive conclusions through handling of juxtaposition and framing devices.

Although it follows the structural pattern of Petrarch's version of the Griselda story, the *Clerk's Tale* encourages an emotional involvement with the characters which is in uneasy tension with the structure of the original tale. There is no moment of actual martyrdom for Griselda to end the tale with a climax, but at the denouement in her rediscovery of her children – once the testing embodied in the story-shape is past – Chaucer works up to a climax of pathos in the mother's repeated swoons. The narrative climax brims with a fullness of released emotion, but the poem of the *Clerk's Tale* is larger and longer than the old story of Griselda it contains,[14] and before the poem's structure releases us we must first step successively through several frames, turning to look back at the story itself now framed within frames. First, the narrative is framed by sinking back into an exemplary past: Griseldas are no longer made; anyway, it would be intolerable if women were to follow her example literally. But the marvellously spirited 'Envoy', which then rounds off the tale by instead urging women to terrorize their husbands, seems by its very excess to allow space retrospectively to the value of Griselda's provoking example. In their structural juxtaposition, the striking transition from framed story into an adjuring envoy allows an exhilarating effect of release, as is also experienced through the device of the final envoy in some of Chaucer's short poems like the poised *Envoy to Bukton*, with its ironic closing advice on freedom: 'The Wyf of Bathe I pray yow that ye rede...'

If the framed structure to the tale of Griselda subverts the Wife of Bath's view that 'it is an impossible / That any clerk wol speke good of wyves' (III, 688–9), the idiosyncratic structure of her own romance tale reflects both the Wife's inclination to clerkly talk and the different role of some of Chaucer's endings as the attempted resolution of a problem – particularly in such romances as the tales of the Wife, Franklin and Knight. The climax to the structure of the Wife's version of her traditional tale is less the knight's discovery of the answer to the question about what women most desire (for this occurs around the middle of the tale), but rather his acceptance of his wife's arguments. To correct the knight's objection to his wife's low birth and old age Chaucer here introduces for the lady the lengthy 'pillow-lecture' (roughly a quarter of the whole tale's volume). The presence of this long lecture within the tale's structure rests more on thematic than psychological aptness. Size is emphasis. Proportion effects re-interpretation. By including this moral speech within the traditional story-shape of the romance, Chaucer attempts to lift the original fairy-tale resolution of the story through a magical transformation on to a new level of reward, from which the Wife, however, briskly moves to her pragmatic final prayer ('and Jhesu Crist us sende / Housbondes meeke, yonge, and fressh abedde': 1258–9).

Variations – however ironic or perfunctory – on the deeply traditional medieval device of ending with a prayer conclude many of the *Canterbury Tales*,[15] for the very act of ending prompts a prayerful sense of all ending, just as an ending usually promises a conclusion, which completes and fulfils the meaning of the preceding structure. Chaucer's bold structural techniques within his poems set up a momentum which the ingenuity of his framing structures can catch and bring to memorable conclusion. Yet to find a way of resolving the questions prompted by his re-structuring of a received story is demanding in proportion to the ambiguities created through Chaucer's reconstruction of a poem.[16]

At the close of the *Knight's Tale*, Chaucer's problem in concluding reflects the implications of the structural pattern he has crystallized out from a less pointedly structured source.[17] Chaucer releases the force he sees in the *Teseida* by replacing the essentially external structural features of Boccaccio's poem with structural patterns that expose much more intensely the conflicting feelings and interests intrinsic to the story's shape. The trappings of *Teseida* are relinquished, and whole books and episodes disappear, while the patterns of pairing, division, and juxtaposition in the lives of the characters swim up much more sharply into focus. The proportional relation between what is kept expresses Chaucer's thematically important structural decisions: the third quarter of his poem actually involves the construction of magnificent buildings which project the conflict within the story in the solidity of symbolic architectural structures. Yet such attempted imposition of order and structure only emphasizes the arbitrary injustice of Arcite's end, and the difficulty for Chaucer's Theseus to make some concluding sense of the ending. To that difficulty Chaucer rises by interpolating Theseus' oration, another large set-piece 'block' within one of Chaucer's structures. But by using the flight of Arcite's soul to the eighth sphere at the end of *Troilus* instead, Chaucer has removed one kind of certainty and knowledge about the afterlife, while adding for Theseus an attempt within the limits of human knowledge and experience to make sense of Arcite's death. Within a much less reassuring structure, formal assurance is to be attempted, and the juxtaposition of Theseus' rhetoric of resignation with the symbolic structure of the preceding tale brings an uneasy close to the opening tale of the pilgrimage of the *Canterbury Tales* – that collection of poems evidently planned to be one poem as well, in a structure which shows Chaucer building with the structural techniques that distinguish all his poems, while moving towards a unity at once ambitious yet casual, finished yet fragmentary.

That the *Canterbury Tales* as it stands is a work frozen at a certain stage of the composition of its whole structure is suggested by the survival of some evidently authentic inconsistencies which presumably any final authorial revision would have resolved. The largest inconsistency in structure involves the tale-telling agreement itself, whereby each pilgrim is to tell two tales on the way to Canterbury and two on the way back to London (I, 791–5). But when Harry Bailly invites the Parson to tell his tale and close the collection 'as we were entrying at a thropes ende' and presumably drawing towards Canterbury, the Host declares 'For every man, save thou, hath toold his tale' (x, 25). As the *Tales* stand most pilgrims have in fact told just one tale, although some have not yet told any, and it is hard to imagine how the Knight, or indeed many of the pilgrims, could follow the effect of their first tale.[18] Two incompatible structures for the story-telling are thus apparently accepted at either end of the work, just as in the *Manciple's Prologue* the Host speaks as if in ignorance of the *Cook's Tale*, for which a slot has clearly been created much earlier in the whole structure.

Signs of an unrevised but authentic text similarly emerge from matchings of tale to teller so hasty that even the gender or profession of the teller has not been brought into line with the tale. The *Shipman's Tale* – probably originally to be told by the Wife of Bath – has been shifted to its new teller without revision of the internal signs of a female teller (VII, 11–19). The Second Nun in her Prologue refers to herself as an 'unworthy sone of Eve'(VIII, 62), presumably because Chaucer did not look through line-by-line to remove inconsistencies in a work possibly written before the *Tales* and re-used here. Such oversights suggest a busy artist, concerned at some stage in shifting and linking blocks of familiar material, and preoccupied then with larger rather than smaller connections and effects, which may also explain the survival within the *Merchant's Tale* of signs that it was originally intended for a religious teller (1251, 1322).[19]

It was perhaps such a shifting about of existing tales within the structure of the whole that has left the Man of Law in his Introduction announcing his intention to tell a tale in prose, but then telling the tale of Custance in stanzaic verse. This interesting prologue, in which the Man of Law makes disparaging remarks about Chaucer's abilities as a poet, apparently reflects several authentic layers of authorial intention, and was possibly once intended to introduce the opening tale of the whole pilgrimage, for the elaborate passage of time-telling by the Host (II, 1–14) is matched in the *Tales* only by the comparably elaborate passage when the Host calls on the Parson to tell the last tale (x, 2–11). Chaucer perhaps once thought of these two time-tellings standing symmetrically at either end of the tale-telling, for the Man of Law's discussion in his prologue of the proper subjects for literature, and his enumeration of Chaucer's other works, focus on matters very fitting for the outset of the *Tales*. His own tale in prose which once was to follow and perhaps open the whole *Canterbury Tales* was very possibly the prose *Melibee* – which the *poet* himself now tells – or even Chaucer's lost translation of *De Contemptu Mundi* mentioned in the *Prologue* to the *Legend of Good Women* (G 414), so that the *Man of Law's Prologue* apparently reflects a mixture surviving there together of several layers or strata of the poet's intentions for the structure of the *Tales*.

It is striking that such apparent survivals of Chaucer's uncancelled draftings occur not within the tales but in the link passages, the prologues, epilogues, and endlinks, where the disposition of the Host – which itself contributes powerfully to the structure of how the *Tales* connect together – evidently prompts Chaucer to write and re-write. The first ending of the *Clerk's Tale* – Harry Bailly's response (1212a–g) – is later replaced by the Clerk's envoy. The prologue to the *Monk's Tale* and the epilogue to the *Nun's Priest's Tale* reveal how a framing idea which strikes Chaucer in one place is shifted to another context with more potential: the Host's innuendo about the teller as himself a 'tredefoul' in the sketchy yet authentic epilogue to the Priest's tale of the cock (VII, 3451) achieves its full realization as the Host's teasing in the *Monk's Prologue* (1945), but the unacceptably repetitious overlap between the two contexts is unlikely to have survived a final revision of the structure of the *Canterbury Tales*.

It is another of Chaucer's drafted link-passages built around the Host's responses – the epilogue to the *Man of Law's Tale* – which has stimulated much debate about what structures and order of tales Chaucer envisaged. After the *Man of Law's Tale*, when the Host calls on the Parson to tell a tale and is rebuked for his swearing, another pilgrim interrupts to insist on telling a livelier tale. Some manuscripts attribute this interjection to the Summoner or the Squire, but it is unlikely that Chaucer would ever have intended so to introduce their existing tales here. One otherwise undistinguished manuscript however, attributes this intervention to the Shipman (whose tale, after all, was probably the Wife's first tale), and upon this slender evidence it has been conjectured that the whole Fragment VII, which is opened by the *Shipman's Tale*, should be shifted forward to follow the *Man of Law's Tale* and precede the Wife's present tale, although this particular sequence is found in no extant manuscript.[20]

The appeal of such conjectural emendation lies not simply in finding a coherent role for the evidently authentic epilogue to the *Man of Law's Tale* (which now stands like a staircase without a house), but in structuring the sequence of tales so that the sporadic allusions to geographical place in the links occur in their proper geographical sequence. The Summoner's threat to tell 'tales two or thre / Of freres, er I come to Sidyngborne' (III, 846–7) could then follow instead of preceding the Host's comment in the *Monk's Prologue*: 'Loo, Rouchestre stant heer faste by!' (VII, 1926). To shift Fragment VII forward would thus remove an apparent confusion over geographical sequence – for of course Rochester comes before Sittingbourne on the road to Canterbury – although this is to interpret the Summoner's blustering words very literally to mean that Sittingbourne is actually the next place on the itinerary.

Chaucer's references to time and place as structuring features of the *Canterbury Tales* are in fact so imprecise as to suggest he lacked time or interest to work through the links plotting a careful structure of chronological and geographical references, foregrounding the *Tales* as an actual pilgrimage on a particular route. Indeed, in the *Man of Law's Prologue* the Host notices that it is 18 April, yet many tales later in the *Parson's Prologue* the date is indicated to be 17 April,[21] although this is only in keeping with the vagueness of allusions to time and place throughout. Chaucer gives little sense of the days of the journey, none of places visited or lodged in. The beginning at the Tabard is realized, but on a pilgrimage to Canterbury the pilgrims' arrival at the shrine is never enacted or described.

Taking the 'meta-tale' of Canterbury – which aims to enable all the tales to be read both in themselves and as one work – as the tale of a pilgrimage during which a collection of stories are related by the pilgrims, modern conceptions of the structure of the whole *Tales* have stressed both dramatic and symbolic unity: the dramatic continuum of the frame of links, and the spiritual unity provided by the purpose and associations of pilgrimage. Whether or not the forgetfulness of spiritual pilgrimage and absorption in story-telling between the beginning and end of the whole structure of the *Tales* reflects on the pilgrims' need for true pilgrimage, these dramatic and spiritual structures operate differently in different parts of the *Canterbury Tales*. The electricity released by Chaucer's conception of a socially very mixed group of tellers involved in a competitive story-telling has often been favourably compared with the socially homogeneous party who tell tales as a pastime in the more two-dimensional frame of Boccaccio's *Decameron*. But the dramatic continuum that Chaucer constructs is of a sharply focussed kind, spotlighting two- or three-way exchanges between the pilgrims.

In the inter-tale continuity passages of the *Canterbury Tales* it is indeed interruption which forms one of the most dramatic devices of structuring: plans and patterns are recurrently not allowed to pursue their course to a conclusion. Most pointedly, the poet-figure himself is brusquely interrupted in relating his *Thopas* and forbidden to continue it. The Host's intention that the Monk should follow the Knight is overborne by the drunken Miller (I, 3118ff). The Pardoner interrupts the *Wife of Bath's Prologue* (III, 163ff), and at its conclusion the Friar and Summoner have an altercation (829ff), not long after which the Summoner breaks into the *Friar's Tale* (1332ff). The *Monk's Tale* is cut short by the Knight (VII, 2767ff), and the whole sudden arrival and tale-telling of the Canon's Yeoman is an interruption into the pilgrimage. Whether the response to the *Squire's Tale* which Chaucer has written for the Franklin (V, 673ff) was positively intended to act as an interruption of the *Squire's Tale* – which stands in the manuscripts unfinished and perhaps unfinishable – is an instance of the ambiguity of interpreting an unfinished unity like the *Canterbury Tales*, in which dramatic unity often lies in such juxtaposition of tales, in interruption and the denial of an ending.

Juxtaposed pairings, into which tales are structured by the responses of their tellers or the Host, form one of the most recurrent patterns in the structure of the *Canterbury Tales*. The Miller's and Reeve's tales, and the Friar's and Summoner's, are locked together by the antagonism of their tellers, the determination of the second teller to 'quit' or pay back the first for his tale. In the prologues to the Cook's and Manciple's tales there are hints that such clashes of tales might have been developed between the Cook and Host, and the Cook and Manciple, because of professional rivalries. The *Clerk's Tale* may be seen as a response to the Wife's comments about clerks, while the *Merchant's Tale* follows on as a response to the Clerk's preceding tale. It is Harry Bailly's responses which link the Physician's and Pardoner's tales, and the tales within Fragment VII. Indeed, it is striking how – as the fragments of the *Canterbury Tales* stand – Chaucer seems to have been working out towards the continuity of the *Tales* as a whole from local unities first established in sequences of pairs. Four (or five) fragments out of the existing nine (or ten) work on this principle: (IV) Clerk–Merchant; (V) Squire–Franklin; (VI) Physician–Pardoner; (VIII) Second Nun–Canon's Yeoman; (IX and X) Manciple–Parson. This apparent pattern of the poet-at-work, preserved in the structure of the completed links, suggests how for Chaucer the essential continuum of the *Canterbury Tales* arises out of the potential for dialogue and pairing between tellers and tales, unities which may be dramatic or thematic, pairings of juxtaposed tales which complement and comment on each other and, cumulatively, on those which have already been told by previous tellers.

These structural patterns in Chaucer's exploiting of the devices of interruption and of pairing can be seen in the placing of the *Melibee* as the poet-figure's second attempt at a tale after the interruption of his *Thopas*. If the structure of the whole *Canterbury Tales* as it stands represents a cross-section of a particular stage of the poet at work, then the altered role of the *Melibee* offers a clue to Chaucer's shifting conception of the unity of the *Tales*. The use of dramatic interruption can allow within the wholeness of the *Tales* some instances (like the *Monk's Tale*) of forms and attitudes which anticipate no necessary end and might continue interminably. The poet's *Thopas*, although comparably directionless and irreversibly cut short, does already anticipate a progressively diminishing structural pattern.[22] It would have dwindled away to nothing, if it had not been interrupted and paired with the *Melibee*, a structure of an altogether different completedness and resolution. In the *Melibee* an opening allegorical narrative, in which enemies break into Melibeus's house and wound his daughter, provides the impetus for the rest of the tale's structure as a book of moral counsel, through his wife Prudence's eventually successful persuading of Melibeus to overcome with forgiveness his impulse for revenge, and to seek reconciliation.[23] If this noble and beautifully written work, with its lesson of patient and loving forbearance, did indeed once initiate the *Canterbury Tales*, it would have contributed to a distinctly different thematic structure for the whole poem. That it should now be positioned very much in the midst of the sequence of tales, and voiced by the poet as his second-choice attempt, points to the strikingly open form of structure which Chaucer was working on for the tales. The humiliating interruption of the poet-figure's own bad poem, and the difficulty even for a strong character like the Host in keeping the company in order, only emphasize how local and relative seems all authority within the framework of the *Tales*. In the Knight's and Parson's tales Chaucer has clearly demarcated in particular ways an opening to the tale-telling and a close to the pilgrimage,[24] but between these two points there is more sense of the local unities of juxtaposition and pairing in the 'quitting' of tales than in a structure 'progressive' in time, place, or moral 'development' among the pilgrim-tellers. In this sense, the framework of the *Tales* aims at a structure 'realistic' in reflecting the unpredictable, accidental, disconnected qualities of life, although patterns of theme both within and across the existing Fragments point to an underlying structure of reiterated concerns and approaches (like those brought together in the *Melibee*) that counterpoints the continuity of clash and quarrel but does not surface into a linear progress of formal debate and resolution.[25]

Yet in having the Host invite the Parson at the end of the tale-telling to 'knytte up wel a greet mateere', and in making the Parson respond by declining to tell a tale as such at all but instead providing a treatise on penance, Chaucer closes the structure of the whole *Canterbury Tales* with the resolution of faith.[26] In the context of contemporary penitential manuals of its type, the *Parson's Tale* shows a careful and serious structure of its own, reflecting Chaucer's thoughtful coordination of a number of sources into a analysis of sinfulness and the potential for emendation, which in medieval terms offers a very full understanding of human experience.[27] Indeed, the universal relevance of its application has inevitably prompted attempts to interpret the role of the *Parson's Tale* in the structure of the *Canterbury Tales* as one that unifies backwards from a finally achieved vantage-point of spiritual values, by offering retrospective commentary and judgement upon the relevant instances of sin in the preceding tales and their tellers.[28] But the scope of the *Parson's Tale* makes an overlap with aspects of the tales inevitable rather than specific, while the *Parson's Prologue* with its renunciation of the fiction of 'fables' suggests a decisive turning-point of transition and transcendence from the preceding continuum of the tale-telling, a change of plane borne out in the changed demands on the reader in the instructional mode of this 'tale' which is no tale. This instructive strategy of the tale in promoting a penitent sense of purpose itself anticipates a spiritual movement which is the true fulfilment

of the idea of pilgrimage in the whole structure of the *Canterbury Tales* (as
the Parson undertakes: 'To shewe yow the wey, in this viage, / Of thilke
parfit glorious pilgrymage / That highte Jerusalem celestial': 49–51).[29]
The outward and literal end of that particular fictional pilgrimage to
Canterbury is never completed, but to end in a penitential manual offers
to each reader the opening of a true inward pilgrimage beyond the
experience of this book of tales. In this spiritual authority as teaching the
Parson's Tale draws together the closural and judgemental associations of
its context and its content, leaving irreversibly behind as evening falls the
idiosyncrasies and divisions of temporal experience in the *Tales*, and
through the very orderliness and comprehensiveness of its analytical mode
projecting those timeless and unchanging verities which should be the goal
of all.

For Chaucer – to whom the artistic problems of concluding seem to have
been a symptom of the significance he created in his fictional structures –
the placing of the *Parson's Tale* at the conclusion of the *Canterbury Tales*
must be an ending to all endings, an absolute ending, for it ends with the
absolute, with that truth which is our ultimate end. As Chaucer had read,
and himself translated into English, in Boethius' *Consolation of Philosophy*:
'of thinges that han ende may ben maked comparysoun, but of thynges
that ben withouten ende to thynges that han ende may be makid no
comparysoun...' (*Boece*, II, pr. 7, 105–8).

Notes

1 Cf. Elizabeth Salter, *Fourteenth-Century English Poetry: Contexts and Readings*
(Oxford, 1983), p. 116: '[Chaucer's] endings and reconciliations are often
made in a spirit of stoicism or weariness, with rarely the sense that they are
the ineluctable consequence of what has gone before, and often coming with
surprising suddenness...'. For a stimulating study of the art of ending in
poetry, cf. Barbara Herrnstein Smith, *Poetic Closure* (Chicago, 1968). Cf. also
E. R. Curtius, *European Literature and the Latin Middle Ages*, trans. W. R. Trask
(London, 1953), pp. 89–91 ('Topics of the Conclusion').

2 On the traditional context of the ending of the *Troilus*, cf. John M. Steadman,
Disembodied Laughter: Troilus and the Apotheosis Tradition (Berkeley, Ca., 1972),
and J. S. P. Tatlock, 'The Epilog of Chaucer's *Troilus*', *Modern Philology*, 18
(1921), 625–59. For a critical discussion, see E. T. Donaldson, 'The Ending of
Troilus', in his *Speaking of Chaucer* (London, 1970). For further references, see
my edition, *Geoffrey Chaucer: 'Troilus and Criseyde': A New Edition of 'The Book
of Troilus'* (London, 1984), pp. 556–63.

3 Piero Boitani, *Chaucer and the Imaginary World of Fame* (Cambridge, 1984),
p. 208, notes that the *Parliament of Fowls*, *Troilus*, the *Legend*, and the *Canterbury Tales* 'have disturbing, unsatisfactory, ambiguous, problematic, incomplete conclusions. This is perhaps the reason why twentieth-century
readers – used as they are to "open" forms of art – feel that his failures are,
beginning with this in-finite *House of Fame*, his most exciting successes...'.

4 For the background, see Olive Sayce, 'Chaucer's "Retractions": the Con-

clusion of the *Canterbury Tales* and its Place in Literary Tradition', *Medium Aevum*, 40 (1971), 230–48.

5 The Ellesmere manuscript's order of tales is:

    I   (A) General Prologue, Knight, Miller, Reeve, Cook
    II (B¹) Man of Law
    III (D) Wife, Friar, Summoner
    IV (E) Clerk, Merchant
    V   (F) Squire, Franklin
    VI (C) Physician, Pardoner
    VII (B²) Shipman, Prioress, Thopas, Melibee, Monk, Nun's Priest
    VIII (G) Second Nun, Canon's Yeoman
    IX (H) Manciple
    X   (I) Parson

Cf. Larry Benson, 'The Order of the *Canterbury Tales*', *Studies in the Age of Chaucer*, 3 (1981), 77–120: E. T. Donaldson, 'The Ordering of the *Canterbury Tales*' in *Medieval Literature and Folklore Studies: Essays in Honor of Francis Lee Utley*, eds. Jerome Mandel and Bruce A. Rosenberg (New Jersey, 1970), pp. 193–204; Helen Cooper, *The Structure of the Canterbury Tales* (London, 1983), ch. 2 ('The Ordering of the *Canterbury Tales*'); Derek Pearsall, *The Canterbury Tales* (London, 1985), ch. 1. For the background of the early MSS, see A. I. Doyle, 'The Production of the *Canterbury Tales* and the *Confessio Amantis* in the early Fifteenth Century' in *Medieval Scribes, Manuscripts and Libraries: Essays presented to N. R. Ker*, eds. M. B. Parkes and Andrew G. Watson (London, 1978), pp. 163–210. For different views which question the authority of the Ellesmere tale-order, cf. A. I. Doyle and M. B. Parkes, 'A Paleographical Introduction' in *The Canterbury Tales: A Facsimile and Transcription of the Hengwrt Manuscript*, ed. Paul G. Ruggiers (Norman, Okla., 1979), and *The Canterbury Tales by Geoffrey Chaucer Edited from the Hengwrt Manuscript*, ed. N. F. Blake (London, 1980).

6 Cf. S. B. Meech, *Design in Chaucer's Troilus* (Syracuse, NY, 1959), and John P. McCall, 'Five-Book Structure in Chaucer's *Troilus*', *Modern Language Quarterly*, 23 (1962), 297–308. The page-format of my edition (London, 1984) is designed to illustrate Chaucer at work on structuring the *Troilus* as he composes from his source, Boccaccio's *Filostrato*.

7 See R. M. Jordan, *Chaucer and the Shape of Creation: The Aesthetic Possibilities of Inorganic Structure* (Cambridge, Mass., 1967). For a more general study, see William W. Ryding, *Structure in Medieval Narrative* (The Hague, 1971).

8 Cf. Robert O. Payne, *The Key of Remembrance* (New Haven, Conn., 1963), ch. 4, 'The First Structural Stereotype', p. 145: 'The great originality of these [dream] poems is in their attempt to exploit the possiblities of *dispositio* – overall structural arrangement – in ways more complex and meaningful than anything the [rhetorical] manuals suggest in their perfunctory treatments of it'. See also *Chaucer's Dream Poetry: Sources and Analogues*, ed. and trans. B. A. Windeatt (Cambridge, 1982), pp. ix–xvii.

9 Cf. Sheila Delany, *Chaucer's House of Fame: The Poetics of Skeptical Fideism* (Chicago, 1972), p. 49: 'Explicit content, then, may be less central to meaning than method or structure, and that structure may be grasped at various points in the work'.

10 Cf. George Henderson, *Gothic* (Harmondsworth, 1968), p. 115: 'A Gothic building cannot simply stop, it has to fade away. Hence the familiar flurry of curves and spikes, by which the physical presence is gradually withdrawn and the dense material mass is dissolved into the empty air'; quoted in discussion

of the *Book of the Duchess* in A. C. Spearing, *Medieval Dream-Poetry* (Cambridge, 1976), p. 53.

11 Cf. *The Parlement of Foulys*, ed. D. S. Brewer (London, 1960), p. 25: 'Nothing has been resolved – ordinary logic is defeated or unimportant – but we are aware of a completed structure, of opposites balanced if not entirely reconciled.'

12 Cf. Derek Brewer, 'Structures and Character-types of Chaucer's Popular Comic Tales' in his *Chaucer: The Poet as Storyteller* (London, 1984), pp. 80–9.

13 Cf. V. A. Kolve, *Chaucer and the Imagery of Narrative: The First Five Canterbury Tales* (London, 1984), especially ch. 2 ('Chaucerian Aesthetic: The Image in the Poem').

14 Cf. Derek Brewer, *Chaucer: The Poet as Storyteller*, ch. 4 ('Towards a Chaucerian Poetic') and ch. 6 ('The Nun's Priest's Tale as Story and Poem').

15 On prayers as endings, cf. Matthew of Vendôme, *Ars Versificatoria* in *Les Arts poétiques du XIIe et du XIIIe siècle*, ed. E. Faral (Paris, 1924), p. 192.

16 Cf. P. M. Kean, *Chaucer and the Making of English Poetry*, 2 vols. (London, 1972), vol. 2, ch. 2 ('The *Canterbury Tales*: the problem of narrative structure'): 'It seems likely that [Chaucer] would have understood...a type of structure in a long narrative work which depended on the development of ideas and of themes, rather than on the devising of a plot with appropriate characters. If so, this would have reinforced any feeling that narrative structure was dependent on a more total and intimate organization of the material than could be achieved by a construction which was based on the story line alone' (p. 71).

17 Cf. Elizabeth Salter, *Chaucer: The Knight's Tale and the Clerk's Tale* (London, 1962), pp. 35–6, and *The Knight's Tale*, ed. A. C. Spearing (Cambridge, 1966), pp. 75–8.

18 For an argument that Chaucer did not abandon the two-way-journey scheme, see Charles A. Owen, *Pilgrimage and Storytelling in the Canterbury Tales* (Norman, Okla., 1977).

19 Cf. Jordan, *Chaucer and the Shape of Creation*, p. 117: 'Such imperfections of adjustment...reveal the essential character of Chaucer's art. It is an art of superimpositions, adjustments, accommodations.'

20 This is the 'Bradshaw Shift', suggested by the reading 'Shipman' in Bodleian MS Arch. Selden B. 14.

21 Cf. Sigmund Eisner, 'Chaucer's Use of Nicholas of Lynn's Calendar', *Essays and Studies*, 29 (1976), 1–22.

22 Cf. J. A. Burrow, 'An Agony in Three Fits' in his *Essays on Medieval Literature* (Oxford, 1984): 'The poem seems to narrow away, section by section, towards nothingness' (p. 65).

23 Cf. W. W. Lawrence, 'The Tale of Melibeus' in *Essays and Studies in Honor of Carleton Brown* (New York, 1940), pp. 100–10; Paul Strohm, 'The Allegory of the *Tale of Melibee*', *Chaucer Review*, 2 (1967–8), 32–42; C. A. Owen, Jr., 'The *Tale of Melibee*', *Chaucer Review*, 7 (1972–3), 267–80; Dolores Palomo, 'What Chaucer really did to *Le Livre de Melibee*', *Philological Quarterly*, 53 (1974), 304–20; Glending Olson 'A Reading of the *Thopas–Melibee* Link', *Chaucer Review*, 10 (1975–6), 147–53; Diane Bornstein, 'Chaucer's *Tale of Melibee* as an example of the *style clergial*', *Chaucer Review*, 12 (1977–8), 236–54; Paul G. Ruggiers, 'Serious Chaucer: The *Tale of Melibeus* and the Parson's Tale' in *Chaucerian Problems and Perspectives: Essays Presented to Paul E. Beichner*, eds. Edward Vasta and Zacharias P. Thundy (Notre Dame, Ind., 1979), pp. 83–94.

24 Cf. Paul G. Ruggiers, *The Art of the Canterbury Tales* (Madison, Wis., 1965),

pp. 42–50 ('The Range of the Middle'), and also his 'The Form of the *Canterbury Tales: Respice Fines', College English*, 17 (1955–6), 439–44.

25 Cf. Helen Cooper, *The Structure of the Canterbury Tales* (London, 1983), ch. 5 ('Links within the Fragments'). Cf. also Donald R. Howard, *The Idea of the Canterbury Tales* (Berkeley/Los Angeles, Ca., 1976), ch. IV ('Memory and Form') and ch. V ('The Tales: A Theory of their Structure'), and Judson Boyce Allen and Theresa Anne Moritz, *A Distinction of Stories: The Medieval Unity of Chaucer's Fair Chain of Narratives for Canterbury* (Columbus, Ohio, 1981).

26 Cf. Traugott Lawler, *The One and the Many in the Canterbury Tales* (Hamden, Connecticut, 1980), ch. 5 ('Closure') and ch. 7 ('Closure II: the Parson's Tale and Chaucer's Retraction'). Cf. also Carol V. Kaske, 'Getting Around the Parson's Tale: An Alternative to Allegory and Irony' in *Chaucer at Albany*, ed. Rossell Hope Robbins (New York, 1975), pp. 147–77.

27 Cf. Siegfried Wenzel, 'The Source for the "Remedia" of the Parson's Tale', *Traditio*, 27 (1971), 433–53; 'The Source of Chaucer's Seven Deadly Sins', *Traditio*, 30 (1974), 351–78. Cf. also Lee W. Patterson, 'The "Parson's Tale" and the Quitting of the "Canterbury Tales"', *Traditio*, 34 (1978), 331–80, for a valuable discussion. In his 'Notes on the *Parson's Tale*', *Chaucer Review*, 16 (1981–2), 237–56, Siegfried Wenzel comments: 'In writing [the *Parson's Tale*] Chaucer translated substantial sections from the identified sources. But it is equally accurate to point out that in doing so he not only worked selectively, but also made changes and additions which reveal intelligence, purposiveness, and a fairly exact familiarity with the pastoral–theological thought and language of his time.'

28 Professor Patterson ('The Quitting of the "Canterbury Tales"', pp. 357–70) lists some thirty-five passages in the *Parson's Tale* which echo passages in the preceding tales. Ten such echoes are of conventional phrases and ideas: *ParsT* 1068, *MerchT* 1315, *ShipT* 9; *ParsT* 940, *WBProl* 129–30, *MerchT* 2048; *ParsT* 957, *KnT* 1323; *ParsT* 472, *KnT* 1255–6, *Pard Prol* 294–96; *ParsT* 473, *ClT* 995–1001; *ParsT* 389, *MerchT* 1640–1; *ParsT* 857–8, *RvProl* 3879–81, *WBProl* 291; *ParsT* 630, *WBProl* 244; *ParsT* 603, *Pard Prol* 350–1; *ParsT* 368, *Mel* 1079. A further twenty-one passages show the *Parson's Tale* overlapping with some of the preceding tales in drawing on the same traditional homiletic materials: (1) *ParsT* 93, *PhysT* 286; (2) *ParsT* 155–7, *WBProl* 784–5; (3) *ParsT* 407, *GP* 377, 449–52; (4) *ParsT* 484, *PhysT* 114–16; (5) *ParsT* 564, *SumT* 2009; (6) *ParsT* 589, 592, *PardT* 633–7; (7) *ParsT* 591, *PardT* 472–5; (8) *ParsT* 593, *PardT* 648–50; (9) *ParsT* 617, *SumT* 2075; (10) *ParsT* 631–4, *WBProl* 278–80, *Mel* 1086; (11) *ParsT* 710, 714, *SNProl* 1–3; (12) *ParsT* 721, *PhysT* 101–2; (13) *ParsT* 793, *PardT* 591–4; (14) *ParsT* 819, *PardT* 504; (15) *ParsT* 819–20, *PardT* 529–33; (16) *ParsT* 822, *PardT* 558–9; (17) *ParsT* 836, *PardT* 481–4, *PhysT* 59, *WBProl* 464; (18) *ParsT* 859, *MerchT* 1839–40; (19) *ParsT* 884, *MerchT* 1438–40; (20) *ParsT* 929, *MerchT* 1384; (21) *ParsT* 100, *Mel* 1054. The four remaining echoes are rather more substantial: *ParsT* 464, 154, 73, *WBT* 1158; *ParsT* 600, *PardT* 631–2; *ParsT* 1008, *SumT* 2098; *ParsT* 938–9, *MerchT* 1441–51.

29 Cf. Ralph Baldwin, *The Unity of the Canterbury Tales*, Anglistica, 5 (Copenhagen, 1955).

13   Chaucer's narrator: *Troilus and Criseyde* and the *Canterbury Tales*

Chaucer's narrator is the discovery of a fairly recent generation of critics. Earlier readers had, of course, noticed the very personal tone of most of Chaucer's poems, but it had not really occurred to them to make a consistent distinction between Geoffrey Chaucer the poet and the 'I' speaking in his works. Modern theories of narrative, however, most influential among them Wayne Booth's *The Rhetoric of Fiction*, have pointed out that there is such a thing as an 'unreliable narrator' and that it is very unsophisticated if not misleading to identify the narrator with the author.[1] This approach was first of all applied to the modern novel, where it certainly led to a much better understanding of many texts and auctorial strategies, but it also seemed helpful in reading earlier authors, and for a time the analysis of narrators became a fashionable critical occupation, which yielded many valuable insights, but was (as often happens with critical fashions) sometimes overdone.

There are, presumably, many cases of authors being no less naive than the majority of their readers and genuinely trying to speak to us in their own voice, without any more complicated intention. This is especially likely in autobiographical poems or passages, and though in the Middle Ages, more than in some other periods, we have to take into account the force of stylistic conventions, we have to beware of the 'conventional fallacy', that is, the mistaken notion that what is conventional cannot be sincere and true.[2]

The most interesting aspect of Chaucer's narrator is not what he reveals about the author's personal life and opinions, but the way he directs our responses and controls the narrative situation. This is observable as early as the *Book of the Duchess* whose 'obtuse' narrator has been subjected to subtle analysis more than once.[3] He tells us one or two intriguing things about himself, such as the fact of his eight years' sickness. It seems an obvious reference to unsuccessful love, but whether it is a conventional pose, or a personal confession his first audience would know how to interpret, will, I suppose, always remain a mystery.

More important is the function of this narrator for the effect of the whole poem; he is a sympathetic listener, and his brief expression of condolence after the Black Knight's elaborate account of his suffering strikes the reader as a genuine and spontaneous attempt to share the bereaved lover's despair. The narrator is a far more individualized figure than many of the conventional dreamers, and the same applies to Chaucer's other dream-allegories, such as the *House of Fame*, the *Parliament of Fowls*, and the *Legend of Good Women*. In all these poems, the poet presents himself as a rather bookish, impractical person whose knowledge of love and of poetry comes from reading rather than from experience and who is granted a sight of the 'real thing' without getting actively involved in the service of love. This aspect is most pointedly expressed by Africanus who acts as the poet's guide in the *Parliament of Fowls*:

> 'But natheles, although that thow be dul,
> Yit that thow canst not do, yit mayst thow se.
> For many a man that may nat stonde a pul,
> It liketh hym at the wrastlyng for to be,
> And demeth yit wher he do bet or he.
> And if thow haddest connyng for t'endite,
> I shal the shewe mater of to wryte.'   (162–8)

The point is not so much whether Chaucer really was that kind of man, but rather the dramatization of the contrast between written tradition and immediate reality, or the confrontation of literary convention with personal involvement.

In the *House of Fame*, the literary aspect is made more explicit: the narrator is an author who is very much concerned with the subject of his poetry, to the extent of losing sight of reality while poring over his books:

> 'But of thy verray neyghebores,
> That duellen almost at thy dores,
> Thou herist neyther that ne this;
> For when thy labour doon al ys,
> And hast mad alle thy rekenynges,
> In stede of reste and newe thynges,
> Thou goost hom to thy hous anoon;
> And, also domb as any stoon,
> Thou sittest at another book
> Tyl fully daswed ys thy look,
> And lyvest thus as an heremyte...'   (649–59)

Again, there is no telling whether this famous passage is an accurate description of Geoffrey Chaucer as he appeared to his contemporaries – in view of his demanding public responsibilities it seems highly unlikely. In any case, the poet-narrator is presented here as a dramatic character, hardly less distinct and memorable than the garrulous Eagle, and his impractical and unsociable bookishness is an important foil for the other attitudes suggested by the poem. Moreover, the narrator's own unconcern for any fame in the traditional sense adds a critical perspective to the exploration of the capricious workings of Fame and the arbitrary nature of 'tydinges'. Lastly, the reader is alerted to the many ironies of the poem by the most obvious irony of the speechless and almost intimidated poet, lectured at by the voluble Eagle, the same 'Geffrey' (729), of course, who is the daringly original creator of the whole book.

In the *Prologue* to the *Legend of Good Women*, the narrator is again publicly identified with the poet himself; indeed, we are even provided with a kind of annotated Chaucer-bibliography. The explicit references to his work as a poet and a translator make the relationship between poet and narrator all the more teasing. On the one hand, there seems to be no reason to doubt that Chaucer is speaking in his own voice when he defends his good intentions; on the other hand, the whole situation is so obviously fictitious and partly comic that we get a strong sense of the author's superior sophistication and detachment: the text is evidently so much more complex and rich in conflicting meanings than the narrator himself seems to be aware of, and this involves the reader in a fascinating game of trying to isolate the 'real' voice behind all this half-serious exchange. Our attitude to this narrator also has some bearing on how seriously we take the following 'legends' and the author's 'penaunce'.[4]

More intriguing still and more crucial for our response to the text is the function of the narrator in *Troilus and Criseyde*. Many readers have felt that this narrator is one of Chaucer's most original poetic creations and that he becomes almost as lively a presence in our minds while we are perusing the poem as the characters in the story.[5]

The first of this narrator's effects on the reader is that we are never allowed to enter fully into the action of the poem without being conscious of its historical distance from us and the narrative medium in which we encounter it. There is hardly anything like it in Boccaccio's *Filostrato*; in that poem, the narrator introduces himself, states the purpose of his work, and then largely retreats behind the story.[6] Chaucer's narrator, in contrast, has no personal axe to grind, and all his problems are connected with his literary labours. His continually changing attitudes towards his material and the poem in hand reflect his difficulties, and he is quite unique among medieval English narrators in sharing these difficulties with his audience.

There is no doubt that all this has a profound influence on the way the reader responds to the story. From the very beginning, he is made to feel that he is taken into the narrator's confidence, that he is not just the object of superior instruction or entertainment by an omnipotent author. The most important aspect of this narrator is his modesty and his sympathetic understanding for people who are very different from himself; this applies to the reader as well as to the characters of the story. His own attitude to both is determined by the fact that he claims to have no personal knowledge and experience of love, while he is trying to tell a love-story, but he assumes that there will be many lovers in the audience who know more about 'fin amors' than he does. To their sympathy he appeals from the very outset, not only for his own benefit, but also on behalf of the actors in the tragedy. This illusion of a personal relationship between author and reader is of crucial importance for our reaction to the poem. In a sense, of course, we are also made aware of the fact, often disguised by less communicative narrators, that we are all the time at the author's mercy. He can only try to make the best of the material in front of him, but at least we are persuaded that he is honest and sincerely tries to make us understand this ancient tale.

Throughout the poem, we hardly ever lose sight of the narrator. This is partly due to the frequency of conventional rhetorical formulas that remind us of the author's craft, such as the following stanza, added by Chaucer to Boccaccio's account:

> But how this town com to destruccion
> Ne falleth naught to purpos me to telle;
> For it were here a long digression
> Fro my matere, and yow to long to dwelle.
> But the Troian gestes, as they felle,
> In Omer, or in Dares, or in Dite,
> Whoso that kan may rede hem as they write.   (*Troilus* I, 141–7)

We are made to realize that the poet has to arrange his material, select certain details and omit others, and this alone prevents us from a naive and uncritical identification with the story.

Another, more conventional form of address to the audience is the direct didactic exhortation, extracting a more or less obvious moral from the story and passing it on to the reader. This may not be particularly original, but Chaucer does not use the device indiscriminately, and it is obvious that the narrator wants to draw our attention to the moral implications of Troilus' fall in a way Boccaccio does not. The following stanza, one of seven interpolated by Chaucer, has no parallel in the *Filostrato*:

> Forthy ensample taketh of this man,
> Ye wise, proude, and worthi folkes alle,
> To scornen Love, which that so soone kan
> The fredom of youre hertes to hym thralle;
> For evere it was, and evere it shal byfalle,
> That Love is he that alle thing may bynde,
> For may no man fordon the lawe of kynde.   (I, 232–8)

Much more surprising and new, in English poetry at least, is the narrator's digression on the differences in language and manners; it is a powerful appeal to our historical imagination, and again we are asked to

make a particular effort to give our full sympathy to characters we may
find very unfamiliar at first:

> And forthi if it happe in any wyse,
> That here be any lovere in this place
> That herkneth, as the storie wol devise,
> How Troilus com to his lady grace,
> And thenketh, 'so nold I nat love purchace,'
> Or wondreth on his speche or his doynge,
> I noot; but it is me no wonderynge.   (II, 29–35)

It is clear that this narrator wants to warn us against hasty judgement
and ahistorical identification, but he also prepares the way for an emotional
participation that is no less deep for being critically controlled and self-
conscious.

The ending of Book II is another brilliant example of narratorial
intrusion: this time, his direct appeal seems to invite us to identify with
the hero in his feverish expectation of the first meeting with Criseyde, but
the effect is complicated by the abrupt breaking off and the complete
change of tone with the beginning of the next book. Any emotional
identification is cut short, and we are sharply reminded of the literary
artifice behind the dramatic moment:

> But now to yow, ye loveres that ben here,
> Was Troilus nought in a kankedort,
> That lay, and myghte whisprynge of hem here,
> And thoughte, 'O Lord, right now renneth my sort
> Fully to deye, or han anon comfort!'
> And was the firste tyme he shulde hire preye
> Of love; O myghty God, what shal he seye?   (II, 1751–7)

The most important effect is that we are continually forced to supply from
our own experience and imagination what the narrator leaves out. He
knows and freely admits that even the best poet can never give an adequate
idea of the complexity of human behaviour and the intensity of emotions.
This can be achieved only by the active cooperation of the reader, by a
critical dialogue between author and audience.

Some of the most interesting interventions of the narrator concern our
moral judgement and our evaluation of the characters. The narrator shares
these problems with us by refusing, for instance, at some critical points
of the story, to offer a definite verdict. His deliberate reticence as to
Criseyde's possible complicity in Pandarus' plans is an obvious case
(III, 575–81). He tells us that he cannot find any more precise information
in his source, but it is evident that he only creates the problem by being
so apologetic about it, and that our own attitude to Criseyde is deeply
affected by this artificial uncertainty. It is not that she is either excused

or condemned by an ironic disclaimer, but that our own judgement is appealed to and we are challenged to assess her behaviour by our own moral standards, our experience of human psychology, and our historical imagination.

In Book II, the reader, or listener, has already been attacked more directly and even threatened with the narrator's curse if he dares to criticize Criseyde for falling in love when she does:

> Now myghte som envious jangle thus:
> 'This was a sodeyn love; how myght it be
> That she so lightly loved Troilus,
> Right for the firste syghte, ye, parde?'
> Now whoso seith so, mote he nevere ythe!   (II, 666–70)

Again, the point is not so much that the heroine is being exonerated of any blame in the story, but that we are made to react to her emotions as if she were a near acquaintance. We are, in fact, invited to create her character in our minds. This is not unlike Fielding's technique of characterization in *Tom Jones*; he, too, denounces the reader who draws the wrong conclusions from the story and forces him to reconsider his verdict: 'Of readers who from such conceits as these, condemn the wisdom or penetration of Mr Allworthy, I shall not scruple to say, that they make a very bad and ungrateful use of that knowledge which we have communicated to them' (III, 5).

The narrator does not, however, remain in the position of a detached observer throughout the whole poem. There are passages where, for all his literary professionalism, he seems completely carried away by his story. The most striking example is his seemingly uncritical identification with the lovers when they have finally come together (see III, 1317–23). Some critics have felt that Chaucer wants to alert the reader by confronting him with a naive narrator who is taken in by the short-lived bliss of these star-crossed and sinful lovers; but I think this is a rather too simple and moralistic reading of the whole episode.[7] There is no suggestion that the lovers are either guilty or deceived at this point. They experience the true happiness of mutual love, and the narrator's envy is not a sign of his simplicity, but a demonstration of the enchanting power of poetry. Even the poet who knows that he is only translating an ancient story, is so ravished by his subject that he appears to forget these are but fictional creatures. He has told us at the beginning of the poem that he has no personal experience of love; he can only repeat what he finds in books, but it turns out that the book is as good as the real thing when it comes to arousing sympathy and conveying to us a sense of perfect bliss.

It is just because this happiness is so complete and unclouded by any sense of guilt or foreboding that the reversal of fate is so shattering.

Criseyde's betrayal is so hard to comprehend that the narrator does not know how to give an adequate account of it. As we approach the tragic catastrophe, the narrator becomes an increasingly prominent figure who plays an important part in manipulating our response to the story. Boccaccio's narrator is far less noticeable at this point. He simply relates the sad events, adding his own commentary at the end. Chaucer's narrator cannot leave the story alone. He is too deeply affected by what he has to translate to keep his artistic distance. He cannot possibly alter the course of the action – at least this is the impression the poet wishes to produce – but he can make clear how deeply he himself is upset and bewildered by Criseyde's behaviour and he can make the reader aware of the moral and aesthetic problems involved.

Thus, the last part of the poem presents simultaneously the events of the classical story and the desperate efforts of the poet to come to terms with them and to prevent the reader from being unjust to the unfortunate actors or victims. Critics have responded very controversially to Chaucer's narrative method. The simpler reading insists on Chaucer's sympathy for Criseyde, his wish to excuse her and to shield her from the harsh condemnation of posterity. More sophisticated readers have felt that, on the contrary, Chaucer is being subversively ironical here by pretending to exonerate Criseyde while, in fact, damning her behind the mask of a naively credulous and easily deceived narrator.[8] Neither response seems to me quite adequate, because the main function of the narrator is not to force a particular interpretation on us, but to make us critically conscious of the process of composition and transmission. We are not allowed to get carried away by the poetical illusion or to identify with the characters, but we are to understand the poem as an example of 'auctoritee' in the Chaucerian sense, with its far from simple relationship to 'experience'. It is all very well to follow your author as faithfully as you can; but, as Chaucer has already shown in the *House of Fame*, books can be just as full of lies as other 'tydynges / Of Loves folk' (644–5), and this makes the responsibility of the author and translator all the more daunting.

The nearer we get to the poem's conclusion, the more prominent the narrator becomes, until, in the last fifteen stanzas, the narrator's problems seem to be as acute as those of the characters themselves. In a brilliant essay on 'The Ending of Chaucer's *Troilus*', E. T. Donaldson has described how the poet-narrator appears to try out various conventional endings, rejecting each in turn because none of them seems adequate to the magnitude of his task.[9] This is, perhaps, a little too dramatic, but the fact is that our reaction to the poem is bound to be profoundly affected by the way it is presented as a conscious labour, performed by one who is deeply worried about the transmission of the story and possible misconceptions about it. He offers a variety of comments, some of them much too trite for this sophisticated performance; he addresses the audience, the friends to whom the work is dedicated, and even the book itself, whose fate he knows to be beyond his control once it has passed into the hands of copyists and readers unfamiliar with its idiom.

No English writer before Chaucer has made the art of narrative part of his subject, and one of the most remarkable things about this narrator is that he seems to be at the same time an entertainer, telling the story to a circle of acquaintances, and a scholar, translating a written source and producing a decidedly literary work of art. The poem is addressed simultaneously to listeners and to readers, and this is why it combines conversational informality with consummate stylistic artifice.

When we turn to the *Canterbury Tales*, the problem of the narrator is quite different because there is such a variety of narrators, none of them quite like the other, yet all of them obviously concerned with the art of telling a story. From the start, when the Host promises a dinner to the most successful narrator, there is an element of competition, and indeed, every narrator gives the impression of trying to do his best. Critics will go on disagreeing about the extent to which each tale has to be read as the performance of a particular narrator; but there cannot be any doubt about the prominence of the narrative situation throughout the whole collection. Story-telling is the subject of this unfinished compilation as much as any of the themes that are taken up by pilgrims in their tales or any of the general 'ideas' that have been suggested as unifying concepts.

Apart from the pilgrim-narrators, briefly characterized in the *General Prologue* and the links between tales, but above all by their contributions to the story-telling contest, there is, of course, Chaucer himself as the narrator of the whole collection, and he appears in various guises: he is, first of all, one of the pilgrims who introduces us to the company, describes his fellow travellers, and proceeds to give an account of the story-telling. This aspect of the narrator has had more than its fair share of attention: the narrator of the *General Prologue* has been called a satirist and a naive innocent, but I do not think he is really meant to be a very distinct personality who might distract the reader from the real subject of this introduction. The narrator is not the recipient of important revelations, as is the 'I' in the dream visions, and his chief concern is to describe the pilgrims to us. There is, of course, a fair amount of subversive irony in these portraits of cheats, rogues, and hypocrites, but the remarkable thing is that the satire is so gentle and indirect and that the narrator most of the time lets the characters speak for themselves rather than unmasking them with the satirist's proper anger or scorn.[10]

The narrator presents himself as a sociable person who is able to find out the relevant facts about more than twenty fellow pilgrims in the course of an evening, but also as an author who promises to give us all the details in their appropriate order and uses traditional rhetorical formulas.

Once the story-telling contest has begun in earnest, there are only two other places where the narrator becomes a more prominent part of the fiction. He is addressed by the Host in a way that suggests again the bookish and unsociable 'Geffrey' of the *House of Fame* (VII, 695–706), and, unlike any of the other pilgrims, he is given the chance to tell two stories, one after the other – stories that represent the two extremes of oral and literary narrative, of popular entertainment and bookish instruction. Modest and shy as the author appears to the Host, his two contributions give an impression of complete self-assurance and of wide literary interests. The *Tale of Sir Thopas* can be appreciated only by a reader who is thoroughly familiar with the clichés of popular romance, and it is obvious that the Host fails to see the point of this brilliant parody. The text does not make quite clear how seriously the pilgrim-narrator himself takes this ridiculous story; but there is certainly no deliberate impression of an unreliable narrator nor any reason to doubt that this narrator, like Chaucer himself, knows what he is doing. More relevant than any sophisticated narrative strategy is the contrast between 'the beste rym I kan' (VII, 928) and the 'litel thyng in prose' (VII, 937) which turns out to be as long as the *Knight's Tale* and, apart from the *Parson's Tale*, the most undiluted specimen of 'sentence' in the whole of the *Canterbury Tales*. Whatever else the author's own two contributions to the story-telling contest achieve, they draw attention to the literary aspects of this mixed collection and to his stylistic versatility. Again, the narrator is not presented as an individualized character in his own right, but primarily as a writer and story-teller.

This also applies to his most personal and appealing appearance in the whole work, that is, the *Retractions* at the very end. Here the concept of the 'unreliable narrator' breaks down completely. No sensitive reader would seriously suggest that Chaucer is here talking tongue in cheek, and yet it would be much too simple to take the *Retractions* as a straight-forward confession or even a sign of Chaucer's final conversion.[11] It is, after all, not a public circular, sent round to all the owners and readers of Chaucer's Collected Works, but an integral part of the work, copied along with all the other stories in most of the important manuscripts. It is, therefore, part of the fiction, an utterance by the narrator, not by the man Geoffrey Chaucer. Within the fictional world of the *Canterbury Tales*, it is one and the same author-narrator who in the *General Prologue* addresses us,

> Now have I toold you soothly, in a clause,
> Th'estaat, th'array, the nombre, and eek the cause
> Why that assembled was this compaignye...   (715–17).

and who, at the end, takes his leave:

Now preye I to hem alle that herkne this litel tretys or rede, that if ther be any
thyng in it that liketh hem, that therof they thanken oure Lord Jhesu Crist...

(x, 1081).

Earlier, in the *Miller's Prologue*, he had already expressed his concern for
the proper reception of his work:

> And therfore every gentil wight I preye,
> For Goddes love, demeth nat that I seye
> Of yvel entente, but for I moot reherce
> Hir tales alle, be they bettre or werse...   (3171–4)

The *Retractions* is not, then, a wholesale repudiation of his poetry or an
attempt to cancel what he had written, but a final appeal to the reader to
make the proper use of the author's labours and to reflect on the powerful
vitality of literature for good or evil. The narrator is, until the last, deeply
concerned about the effect of his book on the reader. Indeed, the moral
responsibility of authors and the close interrelationship between teller,
tale, and audience are among the most prominent themes of the
Canterbury Tales and Chaucer's brilliant use of narrators is a significant
contribution to the debate on these themes implied in the story-telling
contest.

The poet as narrator is but one aspect of it; another is the provocative
diversity of story-tellers and of narrative styles. This is a large and complex
subject because the interpretation of each tale depends, of course, on the
importance we attach to the narrative situation and the narrator's
reliability, but I think very few of the *Canterbury Tales* can be read without
some awareness of their narrators, if we are not to ignore an important
part of their full meaning. It is evident that Chaucer was particularly
interested in the problem of 'unreliable' narrators and that he experimented ingeniously with various possibilities and with degrees of
subjectivity.

The most obvious instances are the unguarded confessions of villains,
like the Pardoner, or figures of fun, like the Wife of Bath, where it is
impossible to miss the satiric effect produced by this form of first-person
narrative. The reader knows all the time that the 'I' of these confessions
is not the author and that he or she is not to be trusted or at least not to
be taken seriously. We never forget the speakers, as we read these
remarkable revelations, and though we may disagree about the violence
or the consistency of the satire, we never fall into the error of taking these
narrators at their word without keeping our critical distance.

This also applies, though perhaps not to the same extent, to their actual
tales. It is an important function of these unashamed confessions to alert
the reader to the highly subjective character of most individual utterances

and to sharpen our ears for misplaced emphasis, exaggerated pathos, empty rhetoric, or faulty reasoning. Thus, many stylistic devices that would be perfectly normal and innocent in a different context, suddenly take on a more complex meaning because we see them in relation to other modes of expression and begin to question their sincerity and their innocence. It is, of course, very easy for the modern reader to be too sophisticated in this respect, and Saul Bellow's warning, 'Deep Readers of the World, Beware!' is as relevant for Chaucer-critics as it is for obsessive irony-hunters in other fields of literature.[12] Yet the stylistic contrasts and the degrees of refinement, intelligence, and tolerance within the *Canterbury Tales* are so obvious that it is hard to believe they were not meant to reflect degrees of insight and credibility and to keep us constantly aware of the fact that all the narrators, like the author, represent but single and necessarily limited points of view. As the Nun's Priest reminds us, anticipating adverse criticism of his fable: 'Thise been the cokkes wordes, and nat myne' (*Nun's Priest's Tale*, 3265). It is a caveat that describes a fundamental principle of Chaucer's narrative technique in the *Canterbury Tales*, from the drunken Miller for whom the narrator feels obliged to apologize, to the learned Clerk who, like Chaucer himself in *Troilus and Criseyde*, produces a 'translation' of a story he finds disturbing and in need of some personal comment.[13]

To illustrate this in detail would be equivalent to a full-scale interpretation of the *Canterbury Tales*. Some of them have often been taken at their face value and without regard to their context; it is also very likely that Chaucer made use of some older stories when he began to gather the items for his collection. Nor does it seem to me very profitable to look for precise psychological correspondences between the portraits in the *General Prologue* and the style of the respective tales: as David Benson's essay in this collection suggests, it is more a question of social rank, general type, and appropriate genre. Within these wide and flexible categories, however, there are enough significant contrasts and idiosyncrasies to give the impression of story-telling as a very subjective and unpredictable activity and to create a strong sense of dialogue between narrators and listeners or readers.

Many of the links between the tales are tantalizingly brief, and the textual situation often does not even allow us to say confidently which tales are meant to be linked or who the speakers are;[14] but by and large, all the surviving fragments of the frame add further substance to the fiction of a succession of narrative situations and a provocative diversity of stylistic attitudes. It is in this sense that the question of the fictitious narrator is so important for our appreciation of Chaucer's narrative art. This does not mean that the poet himself is only a completely detached observer without any convictions of his own; it would be anachronistic and ahistorical to suggest anything of the sort. What it does mean is that Chaucer is far more interested in the complex relationships between story-material, author, reader, and personal style than he is in straightforward instruction and unambiguous authorial statement. Whether there are any of the *Canterbury Tales* he would have 'released' separately, in his own name as it were, is a rather hypothetical but not quite irrelevant question. None of the over twenty narrators is to be identified with Chaucer himself as we believe we know him, though some are more like him than others, such as the Clerk, the Knight, the Man of Law, and, perhaps, the Franklin, and nearly all of them share characteristic elements of style, hard to define but unmistakably present.[15] This makes it very difficult to decide on the precise degree of subjectivity in any particular case and is one of the chief reasons for such contradictory interpretations of many tales. If we think of the Prioress as an exemplary representative of her estate and a thoroughly reliable narrator, we shall probably read the *Prioress's Tale* as an unexceptional miracle, but if we consider her portrait to be a satirical attack on a rather too worldly and hypocritical woman we are likely to mistrust her narrative too and begin to wonder whether it is meant as a parody of childish legends or something even more sinister.[16] The alternatives are usually much more subtle than this, and Chaucer's narrative technique is playfully experimental rather than neatly consistent, alerting the reader to the possibility of subversive irony and teasing him into imaginative mental cooperation. It is not surprising that our reaction to many of the tales is no more unanimous than that of the Canterbury pilgrims themselves, nor is complete critical agreement desirable in reading texts that so clearly encourage discussion and reflection rather than certainty and mere receptiveness.

Perhaps the problem is most acute in the case of the Parson and his tale, though most critics and readers are not particularly interested in this last item of the collection. Since the *Parson's Tale* is not really a tale at all, but rather a prose tract, it hardly seems to make sense to speak of a narrator. From what we are told about the Parson, he is an 'estate ideal' and we expect a truly edifying tale from him. In a way, his sermon on penitence is a most fitting summary and conclusion to all that has gone before, but it does not devalue it, just as the Parson's portrait in the *General Prologue* fails 'to upset the confident tone in which the skills of the *Prologue's* rogues are presented'.[17] The unsophisticated moral seriousness of the speaker and his undiluted homily are only another possibility of story-telling, no less subjective and relative than the rest, though obviously more worthy of imitation.[18] Like the *Retractions*, the *Parson's Tale* is not the definite and authoritative answer to everything else in the book, but an offer we may accept or reject. As Chaucer says of the *Miller's Tale*, at the opening of the work:

...whoso list it nat yheere,
Turne over the leef and chese another tale;
...
Blameth nat me if that ye chese amys.   (I, 3176–7, 3181)

In this sense, the Parson is a narrator like the rest of his fellow pilgrims:
he refuses to tell 'fables and swich wrecchednesse' (x, 34) and contributes
instead 'a myrie tale in prose' (x, 46).

Even to the last, Chaucer does not turn his back on this literary principle
of individual viewpoints and personal responsibility. It is the final
demonstration of the poet-narrator assuming a variety of roles in his
constant search for the most effective way of appealing to his audience
by means of 'Tales of best sentence and moost solaas' (I, 798).

Notes

1 See Wayne C. Booth, *The Rhetoric of Fiction* (Chicago, 1961), especially ch. 8,
  'Telling as Showing: Dramatized Narrators, Reliable and Unreliable', pp.
  211–40. Booth is generally concerned with the novel, not with medieval
  literature. He has a brief passage on Chaucer's *Troilus and Criseyde*, as an
  instance of 'reliable commentary' (p. 170).

2 See J. A. Burrow, 'Autobiographical Poetry in the Middle Ages: the Case of
  Thomas Hoccleve', *Proceedings of the British Academy*, 68 (1982), 389–412.

3 For further references see my book *Geoffrey Chaucer: An Introduction to His
  Narrative Poetry* (Cambridge, 1986), ch. 3.

4 On the poetological aspects of the collection see Lisa J. Kiser, *Telling Classical
  Tales: Chaucer and the Legend of Good Women* (Ithaca, NY, 1983).

5 See my 'The Audience of Chaucer's *Troilus and Criseyde*' in *Chaucer and Middle
  English Studies In Honour of Rossell Hope Robbins*, ed. Beryl Rowland (London,
  1974), pp. 173–89; repr. in *Chaucer's Troilus: Essays in Criticism*, ed. Stephen
  A. Barney (Hamden, Conn., 1980), pp. 211–29.

6 Comparison is made easy by the excellent edition of *Troilus and Criseyde. A New
  Edition of 'The Book of Troilus'*, ed. B. A. Windeatt (London/New York, 1984).'

7 For further references see my article, 'The Audience of Chaucer's *Troilus and
  Criseyde'*.

8 See, for instance, E. Talbot Donaldson, 'Criseyde and her Narrator', in
  Speaking of Chaucer (London, 1970), pp. 65–83.

9 In *Early English and Norse Studies Presented to Hugh Smith in Honour of his
  Sixtieth Birthday*, eds. Arthur Brown and Peter Foote (London, 1963), pp.
  26–45, repr. in *Speaking of Chaucer*, pp. 84–101.

10 See Jill Mann, *Chaucer and Medieval Estates Satire. The Literature of Social Classes
   and the General Prologue to the Canterbury Tales* (Cambridge, 1973), especially
   pp. 187–202, and notes, for further references.

11 See Olive Sayce, 'Chaucer's "Retractions": The Conclusion of the "Canterbury
   Tales" and its Place in Literary Tradition', *Medium Aevum*, 40 (1971), 230–48.

12 See Booth, *The Rhetoric of Fiction*, pp. 364–74, for some provocative comment.

13 See Robin Kirkpatrick, 'The Griselda Story in Boccaccio, Petrarch and
   Chaucer', in *Chaucer and the Italian Trecento*, ed. Piero Boitani (Cambridge,
   1983), pp. 231–48.

14 See the Textual Notes in Robinson's edition or the different arrangement of tales and links in the Hengwrt Manuscript as edited by N. F. Blake, *The Canterbury Tales by Geoffrey Chaucer. Edited from the Hengwrt Manuscript* (London, 1980).

15 See Charles Muscatine, '*The Canterbury Tales*: Style of the Man and Style of the Work', in *Chaucer and Chaucerians: Critical Studies in Middle English Literature*, ed. D. S. Brewer (London, 1966), pp. 88–113; Nevill Coghill's essay 'Chaucer's Narrative Art in *The Canterbury Tales*', in the same collection, pp. 114–39, is also relevant here.

16 See Paul G. Ruggiers, *The Art of the Canterbury Tales* (Madison, Wis., 1965), pp. 175–83, for a 'straight' reading, though Ruggiers allows for 'an irresoluble residue of ambiguity' (p. 183). A rather more negative interpretation is offered by Donald R. Howard, *The Idea of the Canterbury Tales* (Berkeley, Ca., 1976), pp. 274–9.

17 See Mann, *Chaucer and Medieval Estates Satire*, p. 67.

18 For some interesting comment on the *Parson's Tale* see Traugott Lawler, *The One and the Many in the Canterbury Tales* (Hamden, Conn., 1980), pp. 147–72.

14   Chaucer's poetic style

The complexity of Chaucer's poetry

THE style is the man: on the surface straightforward, often apparently simple, with varied fresh feeling, pathetic or comic, anxious to please sometimes almost to the point of chattiness; and beneath this transparent yet gleaming surface, the more you look the more there is of ambiguity, paradox, further implication, unexpected depths; the most interesting style, the most interesting poet, in English.

Orality and literacy

Much of Chaucer's fascination arises from the way he is poised between oral and literate cultures, and actively exploits his participation in both. He invites us first into the warm ancient oral world of the listening group of friends, to which we are in imagination joined. Second, he asks us to follow him into the world of books. A great deal of what he wants to say is derived from solitary reading, from that world of literacy where he was in his day an adventurous pioneer. We may sum up Chaucer's own attitudes, and his stylistic effort, as the combination of these two worlds, the absorbing of literacy into orality,[1] blending the new world of literate thought into the old but always current world of personal direct speech and relationship.

Literacy allows Chaucer to pack his texts with the products of his reading. It would seem that Chaucer's own chief passion in life was not love but reading. The results are everywhere apparent in the variety and interest of his subject-matter. The *Book of the Duchess* is in style primarily oral, but the poet almost immediately starts to tell us about his reading. It is the first poem in English ever to do so. The subject-matter is varied, and much of the poem is freely translated from the written poetry of Machaut. The evidence of literacy is everywhere in Chaucer. He reproaches himself, through the Eagle in the *House of Fame*, for too much reading. In *Troilus* he addresses the very 'audience' as 'thow redere' (v, 270). The 'art of speech' referred to in the *Squire's Tale* (104) is partly the art of converting literacy into orality. At the end of the *Miller's Prologue* Chaucer invites the reader who disapproves of any story to

> Turne over the leef and chese another tale.   (3177)

He is thinking only of the reader with his book.

Such instances, however, must be set against the overwhelmingly oral character of Chaucer's style. Literacy supplies much of his subject-matter, and some of his form (for example, Chaucer's development of a narrator-figure – discussed in this collection by Dieter Mehl – can be seen as a result of the detachment of the poet from his audience which is effected by literacy). But the detailed characteristics of Chaucer's style re-create for us the world of the oral poet, in close and intimate contact with his audience and its values. It is on the elements of this oral style that the present essay concentrates.

The speaking voice

In one of Chaucer's earliest poems, the *Book of the Duchess* (1368) he creates in the very first lines the oral world of the poet speaking directly to the audience.

> I have gret wonder, be this lyght,
> How that I lyve, for day ne nyght
> I may nat slepe wel nygh noght;
> I have so many an ydel thoght,
> Purely for defaute of slep,
> That, by my trouthe, I take no kep
> Of nothing, how hyt cometh or gooth,
> Ne me nys nothyng leef ne looth.   (1–8)

We now know that in fact the basis of this introduction is a written poem by Froissart, and most of the rest of the poem is similarly based on other written sources. Chaucer however turns his written source into orality by making the passage into a direct address to an audience present before him, filling out the style with the typical set phrases of colloquial speech inherited from the English rhyming romances.[2] He adds a specific address to the audience, inviting their cooperation, assuming their sympathy and knowledge ('And wel ye woot...'). This is very different both from his written source and from the compression and tortuous richness of a modern poem which relies on the stability of print, in a situation where poet and reader exist each in solitude, unknown to each other.

Chaucer also begins *Troilus and Criseyde* by presenting himself as the poet addressing an audience, and he continues to use phrases which 'create' an audience throughout the poem, from 'ye loveres' (I, 22) onwards. The famous *Troilus* frontispiece was painted after Chaucer's death but it clearly illustrates the sense Chaucer wants to give of a man speaking to men and women;[3] of a poet addressing a courtly, distinguished audience, a warm social group which in imagination we too must join if we are to understand the poem in anything like its original conception.

In the *Canterbury Tales* the whole scheme is based on the concept of oral story-telling within a group listening to each other. It is conventional because such a situation could only be fictional, and we are more than ever aware of the underlying literacy, even to the extent of being invited to 'turn over the leaf' if we disapprove of a particular story. But by a deep paradox that very invitation is delivered in the style of the poet's speaking voice addressed to us. Though the substance is literate the manner is still oral.

Formulas and set phrases

Since spoken words though powerful are evanescent, they need if possible to be fixed. Thus oral poetry such as Homer's *Iliad* has many fixed formulaic phrases. Their familiarity establishes a link between poet and audience, makes attention easier, characters and actions clearer and more memorable. An obvious example of the same characteristics in Chaucer's style is the passage already quoted from the *Book of the Duchess*, stuffed with versions of familiar phrases (here underlined) from the fourteenth-century English rhyming romances:

> I have gret wonder, *be· this lyght*,
> How that I lyve, *for day ne nyght*
> I may nat slepe *wel nygh noght*...

Chaucer moves away from this blatantly easy and almost chatty style as the poem develops, but the ease, familiarity, transparency, and self-projection are in themselves poetic effects conveying warmth, sympathy, anxiety.

The use of familiar phraseology is more common in the style at the beginning of poems, to introduce the poet, establish a bond with the audience, express an attitude to the forthcoming story, and to start it off. Hence the beginning of the *Parliament of Fowls*, where in the first line an ancient proverb is used as a familiar formula – 'The lyf so short, the craft so long to lerne' – and the remainder of the stanza follows in similar vein. The last line of the stanza illustrates the nature of the style very well, being usually given as 'Nat wot I wel wher that I *flete or synke*' (7) – we can see from the fact that some scribes changed this to *wake or wynke* that they recognized it as a formula. It is a good test of sensitivity to Chaucer's style to see why the standard reading is better, but both phrases are of the same fixed kind. Chaucer makes progressively less use of this traditional formulaic style as he develops his art, but the underlying habit of mind conditions much of his writing, so that he does not fear to use the same phrase several times. Some words and phrases are frequently used: for example, 'aventure' appears a number of times in the phrase 'aventure or cas', 'aventure or grace', while 'good aventure' comes quite often. The phrase 'as in this cas' is frequent. The word 'lady' is often followed by 'bright' or 'dere' or 'swete'. Just as he reiterates certain adjectives with certain nouns so he refers more than once, in closely similar phraseology, to the same idea. The outstanding example of Chaucer's willingness to use the same whole line several times is:

> For pitee renneth soone in gentil herte.   (*Knight's Tale*, 1761)

This was originally a set phrase in Italian; Chaucer uses it again, slightly modified, in the *Merchant's Tale* (1986), the *Squire's Tale* (479), and the *Legend of Good Women* (F 503, G 491). It is a beautiful line and a beautiful sentiment, most characteristic of Chaucer. Normally it reinforces our sense of humane values, although it is used in the *Merchant's Tale* in an ironic way which is not typical of oral poetry.

A diction which uses familiar phrases to such an extent is traditionalist, aiming at familiar effects, ready communication, sympathetic attention. It is transparent, does not call attention to itself, is modest, collectivist, not individualized. It rests ultimately on a static concept of the true nature of the world, or of the world as it ought to be, as an harmonious whole, governed by the love of God, 'with feith, which that is stable', as Troilus sings, in words given him by the poet, following Boethius (*Troilus* III, 1751). That the fallen world is clearly not so stabilized and harmonious in every respect is part of its pain, and one of the functions of art and philosophy is to re-establish stability. Traditional style, relying on the collective wisdom of society in its language, attempts to assert the ideal state by its very nature. Disharmony then becomes absorbed into the larger harmony of language and the universe.

Sententiousness

This sense of traditional social wisdom to be articulated by the poet using formulas and set phrases ('What oft was thought' and oft has been expressed) results in a particular tone and style which is nowadays often misunderstood. Some examples have already been given. We may include with them proverbs and what were called in Latin *sententiae*, 'sentences'; remarks long accepted in society for their general truth and applicability. They are still frequently used in ordinary speech, whether or not recognized as proverbial, and most people will know the satisfaction of being able to sum up a particular fraught situation with an apt traditional phrase. This is part of the satisfaction which is poetic and imaginative, as well as complacent and malicious, of being able to say 'I told you so'. 'Now the fat's in the fire!' one might exclaim, as a foolish friend makes the expected foolish inflammatory or revealing remark. Pandarus in *Troilus* is particularly prone to this kind of colloquial sententiousness. He promises Troilus that he will fix everything that night

> Or casten al the gruwel in the fire.   (III, 711)

Not only Pandarus but Chaucer himself enjoys using the sententious style. Proverbial expressions are vivid, compact, salty, sometimes richly though briefly metaphorical. They tend to be clear in meaning. They can be ironical, but are not normally so, and if irony is used it depends on being clearly signalled and exceptional.

The sententious style lends itself to authorial comment of the kind familiar to oral narrative and song. The story-teller or singer comments on his story to the listening audience and his comments may be serious or comic according to the effect desired. To put it in Chaucer's own words, he uses proverbs

> To enforce with th'effect of my mateere.   (*Melibee*, 958)

Chaucer's style is continuously though variably 'sententious' throughout all his work, as indeed is that of our other great oral poet, Shakespeare. No other great English poets are so soaked in the sententious, proverbial style which is common to the whole English (as to any other) people, high or low, whatever their class. There is no space for extensive illustration from Chaucer's work, because it affects almost every passage, but as a single example we may take the moment when the poet contemplates the sorrowful outcome of Troilus' love. He comments:

> And Troilus moot wepe in cares colde.
> Swich is this world, whoso it kan byholde:
> In ech estat is litel hertes reste.
> God leve us for to take it for the beste!   (V, 1747–50)

'Cold cares' is an ancient English concept and expression for sorrow. We all know it, we are all invited to share it. The alliteration hammers home the familiarity. Its generality gives it the kind of power in this particular instance that an entirely novel expression could never deploy. The story has shown us the reason for Troilus' grief, of an entirely familiar kind but none the less painful for that. So the poet-storyteller quite naturally and movingly goes on to draw the obvious conclusion which brings us all together. The passage just quoted is Chaucer's addition to his source. The diction is simple, direct, transparent, with not a word wasted. The metaphors of sight and rest are proverbial. There is no irony here, no foolish Narrator declaiming his pompous commonplaces while the poet sniggers in the background at ordinary human misery. The poet speaks here as he does some eighty lines later, almost at the very end of the poem, in a rhetorical set-piece which reproduces the rhythmical repetition of commonplace so characteristic of oral origins:

> Swich fyn, hath, lo, this Troilus for love!
> Swich fyn hath al his grete worthynesse!
> Swich fyn hath his estat real above,
> Swich fyn his lust, swich fyn hath his noblesse!
> Swich fyn hath false worldes brotelnesse!   (v, 1828–32)

It would be pointless to talk of 'sincerity' here, since that would introduce again a concept inappropriate to the traditional style, but 'genuineness' or 'authenticity' of feeling and comment are the qualities of such poetry.

Repetition with variation: redundancy and eloquence

The passage just quoted illustrates the use of repetition with variation to create heightened feeling. The obvious examples in other English literature are those orally based supreme masterpieces, the Authorised Version of the Bible, especially the Psalms (whose essential poetic structure is based on repetition), and Shakespeare. Hamlet's speech 'To be or not to be' is a set of variations which are repetitions of the same theme. Repetition is too common in emphatic colloquial speech amongst us all to need illustration. Its power to move and inspire even in the mid-twentieth century was extraordinarily vividly illustrated in Churchill's speech in 1940 after the disaster of Dunkirk, when the country was in daily expectation of invasion. 'We shall fight on the beaches, we shall fight on the landing grounds, we shall fight in the fields and in the streets...' No one who was old enough in England to hear those words repeated at that time can forget them. That they were given in *speech*, to listeners in a society united in fear and determination, is of the essence of their style. The social context of orality allows repetition to develop its poetic power to move the heart.

Chaucer shows how to use such high style at appropriate moments, as already noted. At a less intense but still emotional level, we notice time and again the use of repetition with variation as in

> Ther nas no good day, ne no saluying   (*Knight's Tale*, 1649)

or more extensively, aiming at a different, gentler effect:

> And this was on the sixte morwe of May,
> Which May hadde peynted with his softe shoures
> This gardyn ful of leves and of floures;
> And crafte of mannes hand so curiously
> Arrayed had this gardyn, trewely,

That nevere was ther gardyn of swich prys,
But if it were the verray paradys.
The odour of floures...   (*Franklin's Tale*, 906–13)

To complain that such a style is diffuse would be the same as complaining that there are too many *reprises* in a Mozart aria.

This kind of repetitive style, aiming at eloquence and copiousness, may be more technically described as a 'redundant' style. A 'redundant' style uses many words to convey information because the words are doing other things as well, such as elaborating details, creating feelings, evoking attitudes. Like the sententious style, the redundant style is easily misunderstood if its oral origins are forgotten and we attend only to the simple immediate piece of information. Redundancy, having established the central important point, emphasizes it by repetition and then allows the audience to meditate upon its implications.

A beautiful example of the redundant, eloquent, copious style of variation with repetition is offered by Chaucer's best known lines, the opening of the *Canterbury Tales*, which need not be quoted here. The basic message is simple: in spring people get restless. The message is conveyed in a variety of different ways. It is a truth we easily agree to from experience, and we enjoy the music of the elaboration, in itself varied and fresh, but conveyed in traditional details. The winding repetitions gather the whole cosmos together with poet, audience and pilgrims in the vitalizing, humanizing warmth of the poet's words. No poetry without the social oral base could create such an effect, which draws much of its richness from Chaucer's ability to turn literate learned matter into an oral style.

Chaucer's redundancy is naturally best seen, or rather, most naturally used for, the lyric expressiveness of many of Troilus' speeches, in which he returns time and again, like the opera singer, with variations, to the same point. Such speeches have to be read with the ear, without impatience to get on with the action. The same style occurs in some but not all of the *Canterbury Tales*. Its leisurely progress is heard in the *Knight's Tale* where the poet asks

Why sholde I noght as wel eek telle yow al
The portreiture that was upon the wal
Withinne the temple of myghty Mars the rede?   (1967–9)

When listening, an audience needs such guide-lines to what is going on, preliminary notice of the next subject, and appreciates the sense of leisurely collaboration.

Addition and association (metonymy)

Common speech, and oral verse and prose, tend to proceed, as the above example suggests, by the *addition* of material or events, rather than by analysis. There are very lively character-sketches in the *General Prologue* but they are not analytical. One detail is added to another. Much the same is true of the sequence of events in traditional stories. In general the oral poet is not much interested in causation, because he uses pre-existent underlying patterns and structures. Analysis of character or of how one event can cause another is a concern which is one of the chief assumptions governing the understanding of the novel, whereas causation and analysis have little place when the whole shape of the story and the general nature of the characters are already known to poet and audience.

The result of an additive, non-analytical habit of mind in traditional style is lack of grammatical subordination, preference for loosely strung sentence structure, conventional epithets, lists. The first chapter of Genesis, in the closely literal translation of the Authorised Version, with its sequence of 'ands', is a classic case of additive, non-analytical style. There are few subordinate clauses, and every detail seems to be presented with the same prominence. There is as it were no perspective. All is evenly demonstrated. The series proceeds by aggregation. It is a sort of list. In Genesis I the effect is one of noble stately irresistible regular steps. The modern translators of the New English Bible show how uncomfortable this is to the modern mind by minimizing the solemn gravity and inserting pseudo-subordinative words such as 'then', with other trivializing devices. Chaucer is not so modern-minded, and his style is nearer the effect of the Authorised Version when he wishes, for example, to describe in solemn moving terms the meeting of Criseyde, accompanied by Troilus, with Diomede. The riding out and the meeting are described with powerful simplicity which adds details merely with a sequence of 'ands':

> And right with that was Antenor ycome
> Out of the Grekis oost, and every wight
> Was of it glad, and seyde he was welcome.
> And Troilus, al nere his herte light,
> He peyned hym with al his fulle myght
> Him to withholde of wepyng atte leeste
> And Antenor he kiste, and made feste.
>
> And therwithal he moste his leve take,
> And caste his eye upon hire pitously,
> And neer he rood, his cause for to make,
> To take hire by the honde al sobrely.
> And Lord! so she gan wepen tendrely!
> And he ful softe and sleighly gan hire seye,
> 'Now holde youre day, and do me nat to deye'.   (v, 71–84)

The word 'and' occurs thirteen times in these fourteen lines. There are three short subordinate clauses. The power of this piece lies in the simplicity of the syntax, the concentration on essentials, the juxtaposition of crucial contradictory elements with so little subordination.

Such a style is not necessarily solemn. The immediate effect depends on the subject-matter. There is a passage describing the fight in the bedroom in the *Reeve's Tale* which is hilarious farce (4292–307).[4] The power still derives from the same sources, a high proportion of nouns and verbs, few, familiar and simple adjectives, a few guiding adverbs. The vocabulary is familiar. In the sixteen lines of the passage from the *Reeve's Tale*, nine begin with 'and' and two more with the functionally similar 'but', and subordinate clauses occupy only one and a half lines.

The style is additive but it is not shapeless. The structures are not created by analysis or causation but by underlying pattern and association. Pattern is created by the event, which in the *Troilus* passage depends on the contrasts between Troilus and Diomede, between joy and sorrow in various forms. Association, more technically called metonymy, is created by, or rather here is much the same thing as, juxtaposition.[5]

This may need a word of explanation. All composition depends on connection. Connection can be created by likeness (metaphor) or by metonymy (association either by act or habitual recurrence). Both are fundamental to speech, but metonymy has only recently been recognized. Metonymy is fundamental to oral poetry, which depends on the associations formed by habit (memory and experience) or created by narrative events. Although oral poetry uses metaphor, mainly in brief and proverbial form, it relies more on metonymy, that is, on the associations of words. By metonymy words can be relied on to evoke particular associated accepted ideas and feelings. These naturally depend on social, moral, and intellectual structures, some of which we have lost. We may therefore easily overlook the richness of oral poetry because we do not know, or we neglect, the social, moral, and intellectual context, which is the associative structure. Fortunately for our understanding of Chaucer the stories themselves often supply much of the context we need. At other times the subject-matter is so manipulated that the style tells us enough, as we see in the portraits of the *General Prologue*, which are purely additive and metonymic, or the great descriptions, the 'portreyture', of the *Knight's Tale*, or the lists in the *Parliament of Fowls* and particularly in the *House of Fame*.

Metonymy is only a part of style and may be seen working in conjunction with other aspects. Although metonymy depends on association and addition, not likeness, to make connections, it may join with likeness and re-inforce that independent, self-contained, aspect of language which results in the various kinds of wordplay which characterize oral poetry. Of these, puns are a striking example, where likeness of sound associates two totally disparate meanings, often but not always with a comic effect. As literacy progressed and became dominant from the seventeenth century onwards puns became despised and other wordplay disliked.[6] They could not be ignored in Shakespeare, where they were regarded as a fault, but were overlooked in Chaucer until recently.

Hyperbole

Another oral characteristic is hyperbole – that is, exaggeration in description, effects, numbers. In traditional literature, for example in the Bible, numbers are usually wildly and hyperbolically impossible, as when after David has slain Goliath (and only Goliath) the women sing

> Saul hath slain his thousands
> And David his ten thousands.   (1 Samuel 18. 7)

Traditional epic and romance also use such imaginative or emotive exaggerated number. Thus in the *Knight's Tale* when Palamon and Arcite are fighting in the grove like cruel tiger and wild boar, we are told

> Up to the ancle foghte they in hir blood.   (1660)

In a literalistic sense this would be an absurd exaggeration. But no clear precise visual image is attempted. There is no way in which this line can be rationalized in accordance with a label theory of language. It is passionate, dramatic. It tells the audience of desperate wounds, fanatical courage, extreme danger, and makes no attempt in any precise way to measure the depth of the lake of blood in which the knights paddled. Poetic hyperbole sweeps us away on the tide of feeling.

There is more of this hyperbolical vein in Chaucer's style than is usually consciously recognized. For example we tend to take it for granted, accepting the implicit hyperbole, that all the characters in the *General Prologue* are the best of their kind. Another kind of example is the extremity of feeling, the hyperbole of emotion, portrayed in *Troilus*. B. A. Windeatt has shown how constantly Chaucer adds emphasis and exaggeratedly emotional behaviour and language to the Italian original which he is closely following.[7] In this case the Englishman is more emotional than the Italian. That may well be because Chaucer is much closer to the oral style than is Boccaccio, who was the product of a culture much more advanced in literacy than Chaucer's England.

Hyperbole is a fundamental human characteristic which gives ordinary speech much of its emotional and imaginative impact. In animated informal conversation people still say 'There were *thousands* of them', meaning an unexpectedly large number, say several dozens. One may say, and be perfectly well understood, 'I'm frozen', meaning uncomfortably cold, or 'My feet are killing me', meaning they hurt. A literalistic label theory of language and style can make nothing of the poetry of such everyday speech. These vivid compact familiar phrases are rich in hyperbole. They are dramatic, emotive, relating speaker to audience, clear in meaning because of the context, not to be taken literalistically. This is not to say that Chaucer's poetry is built up of the clichés of ordinary life, but that this is the nature of this style, to which he brings discipline, point, heightening.

The hyperbolical style necessarily involves the description of hyperbolical feelings and actions – the extremity of love in romances, the extreme patience of Griselda and cruelty of her husband, and so forth. To say that the action is 'hyperbolical' does not mean that we should not give it our full sympathy. Quite the reverse; we are moved the more, as we are by the depth of feeling in someone speaking with passionate exaggeration of love or fear or terror or dismay. We take the message of the medium without requiring an everyday plausibility of event or character, because of the independence of the spoken word, the 'gap' between word and referent, signifier and signified, which the oral style allows – a gap filled with feelings, attitudes, intentions. Cultural developments since the fourteenth century and the prevalence first of writing and then of print have narrowed that gap for us and emphasized the literalistic descriptive element in language. Some 'literalism', some real relation between 'word' and 'thing' there must always be, even in purely oral forms, or we are in the realm of lies or self-indulgent fantasy or ignorance. Literacy emphasizes the literalistically precise use of descriptive language, and Chaucer became progressively more conscious of this. The derisive envoy to the *Clerk's Tale* shows how uncomfortable he could be with hyperbolical action, while at the same time relishing it. When he creates the Pardoner's ranting style of preaching at the beginning of his tale Chaucer shows his distrust of inflammatory exaggerated speech. But he starts from orality, even if he finishes by distrusting it.

Kinetic imagery

The prevailing generality of an oral style causes imagery to be rich, but by literalist standards imprecise. Mixed metaphors are common and may, like Shakespeare's, seem ridiculous if they are expected to create a naturalistic comparison. An outstanding example is

> This Troilus, with herte and erys spradde,
> Herde al this thyng devysen to and fro. (*Troilus*, IV, 1422–3)

The intensity of Troilus' desire to hear is expressed by the image of spread-out heart and ears which immediately captures the sense of emotional and physical strain, and which does not seem, from the context, intended to be in any way comic. It is kinetic in the sense that it represents action rather than static comparison, and if it is paused on for naturalistic visualization it may seem grotesque.

Imagery of the heart is traditionally of such a kind. St Paul speaks of 'the eyes of the heart' (Ephesians 1. 18). Biblical imagery in general is markedly kinetic; metaphors are mixed and non-mimetic. Chaucer uses much imagery of the heart in *Troilus*, and almost all of it is traditional mixed metaphor and metonymy: the heart is on fire, is the eye of the breast, frequently dear, ready to burst, the source of thought, is playing, felt to weep, soft enough for thoughts to sink into, is warm or cold, gay, torn out, exchanged with another, capable of bleeding, is dancing, laughing, could be of stone, personifies a dear or sweet person, is able to be steered, shut in by sorrow, seeming to die, capable of being opened, weeps bloody tears, can be deeply engraved, floats in joy, contains the beloved, is gnawed by woe, can speak to oneself, can be stern and cruel, contain a weeping spirit, can be burnt to a powder, is the memory, has a visage to be turned up to God, and so forth. Here is the poetry of the common mind in English speech, nourished by centuries of thought and feeling, and though based on an entirely mistaken physiology is still easily recognizable today.

The common speech is of the same kind as the poetry, though poetry intensifies it, like a waterfall gathering together meandering streams into a force whose effect is in appearance strikingly simple, though it is the product of complex sources and is itself when closely examined a highly complex structure. Such poetry looks 'easy', and so in a sense it is, for enjoyment and understanding; but what other poet, apart from Shakespeare, has been able to draw such wealth from the stream of common language? What is true of this one image of the heart is also true, if less extensive, for other traditional words and phrases, often repeated yet never dull.

Timeless and essentialist

The traditional style, general, based on long-felt beliefs and relying on accepted knowledge, with its fixed recurrent epithets, reflects a habit of thought which is less conscious of the passing of time. Change cannot be denied in human experience but for the oral mentality it produces only addition or loss, not intrinsic alteration. Whatever is not present, or in present memory, is lost. No pages can be turned back to check consistency or revive what has died. There is therefore little representation of linear time. Certainly the days pass and the year progresses, but the seasons recur in an apparently continuous cycle. Though there is variation there is essential repetition. Why should epithets change? Even human life can be

seen as cyclical, and in an oral world the belief that the true world is beyond
present appearances, and outside time, is strong. The whole of a traditional
story from beginning to end is known to the community before it is started,
and in *Troilus* Chaucer even makes sure of that, by summarizing for us
the shape and outcome of his narrative in the very first line of the poem.
Characters do not age, though they may love for twenty years; nor do
personalities develop.

In style, timelessness is reflected by redundancy, by the enunciation of
traditional wisdom – 'Such is this world', and by recurring epithets. Ladies
are always 'fresh', 'dear', 'sweet'; grass is green; flowers are of simple
colours, red, white, yellow, and blue. The style reflects the 'real' world of
essence or being, not the changing world of becoming, by employing as
the strongest epithets those that re-inforce what they qualify, as 'manly'
for a man, 'womanly' for a woman. Of the Yeoman in the *General Prologue* the poet says 'Wel koude he dresse his takel *yemanly*' (106). Of the
splendid magic horse in the *Squire's Tale* it is highest praise that it should
be 'Therwith so *horsly*' (194). One development of such an attitude and
style is seen in the praise of Troilus:

So lik a man of armes and a knyght	(II, 631)
God woot wher he was lik a manly knyght	(II, 1263)
This is to seyn, in armes as a knyght	(III, 438)
Welcome, my knyght, my pees, my suffisaunce	(III, 1309)

(which is a brilliant example also of metonymy):

Forthi tak herte, and thynk right as a knyght	(IV, 617)

– and so forth. In such a thought-world, and such a style, simply to call
the knight Troilus a knight is high and sufficient praise, evoking a static
poetic stereotype. (This praise is ironically mimicked in the description of
Diomede swearing to Criseyde 'treweliche...as a knyght': v, 113.) When
adjectives are used to qualify 'knight', they are normally such as
'worthy', 'lusty', 'true', 'noble'. There is indeed a 'false knight' in the
Man of Law's Tale (619, 687) but the discordant adjective is rare and draws
its power from its rarity, which enables it to constitute a self-contradictory
phrase, an oxymoron. In such phrases Chaucer's own literate, individualistic, independent character emerges like a rock out of the sea of orality.
This can lead to irony, as when he uses stock phrases which the immediate
context shows are denied by the truth, as 'worthy limitours', 'holy friars',
which could not be so effective if they did not by implication both endorse
and reverse normal judgement. These ironies are exceptions. The bases of
oral mentality and its poetic style are hyperbolic praise or derision based

on the acceptance of social and moral norms. The Summoner is condemned simply by being called a summoner in a beautifully metonymic line:

> A theef, and eek a somnour, and a baude.   (*Friar's Tale*, 1354)

Literacy

Having described so many characteristics of Chaucer's poetry which take their origins from orality, we may in conclusion briefly return to those features more closely linked with literacy, to avoid giving the impression that Chaucer's style is *only* composed of the simple, the easy and the everyday. The speech of the Eagle in the *House of Fame* is a good example of the fusion of orality with more learned elements.

> 'Telle me this now feythfully,
> Have y not preved thus symply.
> Withoute any subtilite
> Of speche, or gret prolixite
> Of termes of philosophie,
> Of figures of poetrie,
> Or colours of rhetorike?
> Pardee, hit oughte the to lyke!
> For hard langage and harde matere
> Ys encombrous for to here
> Attones; wost thou not wel this?'
> And y answered and seyde 'Yis.'
> 'A ha!' quod he, 'lo, so I can
> Lewedly to a lewed man
> Speke, and shewe hym swyche skiles
> That he may shake hem be the biles,
> So palpable they shulden be.'   (853–69)

The passage is indeed 'easy' with direct address, familiar phrases, repetition with variation. Much of the vocabulary is plain and ordinary. Yet although the Eagle claims he is speaking in a 'lewed' style (866), within seventeen short lines there are a number of learned words. 'Subtilite' is only once recorded before, in the form 'sotelte', used by the mystic Richard Rolle, about 1340; 'prolixite' is first recorded here, as are 'poetrie', 'rhetorike', 'encombrous', 'palpable'. This passage contains the earliest recorded use in these special senses of 'figure' and 'colour' referring to style, while 'term' (in the sense of 'expression') was also just coming into use about this time. This 'lewed' style is not 'lewed' at all in vocabulary. It is full of neologisms and abstractions with precise signification.

Chaucer vigorously developed a large new learned vocabulary. *Troilus* in particular has strings of interesting new words, many of them adopted or adapted from French. Thus a random selection from Book IV gives us 'surplus' (60), 'tretis' (64), 'resport' (86 and 850, and nowhere else), 'redempcioun' (108), 'affeccioun' (153), 'fantasies' (193), 'president' (213), 'substaunce' (217), 'casuel' (419), 'passiones' (468), 'argument' (477), 'felicite' (480), to mention only a few. Chaucer was clearly in the forefront of modern usage of elaborate, abstract, elevated, culturally important new words derived from literacy.

On occasion, this elevated vocabulary is deliberately juxtaposed and contrasted with the commonplace. Thus in the *Parliament of Fowls* the eagles' stately proceedings are described in words of parliamentary, legal or scholastic flavour: 'conclusioun', 'pleyn eleccioun', 'diffyne', ter-myne' (526–30). 'Conclusioun' and 'diffyne' are first recorded in English in Chaucer's own *House of Fame*; and 'termyne' was only just coming into use. By contrast, the vulgar birds speak sharply: '"Wel bourded", quod the doke, "by myn hat!"', (589). Chaucer later became bolder still and in his churls' tales he uses such coarse words as 'swyve' (copulate) 'ers' (arse), etc., for their comic shock effect.

Conclusion

The learned elements in Chaucer's style are however in no way inevitably at odds with its colloquial and familiar elements. More frequently, as in the Eagle's speech, the one is effortlessly absorbed into the other. As a final example we may take Troilus' anguished debate with himself about 'fate, free-will, foreknowledge absolute' within the temple in Book IV of *Troilus and Criseyde*. The material for this is highly literate, drawn from Boethius' *Consolation of Philosophy*. But Troilus is represented as *speaking*, albeit to himself. Moreover, the poet participates so fully in this speech that he turns it into an actual verbal argument, as if he were arguing with someone else who was actually present. Though the style is full Chaucerian-oral it is most unnaturalistic in the dramatic situation if we judge it by the standards of literate consistency. Chaucer resorts to the devices of orality – in par-ticular, personal address and redundancy – for example, when Troilus says

> For if ther sitte a man yond on a see,
> Than by necessite bihoveth it
> That, *certes, thyn* opynyoun sooth be,
> That wenest *or conjectest* that he sit.
> *And further over now ayeynward yit,*
> *Lo, right so* is it of the part contrarie,
> As thus – *nowe herkne, for I wol nat tarie.*   (IV, 1023–9)

There is nothing of this personalized tone of addess in the Latin *Consolatio*, nor in Chaucer's own prose translation. The speech is a major example of Chaucer's recycling of literate material in oral terms. When we think of

the *Wife of Bath's Prologue*, of the 'Boethian' speeches of Palamon and
Arcite in the *Knight's Tale*, of the debate between Chaunticleer and Pertelote on dreams – to mention only a few of the other possible examples –
we realize how widespread is this absorption of literate, learned material
into the idioms and rhythms of popular speech. To express the weighty
concerns of the literate tradition in the fluid easy style of orality was the
achievement of Chaucer's genius.

Notes

1 Cf. Walter J. Ong, *Orality and Literacy: The Technologizing of the Word* (London/
   New York, 1982).
2 See Derek Brewer, 'The Relationship of Chaucer to the English and European
   Traditions' in *Chaucer: The Poet as Storyteller* (London, 1984), pp. 8–36.
3 See Elizabeth Salter and Derek Pearsall, 'Pictorial Illustration of Late Medieval
   Poetic Texts: the Role of the Frontispiece or Prefatory Picture' in *Medieval
   Iconography and Narrative, A Symposium*, eds. F. G. Andersen, E. Nyholm,
   M. Powell and F. T. Stubkjaer (Odense, 1980), pp. 100–23.
4 See Derek Brewer 'The Poetry of Chaucer's *Fabliaux*' in *Chaucer: the Poet as
   Storyteller*, pp. 107–19.
5 See Derek Brewer, 'Some Metonymic Relationships in Chaucer's Poetry' in
   Chaucer: the Poet as Storyteller, pp. 37–53.
6 See Derek Brewer 'Some Observations on the Development of Literalism and
   Verbal Criticism', *Poetica*, 2 (1974), 71–95.
7 *Troilus and Criseyde*, ed. B. A. Windeatt (London/New York, 1984), p. 9.

15 Further reading: A guide to Chaucer studies

1. Bibliography

The first four items in section 1.1 list Chaucer criticism up to 1973; for works published after that date, the annual bibliographies published in the journals listed in section 1.2 should be consulted. The *Year's Work in English Studies* is particularly useful because the items listed are annotated. For quick reference, the Goldentree Bibliography has a very good selection of critical studies on Chaucer's works. Finally, the volume by R. A. Peck is the first in a series of annotated Chaucer Bibliographies, which will facilitate easier access to the prodigious Chaucer criticism produced in this century.

1.1 Collections

Hammond, E. P. *Chaucer: A Bibliographical Manual* (London, 1908; repr. New York, 1933).

Griffith, D. D. *Bibliography of Chaucer, 1908–1953* (Seattle, 1955).

Crawford, W. R. *Bibliography of Chaucer, 1954–63* (Seattle/London, 1967).

Baird, L. Y. *A Bibliography of Chaucer, 1964–1973* (Boston, 1977).

Baugh, A. C. *Goldentree Bibliographies: Chaucer*, 2nd edn (Arlington Heights, Ill., 1977).

Peck, R. A. *The Chaucer Bibliographies: Chaucer's Lyrics and Anelida and Arcite. An Annotated Bibliography 1900 to 1980* (Toronto/Buffalo, N.Y./London, 1983).

1.2. Annual bibliographies

PMLA Annual Bibliography.
Year's Work in English Studies.
Chaucer Review.
Studies in the Age of Chaucer.

243

2. Editions

The standard one-volume edition of Chaucer's works is F. N. Robinson's *The Works of Geoffrey Chaucer*. It is based on eight MSS and the Thynne edition together with collations of the Cardigan and Morgan copies, and is presently in the process of revision for a third printing. The Robinson edition has recently been complemented by an edition prepared by John H. Fisher, who uses a single-base MS for every text with emendations from collations of texts by earlier editors. In contrast to the Robinson edition, the notes and glosses in Fisher are printed at the bottom of each page. In 1940, Manly and Rickert published a critical edition of the *Canterbury Tales* based on all MSS. The definitive edition of Chaucer's works, replacing the old Skeat edition, will ultimately be *The Variorum Edition* in forty-three volumes under the general editorship of Paul G. Ruggiers.

Good selective editions are those by Baugh and Donaldson, who print almost identical selections – that is, all of Chaucer's verse with the exception of the tales from the *Legend of Good Women*, *The Romaunt of the Rose*, *Anelida and Arcite*, and the prose writings. Donaldson's edition also features a good discussion of the individual works.

The continuing popularity of the *Canterbury Tales* is attested by the great number of modern editions. Blake prints the Hengwrt MS; Pratt uses the text of the Robinson edition with readings from other MSS; and Cawley uses the Robinson edition without alterations. Single tales with good introductions and glossaries have been edited by Hussey, Spearing and Winny (*General Prologue*, *Miller's Tale*, *Reeve's Tale*, and *Cook's Tale*, *Wife of Bath's Tale*, *Nun's Priest's Tale*, and *Franklin's Tale*).

The standard edition of the *Troilus* has long been that by Robert K. Root, recently superseded by Windeatt's edition. R. K. Gordon's edition is valuable because it also prints a translation of the *Roman de Troie* and the *Filostrato*. Helen Phillips' edition of the *Book of the Duchess* is excellent, featuring a good introduction with bibliography, the text plus readings from different MSS, copious notes, a translation of the French sources and analogues, and a complete glossary. Derek Brewer's edition of the *Parliament of Fowls* is also recommended, containing an excellent introduction, bibliography, text, notes, and glossary.

2.1. Complete editions and individual works

The Complete Poetry and Prose of Geoffrey Chaucer, ed. J. H. Fisher (New York, 1977).

The Works of Geoffrey Chaucer, ed. F. N. Robinson, 2nd edn (Boston/London, 1957).

The Variorum Edition, ed. P. G. Ruggiers (Norman, Okla., 1979–).
The Complete Works of Geoffrey Chaucer, ed. W. W. Skeat, 2nd edn, 7 vols. (Oxford, 1899).

2.2 Selected editions

Chaucer's Major Poetry, ed. A. C. Baugh (New York, 1963).
The Canterbury Tales by Geoffrey Chaucer, ed. N. F. Blake (London, 1980).
The Parlement of Foulys, ed. D. S. Brewer, 2nd edn (Manchester, 1972).
The Canterbury Tales, ed. A. C. Cawley, rev. edn (New York, 1975).
Chaucer's Poetry: An Anthology for the Modern Reader, ed. E. T. Donaldson (New York, 1958).
The Story of Troilus as Told by Benoît de Sainte-Maure, Giovanni Boccaccio, Geoffrey Chaucer, Robert Henryson, ed. R. K. Gordon (London, 1934).
Selected Tales from Chaucer, eds. M. Hussey, A. C. Spearing and J. Winny (Cambridge, 1965–).
The Text of the Canterbury Tales, eds. J. M. Manly and E. Rickert, 8 vols. (Chicago/London, 1940)
The Book of the Duchess, ed. H. Phillips (Durham/St Andrews, 1983).
The Tales of Canterbury, ed. R. A. Pratt (Boston, 1966).
The Book of Troilus and Criseyde, ed. R. K. Root (Princeton, NJ, 1926).
Troilus and Criseyde: A New Edition of 'The Book of Troilus', ed. B. A. Windeatt (London/New York, 1984).

3. Chaucer's life and world

Approximately five hundred documents referring to Chaucer, the man and civil servant, have been collected by Crow and Olson in *Chaucer Life-Records*. Biographies drawing on these life records and the poet's works are the books by Chute and Brewer (*Chaucer, Chaucer and His World* – a book featuring many fine illustrations). Brewer's third study, *Chaucer in His Time*, is an account of the political and social conditions of Chaucer's England, courtly life, domestic life, and the religious life. D. W. Robertson complements this general outline by a specific study dealing with the economic, political, social, and intellectual conditions of Chaucer's London. Two richly illustrated pictorial companions to the *Canterbury Tales* in particular and to Chaucer's works in general are the books by Hussey and by Loomis. Rickert *et al.*'s volume, finally, presents a fine collection of contemporary documents illustrating such widely divergent areas as London life, training and education, commercial life, entertainment, travel, warfare, and religion.

Brewer D. S. *Chaucer*, 3rd edn (London, 1973).
Brewer, D. S. *Chaucer and His World* (London, 1978).

Brewer, D. S. *Chaucer in His Time* (London, 1963; repr. Westport, Conn., 1977).
Chute, M. *Geoffrey Chaucer of England* (New York, 1946; repr. London, 1977).
Chaucer Life-Records, eds. M. M. Crow and C. C. Olson (Oxford, 1966).
Hussey, M. *Chaucer's World: A Pictorial Companion* (Cambridge, 1967).
Loomis, R. S. *A Mirror of Chaucer's World* (Princeton, NJ, 1965).
Chaucer's World, eds. E. Rickert, C. C. Olson and M. M. Crow (New York, 1948).
Robertson, D. W., Jr *Chaucer's London* (New York, 1968).

4. *Language and style, dictionaries and glossaries, concordance*

Section 4.1 contains a list of studies on the language and style of Chaucer's poetry. Purely linguistic analyses – that is, studies of the phonology, morphology, and syntax of Chaucer's language are made by Kerkhoff, Kökeritz and Ten Brink. For the position of Chaucer's language in the wider context of Middle English the interested reader should consult the handbook by Mossé in section 4.2. The studies by Eliason, Elliott, Masui, and Roscow investigate primarily stylistic features, while Burnley's excellent treatment combines both historical linguistics and stylistics.

A special glossary of the words appearing in Chaucer's works has been assembled by Davis *et al.*, while Ross has provided an index of supposedly lewd words and phrases. Invaluable for the understanding of Chaucer's language is also the *Middle English Dictionary*, now completed up to letter r(raiment). Magoun provides a glossary on the place names, proper names and allusions.

4.1. *Language and style (Chaucer)*

Burnley, J. D. *Chaucer's Language and the Philosophers' Tradition* (Cambridge, 1979).
Burnley, J. D. *A Guide to Chaucer's Language* (np, 1983).
A Chaucer Glossary, eds. N. Davis, D. Gray, P. Ingham and A. Wallace-Hadrill (Oxford, 1979).
Eliason, N. E. *The Language of Chaucer's Poetry: An Appraisal of the Verse, Style and Structure* (Copenhagen, 1972).
Elliott, R. W. V. *Chaucer's English* (London, 1974).
Kerkhoff, J. *Studies in the Language of Geoffrey Chaucer* (Leiden, 1966).
Kökeritz, H. *A Guide to Chaucer's Pronunciation* (Stockholm/New Haven, Conn., 1954; repr. New York, 1962).
Magoun, F. P., Jr *A Chaucer Gazetteer* (Chicago/Uppsala, 1961).

Masui, M. *The Structure of Chaucer's Rime Words: An Exploration into the Poetic Language of Chaucer* (Tokyo, 1974; repr. Folcroft, Pa., 1975).

Ross, T. W. *Chaucer's Bawdy* (New York, 1972).

Roscow, G. H. *Syntax and Style in Chaucer's Poetry* (Cambridge, 1981).

A Concordance to the Complete Works of Geoffrey Chaucer and to the Romaunt of the Rose, eds. J. S. P. Tatlock and A. G. Kennedy (Washington, DC, 1927; repr. Gloucester, Mass., 1963).

Ten Brink, B. *The Language and Metre of Chaucer,* trans. M. Bentinck Smith (London, 1901; repr. New York, 1969).

4.2 *Language (Middle English)*

Middle English Dictionary, ed. H. Kurath, S. M. Kuhn *et al.* (Ann Arbor, Mich., 1954–).

Mossé, F. *A Handbook of Middle English,* trans. J. A. Walker (Baltimore, Md./London, 1952).

5. *Prosody*

The study of Chaucer's prosody is hampered by certain conditions which make it difficult to provide definitive answers in this area of investigation. First, we do not know whether he meant his poetry to be read or recited, or what the scribes had in mind when they wrote their versions of Chaucer's poetry. Secondly, we do not know enough about the spoken language of Chaucer's time to make valid statements about his prosody. And thirdly, modern editors have provided us with texts which reflect their own principles of prosody rather than those that Chaucer may have subscribed to. For these reasons it is not surprising that a protracted debate has been carried on, a debate based on certain assumptions about the prosodic principle of Chaucer's poetry. There are two approaches: (1) the hypothesis of iambic decasyllabic verse as the basis of Chaucerian prosody and (2) word accent and speech rhythms as determinants of the metre of Chaucer's verse. Closely connected with these two approaches is the question to what extent Chaucer modelled his verse on contemporary Italian and French verse and the controversy over the pronunciation of the final unaccented -e. Proponents of the iambic decasyllabic verse theory would subscribe to the influence of Italian and French verse on Chaucer's prosody, Romance poetry being fundamentally syllabic in character; while adherents to the speech rhythm hypothesis would discount this influence, pointing to the accentual nature of English poetry. The same holds true for the pronunciation of the final unaccented -e, which some will pro-nounce for metrical reasons, while others will not, arguing the obsoleteness of this sound in the London standard of Chaucer's time and the preponderance of the natural speech rhythms.

Debate rages also over the meaning of the punctuation in the MSS. Do the virgules (/), colons and dots placed either above or on the line indicate caesuras or rising intonation? Are the lines divided into two hemistichs or not? And is Chaucer thinking in terms of a single verse unit at all?

Finally, the question of how far Chaucer's prose is influenced by the Latin cursus – that is, the cadenced medieval prose characterizing the Latin writings of his time – is still unanswered.

Conflicting views on these and other matters will be found in the studies cited below analysing Chaucer's prosody. The essay by Gaylord is the best assessment of the strengths and weaknesses of the respective positions.

Baum, P. F. *Chaucer's Verse* (Durham/Cambridge, 1961).

Gaylord, A. T. 'Scanning the Prosodists: An Essay in Metacriticism', *Chaucer Review*, 11 (1976), 22–82.

Halle, M. and Keyser, S. A. 'Chaucer and the Study of Prosody', *College English*, 28 (1966), 187–219.

Mustanoja, T. F. 'Chaucer's Prosody', in *Companion to Chaucer Studies*, ed. B. Rowland, rev. edn (New York/Oxford, 1979), pp. 65–94.

Robinson, I. *Chaucer's Prosody: A Study of the Middle English Verse Tradition* (Cambridge, 1971).

Schlauch, M. 'Chaucer's Prose Rhythms', *PMLA*, 65 (1950), 568–89.

Schlauch, M. 'The Art of Chaucer's Prose', in *Chaucer and Chaucerians: Critical Studies in Middle English Literature*, ed. D. S. Brewer (London, 1966), pp. 140–63.

Southworth, J. G. *Verses of Cadence: An Introduction to the Prosody of Chaucer and His Followers* (Oxford, 1954).

Southworth, J. G. *The Prosody of Chaucer and His Followers: Supplementary Chapters to Verses of Cadence* (Oxford, 1962).

6. *Sources and analogues*

The standard work on sources and analogues for the *Canterbury Tales* is still the collection by Bryan and Dempster. For the fabliaux of the *Canterbury Tales* Benson and Andersson's collection of the French, German, Italian, and Latin analogues, accompanied by an English translation, is a very good reference book. Havely provides a new translation of those sections from Boccaccio's works comprising the basis of the *Troilus*, the *Knight's Tale*, and the *Franklin's Tale*. Windeatt makes available in translation the French, Latin, and Italian texts that lie behind Chaucer's dream poems, for example, passages from Froissart, Machaut, Deschamps, Cicero, and Boccaccio. And Dahlberg furnishes a translation of the *Roman de la Rose*.

A source book of a different sort is that by Miller, which combines translations of passages from works Chaucer is known to have used with selections from the works of a large number of writers regarded by Chaucer and his contemporaries as authorities in matters ranging from reading to romantic love, chivalric ideals to antifeminism, and the estates of society to the Last Judgement.

The Literary Context of Chaucer's Fabliaux: Texts and Translations, eds. L. D. Benson and T. M. Andersson (Indianapolis, Ind./New York, 1971).

Sources and Analogues of Chaucer's Canterbury Tales, eds. W. F. Bryan and G. Dempster (Chicago, 1941; repr. New York, 1958).

The Romance of the Rose, trans. C. Dahlberg (Princeton, NJ, 1971; repr. Hanover/London, 1983).

Chaucer's Boccaccio: Sources of Troilus and the Knight's and Franklin's Tales, ed. and trans. N. R. Havely (Cambridge, 1980).

Chaucer: Sources and Backgrounds, ed. R. P. Miller (New York, 1977).

Windeatt, B. A. *Chaucer's Dream Poetry: Sources and Analogues* (Cambridge, 1982).

7. Introductions, handbooks, anthologies, and collections of essays in criticism

Within the past twenty years a number of general introductions have been written to facilitate access to Chaucer's poetry. The books by Coghill, Howard, Hussey, Kane, and Lawlor intend to do just that, that is, they are designed to introduce students to the Chaucer canon. The volumes by Norton-Smith and Mehl, though likewise introductory in nature, are addressed to the advanced student of Chaucer's poetry. Also within the same period a number of companions to Chaucer studies have been assembled to help both students and teachers familiarize themselves with major aspects of Chaucer studies. The four works listed here reflect different approaches as well as different levels, ranging from selective (Cawley) to all-inclusive (Rowland) and from elementary (Hussey, Spearing and Winny) to advanced (Brewer).

In section 7.3 five anthologies of Chaucer criticism are listed. Spurgeon and Brewer print comments on Chaucer's poetry from his own time up to 1900 and 1933, respectively, while Burrow's anthology combines selected statements from all centuries up to the present. The two volumes by Schoeck and Taylor and the anthology by Wagenknecht contain important essays in criticism by twentieth-century scholars.

In section 7.4 a few collections of original essays are listed ranging from specific topics like 'Chaucer and the Italian Trecento' to general discussions such as 'Chaucerian Problems and Perspectives'.

7.1 Introductions

Coghill, N. *The Poet Chaucer*, 2nd edn (London, 1968).
Howard, E. J. *Geoffrey Chaucer* (New York, 1964).
Hussey, S. S. *Chaucer: An Introduction* (London, 1971).
Kane, G. *Chaucer* (Oxford, 1984).
Lawlor, J. *Chaucer* (London, 1968).
Mehl, D. *Geoffrey Chaucer: An Introduction to His Narrative Poetry* (Cambridge, 1986).
Norton-Smith, J. *Geoffrey Chaucer* (London, 1974).

7.2 Handbooks

Writers and Their Background: Geoffrey Chaucer, ed. D. S. Brewer (London, 1974).
Chaucer's Mind and Art, ed. A. C. Cawley (Edinburgh/London, 1969).
Hussey, M., Spearing, A. C. and Winny, J. *An Introduction to Chaucer* (Cambridge, 1965).
Companion to Chaucer Studies, ed. B. Rowland, 2nd edn (Toronto/New York/London, 1979)

7.3 Anthologies of essays in Chaucer criticism

Chaucer's Troilus: Essays in Criticism, ed. S. A. Barney (Hamden, Conn./London, 1980).
Chaucer: The Critical Heritage, ed. D. S. Brewer, 2 vols. (London/Henley/Boston, 1978).
Geoffrey Chaucer: A Critical Anthology, ed. J. A. Burrow (Harmondsworth, 1969).
Chaucer Criticism, eds. R. J. Schoeck and J. Taylor, 2 vols. (Notre Dame, Ind., 1960–1).
Five Hundred Years of Chaucer Criticism and Allusion, 1357–1900, ed. C. F. E. Spurgeon, 3 vols. (Cambridge, 1925; repr. New York, 1960).
Chaucer: Modern Essays in Criticism, ed. E. Wagenknecht (New York, 1959).

7.4 Collections of original essays in criticism

Chaucer and the Italian Trecento, ed. P. Boitani (Cambridge, 1983).
Chaucer and Chaucerians: Critical Studies in Middle English Literature, ed. D. S. Brewer (London, 1966).

Geoffrey Chaucer: A Collection of Original Articles, ed. G. D. Economou (New York, 1975).

Signs and Symbols in Chaucer's Poetry, eds. J. P. Hermann and J. J. Burke, Jr (University, Ala., 1981).

Chaucer the Love Poet, eds. J. Mitchell and W. Provost (Athens, 1973).

Chaucer at Albany, ed. R. H. Robbins (New York, 1975).

New Perspectives in Chaucer Criticism, ed. D. M. Rose (Norman, Okla., 1981).

Essays on Troilus and Criseyde, ed. M. Salu (Cambridge, 1979).

Chaucerian Problems and Perspectives: Essays Presented to Paul E. Beichner CSC, eds. E. Vasta and Z. P. Thundy (Notre Dame, Ind./London, 1979).

8. Criticism

A glance at one of the annual bibliographies will convince anyone quickly that Chaucer criticism within the past years has become a veritable industry. To give it adequate treatment within the limited scope of this summary chapter is impossible. Consequently, the interested reader is advised to consult the essays listed in section 8.1, which will sketch the history of Chaucer criticism from the Middle Ages to the present when read in the following order: Brewer (2), Baugh and Purdy, Crawford, and Ridley. Benson's treatment is more comprehensive.

Although a survey of Chaucer criticism cannot be produced here, it is still possible to establish groupings to which the book-length studies cited below can be assigned. Leaving aside structuralist, semiotic, psychological and anthropological approaches, which make only rare appearances in conventional Chaucer criticism, the bulk of the remainder can be allocated and distributed to the following three categories: 8.2 general criticism; 8.3 literary tradition; and 8.4 historical criticism. Under the heading 'general criticism' are included studies on rhetoric, stylistics, genre theory, narratology, and hermeneutics. In the category 'literary tradition' are assembled works on Chaucer and his place in literary history, be this native English, French, Latin, or Italian. And the grouping 'historical criticism', finally, embraces all those studies which focus primarily on theological, philosophical, art historical, historical, and economic conditions and their supposed influence on Chaucer's poetry. Needless to say, the boundaries between these three divisions are not always clear-cut because studies on Chaucer tend to be multi-faceted and occasionally multi-methodological. In these cases assignment has been made according to what appears to be the dominant character trait. In general, studies from the postwar period have been included here, since the foundations of contemporary Chaucer criticism rarely extend to a period before that time. Seminal books which appeared in this epoch of criticism are marked by an asterisk (*) – the choice made by the author, of course, being a subjective one.

8.1 Surveys of Chaucer criticism

Baugh, A. C. 'Fifty Years of Chaucer Scholarship', *Speculum*, 26 (1951), 659–72.

Benson, L. D. 'A Reader's Guide to Writings on Chaucer', in *Writers and Their Background: Geoffrey Chaucer*, ed. D. S. Brewer (London, 1974), pp. 321–72.

Brewer, D. S. 'The Criticism of Chaucer in the Twentieth Century', in *Chaucer's Mind and Art*, ed. A. C. Cawley (Edinburgh/London, 1969), pp. 3–28.

Brewer, D. S. *Chaucer: The Critical Heritage*, 2 vols. (London/Henley/Boston, 1978), vol. 1, pp. 1–29; vol. 2, pp. 1–23.

Crawford, W. R. *Bibliography of Chaucer 1954–63* (Seattle/London, 1967), pp. xiii–xl.

Purdy, R. R. 'Chaucer Scholarship in England and America: A Review of Recent Trends', *Anglia*, 70 (1952), 345–81.

Ridley, F. H. 'The State of Chaucer Studies: A Brief Survey', *Studies in the Age of Chaucer*, 1 (1979), 3–16.

8.2 General criticism

Burlin, R. B. *Chaucerian Fiction* (Princeton, NJ, 1977).

Cooper, H. *The Structure of the Canterbury Tales* (London, 1983).

Corsa, H. S. *Chaucer: Poet of Mirth and Morality* (Notre Dame, Ind., 1964).

David, A. *The Strumpet Muse: Art and Morals in Chaucer's Poetry* (Bloomington, Ind./London, 1976).

Ferster, J. *Chaucer on Interpretation* (Cambridge, 1985).

Fichte, J. O. *Chaucer's 'Art Poetical': A Study in Chaucerian Poetics* (Tübingen, 1980).

Gordon, I. *The Double Sorrow of Troilus: A Study of Ambiguities in Troilus and Criseyde* (Oxford, 1970).

Howard, D. R. *The Idea of the Canterbury Tales* (Berkeley/Los Angeles, Ca./London, 1976).

Jordan, R. M. *Chaucer and the Shape of Creation: The Aesthetic Possibilities of Inorganic Structure* (Cambridge, Mass./London, 1967).

*Kolve, V. A. *Chaucer and the Imagery of Narrative: The First Five Canterbury Tales* (London, 1984).

Lumiansky, R. M. *Of Sundry Folk: The Dramatic Principle in the Canterbury Tales* (Austin, Ts., 1955).

Meech, S. B. *Design in Chaucer's Troilus* (Syracuse, NY, 1959: repr. New York, 1969).

*Payne, R. O. *The Key of Remembrance: A Study of Chaucer's Poetics* (New Haven, Conn./London, 1963).

Pearsall, D. *The Canterbury Tales* (London/Boston/Sydney, 1985).

Richardson, J. '*Blameth nat me*': *A Study of Imagery in Chaucer's Fabliaux* (Paris/The Hague, 1970).

Ruggiers, P. G. *The Art of the Canterbury Tales* (Madison, Wis., 1965).

8.3 *Literary tradition*

Bennett, J. A. W. *The Parlement of Foules: An Interpretation* (Oxford, 1957).

Bennett, J. A. W. *Chaucer's Book of Fame: An Exposition of the 'The House of Fame'* (Oxford, 1968).

Boitani, P. *Chaucer and Boccaccio* (Oxford, 1977).

*Clemen, W. H. *Chaucer's Early Poetry*, trans. C. A. M. Sym (London, 1963).

Cooke, T. D. *The Old French and Chaucerian Fabliaux. A Study of Their Comic Climax* (Columbia, SC/London, 1978).

Donaldson, E. T. *Speaking of Chaucer* (London/New York, 1970).

Fyler, J. M. *Chaucer and Ovid* (New Haven, Conn./London, 1979).

Kean, P. M. *Chaucer and the Making of English Poetry*, 2 vols. (London, 1972).

McAlpine, M. E. *The Genre of Troilus and Criseyde* (Ithaca, NY/London, 1978).

*Mann, J. *Chaucer and Medieval Estates Satire: The Literature of Social Classes and the General Prologue of the Canterbury Tales* (Cambridge, 1973).

Minnis, A. J. *Chaucer and Pagan Antiquity* (Cambridge, 1982).

Miskimin, A. S. *The Renaissance Chaucer* (New Haven, Conn./London, 1975).

*Muscatine, C. *Chaucer and the French Tradition* (Berkeley, Los Angeles, Ca., 1957).

Schless, H. H. *Chaucer and Dante: A Reevaluation* (Norman, Okla., 1984).

Steadman, J. M. *Disembodied Laughter: Troilus and the Apotheosis Tradition* (Berkeley/Los Angeles, Ca./London, 1972).

Wetherbee, W. *Chaucer and the Poets: An Essay on Troilus and Criseyde* (Ithaca, NY/ London, 1984).

Wimsatt, J. I. *Chaucer and the French Love Poets: The Literary Background of the Book of the Duchess* (Chapel Hill, 1968).

8.4. *Historical criticism*

Baldwin, R. *The Unity of the Canterbury Tales* (Copenhagen, 1955; repr. New York, 1971).

*Boitani, P. *Chaucer and the Imaginary World of Fame* (Cambridge, 1984).

Bowden, M. *A Commentary on the General Prologue to the Canterbury Tales*, 2nd edn (New York/London, 1967).

Curry, W. C. *Chaucer and the Mediaeval Sciences*, 2nd edn (New York, 1960).

Delany, S. *Chaucer's House of Fame: The Poetics of Sceptical Fideism* (Chicago/London, 1972).

Lawlor, T. *The One and the Many in the Canterbury Tales* (Hamden, Conn., 1980).

*Robertson, D. W., Jr *A Preface to Chaucer: Studies in Medieval Perspectives* (Princeton, NJ, 1962).

Wood, C. *Chaucer and the Country of the Stars: Poetic Uses of Astrological Imagery* (Princeton, NJ. 1970).

Chaucer Bibliography since 1986:

The third edition of Robinson's *Works of Geoffrey Chaucer* has appeared as *The Riverside Chaucer*. ed. L. D. Benson (Boston, 1987).

Cooper, H. *Oxford Guides to Chaucer: The Canterbury Tales* (Oxford, 1989).

Dinshaw, C. *Chaucer's Sexual Poetics* (Madison, Wisconsin, 1989).

Leicester, H. M., Jr. *The Disenchanted Self: Representing the Subject in the Canterbury Tales* (Berkeley, 1990).

Mann, J. *Feminist Readings: Geoffrey Chaucer* (Hemel Hempstead, 1991).

Patterson, L. *Chaucer and the Subject of History* (London, 1991).

Pearsall, D. *The Life of Geoffrey Chaucer: A Critical Biography* (Oxford, 1992).

Strohm, P. *Social Chaucer* (Cambridge, Mass., 1989).

Windeatt, B. *Oxford Guides to Chaucer: Troilus and Criseyde* (Oxford, 1992).

Index